Disability, the Environment, and Colonialism

EDITED BY TATIANA KONRAD

Disability, the Environment, and Colonialism

TEMPLE UNIVERSITY PRESS
Philadelphia • *Rome* • *Tokyo*

TEMPLE UNIVERSITY PRESS
Philadelphia, Pennsylvania 19122
tupress.temple.edu

Library of Congress Cataloging-in-Publication Data

Names: Konrad, Tatiana, 1991– editor.
Title: Disability, the environment, and colonialism / edited by Tatiana
Konrad.
Description: Philadelphia : Temple University Press, 2024. | Includes
index. | Summary: "Aligning discourses surrounding hegemonic colonial
visions of the environment and disability, this volume illustrates the
ways in which colonial understandings of disability were and continue to
be defined by relationships with the environment, collectively creating
a form of eco-ableism that continues to this day"— Provided by
publisher.
Identifiers: LCCN 2023044361 (print) | LCCN 2023044362 (ebook) | ISBN
9781439925201 (cloth) | ISBN 9781439925218 (paperback) | ISBN
9781439925225 (pdf)
Subjects: LCSH: Sociology of disability. | People with disabilities—Public
opinion. | Environmental sociology. | Human ecology and the humanities.
| Colonization—Environmental aspects. | Imperialism—Environmental
aspects.

Classification: LCC HV1568 .D5697 2024 (print) | LCC HV1568 (ebook) | DDC
362.4—dc23/eng/20240401
LC record available at https://lccn.loc.gov/2023044361
LC ebook record available at https://lccn.loc.gov/2023044362

9 8 7 6 5 4 3 2 1

Contents

PART III DISABLED BODIES, ECOLOGIES, AND IMPERIALIST SUBJECTIVITIES

PART IV COLONIALISM, (DIS)ABILITY, AND NATURE IN AND THROUGH AMERICA

Foreword

Tsitsi Chataika

have had the privilege of coediting several books in disability studies, including the 2020 Taylor and Francis Outstanding Handbook in the social sciences, *The Routledge Handbook of Disability Activism*. I am aware what it means to put together such an edited volume. The exciting part is signing autographs and hearing feedback from readers. Writing a book is strenuous and, hence, a calling. I congratulate Tatiana Konrad for answering her call to write this well-crafted *Disability, the Environment, and Colonialism*. It was a joy to read this volume that has areas close to my heart, and I have also personally contributed to their bodies of knowledge.

The volume, contributed to by diverse and experienced authors, starts with an introductory chapter, which sets the scene and provides the structure. Specifically, it emphasizes the intersectionalities of the interdisciplinary fields of disability studies, the environmental humanities, and colonialism. Part I includes four chapters focused on justice, imperialism, and eco-ableism. Part II, with three chapters, is centered on redefining blindness and deafness through (dis)ability, colonialism, and the environment. Part III includes three chapters focused on disabled bodies, ecologies, and imperialist subjectivities. The last three chapters, which constitute Part IV, are centered on colonialism, (dis)ability, and nature in and through America.

One of the greatest decisions you can do is to take your time and read this book. I recommend it and urge researchers; students; disability activists; policymakers; development partners; and anyone interested in disability studies, the environmental humanities, and colonialism to read this volume and appreciate how these three aspects intersect.

Disability, the Environment, and Colonialism

Introduction

Unnatural Bodies

Colonialism, Disability, and the Environment

Tatiana Konrad

In their introduction to *Disability Studies and the Environmental Humanities: Toward an Eco-Crip Theory*, Sarah Jaquette Ray and Jay Sibara outline the crucial significance of "bring[ing] into dialogue the interdisciplinary fields of disability studies and the environmental humanities."[1] I propose to add another perspective to this discussion—namely, colonialism—and argue that it is impossible to address disability and environmentalism without uncovering the sociopolitical and cultural intricacies of the colonialist ideology and its permeating, omnipresent significance during both colonial times and today. It is through a careful analysis of the intersection of disability, the environment, and colonialism that one can most effectively understand such issues as eco-ableism, environmental degradation, homogenized approaches to environmentalism or the lack thereof, and climate change.

This edited collection examines the imbrications of disability and the environment in the formation of colonial ideology and in the process of colonization. It traces the emergence of eco-ableist discourses through a careful analysis of such issues as gender, race, imperialism, the environment, and climate, and it probes the ways in which various cultural artifacts from that era effectively construct the definitions of disability and the environment. The book shows that in colonial times, colonizers' perceptions of disability were largely defined by earlier environmental discourses, which treated the environment in much the same way as people with disabilities. Additionally, it demonstrates—drawing on various contemporary literary and media examples—how the perverse nature of colonialism continues to dominate the globe today. It thus designates colonialism as a perpetual instrument through which to construct knowledge about disability and the environment, outlining the ceaseless, tight, and intricate linkages between disability, the environment, and colonialism.

Colonialism is a complex practice that has been exercised by different nations in different time periods and for different purposes. It is, therefore, impossible to provide a comprehensive historical overview of colonization, and the place of disability and the environment therein, in one book alone. This work predominantly focuses on Western colonialism and Anglophone writings. Despite this rather selective approach, the edited collection looks at a broad historical period—from the beginning of the seventeenth century until today—and contributes to the study of colonialism as a practice that, while diverse in its implementation and impacts, has distinct characteristics through which it functions. These are *oppression* of people deemed by colonizers to be less than human, *violence* directed toward dehumanized groups, and *exploitation* of all colonized peoples and lands.

Along with looking at the nations traditionally recognized as former colonies, this book also discusses the United States. Cognizant of the scholarly debate regarding the country's relationship to colonialism,[2] this edited collection looks at the United States from a postcolonial studies lens, recognizing the impact of British colonialism on the New World and of settler colonialism in the United States in particular. Indeed, as Jenny Sharpe notes, America's "history of imported slave and contract labor, continental expansion, and overseas imperialism" outline a clear development of this state as a (post)colonial nation.[3] The United States' own experience with colonialism, ending the American Revolutionary War in 1783, reveals the nation's historical challenges with dependence and freedom.[4] Focusing on the historical period from the second half of the eighteenth century to the beginning of the twenty-first century, the book explores the unique status of America through the lens of (post)colonialism, the environment, and disability.

The essays in this book do not simply articulate the interconnections of the three subjects; crucially, they demonstrate that the colonial understandings of disability and the environment were formed and interpolated in a rather similar fashion through the perverse, discriminating, oppressive, and devaluing ideology of colonialism. The book traces the steady formation of marginalization and subjugation through the notion of the body as a socially constructed and socioculturally and politically defined object, identifying how gender and race were abused to promote colonialist ideologies. Conquering the land and peoples, and dividing bodies and spaces into civilized and uncivilized ones, colonizers established a very peculiar form of ableism that was similarly articulated and exercised both toward people *and* the environment. As the book demonstrates, this structured discrimination and abuse not only helps us understand the relationship between disability and the environment and how one complemented the other in the colonial era but also tackles current issues related to disability and the environment. This, in turn, reveals the unabating power of colonialism to designate bodies in specific ways even in the times of decolonization and postcolonialism. The book thus does not approach colonialism as a historical phenomenon from the past; rather, through the meticulous discussion of the intersection of disability and the environment, it illustrates how the politics of colonialism still dominate our globalized culture. Finally, it presents the longer, uninterrupted history of constructing "knowledge" about disability and the environment. This knowledge, as the book's essays explain, remains one of the major obstacles in fighting ableism and minimizing the effects of environmental degradation and climate change.

In its discussion of these issues, this book is careful to ensure that it does not promote the one-way transfer of knowledge from the North to the South and does not obscure the views of formerly colonized populations. The contributors to this edited collection carefully discuss the issue of positionality, clearly outlining their approaches and intentions as they conduct this important research and foregrounding the voices of scholars from the Global South. Including voices from the communities concerned (people with disabilities, scholars from the Global South) rather than speaking for them is crucial. Although the current environmental crisis impacts the health and well-being of populations worldwide, the struggles of the Global South are much more severe. This book draws on scholarship produced by scholars from the Global South, includes analyses of texts from the Global South, and engages with eco-ableism as a direct outcome of colonialism, examining its effects on peoples and environments during the colonial era and on the postcolonial world today.

Colonial Constructs: Disability and the Environment through a Colonialist Lens

The intersections of disability and colonialism, the environment and colonialism, and even disability and the environment have been brought to the fore by many scholars worldwide. Yet, as this collection demonstrates, it is only through understanding the interdependence of all three concepts that we can fully comprehend each individually. Western colonialism (and later neocolonialism) has profoundly shaped the meanings of disability and the environment through systematic, institutionalized oppression, exploitation, and various forms of abuse. As scholars have recently begun to emphasize,[5] the notions of disability and the environment are not merely similarly constructed; through them, we can better grasp the false dichotomies of normal and abnormal, natural and unnatural, organic and mechanical, humans and nonhumans, and human-made and nature-made. Emphasizing the necessity of clearly articulating the role of colonialism in shaping disability and environmental discourses, this edited collection offers a unique and timely contribution to the fields of disability studies, environmental studies, and (post)colonial studies. The ambition to bring colonialism to recent disability-environment debates not only expands the existing scholarship but also further perpetuates the profound potential of combining disability studies and the environmental humanities.

The colonial aspect is key to the rationale of this book, which does not treat the term as a synonym for capitalism or industrialization but rather clearly distinguishes the political, social, cultural, and economic conditions generated via colonial views and measures the impact they have had on and through other forces of change. Colonialism is thus a superimposed practice that has defined and influenced other transformations, leading to and further intensifying the flourishing of white populations and the subjugation and exploitation of colonized peoples. Additionally, while illustrating the debilitating nature of colonialism, the book foregrounds the endurance and agency of the formerly colonized populations. The focus of several chapters on postcolonialism is intentional, for the book aims to emphasize how inequalities that existed in colonial times remain in place and to illustrate that studying oppression, inequality, and exclusion via disability and the environment can be productive only when considering the colonial ideology and its long-lasting effects. The book thus connects (but does not conflate) colonialism and postcolonialism, drawing a clear distinction between the two and emphasizing how the two inform each other. The way the volume parses this out is engaged later in this introduction.

Colonialism has largely influenced the perception of people with disabilities and the very idea of *being disabled*. Moreover, historical evidence indicates that colonial practices, such as slavery, "produced" both "discursive" and "physical" disability.[6] From the actions of colonizers that directly caused disability in colonized peoples through exhausting toil, abuse, and food deprivation to the culturally and politically problematic reclassification of certain individuals as less than human, *disabling* was an actual, powerful instrument of colonialism. Moreover, the health and well-being of Black, Indigenous, and People of Color (BIPOC) communities are still negatively affected today, revealing how inequality and injustice intersect to harm these populations and sustain their marginalization. The legacies of coloniality remain present to this day, as illustrated in Latin America, for example, by the impact of deforestation on Indigenous populations in Brazil and desertification in Argentina that results in ecological debility.[7] It is through the

literal and metaphoric disabling of the colonized that colonizers have successfully established a hierarchy of oppression. This, in turn, problematized
the very notion of disability that not only has come to mean specific physical
and mental impairments but also defines the sociopolitical and cultural conditions of certain individuals and nations. The perception of disability as not
only a difference but also "a threat," as Sarah Jaquette Ray writes, was intensified in the United States toward the end of the nineteenth century, when
"the purity of the body and the nation" became particularly important, promoting "wilderness, eugenics, and imperialism" in the West.[8] Disability could
not be conceptually incorporated into a world divided by colonialism into
the privileged and the subjugated, and thus "alongside racialized bodies of
American Indians, African Americans, women, and the poor, the disabled
body had no place."[9] Disability was hence not only an individually defined
physical or mental difference; it was a collective identity category—to be sure,
an unwanted one—"defined by the inability to contribute productively to the
capitalist system, to the body politic, and therefore to society."[10]

Indeed, as David T. Mitchell and Sharon L. Snyder demonstrate in their
edited collection *The Body and Physical Difference: Discourses of Disability*,
"disability is as much a symptom of historical and cultural contingencies as
it is a physical and psychological reality."[11] Colonialism has profoundly
shaped the dual meaning of disability through various ableist practices that
both precipitated disablement and labeled it as an unnatural or even evil
category. Colonizers have accomplished this by establishing *the norm* as a
defining category through which to, among other things, justify colonization and how it was achieved. Rosemarie Garland-Thomson's notion of "normate," which "designates the social figure through which people can represent themselves as definitive human beings," is particularly helpful here.[12]
Garland-Thomson argues, "Normate . . . is the constructed identity of those
who, by way of the bodily configurations and cultural capital they assume,
can step into a position of authority and wield the power it grants them."[13]
A disabled individual, in a colonialist perception of the world, is one that
lacks power, symbolizes a certain difference from the norm, and is thus
nonnormate. Colonialism reclassified individuals into bodies and, further,
into bodies that are natural and unnatural. This binary view, which shaped
the colonial project, is a fiction that dramatically redefined the meaning of
the human via nature: people with disabilities have come to be understood
as unnatural—that is, not belonging to nature and the natural order as such.
In contrast, Indigenous perspectives on disability emphasize the artificial
nature of this construct: "Disablement needs two parts: human difference
and human contempt. It is a human decision to label a difference as less-
than, a problem in need of fixing, an unwanted dependence. But this landscape, this mother, these spiny trees and vivid skies, Wako^n'da, they could

not know such a thing. All is one, and all is kin."[14] This viewpoint fore-grounds colonialist premises that make disability a characteristic that justi-fies colonization in the eyes of the colonizers.

Colonialism constructed the meanings of disability and the environ-ment through its exertions of power on both people and the land, includ-ing its more-than-human inhabitants. The environment was transformed, abused, exploited, and oppressed, just as people were. Nature, too, has be-come colonized, a resource for the white man's profit. Through the constant exploitation that has led to environmental degradation and climate change, among other serious issues, the colonizer has redefined the meaning of na-ture from the mother to a slave—an understanding similar to how colonized peoples were viewed.[15] The environment was perceived as a space for a white man's prosperity and benefit, and "environmentalism was riddled with . . . 'hidden attachments' to Manifest Destiny, empire, and whiteness."[16] Fore-grounding the place of the environment in the construction of colonialism, Elizabeth DeLoughrey and George B. Handley claim that the environment is "a nonhuman witness to the violent process of colonialism."[17] This is only further emphasized by Graham Huggan and Helen Tiffin, who, accentuat-ing the broad "ecological gap between coloniser and colonised,"[18] draw at-tention to unequal environmental conditions that have been created via colonization. Destruction, transformation, toxicity, and exploitation of the environment were systemic colonial practices that have led to environmen-tal inequalities and promoted environmental racism that postcolonial na-tions continue to face today. Bonnie Roos and Alex Hunt aptly point out this ongoing inequality, claiming that today, in the time of environmental crisis, the West continues to perform the role of a savior, which maintains the colonial vision of "'white' civilization rid[ing] to the rescue of those needy 'others.'"[19] Environmental inequality in the postcolonial era manifests itself not only in the form of "land-based" imperialism but also via "globalization" and "cultural imperialism."[20]

Indigenous perspectives on the environment and the harm exercised over peoples and territories through colonization are particularly helpful to consider. Jen Deerinwater explains,

> Traditionally, land, water, air, and beings weren't viewed as separate entities from many Indigenous people; we understand that our lives are interconnected with all life. We and our Indigenous nations his-torically and today are our Earth's protector. The "environment" as a concept is truly one of the colonizer. It disconnects people from the land, air, water, and animal relatives in order for primarily West-ern and white supremacist nations to plunder and profit, leaving a wake of devastation.[21]

The result of colonial environmental exploitation is both the destruction of territories where Indigenous peoples live (for example, due to rising sea levels caused by climate change) and harm to the health and even death of people with disabilities. Deerinwater emphasizes the alarming consequences of colonialist and ableist practices: Indigenous people with disabilities simply do not have enough financial means to evacuate from the precarious territories. In fact, many of these people are "denied the right to evacuation through a lack of accessible news, information, resources, transportation, and shelters."[22] Disturbing forms of eco-ablism and environmental injustice result from colonizers' deliberate and violent erasure of people with disabilities and BIPOC communities via, among other criminal acts, stealing their territories, directing environmental toxicity and precarity toward them, and ultimately excluding these people from any decision-making processes. These practices must be decolonized. Decolonization of disability and the environment, however, is possible only when we fully recognize the ways in which colonialism has affected (and continues to affect) communities and lands and take measures to end existing systems of oppression.[23] Deerinwater emphasizes the crucial value of both an intersectional approach to such issues as disability, environmental crisis, and colonial exploitation and the collaborative work of scholars, academics, activists, and politicians to foreground the voices of people with disabilities and BIPOC communities:

> My life has been deemed worthless by colonial society and I'm currently drowning in a sense of despair and the sheer terror of how I'll survive as the climate crisis worsens. I see glimmers of hope though. Indigenous Climate Action is now in the early stages of including a disability framework in their organization. Health Justice Commons is connecting the dots between the need for disability and environmental justice and the end of colonization. Just the fact that this piece will be read by those in academia will hopefully lead to more thorough research on this topic that could be used for swift policy and grassroots action.[24]

By identifying and examining ways in which disability and the environment intersect with colonial practices and politics, this edited collection produces much-needed research on this largely neglected topic.

How do disability and the environment intersect with each other and colonialism, and to what extent does colonialism play a role in approaching the constructed meanings of disability and the environment? Scholar and environmental and disability activist Anthony Nocella II shrewdly observes, "These traditionally oppressed groups—nonhuman animals, people with disabilities, and the ecological world—have much in common and have arguably been marginalized more than any other segment of society."[25] The discrimination, subjugation, and oppression suffered by people with disabilities corresponds with the treatment of the environment (the concept I use to talk about the natural world in general and various species and organisms that inhabit it as well as objects that construct it); this was a systematic policy that, in turn, was the product and the major instrument of colonialism. The white man's domination over the world essentially presupposed arranging it in a way that would celebrate a specific definition of *the human*, with whiteness, masculinity, heterosexuality, and even class being the major identifiers. Anyone and anything that did not fit that description was not viewed as human and was thus constructively and elaborately dehumanized through physical, political, and cultural powers. Colonialism, through these mechanisms of exclusion, largely reimagined what it meant to be human and the role of the human in the world.

Jaquette Ray pinpoints a tight linkage between disability and environmentalism in America, calling it "a material, constitutive relationship" and explaining that through wilderness, "the fit body" was celebrated and promoted as an ideal image of a human being.[26] In that respect, one can argue that considering the current environmental degradation as "a crisis of the body" is directly related to the major tool of industrialization that undergirded colonial expansion—the machine—through which the human-nature relationship was reimagined and an explicit hierarchy of the oppressor and the oppressed was formulated.[27] That hierarchy composed "one complex system of force relations" that was built on the oppositions of "the animal and the mechanical, the organic and inorganic, nature and industry."[28] It is on the material level of the body that environmentalism and disability come together to be understood as similarly constructed issues, equally impacted by colonial oppression. Once we start thinking of nature as a body that was invaded, abused, and transformed, we inevitably step into the discourse of disability. For Jaquette Ray, "Environmental rhetoric claiming that technology corrupted the garden registers disabled figures as unnatural, symbols of the imperfections we must strive to avoid or overcome."[29] While the problem of environmental degradation and the colossal role of the human in causing it should not be undermined, it is important to understand that once we describe nature as a body and view the current environmental crisis as a manifestation of nature's disability, we inevitably imply that disability is a vital threat for humanity and must be eradicated. This tactic is appropriate for amplifying fear of climate change, but it obviously does not foster inclusion or promote diversity and disability rights. Nevertheless, this rhetoric is an effective way to engage with a moral issue that humanity must address regarding the environment and the disabled minority. In a similar fashion, then, both the environment and disability raise the problem of "an ethical way of being in the world."[30]

Discrimination against disabled individuals (ableism) and more-than-humans (speciesism) are practices that have been methodically changing the world, "promoting civilization, normalcy, and intellectualism grounded in modernity, which arose out of the European Enlightenment."[31] It is because of this that critique of "colonization and domination of the environment" is of particular importance not only in environmental discourses but also in disability studies, to facilitate an inclusive and "more sustainable global community."[32] Nocella coins a helpful term to address the long-lasting oppression of people with disabilities and more-than-humans—"eco-ability"— and explains that this notion "combines the concepts of interdependency, inclusion, and respect for difference within a community; and this includes *all* life, sentient and nonsentient."[33] Through this term, one can effectively juxtapose environmental oppression (including the current environmental crisis) and the oppression of people with disabilities as ethical wrongs that were and still are exercised in a similar manner and, consequently, can be solved in a similar way: through the introduction of anti-oppressive, conservationist policies and the transformation of the world around us into an all-inclusive space. "Eco-ability" can thus be adopted as a new way of thinking and perceiving the world—"a philosophy that respects differences in abilities while promoting values appropriate to the stewardship of ecosystems."[34] After all, as Nocella correctly pinpoints, "the inherent philosophy within the natural world is that the environment strives to be in harmony and balance. The ecological world, or biosphere, is itself an argument for respecting differing abilities and the uniqueness of all living beings."[35] Domination and abuse of power by certain individuals and by humanity as a species largely unbalances the natural order and, as can be observed today, leads to environmental degradation and inequality.

The influence of colonialism on people with disabilities and on the very formation of the disability history was profound. Colonization "changed the natural and human landscape forever."[36] Such a transformation was enabled through the introduction of new viruses and illnesses in colonized territories, enslavement and forced labor, resource manipulation leading to undernourishment, and more. "As the colonizer encountered the Other," writes Shaun Grech, "it had to construct the Other, racially, culturally, bodily, and spiritually."[37] It is through this cultural, political, and physical reconstruction of the colonized subject that the definitions of disability and people with disabilities were formulated. An important note to make here, however, is a distinction between colonialism and settler colonialism and the differences that the two practices entailed on colonized bodies. While the aim of "more administrative forms of colonialism," such as the case of British colonization of India, was "to exploit or control" the colonized, the goal of settler colonialism was "to exterminate indigenous people or push them out."[38] In both cases, colonizers recognized Indigenous people as inferior; yet the process of dehumanization functioned on different levels. Settler colonialism led to immediate, complete eradication of the body, whereas other forms of colonialism disabled and exploited the body until it was dead.

Colonizers promoted ableism and anti-environmentalism by various means. While racism and sexism could be viewed as distinct types of oppression on their own, they also helped reinforce discrimination against people with disabilities, in addition to speciesism. The potency of such biases was amplified with the emergence of the pseudoscience of eugenics in the West, which was "of strategic importance to the imperial colonial project."[39] According to those who practiced and followed the doctrines of eugenics, "Women and people of color had smaller brains, were 'by Nature' less intelligent, psychiatrically inferior to men (labels such as 'hysterical' were applied), and less than human."[40] Such views doubtless helped perpetuate colonialism, widening the gap between the colonizer and the colonized, the white able-bodied man and all other humans. Initially, however, the fundamental instrument through which this gap was outlined was the colonialist justification of atrocities that produced not only physical victims but also long-lasting cultural, political, and social transformations in the colonized territories. That was the result of the white man's mission of fighting the assumed barbarism of the colonized and, as it was believed, enlightening those peoples with the grace of civilization. Nocella notes that in that time of irrevocable historical and cultural transformation, the very mission of civilizing the colonized established a clear "divide between nature and humans": "Those considered wild, savage, or primitive were situated on one side, and those considered civilized, privileged, and normal on the other."[41] The association of the colonized with nature was a good enough justification for colonizers to handle the environment and its inhabitants in a similar manner. In turn, the parallelism between the colonized and nature as less than human, and thus abnormal, gave rise to a peculiar form of ableism that I, paraphrasing Nocella, would call eco-ableism. Eco-ableism essentially functioned in a way that allowed the oppression of the environment and (disabled) individuals on ideological, cultural, and political levels.

Through eugenics, the concept of the body was considerably reimagined. Eugenics not only contributed to the construction of the belief that the true natural, ideal body is that of a white man (as opposed to, for example, white female and Indigenous bodies) but also, in combination with other perverse principles of colonialism, suggested that the white man had superior power because of his culturally, politically, economically, physically, and medically dominant body. Donna Haraway's discussion of the American Museum of Natural History in New York and how it constructed the meaning of "the natural body of man" profoundly illustrates these changing ideas about the body.[42] Even before entering the museum, the visitor witnesses the clear distinction between the bodies of the colonizer and the colonized, in the shape of a bronze statue positioned outside its doors: "To enter the Theodore Roosevelt Memorial, the visitor must pass by a James Earle Fraser equestrian statue of Teddy majestically mounted as a father and protector between two 'primitive' men, an American Indian and an African, both standing and dressed as 'savages.'"[43] Present at the entrance to the museum since 1940, the statue was removed in 2022 after a flurry of anti-racist activism, sparked in 2020 by the killing of Black American George Floyd by white police officer Derek Chauvin.[44] Along with dehumanizing portrayals of people of different races and ethnicities, Haraway draws attention to the cultural controversy that the objects in the museum convey, especially taxidermic animals. There is likewise a history of mounting human skins as museum specimens.[45] Taxidermy, particularly at the end of the nineteenth and beginning of the twentieth centuries, was a way to reinforce the legitimacy of the white man's body and emphasize the white man's control over the bodies of the other beings. Certainly, that was one of the ways to question the ecology of the body. By means of oppression and domination, the issue of difference—bodily, but also ecological difference—was foregrounded as the key principle of division between the privileged and deprived. There are multiple ways in which this very idea of the true ecological body continues to permeate today's culture. This, for example, is still very pronounced in discriminatory norms of "compulsory heterosexuality, compulsory able-bodiedness."[46] This is also apparent in the "extreme margin[alization]" of vegans.[47] The choice to be or become an ecologically different body is majorly perceived as a form of deviance. Bob and Jenna Torres's titular reference to a "vegan freak" effectively communicates both anti-environmentalism and ableism.[48] Despite the power of the vegan diet to solve a variety of environmental issues, vegans are continuously referred to or perceived as "freaks."[49] At the same time, the term *freak* is an infamously derogatory concept associated in disability studies with "everyday stigmatization endured by people with disabilities."[50] Various "discourses of the body" thus continuously shape and strengthen the phenomenon of "cultural disgust" that "distinguishes between good ecological subjects and impure, dirty, unnatural 'ecological others.'"[51]

Scholars throw into bright relief "the lasting effects of colonial power on subjectivity and culture."[52] Yet I also want to emphasize the persistent influence of colonialist ideologies that continue to fuel ableist and anti-environmental views even after colonialism is over. I am not the first one to note that with the official dismantling of colonialism as an institutionalized, systematic practice, the very ideology did not disappear.[53] Discrimination, oppression, abuse, and subjugation became so deeply rooted in culture, in the very understanding of being human, that in its inertia it continued to constitute the global culture. The effects of colonialism were also so profound that the transformations it had violently and forcefully imposed simply could not be undone. When discussing the cultural history of disability and environmentalism through the prism of colonialism, therefore, I do not refer to the periods after colonies gained independence as postcolonial or decolonial times—although I do not refute the legitimacy of these terms. Rather, I view the ableist and anti-environmental ideologies and actions that have been taking place since then as continuously influenced and shaped by colonialism and its aftereffects. I believe that the term *neocolonial* might be useful here to acknowledge the official ending of colonialism. Yet, for the purposes of my argument—that is, that the attitudes toward disability and the environment were and continue to be shaped by colonialist ideologies and cultures, I find it legitimate to use the term *colonialism* even when referring to instances from the second half of the twentieth century and the first two decades of the twenty-first century.

Walter D. Mignolo's discussion of the ceaseless influence of colonialism is particularly helpful here:

> The idea of America . . . is a modern European invention and limited to Europeans' view of the world and of their own history. In that view and in that history, coloniality, naturally, was (and still is) ignored or disguised as a necessary injustice in the name of justice. Coloniality names the experiences and views of the world and history of those whom Fanon called *les damnés de la terre* ("the wretched of the earth," those who have been, and continue to be, subjected to the standards of modernity). The wretched are defined by the *colonial wound*, and the colonial wound, physical and/or psychological, is a consequence of *racism*, the hegemonic discourse that questions the humanity of all those who do not belong to the locus of enunciation (and the geo-politics of knowledge) of those who assign the standards of classification and assign themselves the right to classify. The blindness toward histories and experiences lying outside the local history of Western Christianity, as shown by secular Europeans, grounded in the Greek and Latin languages, and unfolded in the six vernacular imperial languages (Italian, Spanish, Portuguese, French, German, and English), has been and continues to be a trademark of intellectual history and its ethical, political, and economic consequences.[54]

Mignolo thus explains the continuous presence of colonialist ideology in the world through the term *coloniality*, suggesting that nations, individuals, and even territories are still divided into the oppressor and the oppressed, where equality—including disability rights and eco-friendly existence—is yet to be achieved. Colonialism is part of our current life, for it "continues to provide the ideological-cultural and material foundations for continuing domination."[55] As Mignolo asserts, colonialism, or rather, "coloniality," was part of a larger reality that included "modernity" and "capitalism" "as we know them today," though the emergence of this very cluster dates back to the beginning of the triangular trade.[56] With decolonization largely taking place in the twentieth century, "the myth of a 'postcolonial' world" was established, yet "the juridical-political decolonization" of the world did not lead to the elimination of the colonial history, ideology, and culture, and, as a result, "we continue to live under the same 'colonial power matrix.'"[57] This is of particular concern to Indigenous scholars who debate the prefix in the term *postcolonialism*, corroborating the problematic nature of the notion with the observation that "colonization has not ended."[58]

That coloniality is still part of our reality has become acutely noticeable in the times of globalization when various countries must "question their role as modern states."[59] Indeed, several countries, nations, and even larger territories continue to experience the effects of their colonial designations in the neocolonial era. Analola Santana uses the powerful term *abjection* to characterize those feelings of differentiation and being different, and, via the example of Latin America, elucidates the long-lasting power of colonialism:

> Within the discourse of coloniality, Latin American subjectivity has historically been formatted within the domain of abjection; these are bodies that threaten the expansion of a project of colonization in the name of modernization. In order to justify a system of imperial domination, Latin America had to be condensed into a single, homogeneous identity. In the beginning, these undesirable subjects were generalized categories such as the indigenous native, the black slave, the peasant, and the woman. In contemporary society they now include the lower classes, the political dissident, the immigrant, and the queer. These bodies have been made into a spectacle of difference exhibited as the monstrous and the freak, that which will destroy the social order if not controlled.[60]

Santana's apt observation can be applied to other formerly colonized peoples and territories.[61] What is important here then is, first, that colonialism has fluidly transformed into neocolonialism when essentially the same principles and systems of inequality are preserved, and, second, that these inequalities continue to center the body as the primary agent through which ableism and anti-environmentalism are promoted, through ideologies denoting the purity, privilege, and exceptionalism of some and the reverse of others.

This idea of neocolonialism, "coloniality," is a continuous colonialism that exists within and with capitalism, which, as the central economic system adopted by the West, has rather successfully been spread throughout the globe.[62] And here one can observe how colonialism, capitalism, ableism, and environmental crisis entwine into one single complex web, making the parallels between disability rights and environmentalism even more pronounced. Nocella sees the direct link between the colonization of the world by European nations and capitalism. The scholar claims,

> With European colonialism spreading across the world, an economic system that upheld the values of capitalism was created, placing a value on everything and everyone. For example, whites were more valuable than people of color, birds, trees, water, and even land. All of nature was viewed as a natural resource, a commodity, and typically marked as property—something owned by someone—to be used any which way its owners saw fit. Over time everything, including people (such as slaves), had an inherent worth and was viewed as a commodity.[63]

The commodification of the environment and of certain individuals that took place in the colonial era further intensified with the emergence of capitalism, particularly so in the twentieth century when the world as we know it today was built. This is what energy humanities scholars have been vigorously lamenting about, peeling back to the true nature of capitalism, its interminable production and insatiable consumption, that brought us into the current environmental collapse, with the attendant problems of cheap energy, climate change, and animal rights abuses, among many others, in the forefront. Thus, Stephanie LeMenager claims that in twentieth-century United States "energy, perhaps the most essential quality of biological life, has supplanted personhood, the social 'face' of the individual human body."[64] Energy humanities scholars Sheena Wilson, Adam Carlson, and Imre Szeman foreground "the colonial and ongoing neo-colonial rationalization of the dispossession of Indigenous lands and the assimilation of Indigenous peoples into capitalist modernity."[65] Wilson draws attention to "bodies (human and otherwise) [that] are managed, (im)mobilized, and (dis)connected in the name of those extractivist, patriarchal, and colonial worldviews that perpetuate the (North) American Dream(s) of nationhood, prosperity, and petrocolonial futurity."[66] What all these scholars, and many others, accentuate is that "colonization tightly interweaves with the petromodernity of the present."[67] It is the tangled ball of colonialism, capitalism, fossil fuels, climate change, and inequality that we are dealing with today.

Capitalism has largely entered the Western world through industrialization, which was itself, in the words of Timothy Mitchell, "a colonial [phenomenon]."[68] It is therefore plausible to argue that one of the ways that colonialism continues to exercise its power in today's world is through capitalism. In *After Globalization*, Eric Cazdyn and Imre Szeman make a significant claim: "Capitalism is now everywhere, which seems to confirm not only its permanence and effectiveness, but also its legitimacy. Without any competing system against which to now measure it, capitalism is no longer up for debate. This doesn't mean that everyone is satisfied with it, or that we can't analyze its problems and failures, but that its reality as a system has disappeared into the background of everyday life."[69] Through capitalism, the systems of oppression that existed in the colonial era, as well as newly emergent ones, continue to destroy the environment and widen the gap between the privileged and the poor, white people and BIPOC communities, the West and the East, and the Global North and the Global South. I fully concur with the prominent postcolonial and environmental studies scholar Dipesh Chakrabarty that problems like climate change "cannot be reduced to a story of capitalism," for, as Chakrabarty notes, "unlike in the crises of capitalism, there are no lifeboats here for the rich and the privileged"; yet climate change, as well as various other environmental issues, and the global injustice to which they contribute "accentuate the logic of inequality that runs through the rule of capital."[70]

The destruction of the environment as well as the inequality from which people with disabilities suffer the most are some of the major outcomes of capitalism, neocolonialism, and neoliberalism. Jos Boys foregrounds "the economic and social disadvantage created by neocolonialism and capitalist exploitation."[71] In turn, Karen Soldatic, one of the most prolific disability studies scholars, views "disability and disablement as socially produced and reproduced oppression" in a neoliberal state.[72] Grech notes in his exploration of the linkages between disability and colonialism that neoliberalism and globalization along with capitalism (or as part of it) "embody and perpetuat[e] the neocolonial."[73] This becomes particularly visible through the violence that people from the postcolonial world experience. This is, for instance, "slow violence"—the term that Rob Nixon coins to describe "a violence that occurs gradually and out of sight, a violence of delayed destruction that is dispersed across time and space, an attritional violence that is typically not viewed as violence at all."[74] One such example is, of course, climate change, and the general environmental devastation, that has disproportionately impacted postcolonial territories, and which the people living there have no means to mitigate. "Slow violence" harms not only individuals who live in the regions most affected by climate change but humanity in general; after all, we all share this planet, and thinking that some people might survive environmental collapse just because of their geographic location is not only unproductive but profoundly wrong. The term *slow violence* also illuminates the horrific transformations of the environment. Stacy Alaimo describes this as the result of humanity's conquering and subjugating nature: "The *environment* has been drained of its blood, its lively creatures, its interactions and relations—in short, all that is recognizable as 'nature'—in order that it become a mere empty space, an 'uncontested ground,' for human 'development.'"[75] Another effective example of violence is more immediate and directly visible: war. Grech examines the powerful entanglement of war, environmental crisis, and disability, on the one hand, and (neo)colonialism, on the other:

> Often steered by the Western hand, violent conflict remains a major cause of impairment and death throughout the world and shatters the lives of those who live through it. . . . The neocolonial also emerges and breathes through the environmental degradation—a major source of poverty, destitution and ill-health—caused by rich countries, and again among the hardest hit are disabled people. Research, media and other representations such as movies, documentaries, books and development discourse also embody and perpetuate the neocolonial. These blatant or subliminal messages, [sic] are insidious in constructing a Southern subject that is degenerate, sexual, ignorant, violent, uncivilized- [sic] calling for, and even desiring an illuminated and civilized intervention that can only be offered by the Western hand. Developing and humanizing the Other, therefore becomes a moral obligation.[76]

Realizing the profound influence of "neocolonialism, neoliberalism, and transnational capitalism" on our values, our institutions, and our very way of living, "we can see the effects of the colonialism that has never really been 'post-' among indigenous people worldwide."[77]

Though the colonialist terminology used to describe the colonized as "the savage, the cannibal, and the monstrous other"[78] might seem archaic today, it has not completely disappeared from Western/Northern thought and continues to sustain inequality. Disability studies scholars show a great concern regarding people with disabilities born in Third World countries because of the neocolonialist and imperialist practices of wealthier, more powerful nations. In Iraq, for example, there is a visible influence of such practices on children's health: "Rather than being the natural consequence of Third World instability and violence, these birth anomalies [congenital heart defects] are the material result of imperialist foreign policy and its attendant environmental destruction, and thus present urgent questions to our understanding of environmental justice in the context of ongoing imperialist violence."[79] The prognoses for people with disabilities born or living in Third World countries are rather depressing: "Disabled people in the Third World are at risk of becoming invisible in global media and within their own societies through the erosion of social services; this invisibility engenders further dehumanization."[80] What scholars foreground through these instances of disability (and environmental devastation) is the perpetual, ongoing colonialist ideology that allows certain nations to think higher of themselves than others, certain individuals to perceive themselves as being more human than others, and certain territories and living environments to be conceived as less valuable than others. This, paradoxically, has led to the fact that social, political, medical, and environmental calamities in the postcolonial world have become classified as norms. Scholars point out that the "statistical invisibility" of people with disabilities from the Third World goes hand in hand with "a kind of hypervisibility that naturalized these disabilities as the result of violence."[81] Through this, the colonialist division of the world into the civilized and the barbaric continues to be manifested in the second half of the twentieth and the first two decades of the twenty-first centuries.

In a world dominated by (neo)colonialist views, our interaction with each other through the materiality of the body and our relationship to the environment we inhabit become crucial in redefining the body as an ecological self. Mitchell and Snyder comment on humanity's connection to the environment as follows: "We are vulnerable embodied beings who interact with our environments; thus we experience ourselves and others through a defining porosity: we are not only affected by the places we inhabit, but we also leave our imprint on these locations. Marginalized subjects, including disabled people, often experience their lives in greater proximity to environmental threats such as toxicity, climate change, generational exposures to unsafe living conditions due to poverty, militarization, body-exhausting labors as in the case of migrant workers, and more."[82] Indeed, the environment we inhabit directly influences who and how we are; the destruction of the environment is essentially the destruction of, among other things, ourselves. Disabling the environment disables the able-bodied majority and intensifies the impairments of disabled individuals. Here again we can witness how neocolonial practices and capitalism influence the environment and disability. To borrow from Kelly Fritsch, "the material-discursive production of disability is intimately linked to forms of neoliberal biocapitalism that have consequences for how we think toxicity [from and through the environment] and disability together."[83] It thus becomes imperative to understand this codependence of disability and the environment, on the one hand, and colonialist views toward certain peoples and territories, on the other. A greater task for humanity in promoting environmental justice and equality is "that we work to ensure that people are not exposed to those environmental assaults that lead to the creation of 'the disabled' or 'disability.'"[84] Fighting against inequality and environmental degradation can thus help dismantle oppressive views, policies, and actions that stem from neocolonialism, neoliberalism, and capitalism.

What only reinforces the oppressive condition of the South/the East/the postcolonial world is the unjust vestment in the authority of Western knowledge as such—which this book works against, drawing on scholarship from the Global South and explicating, among other issues, examples of injustice in the Global South. This can be perceived not only through the lack of interest, care, and support regarding environmental issues and disability in formerly colonized territories (though these largely emerged due to the actions of wealthier nations) but also through the prevalence of scholarship from the West/North regarding issues like disability and the environment. In their discussion of the relationship between disability and colonialism, Grech and Soldatic note that "the hegemonic global North disability studies has not done much to improve" the problem of disengagement with disability in various scholarly fields, and "it remains detached from the global South, the histories, contexts and cultures, and epistemologies of these specific geopolitical spaces, and how disability is ontologically constructed and lived through a history replete with signifiers of power and empire that frame the global."[85] Indeed, the very emergence of the so-called "southern disability theory" that Soldatic refers to in *Routledge Handbook of Disability Studies* published in 2020 reveals the prior exclusive focus on and by the Global North and further calls for recognition of disability as understood and lived in the Global South.[86] The experiences of being disabled in the Global North and the Global South differ dramatically, primarily because of the financial and health conditions of the nations in general.[87] Learning about disability through and beyond colonialism, adopting an all-inclusive global approach can, to a large degree, change "the contemporary disability landscape"; this will lead to a much-needed "(re)positioning [of 'the disability narrative in the global South'] . . . and to a new understanding of disability as a global historical narrative."[88] In addition to that, this will open a new perspective on colonialism and neocolonialism as such, making it "possible to examine imperialism through the lens of disability, and provide useful avenues for engagements with disability in fields such as postcolonial studies."[89]

Organization of the Book

The book is divided into four parts—"Justice, Imperialism, and Eco-Ableism," "Redefining Blindness and Deafness through (Dis)Ability, Colonialism, and the Environment," "Disabled Bodies, Ecologies, and Imperialist Subjectivities," and "Colonialism, (Dis)Ability, and Nature in and through America"— each tracing the intricate relationship between disability, the environment, and colonialism from the historical past to the present day.

The book begins with a theoretical analysis of the intersection of disability and the environment, emphasizing the tight connection of eco-ableism with various types of inequality that were formulated and promoted during colonial times and remain in place today. Part I opens with Andrew B. Jenks's "Disability Rights as a 'Global' Norm: Environmentalism, Post-Colonialism, and the Meaning of Disability in the Majority World." Jenks observes that although social movements advancing understandings of disability as socially constructed phenomenon have been emancipatory for those living in the minority world of the Global North, for many living in the majority world of the Global South, the potential of the UN Convention on the Rights of Persons with Disabilities (CRPD) to ensure equal rights has been questioned by feminist and postcolonial scholars. Using feminist and critical disability studies lenses in analyzing discourse surrounding the convention, Jenks explores an alternative to what Katharina Heyer has termed "rights enabled" by looking to the ways in which official understandings of disability imported from the minority world further "disable" individuals it purports to protect, through official stylized, mainstreamed meanings of disability. Recognizing the onto-formative characteristics of the current regime surrounding disabled peoples' human rights, this essay asks whether the new era of disability rights is a positive change for the position of the disabled in society or whether it reinforces binaries between the minority and majority worlds. By pushing back against the same ableism that defined not only disability but also colonial subjectivities, just environmental policy must be formed through processes that do not view disability only as a problem to be solved.

The section proceeds with Nancy J. Hirschmann's "Disability, Colonialism, and Environmental Theory: A Political Theory Perspective." Hirschmann considers the intersections of environmentalism with disability. The author observes that disability is rarely mentioned, much less engaged, by environmental political theory. Yet disability studies has long maintained that disability is a condition not of bodies but rather of the lack of receptivity of human-made environments to certain kinds of bodies: for instance, architecture that adopts stairs instead of slopes or ramps disables bodies that use wheelchairs for mobility. Similarly, the human-made environment can cause disabling impairments, both directly (when landmines blow off limbs or when fetal exposure to air pollution causes developmental disabilities in children) and second-arily (when flooding caused by rising sea levels makes wheelchair mobility impossible). Hirschmann claims that insights of disability studies can make important contributions to environmental theory. For instance, ableism can result from environmentalist efforts at sustainability, such as the elimination of plastic straws that are helpful to people with upper-body impairments, or accommodation can appear to harm the "natural" environment, such as when hardscape surfaces are built in beaches or forests. Can efforts toward sus-tainability and disability accommodation be reconciled, or are they inevitably at odds? Will disabled persons be sacrificed on the altar of consequentialism in the face of global disaster, or are there different and inclusive solutions?

Memona Hossain's "(Post)Colonialism, Eco-Ableism, and the Produc-tion of Knowledge" explores how the colonial narrative continues to illus-trate an erasure of one voice and the dominance of another, undermining access and engagement to environmental consciousness by people with dis-abilities. Hossain argues that a disabled person's access to environmental activism and to responding to Earth's climate crisis is defined by the colonial able-bodied model. Hossain is thus interested in the intersectionality of im-perialism, disability, and environmental consciousness through engagement with what constitutes truth. The essay's primary concern is how we can rede-fine our locus of knowledge production to engage participation and empow-erment rather than discouraging or creating impediments to engagement through means of omitting a people's narrative. Hossain provides insight from ecopsychology to illustrate how the access point to environmental con-sciousness can no longer assume a power differential but rather becomes accessible to all who are invested in understanding their relationships with nature.

This section concludes with Alice Wexler's "Rights and Responsibilities in Australia: Debility and Dispossession in Settler Colonialism." The author provides a thorough analysis of disability/debility as inseparable in Indig-enous Australia with economic disempowerment and dispossession of land. Commonalities between disability/debility and Indigeneity also exist in how bodies are valued in Western capitalist society. The land is critical to the Indigenous body as the source of various assets. Displaced from land and herded to country in which they had no connection, Indigenous peoples were dependent on the paternalistic policies that deepened and entrenched them in a cycle of poverty. Against this backdrop, Wexler discusses the con-tentious philosophy and politics of the Indigenous attorney and scholar Noel Pearson, a brutal realist who was tired of losing. The core of Pearson's prag-matic philosophy is that rights and responsibilities are inseparable. While the underlying reason for substance abuse and domestic violence is osten-sibly dispossession, racism, unemployment, and trauma, Pearson risks the ire of Indigenous peoples by recommending that they confront the disease as an epidemic with immediate action. He suggests that the passive welfare mentality is the cause of addiction and social and economic decline. Wexler analyzes Pearson's radical position as it interfaces with disablement caused by a lack of resources, sovereignty, and self-representation.

The book then moves to specific examples of disability (blindness and deafness) to illustrate the intersection of disability, the environment, and colonialism. Here, the focus is geographically broad, to capture the nature of the tight connection between eco-ableism and colonialism across many colonized places. Part II begins with Iain Hutchison's "Blind Horizons: The Worlds of People with Sight Loss during Scotland's Long Nineteenth Century." Focusing on blindness and sight loss within a historical context from the end of the eighteenth century to the beginning of the twentieth century in Scotland—notably its capital city, Edinburgh, and the surrounding rural hinterland—the essay uses the archival records of two sometimes complimentary but often competing entities that endeavored to both support and direct the lives of the people with sight loss. One of these operated within a residential and nonresidential framework, catering to what it saw as the able-bodied blind and therefore operating through the provision of work as well as welfare support; the other focused on the "outdoor" blind—that is, blind people who lived in their own homes rather than in or near institutional settings but who were considered unable to work. Hutchison interprets the environment in his analysis from several perspectives: geographical environment (urban/rural); familial versus institutional environments; top-down cultural environments from often well-meaning but agenda-driven interventionists such as religious evangelists and philanthropists/benefactors; and blind perspectives on interventions in their lives where environments of gratitude toward outside benevolence were created but where there were also environments of rejection and rebellion against well-intended, or gender-driven, external benevolence.

In "Curing a 'Toxic Condition': Deafness and Public Health Policy during the Porfiriato," Holly Caldwell explores how governing authorities in modernizing Latin American states used medicine and science as instruments of social control to manage marginalized populations. As an elite group of government officials, prominent citizens, and urban professionals—collectively known as *científicos*—drew on models of European colonialism to classify, diagnose, and cure their own population of perceived backwardness, they forged close links between ideals of order, cleanliness, and hygiene. Deafness, and its perceived associated causes—poverty, disease, and immorality—represented a central part of these late nineteenth-century concerns and was thus considered an obstacle to building a disciplined and "pure" nation. Established in 1868, Mexico's first school for the deaf, the Escuela

Nacional de Sordomudos (ENSM), was created in response to growing social concerns over how to educate this population; this coincided with the advent of the professionalization of medicine and public health, the development of notions of "normality" and "abnormality," and the increasing medical surveillance of "deviant" bodies. In addition to categorizing and classifying marginalized populations through scientific methods to achieve "progress" and "civilization," the Díaz administration drew on colonial models as it developed extensive engineering projects to reshape Mexico City's urban environment. Caldwell examines how Porfirian policymakers enacted a multifold mission to improve public health conditions and the ways in which their goal to rid the urban environment of "degenerate" characteristics that directly or indirectly caused deafness introduced a series of failed sanitation reforms at the ENSM.

The section concludes with Aubrey Tang's "The Blindness of Colonial Modernity: *A Blind Man's Remembrance of Things Past*." Tang examines the 1976 Cantonese autobiographic operatic song *Yik Wong/Yiwang* 憶往 (A Blind Man's Remembrance of Things Past), written by *Dou Wun/Duwun* 杜煥 (1910–1979), the most acclaimed blind musician from the tradition of Cantonese *Naamyam/Nanyin* 南音 (sound from the South). This song chronicles Dou's life not only as a legendary musician but also as a blind man living in British colonial Hong Kong between the 1920s and 1970s. Through this forty-nine-minute song, this essay calls into question Hong Kong's development from a preindustrial southern Chinese modernity to an industrial–financial British colonial modernity, when blind Cantonese people lost their mobility and livelihood along with the accompanying biocultural changes. It explores the ways in which industrialization was an ableist colonial endeavor favoring the sighted at the expense of the native blind people. The essay employs a phenomenological approach to investigate how colonialism strips away the native people's bodily agency in the modern age.

The book then pays close attention to the body and its representation in literature—from Shakespeare to Sinha—and the ways in which physical disability can be understood through imperialism and ecology. Focusing on a broader period, this section conceptualizes colonialism as a set of practices, policies, and sociocultural measures aimed at subjugating certain peoples and environments for the prosperity and well-being of others. Thinking of colonial times in this way helps connect colonialism to postcolonialism and illuminates the ongoing impact of colonial oppression. Part III opens with John Gulledge's "Dis/Enabling Spaces: Crip-Ecologies of Shakespeare's *The Tempest*." Gulledge argues that for *The Tempest*, Shakespeare's dramatic commentary on imperial expansion and early colonialism, the "cripping" of ecologies begins with the linguistic usurpation of the *Other*'s material and discursive history. Gulledge examines the play as a rich site for extended consideration on crip-ecologies and explores how the intrusion of privileged minds and bodies disrupts the habitude of markedly different minds and bodies. The author traces the development of Ariel and Caliban specifically as two body-texts that both reflect and represent the island's ecology. As symbolic embodiments of the natural elements—Ariel of air and fire, Caliban of water and earth—they both figuratively and literally become interdependent parts of the healthy body and the healthy landscape; they are, in effect, the humors balanced. Prospero's alteration to their ecological functions and abilities frustrates their interactions with the Island space, transforming it from enabling to disabling. Gulledge deliberately locates the "normate" Prospero against what he sees as the ecologically committed bodies of Ariel and Caliban to propose a turn: through a possibly anachronistic reading of Shakespeare in a deeper shade of green and through a disability lens, we might recognize Prospero's own inabilities, his own interdependencies, and his own potential status as *Other*.

In "The Superfluous Who 'Neither Produce like the Poor nor Consume like the Rich': Eugenics and the 'Coloniality of Ability' in Edward Thomas's *The Happy-Go-Lucky Morgans* (1913)," Anna Stenning argues that the Anglo-Welsh poet and critic Edward Thomas's novel *The Happy-Go-Lucky Morgans* contributes to our understanding of both Thomas's poetry and what Walter D. Mignolo describes as "the darker side of Western modernity"—the influences of colonialism and coloniality on Liberal thought. Stenning focuses here on what Mignolo terms "the coloniality of being," which is the lived experience of colonization and its impact on language. She argues that Thomas's politics must be understood through his status as the son of a high-ranking British Liberal party member and his readings of H. D. Thoreau. This means that the Superfluous Man—an epithet that Thomas applied to himself—informed Thomas's critique of a logic of domination that underpinned leftist politics, despite his egalitarianism. When Thomas was writing *The Happy-Go-Lucky Morgans*, the Liberal Party invested in the pseudoscience of eugenics. This interest—which underpinned early efforts to form a welfare state—united a party formerly divided over the issue of Irish home rule. Stenning argues that this informed his observations of rapidly changing social attitudes toward both people and nature, manifest in general scorn for the socially "unnecessary," which was encoded in the "Mental Deficiency Act" of 1913 and the development of "no man's land" around towns and cities. According to Stenning, through *The Happy-Go-Lucky Morgans*, Thomas creates an analogy for a world where human beings and the natural world are no longer exploited in the relentless quest for wealth accumulation or private advancement, akin to Thoreau's philosophy of "extra-vagance."

The section concludes with Suha Kudsieh's "The Damaging Effects of Western Neoliberal Policies and Local Corruption in Indra Sinha's *Animal's*

People." Kudsieh claims that when India embraced transnational neoliberal policies that were promoted by the World Bank and opened its doors to Western corporations in the 1970s, environmental issues became a salient theme in South Asian fiction, as evidenced in the novels written by Amitav Ghosh, Arundhati Roy, and Ruchir Joshi. Disability also became a prominent theme, as can be seen in the novels written by Salman Rushdie, Bapsi Sidhwa, and Rohinton Mistry. Indra Sinha is unique among those authors in this regard because he combines both themes to retell the tragic aftermath of the gas leak that took place in a pesticide plant owned by a Western corporation in Bhopal, India. The leak caused the death of the poor people who lived nearby and blinded others while other victims developed incurable respiratory conditions. Sinha sheds light on the struggle of those victims by detailing the mercurial efforts of Western companies to shift the blame, which renders the quest for justice almost an impossible mission. Subsequently, the theme of disability, according to Kudsieh, becomes a convenient tool in the novel both to examine the issues of injustice between the marginalized poor and the rich and between the able bodied and the disabled and to depict the ease with which Western corporations are held responsible in the West for work accidents, whereas they flaunt the same laws in the ex-colonies. Although a decisive victory seems elusive in the novel, change is possible if one starts planning for the future and embraces hope as Animal, the titular narrator, does. Both actions, thinking of tomorrow and being hopeful, are integral to the human condition. The theoretical framework for this essay draws on the works of Rob Nixon, Edward Said, Upamanyu Pablo Mukherjee, and Justin O. Johnston, among many others.

Finally, the book introduces several essays on the representation of disability, the environment, and colonialism in and through the United States. This section not only engages with the colonial and postcolonial legacies of the United States but also reflects the breadth of scholarship occurring there. This section outlines the specific examples of the United States' colonialist practices, from the reflection of eco-ableism in colonial science, the eradication of American bison, and the use of disability to promote the conquest of the American West to the examples of U.S. nuclear colonization and its dramatic effects on the environment. Via this section, the book makes an important contribution to the study of colonialism, disability, and the environment, demonstrating that the United States can and should be considered from these three perspectives and that certain political decisions and actions made by the United States must be viewed as clear forms of colonization that have had dramatic consequences on peoples and environments.

Part IV begins with Gordon M. Sayre's "American Degeneracy: Colonial Science and Environmental Anxiety in the Eighteenth Century." The essay's primary interest concerns a debate that raged in the second half of the eighteenth century about the American environment that had an impact on European emigration, the Creole Revolutions, and even the philosophies of Immanuel Kant and Georg Wilhelm Friedrich Hegel. Travel writers and natural historians such as Pehr Kalm and the Comte de Buffon claimed that American Indians were weak and infertile, that livestock brought from the Old World became smaller in America, and that Creole colonists aged quickly and died younger than Europeans. This was "The Dispute of the New World," to use the title of the book by Antonello Gerbi, or *La Querelle d'Amérique* according to Alexander von Humboldt. Yet Sayre prefers the term "American Degeneracy" as used by Cotton Mather and Thomas Jefferson. In his essay, Sayre reconsiders American degeneracy as a form of environmental anxiety affecting colonists and Creoles. If the American climate was excessively humid and cool, as Buffon claimed, or its soil and climate deleterious to growth and fertility, as Kalm wrote, Americans faced a disability that must be overcome if they were to compete with Europe economically or intellectually. Identifying the ways in which this phenomenon is comparable to influential concepts in the environmental humanities introduced by Lawrence Buell, Stacy Alaimo, and Ulrich Beck, Sayre argues that American degeneracy resembles climate change as much as it does toxic pollution, because the evidence that inspired it came from fossils and bones of a prehistoric past, and the controversy helped to establish the epistemologies of deep time that have been decisive for climate science.

The next essay in this section is Matthew J. C. Cella's "The Bison and the Plow: Eco-Ableism and the Conquest of the Great Plains," in which the author examines two icons of the Great Plains—the bison and the plow—through the dual lenses of disability studies and ecological criticism. Cella explores the U.S. government's attempted eradication of American bison during the nineteenth century and how the trope of disability was deployed as a defense for the conquest of the American West. First, the essay demonstrates how the destruction of the bison population during this period was part of an overall attempt to regulate the deviance of Native American bodies, subduing and eradicating what was perceived as the pathology of Native savagery. Second, it explores the colonizing act of bison destruction from the Native perspective, highlighting how Native authors like Zitkala-Ŝâ (Yankton Dakota Sioux) and Charles Eastman (Santee Dakota) present colonization as a debilitating phenomenon that socially constructs disability within the colonized Native population. Third, the essay demonstrates how the near destruction of bison herds and the subsequent colonization of the Plains Indians was motivated by an eco-ableist paradigm that regarded the arid grasslands—and the bison-hunting culture it supported—as a nonnormative landscape that needed to be conquered, subdued, and rehabilitated. This manipulation of the environment to make it adhere to Euro-American standards of economically appropriate land-use practices, Cella notes, led to long-term degradation of the regional landscape. The parallel depletion of bison herds and the emergence of the plow as an environmental corrective device are interpreted in the context of Progressive Era thinking surrounding disability. Finally, the essay ponders the return of the American bison to the Great Plains at the turn of this century as an ironic symbol for the ecological rehabilitation of a region ravaged by over a century of aggressive cultivation.

Finally, the section, and the book itself, concludes with "The (Un)Making of Voice: Nuclear Colonialism, Disability, and Toxic Environmentalism in Marshallese Music," where Jessica A. Schwartz explores Marshallese "radiation songs" or songs that address a complex of colonial entanglements through extant consequences of U.S. nuclear colonization to share the problematic individuation of disability and its separation from the environment. Radiation songs, Schwartz argues, evince the interconnections of environmental degradation and collective-personal disablement at the level of the throat, which is the connective nexus of the collective (more-than-human world) and personal spirit. Through song, this essay shares how nineteenth-century development of the German copra trade in the Marshall Islands saw the formation of a distinct "working class" while Protestant missionaries aimed to convert commoners through humancentric hymn-singing. Marshallese singing voices waiver in and out of audibility throughout songs that detail their compulsory disablement, where the (un)making of their voices speaks to the collusion of nineteenth-century projects of German colonial-capitalism (economy) and American missionary-democratic (political) projects, such as severing "humans" from the "environment," which destabilized matrilineal culture. Refusing voice-based, individualistic productivity as ability, Schwartz contends, these songs offer decolonial reflection on the failures of human agency in the making of "the environment," prompting critique on the medical model and environmental understandings of disability via the human body. Listening to collectivized disability as throat-based movements displaces colonial hierarchical "voice" to resituate more-than-human political action and rethink the ableist Eurocentric tenets of democracy (that centers power in the people).

Conclusion

This collection does not attempt to equate today's world with the historical colonial reality, nor does it aim to undermine our achievements in both environmental and disability struggles. It does, however, call for recognizing the persistent influence of practices and views that were formulated during the colonial era and continue to dominate the sociocultural and political consciousness of today, sustaining and promoting ableism, environmental degradation, and global inequality. There has been gradual progress in disability discourse, from the rejection of concepts like "freak" and "monstrosity," to the industrial-era reimagining of the body, and to the reconceptualization of disability from a "pathology" to "a paradigm for all bodies as lacking capacities that are in need of market-based solutions—particularly those peddled within a new era of biopolitics by an increasingly globalised pharmaceutical industry."[90] Similarly, the environment is a concept that has been approached in various ways, from Mother Nature, to a subject that could be abused and oppressed (a view that became particularly pronounced during the Industrial Revolution), to our current recognition of the vital necessity of mitigating the ramifications of environmental degradation. What we observe today, however, is that the attachment to the idea that the world is dominated and governed by white, able-bodied, heterosexual men continues to jeopardize attempts to build a new world that celebrates diversity and appreciates and cares for the environment, including the humans and more-than-humans that inhabit it.

As we scrutinize the problem closer, the intersection of disability, the environment, and colonialism becomes strikingly apparent. Disability and the environment were marginalized in the colonial era through policies of oppression over natural and colonized bodies, when, for example, the ideas of "able, fit, disciplined, industrious and productive bodies and minds . . . always stationed disability *and* indigeneity at its door."[91] Matthew J. C. Cella thus sees strong potential in conjoining ecocriticism and disability studies, for "each field has become increasingly invested in exploring the relationship between the two sides of the ecosomatic coin: the body and the environment."[92] A better-known way of how the environment becomes part of disability discourse is through the discussions of "the built environments and sociopolitical transformations of space into places," where disability is welcome or not, that make disability a negative category or celebrate it as a difference.[93] In short, these are environments that "can both '*enable* activity' or '*impede* functioning of the individual.'"[94] But it is through disability and the environment that such crucial issues as a "habitable body" and a "habitable world" come to the fore.[95] And it is through the intersection of these notions that we can fully learn about "the interconnections, interchanges, and transits between human bodies and nonhuman natures."[96] Additionally, the struggle of both fields with the term *the Other* perhaps most prominently signals the footprint of colonialist ideology on the two. In disability studies, there has been an ongoing effort "to remove the consistent representation of it [disability] as 'the other,'" thus eradicating the negative association of disability with deviance.[97] In the environmental humanities, scholars continue to grapple with the problem of *othering* nature and more-than-humans, from the more evident perception of humanity being part of nature (that recognizes and tries to rectify the problematic anti-environmental views of the human as oppressor and governor of the natural world), to the attempts to celebrate nature's otherness. Consider, for example, Timothy Morton's call to recognize nature's secret sides in his interpretation of an "animal": "Instead of 'animal,' I use *strange stranger*. This stranger isn't just strange. She, or he, or it—can we tell? how?—is strangely strange. Their strangeness itself is strange. We can never absolutely figure them out. . . . They are intrinsically strange."[98] It is thus the aim of this collection to point out the major overlaps in constructing and perceiving disability and the environment historically and the influence of (neo)colonialist views on these processes.

Providing theoretical interventions in eco-ableism and colonialism, this book draws on specific disabilities and examines them from the perspectives of colonial studies and the environmental humanities. It explores the body as a site of colonial oppression and environmental exploitation and investigates the intersection of disability, the environment, and colonialism in the United States. These important contributions offer a unique approach to the study of the three concepts of disability, the environment, and colonialism. Drawing on existing research, the current edited collection connects eco-ableism, disability, and environmental inequality to colonialism, explicating the ways in which colonialism has shaped them. This book thus emphasizes that while it is important to study disability at the intersection of the environment, it is also impossible to fully address this issue without explicitly acknowledging both the impact of colonialism on disability and the environment and the ramifications that the postcolonial world continues to experience today.

NOTES

1. Sarah Jaquette Ray and Jay Sibara, "Introduction," in *Disability Studies and the Environmental Humanities: Toward an Eco-Crip Theory*, ed. Sarah Jaquette Ray and Jay Sibara (Lincoln: University of Nebraska Press, 2017), 1.

2. See, for example, Bill Ashcrof, Gareth Griffiths, and Helen Tiffin, *The Empire Writes Back: Theory and Practice in Post-Colonial Literatures* (London: Routledge, 1989); Elleke Boehmer, *Colonial and Postcolonial Literature* (Oxford: Oxford University Press, 1995); and Gesa Mackenthun, "America's Troubled Postcoloniality: Some Reflections from Abroad," *Discourse* 22, no. 3 (2000); 34–45, accessed July 15, 2021, https://doi.org/10.1353/dis.2000.0008.

3. Jenny Sharpe, "Is the United States Postcolonial? Transnationalism, Immigration, and Race," *Diaspora: A Journal of Transnational Studies* 4, no. 2 (1995): 181, accessed July 15, 2021, https://doi.org/10.1353/dsp.1995.0004.

4. Kariann Akemi Yokota, *Unbecoming British: How Revolutionary America Became a Postcolonial Nation* (Oxford: Oxford University Press, 2011), 9.

5. Some examples here include such edited collections as Sarah Jaquette Ray and Jay Sibara's *Disability Studies and the Environmental Humanities: Toward an Eco-Crip Theory*

and Matthew J. C. Cella's *Disability and the Environment in American Literature: Toward an Ecosomatic Paradigm* as well as monographs like Stacy Alaimo's *Bodily Natures: Science, Environment, and the Material Self* and Sarah Jaquette Ray's *The Ecological Other: Environmental Exclusion in American Culture.*

6. Stefanie Hunt-Kennedy, "'Had His Nose Cropt for Being Formerly Runaway': Disability and the Bodies of Fugitive Slaves in the British Caribbean," *Slavery & Abolition: A Journal of Slave and Post-Slave Studies* 41, no. 2 (2020): 213–14.

7. See also Eleni Kefala, *Peripheral (Post) Modernity: The Syncretist Aesthetics of Borges, Piglia, Kalokyris and Kyriakidis* (New York: Peter Lang, 2007), 21–23, on "peripheral modernity" and Latin America.

8. Sarah Jaquette Ray, "Risking Bodies in the Wild: The 'Corporeal Unconscious' of American Adventure Culture," in *Disability Studies and the Environmental Humanities: Toward an Eco-Crip Theory*, ed. Sarah Jaquette Ray and Jay Sibara (Lincoln: University of Nebraska Press, 2017), 47.

9. Ibid.

10. Ibid., 47–48.

11. James I. Porter, "Foreword," in *The Body and Physical Difference: Discourses of Disability*, ed. David T. Mitchell and Sharon L. Snyder (Ann Arbor: University of Michigan Press, 1997), xiv.

12. Rosemarie Garland-Thomson, *Extraordinary Bodies: Figuring Physical Disability in American Culture and Literature* (New York: Columbia University Press, 1997), 8.

13. Ibid.

14. Caroline Lieffers, In'aska (Dennis Hastings), and Margery Coffey (Mi'onbathin), "Inseparable: Lands and Peoples in Sacred Connection," *Disability Studies Quarterly* 41, no. 4 (2021): n.p., accessed January 24, 2023, https://dsq-sds.org/index.php/dsq/article /view/8462/6295.

15. For more on "controlling nature," see, for example, Kimberly K. Smith, *African American Environmental Thought: Foundations* (Lawrence: University Press of Kansas, 2007), esp. chap. 1, "Strange Readings of Nature."

16. Jaquette Ray, "Risking Bodies in the Wild," 32.

17. Elizabeth DeLoughrey and George B. Handley, "Introduction: Toward an Aesthetics of the Earth," in *Postcolonial Ecologies: Literatures of the Environment*, ed. Elizabeth DeLoughrey and George B. Handley (Oxford: Oxford University Press, 2011), 8.

18. Graham Huggan and Helen Tiffin, *Postcolonial Ecocriticism: Literature, Animals, Environment* (London: Routledge, 2010), 2.

19. Bonnie Roos and Alex Hunt, "Introduction: Narratives of Survival, Sustainability, and Justice," in *Postcolonial Green: Environmental Politics and World Narratives*, ed. Bonnie Roos and Alex Hunt (Charlottesville: University of Virginia Press, 2010), 2.

20. See Laura Wright, *Wilderness into Civilized Shapes: Reading the Postcolonial Environment* (Athens: University of Georgia Press, 2010), 14.

21. Jen Deerinwater, "Colonial Forces of Environmental Violence on Deaf, Disabled, & Ill Indigenous People," *Disability Studies Quarterly* 41, no. 4 (2021): n.p., accessed January 24, 2023, https://dsq-sds.org/article/view/8479/6296.

22. Ibid.

23. See also Nicole Ineese-Nash, "Disability as a Colonial Construct: The Missing Discourse of Culture in Conceptualizations of Disabled Indigenous Children," n.p., accessed January 24, 2023, https://cjds.uwaterloo.ca/index.php/cjds/article/download /645/899.

24. Deeriwater, "Colonial Forces of Environmental Violence," n.p.

25. Anthony J. Nocella II, "Defining Eco-ability: Social Justice and the Intersectionality of Disability, Nonhuman Animals, and Ecology," in *Disability Studies and the Environmental Humanities: Toward an Eco-Crip Theory*, ed. Sarah Jaquette Ray and Jay Sibara (Lincoln: University of Nebraska Press, 2017), 141–42.

26. Jaquette Ray, "Risking Bodies in the Wild," 48.

27. Ibid., 49.

28. Allen MacDuffie, *Victorian Literature, Energy, and the Ecological Imagination* (Cambridge: Cambridge University Press, 2014), 90.

29. Jaquette Ray, "Risking Bodies in the Wild," 58–59.

30. Ibid., 62.

31. Nocella, "Defining Eco-ability," 149.

32. Ibid., 141.

33. Ibid. (italics in original).

34. Ibid., 143.

35. Ibid.

36. Shaun Grech, "Decolonising Eurocentric Disability Studies: Why Colonialism Matters in the Disability and Global South Debate," *Social Identities* 21, no. 1 (2015): 9.

37. Ibid.

38. Siobhan Senier, "Blind Indians: Káteri Tekakwí:tha and Joseph Amos's Visions of Indigenous Resurgence," in *Disability Studies and the Environmental Humanities: Toward an Eco-Crip Theory*, ed. Sarah Jaquette Ray and Jay Sibara (Lincoln: University of Nebraska Press, 2017), 271.

39. Karen Soldatic, *Disability and Neoliberal State Formations* (London: Routledge, 2019), 1.

40. Nocella, "Defining Eco-ability," 142.

41. Ibid., 144–45.

42. Donna Haraway, "Teddy Bear Patriarchy: Taxidermy in the Garden of Eden, New York City, 1908–1936," *Social Text*, no. 11 (1984–1985): 21, accessed February 11, 2020, https://www.jstor.org/stable/466593.

43. Ibid.

44. Robin Pogrebin, "Roosevelt Statue to Be Removed from Museum of Natural History," *New York Times*, updated January 19, 2022, accessed January 23, 2023, https://www.nytimes.com/2020/06/21/arts/design/roosevelt-statue-to-be-removed-from-museum-of-natural-history.html.

45. See, for example, "The Man Stuffed and Displayed like a Wild Animal," *BBS News*, September 16, 2016, accessed July 14, 2021, https://www.bbc.com/news/magazine-37344210.

46. Alison Kafer, "Compulsory Bodies: Reflections on Heterosexuality and Able-Bodiedness," *Journal of Women's History* 15, no. 3 (2003): 79.

47. Laura Wright, *The Vegan Studies Project: Food, Animals, and Gender in the Age of Terror* (Athens: University of Georgia Press, 2015), 32.

48. Bob Torres and Jenna Torres, *Vegan Freak: Being Vegan in a Non-Vegan World* (Oakland, CA: PM Press, 2010).

49. Julie Doyle, "Celebrity Vegans and the Lifestyling of Ethical Consumption," *Environmental Communication* 10, no. 6 (2016): 777–78.

50. David Church, "Freakery, Cult Films, and the Problem of Ambivalence," *Journal of Film and Video* 63, no. 1 (2011): 4, accessed February 13, 2020, http://www.jstor.org/stable/10.5406/jfilmvideo.63.1.0003.

51. Sarah Jaquette Ray, *The Ecological Other: Environmental Exclusion in American Culture* (Tucson: University of Arizona Press, 2013): 1, 2.

52. Analola Santana, *Freak Performances: Dissidence in Latin American Theater* (Ann Arbor: University of Michigan Press, 2018), 2.

53. On the role of the United Nations in decolonization, see "Decolonization," *United Nations*, accessed April 23, 2023, https://www.un.org/en/global-issues/decolonization.

54. Walter D. Mignolo, *The Idea of Latin America* (Malden: Blackwell, 2005), 8 (italics in original).

55. Grech, "Decolonising Eurocentric Disability Studies," 13. For more on the influence of colonialist ideology today, see also Mark Jackson, ed., *Coloniality, Ontology, and the Question of the Posthuman* (London: Routledge, 2018).

56. Walter D. Mignolo, "The Geopolitics of Knowledge and the Colonial Difference," in *Coloniality at Large: Latin America and the Postcolonial Debate*, ed. Mabel Moraña, Enrique Dussel, and Carlos A. Jáuregui (Durham, NC: Duke University Press, 2008), 247–48.

57. Ramón Grosfoguel, "Decolonizing Post-Colonial Studies and Paradigms of Political Economy: Transmodernity, Decolonial Thinking, and Global Coloniality," *Transmodernity: Journal of Peripheral Cultural Production of the Luso-Hispanic World* 1, no. 1 (2011): 13, accessed February 10, 2020, http://escholarship.org/uc/item/21k6t3fq.

58. Karen Soldatic, "*Post*colonial *Re*productions: Disability, Indigeneity and the Formation of the White Masculine Settler State of Australia," *Social Identities* 21, no. 1 (2015): 56.

59. Santana, *Freak Performances*, 4.

60. Ibid., 9–10.

61. For example, for more on Africa, see Diana Adesola Mafe, "(Mis)Imagining Africa in the New Millennium: *The Constant Gardener* and *Blood Diamond*," *Camera Obscura* 75.25, no. 3 (2011): 69–99.

62. For more on (post)colonialism, capitalism, and modernity, see Dipesh Chakrabarty, *Provincializing Europe: Postcolonial Thought and Historical Difference* (Princeton, NJ: Princeton University Press, 2000).

63. Nocella, "Defining Eco-ability," 145.

64. Stephanie LeMenager, *Living Oil: Petroleum Culture in the American Century* (Oxford: Oxford University Press, 2014), 107.

65. Sheena Wilson, Adam Carlson, and Imre Szeman, eds., *Petrocultures: Oil, Politics, Culture* (Montreal: McGill-Queen's University Press, 2017), 22.

66. Sheena Wilson, "Trafficking in Petronormativities: At the Intersections of Petrofeminism, Petrocolonialism, and Petrocapitalism," in *Transportation and the Culture of Climate Change: Accelerating Ride to Global Crisis*, ed. Tatiana Prorokova-Konrad (Morgantown: West Virginia University Press, 2020), 227.

67. Tatiana Prorokova, "Pre-Apocalyptic Horror of Climate Change: Colonization and Oil Drilling in *The Last Winter*," in *Exhaustion and Regeneration in Post-Millennial North-American Literature and Culture*, ed. Julia Nikiel and Izabella Kimak (Berlin: Peter Lang, 2019), 74.

68. Timothy Mitchell, "Carbon Democracy," in *Energy Humanities: An Anthology*, ed. Imre Szeman and Dominic Boyer (Baltimore, MD: Johns Hopkins University Press, 2017), 160.

69. Eric Cazdyn and Imre Szeman, *After Globalization* (Malden: Wiley-Blackwell, 2013), 7.

70. Dipesh Chakrabarty, "The Climate of History: Four Theses," in *Energy Humanities: An Anthology*, ed. Imre Szeman and Dominic Boyer (Baltimore, MD: Johns Hopkins University Press, 2017), 50.

71. Jos Boys, "Theoretical Reflections: Rurality, Gender and Disability," in *Disability and Rurality: Identity, Gender and Belonging*, ed. Karen Soldatic and Kelley Johnson (London: Routledge, 2017), 148.

72. Soldatic, *Disability and Neoliberal State Formations*, 1.

73. Shaun Grech, "Disability and the Majority World: A Neocolonial Approach," in *Disability and Social Theory: New Developments and Directions*, ed. Dan Goodley, Bill Hughes, and Lennard Davis (Basingstoke: Palgrave Macmillan, 2012), 56.

74. Rob Nixon, *Slow Violence and the Environmentalism of the Poor* (Cambridge, MA: Harvard University Press, 2011), 2.

75. Stacy Alaimo, *Bodily Natures: Science, Environment, and the Material Self* (Bloomington: Indiana University Press, 2010), 1–2 (italics in original).

76. Grech, "Disability and the Majority World," 56.

77. Senier, "Blind Indians," 272.

78. Santana, *Freak Performances*, 2.

79. Julie Sadler, "War Contaminants and Environmental Justice: The Case of Congenital Heart Defects in Iraq," in *Disability Studies and the Environmental Humanities: Toward an Eco-Crip Theory*, ed. Sarah Jaquette Ray and Jay Sibara (Lincoln: University of Nebraska Press, 2017), 338.

80. Ibid., 344.

81. Ibid.

82. David T. Mitchell and Sharon L. Snyder, "Precarity and Cross-Species Identification: Autism, the Critique of Normative Cognition, and Nonspeciesism," in *Disability Studies and the Environmental Humanities: Toward an Eco-Crip Theory*, ed. Sarah Jaquette Ray and Jay Sibara (Lincoln: University of Nebraska Press, 2017), 553.

83. Kelly Fritsch, "Toxic Pregnancies: Speculative Futures, Disabling Environments, and Neoliberal Biocapital," in *Disability Studies and the Environmental Humanities: Toward an Eco-Crip Theory*, ed. Sarah Jaquette Ray and Jay Sibara (Lincoln: University of Nebraska Press, 2017), 360.

84. Valerie Ann Johnson, "Bringing Together Feminist Disability Studies and Environmental Justice," in *Disability Studies and the Environmental Humanities: Toward an Eco-Crip Theory*, ed. Sarah Jaquette Ray and Jay Sibara (Lincoln: University of Nebraska Press, 2017), 83.

85. Shaun Grech and Karen Soldatic, "Introduction: Disability and Colonialism: (Dis) encounters and Anxious Intersectionalities," *Social Identities* 21, no. 1 (2015): 2.

86. Karen Soldatic, "Social Suffering in the Neoliberal Age: Surplusisty and the Partially Disabled Subject," in *Routledge Handbook of Disability Studies*, ed. Nick Watson and Simo Vehmas (London: Routledge, 2020), 237.

87. Tom Shakespeare, "Disability in Developing Countries," in *Routledge Handbook of Disability Studies*, ed. Nick Watson and Simo Vehmas (London: Routledge, 2020), 322.

88. Grech, "Decolonising Eurocentric Disability Studies," 8.

89. Ibid.

90. Stefanie Kennedy, "'Let Them Be Young and Stoutly Set in Limbs': Race, Labor, and Disability in the British Atlantic World," *Social Identities* 21, no. 1 (2015): 37; David Mitchell and Sharon L. Snyder, "Minority Model: From Liberal to Neoliberal Futures of Disability," in *Routledge Handbook of Disability Studies*, ed. Nick Watson and Simo Vehmas (London: Routledge, 2020), 45–46.

91. Soldatic, "*Postcolonial Reproductions*," 54 (italics in original).

92. Matthew J. C. Cella, "Introduction: The Ecosomatic Paradigm and the American Environmental Imagination," in *Disability and the Environment in American Literature:*

Toward an Ecosomatic Paradigm, ed. Matthew J. C. Cella (Lanham, MD: Lexington, 2016), 4.

93. Matthew J. C. Cella, "The Ecosomatic Paradigm in Literature: Merging Disability Studies and Ecocriticism," in *Disability Studies and the Environmental Humanities: Toward an Eco-Crip Theory*, ed. Sarah Jaquette Ray and Jay Sibara (Lincoln: University of Nebraska Press, 2017), 174.

94. Erin E. Andrews, *Disability as Diversity: Developing Cultural Competence* (New York: Oxford University Press, 2020), 30 (italics in original).

95. Cella, "Ecosomatic Paradigm in Literature," 168–69.

96. Alaimo, *Bodily Natures*, 2.

97. Helen Meekosha and Karen Soldatic, "Human Rights and the Global South: The Case of Disability," *Third World Quarterly* 32, no. 8 (2011): 1385.

98. Timothy Morton, *The Ecological Thought* (Cambridge, MA: Harvard University Press, 2010), 41 (italics in original).

I

Justice, Imperialism, and Eco-Ableism

1

Disability Rights as a "Global" Norm

*Environmentalism, Post-Colonialism, and the Meaning of
Disability in the Majority World*

ANDREW B. JENKS

L iberal human rights discourses, both in policy and in academic scholarship, tend to obscure just how deleterious a reliance on universalisms
can be to those they purport to help. In the context of environmentalism and the case of disability, these imposed universalisms are especially
troubling, as they can obscure the political needs of those who are oft recognized as being the planet's most needy, disabled people. As policymakers
working within the state and international organizations seek to collectively stave off the effects of ever-growing environmental threats through commitments that are just to our planet, they must not put aside the question of
how their choices could disproportionately negatively affect the roughly
eight hundred million people who live with a disability in the majority
world,[1] often referred to as the "Global South." If scholars, practitioners,
activists, and policymakers in the minority world of the "Global North"
wish to support all people with disabilities through the creation and affirmation of a truly "global" norm of disability rights, they must work to break
the legacies of ableism that enabled centuries of colonial violence and still
drastically impact the lives of those living in postcolonial contexts.[2] This
chapter asks the question of whether the diffusion of an international norm
of disability rights, which understands disability as a socially constructed
phenomena, is a positive change for the position of the disabled in society
as it relates to environmentalism and the threats of climate change, or
whether it reinforces binaries between the minority and majority world,

importing hegemonic interpretations of problems and solutions "from above" in a one-size-fits-all model.

This chapter argues that the same kinds of hegemonic knowledge regimes around disability rights, which claim that disability rights have become forefront in the lives of disabled people around the world, are in fact replicating the same ableism endemic to the colonial project in the majority world. Through the environmental justice and the disability rights paradigms, the social processes that actually produce and replicate "disability" have obfuscated the fundamental problem on which we must focus: the legacy of poverty, stigma, and structural violence that fuels disability in the postcolonial world. Colonialism and neoliberalism's insidious reach present themselves at nearly every stage of the process in the fixing of meanings of disability in a global context. Important to this conversation is the adoption of the 2006 United Nations Convention on the Rights of Persons with Disabilities (UNCRPD) and the ratification of the convention and its Optional Protocol as well as other rights-based social policy, generally lauded as the final step toward ensuring full and equal human rights for disabled people by policymakers and scholars alike. While social movements advancing understandings of disability as socially constructed phenomenon have certainly been emancipatory for those living in the minority world, for many living in the majority world, the emancipatory potential of rights has been questioned by feminist, disability studies, and postcolonial scholars, and these critiques have an important place in charting a path forward as many of the greatest social threats to our planet become intertwined with environmental threats.

This chapter proceeds in three substantive sections before concluding with a discussion on how reframing "global" disability rights is necessary moving forward. It first summarizes the emergence of disability rights movements, including the activism and the raising of disability rights consciousness internationally by the introduction of a social constructionist understanding of impairment and disability, the social model of disability. It then sketches the ways in which disabled identities in the majority, largely postcolonial world is often poorly represented by the "universal form of knowledge" on disability imported from the minority world, which only holds a fraction of the one billion people estimated to be living with a disability globally,[3] focusing in part on the UNCRPD and the discourse surrounding its production. This mode of understanding disability is one that may not truly be emancipatory for those living with a disability in the majority world.[4] Taking seriously the incongruities between the document and the lived experience of disabled people in the majority world more than a decade after its widespread adoption, the CRPD is confronted with the problem of not "doing the doing."[5] The third section focuses on the myriad challenges faced in the daily lives of disabled people in the majority world in accessing protections of the CRPD. Feminist and postcolonial theorizing on the role of postcolonial and neoliberal violence, including ongoing conflicts, are of particular importance. Karen Soldatic notes that these processes are the "invisible visible" causes of disability in the Global South.[6] Finally, I echo the calls of many scholars in suggesting that a politics of disability attuned to the ontoformative nature of disabled embodiment, combined with a phenomenological approach to the "problem" of disability, can work to create a better future for people with disabilities who live in the majority periphery of the global disability community.

This chapter intends to help set the context for the rest of the book by disrupting commonly held assumptions about disability rights in the postcolonial context that are important foundations for many discussions of environmentalism at the nexus of these two topics. Much of this chapter is not explicitly concerned with environmentalism, but it helps inform readers as to how existing knowledge regimes have and will continue to fail disabled people if we rely on the virtue of the universalisms they assume.

Disability Rights in the Minority World

In her 2015 book, *Rights Enabled: The Disability Revolution, from the US, to Germany and Japan, to the United Nations*, political scientist Katharina Heyer "follows the journey of the disability rights model across national and ideological boundaries"[7] and argues that disability has moved on to become an international human rights issue by giving disabled people a frame within which to advocate and achieve equality. Heyer's comprehensive analysis of disability rights in a comparative context does an excellent job of tracing the roots of a disability rights consciousness rooted in a social model understanding of disability from the United States to norm entrepreneurs in Germany and Japan and finally to the UNCRPD. Yet this "global" movement has come at a price, as critical disability studies, feminist, and postcolonial scholarship has noted; the actionable shift for an emancipatory politics of disability in the majority world is now stymied by imported interpretations of disability from a particular interpretation of disability, borne in response to threats from neoliberalism in the minority world. Further, global pushes for policy, like single-use plastics bans, have created further marginalization for those who typically find themselves poorer and more disabled than their peers.[8]

What is disability? The need to define disability has historically been one felt by the state. Oliver and Barnes note that the United Kingdom did not begin to officially use the term *disabled* to describe some of its citizens until after World War II.[9] Throughout much of human history, disabled people have been treated as objects of pity and charity, generally pushed to the margins of society.[10] The rise of a global capitalist system introduced and has since reinforced the practice of valuing bodies based on how much they can produce.[11] Thus bodies rendered sick, ill, or weak have been considered less meaningful and able to contribute to a productive society. Neoliberalism further contributed to the devaluing of the disabled body, a resurgence of practices from the industrial revolutions in early industrializing nations like the United States and the United Kingdom, where bodies were valued for how much they could produce.[12] Neoliberal rationality and economization of the individual has permeated nearly all facets of human life, where economic rationality dictates that certain bodies are less valuable than others. This rationality does not only affect those living in the minority world. It has for centuries also dominated life in the majority world, especially in the colonial context.

The medical model of disability is an approach to disability that understands disabilities as occurring from impairments that result from an underlying disease or disorder.[13] The social model of disability, credited to sociologist Mike Oliver[14] and others, proposes a separation between body and culture, impairment, and disability. Put succinctly, Jenks notes, "the medical model emphasizes changing the person to fit the environment, whereas the social model emphasizes changing the environment to fit the person . . . those fighting for the rights of the disabled argue that disability is not the main barrier to participation in society for disabled individuals: society's practices construct the barriers."[15] The CRPD embraces a social model understanding of disability focusing on how impairment interacts with the social world, and it embraces the concept of disability as one held within society and not individual. Persons with disabilities under the CRPD are defined as "those who have long-term physical, mental, intellectual, and sensory impairments which in interaction with various barriers may hinder their full and effective participation in society on an equal basis with others."[16] This definition replaces the global standard previous to the CPRD, the World Health Organization's *International Classification of Impairment Disability and Handicap* definition of disability from 1980, which relates impairment in the individual to his or her ability to "perform an activity in the manner or within the range considered normal for a human being."[17] The shift toward a social model understanding of disability in conventions like the CRPD represents a shift in global discourse and official stylized understandings of disability that originate in the minority world, largely eschewing the medical model of disability.

The latter third of the twentieth century saw the concurrent rise of the independent living movement in the United States and Canada as well as both bottom-up and top-down pushes from activists and policymakers to guarantee civil and human rights for disabled people. Reactions from members of disabled communities in the United Kingdom like the Union of the Physically Impaired Against Segregation (UPIAS) to the forced institutionalization into group homes of people who used wheelchairs became a focal point for a new disability politics there.[18] This emancipatory politics of disability was an attempt to shift understandings of disability as a phenomenon that resided within the body of the individual, an impairment, to one that located the conditions that disable people in society. The differentiation between this new understanding of disability and the traditional understandings with which governments in the minority world had previously approached disabled peoples' issues became a focal point for the emerging field of disability studies in the 1970s. This does not mean disabled people from the majority world were not involved in either domestic or transnational forms of disability activism, as unions of single impairment and cross-impairment groups like Disabled People's International had global memberships that advocated for rights-based protections.[19]

Oliver and Barnes[20] discuss the rise of a broadly focused, loosely associated Disabled People's Movement (DPM) in the 1970s to its height in the 1990s as a formative era in what can be thought of as the beginning of an era of "disability politics." The rise of the modern state in Europe and North America saw the creation of segregated spaces for people with any number of impairments, physical, sensory, intellectual, developmental, mental health, and so on. Often when these individuals did not have families or their families could not care for them, they were pushed into institutions to be cared for by state- or church-run institutions.[21] Major shifts occurred with the rise of the eugenics movement in the early 1900s, when states attempted to medicalize impairment and disabled people became more visible.[22] After World War II, another shift occurred, especially in states like Germany, the United Kingdom, the United States, Canada, and Australia. Rehabilitation became the focus, as disability became less of an unfortunate malady that affected those who were sick or weak and more of a broader one where fit, young men were the ones impaired.[23] Finally, the shift toward a new era of understanding of disability, considered emancipatory by disability studies scholars and activists alike, is that of "postmedicalization." This was a time when disabled people began to affect change in the politics that governed their bodies. Social movements made up of people with disabilities in the United States, Canada, and the United Kingdom are well documented, and this helped usher in the current wave of disability politics.[24]

Heyer contends that this movement has led to a shift in the ways in which people think about disability and disability rights, raising a global rights consciousness among and toward people with disabilities.[25] Consciousness in this academic literature refers to understandings and meanings of law [and rights] circulating in social relations.[26] Stemming from the Durkheimian notion that law is the result of what a society deems to be criminal: "an act is criminal when it offends the strong, well-defined states of the collective consciousness."[27] The study of legal consciousness is a related concept (and perhaps more familiar). If law forms from a Durkheimian collective conscious-ness where socially held conceptions of what is legal or not are translated to law, legal consciousness addresses how *individuals* interact with and under-stand the law. Legal consciousness "documents the forms of participation and interpretation through which actors sustain, reproduce, or amend the circulating (contested or hegemonic) structures of meanings concerning law[28] . . . [and] the ongoing, dynamic process of constructing one's under-standing of, and relationship to, the social world through use of legal con-ventions and discourses."

Suggesting that this relatively new way of understanding disability has become a global norm, Heyer notes the importance of the work of disability groups in the United States in helping create the CRPD as evidence of the adoption of a new norm in the politics of disability, one that is emancipa-tory for disabled people transnationally.[29] Relating this type of transnation-al movement to Finnemore and Sikkink's[30] model of transnational norm diffusion, where disability activism inspired a global norm for how disabil-ity was understood, is an overstep. While the global Disabled People's Move-ment (DPM) has had an impact in changing how states conceptualize dis-ability, from monitoring and measuring to enacting policies to create more inclusive and less discriminatory environments for disabled people to fully participate in society, this is not the case for *most* disabled people.[31] In no way should the accomplishments of groups like DPI (Disabled People Inter-national), the UN Ad Hoc Committee on Disabled Persons, or the Washing-ton Group[32] nor the work of generations of disability rights activists around the world be dismissed. But we must more fully engage disability in the ma-jority world before discussing such universalisms.

Disability in the Majority World

Of the estimated one billion people worldwide living with a disability, 80 percent of them live in the majority world.[33] While the focus on disability rights has been a movement with truly global roots, where strong pushes for international treaties have come from states like the Philippines and Mexico, it has not been of great focus to those doing disability studies more gener-ally until the last decade. These accounts often come from a minority world perspective and work (often unintentionally) to universalize the disability experience in the United Kingdom, the United States, or Canada as one that exists globally. What makes disability different in the minority world? Who are the people with disabilities? What other identities interact with their im-pairments to disable or further disable them? And how could these differ-ences impact the "universal" nature of disability rights?

Many states in the majority world use data taken by census as the sole means of data collection, as Me and Mbogoni note in their review of practices in developing states.[34] A huge disparity is seen in the reported rates of disability in developing states, with disability rates being reported between just 0.17 percent and 9.76 percent, compared to data from the United States, Australia, the Netherlands, the United Kingdom, and New Zealand ranging from 11.6 to 20.0 percent.[35] This is due to differences in how disability is defined and measured in these states. Possible factors that influence the results of census data and limit the validity of results are attributed to culturally defined concepts of disability that may limit the types of questions asked as well as limitations imposed by who is asking questions and who is answering them.[36] Though census takers have asked questions about deafness, blindness, physical and mental impairment, and mental health since the eighteenth century, collecting accurate information is still problematic.[37] For instance, all seven Caribbean states in the UN Disability Statistics Database (DISTAT) rely solely on census data, as do two-thirds of African and one-third of Asian and Latin American states.[38] Some languages lack a word for "disability" as a concept. Or health status is used as a proxy for disability. Groce[39] points to problems in reliable measurement related to the interaction between census takers and those from whom they are collecting information in societies that have deep ethnic, class, tribal, or caste divides as being determinants of why data in many states is unreliable. Collecting household-level data can be problematic, as the head of household, often male, may not know the extent to which disability is a limiting factor and may not recognize the care work taken on by the majority female caretakers in the household.[40] Finally, fear of stigma, government intervention into the private sphere, and a change in eligibility of services or programs can prompt individuals to lie about the disability status of members of their households.[41] Possible positive cases of more accurate disability measurement, like Caribbean states that have disability rates between 5.5 and 7.6 percent, rely on individual rather than household data.[42]

While rates of disability may be under- or misreported in the majority world, there are a myriad of social, economic, and political barriers for disabled people in participating fully in society. Section *t* to the preamble of the CRPD recognizes "the fact that the majority of persons with disabilities live in conditions of poverty, and in this regard recognizing the critical need to address the negative impact of poverty on persons with disabilities."[43] The nexus between poverty and participation in economic life, and how it interacts with employment, education, and development, is one that presents itself as a common theme on proposed solutions for the eradication of the cycle of being disabled and poor.

Being disabled and being poor are often characterized as vicious cycles.[44] Disabled people experience relative poverty, which does not imply that physical human necessities like nutrition, health, and shelter cannot be met but rather that standards by which disabled people live are comparably less than what is common in society.[45] Eliminating relative poverty for the disabled is an explicit goal of the CRPD and the Sustainable Development Goals (SDGs). In a case study of people with physical and sensory impairments in Jordan, Turmusani[46] notes this cycle as being twofold: poverty causes disability, and people with disability experience poverty at higher levels.

Preventable disease, malnutrition, and nonvaccination create incredibly high levels of disability.[47] Onchocerciasis or "river blindness" caused by flesh-eating black flies accounts for blindness in over 50 percent of men over the age of forty in some West African communities.[48] Of the world's estimated 285 million people who are blind or visually impaired, 90 percent live in low-income settings, and 80 percent have preventable visual impairments.[49] Efforts to combat common causes of visual impairments like cataracts and glaucoma have led to the reduction in these rates since the 1990s (WHO, 2017). Oftentimes people who are from areas affected by these "preventable" causes of disability cannot afford to travel for medical treatment, cannot afford to miss work, or are often stigmatized by their disability and are unwilling to seek attention.[50] Two types of approaches to studying the topic of disability and poverty, macro and grassroots, can serve to better understand what shapes the relationship between them.

Macro perspectives that use large datasets to analyze the relationship between disability and poverty, while lamented for the quality of the data on which they rely, provide correlations that can identify areas to target to end the vicious cycle of poverty and disability. Kamal Lamichhane's *Disability, Education, and Employment in Developing Countries* uses comprehensive datasets to analyze the relationships between the factors listed in the title and offers suggestions on how best to increase the participation of disabled people in the economy of developing countries. They note that overall, people with disabilities are more likely to be self-employed or to work in the informal economy at rates from 3 to 12 percent.[51] Their case study of Cambodia provides an excellent example of some of the problems with this type of data and offers evidence of the "big" issue with disability and poverty being one of relative poverty, addressed in the preamble to the CRPD. Data used was collected by USAID, and while the number of people with disabilities is estimated at being 9 percent, only 0.68 percent of survey respondents reported having a disability. Data show people with physical disabilities having on average two years less of schooling and attending secondary education at roughly 60 percent the rate of their nondisabled peers. Looking to law in Cambodia, Lamichhane[52] sees the need for greater explicit protection and suggests that quotas introduced in 2009 for hiring disabled people can help alleviate this cycle. This study itself is expressed in terms familiar to those in the minority world. Rehabilitation experts can look at these numbers, understand them, take them as a holistic representation of disability in the majority, then make policy recommendations as how to best address the "problem" of disability.

While poverty, state capacity, and myriad other issues can contribute to the overwhelming concentration of disability in the majority) world, the focus of the rest of this essay, and the crux of the argument it makes, is on structural violence. This structural violence is not only what has disabled in the past and continues to disable today but is also a creation of societal forces that we continue to perpetuate—namely, the ableism that permeates devaluation of the lives of people living in the majority world.

Structural Violence and Disability in the Majority World

Modern warfare is worse than "we," the manufacturers of "smart" bombs and jet fighters can think of. The pain and fear of children torn to pieces at home—in their habitus, inside their safe harbor with the smell of boiling rice in their nostrils—is beyond imagination. How can we understand the hopelessness of a mother who has lost children to land mines, and still has to wait for the next bang with more children mangled or dead? And it is even harder to understand the price of endurance the poor peasants have to pay—for there is not just one bomb, but many; not one land mine, but thousands; not one war, but repeated wars of colonisation fought by "us" against "them." Guernica, Dresden, My Lai, Gaza, Helmand, Fallujah, Abu Graib: structural poverty is killing millions of children yearly. In this dirty context, *few* and *many* represent different qualities because each massacre modifies conditions for recognition. Herein lays the urgency of giving voice to the voiceless if we are to seek a serious understanding.[53]

Husum and Edvardsen's powerful passage when discussing the "methodological problems when reality gets ugly" is a sobering reminder of the lived realities of disabled people in places where the most basic human right, personal security, is routinely violated not only by the state in which those individuals live but by the minority world on those living in the majority world.[54] Grassroots studies of disability and poverty provide a useful frame for understanding this structural violence. They attempt to locate both the effects of social suffering and structural violence on impairment and disability, which lead to this cycle of poverty and disability.

Rod Michalko[55] explains, "We do not suffer the condition of our impairments as medicine and the rest of society would have it, we 'suffer' our society. We suffer what our society makes of our impairments."[56] By seeing suffering as social, the blame and guilt is taken away from those who are suffering and placed on outside forces.[57] I have echoed calls for disability studies scholars to understand disability as grounded in an "ontology of impairment," where not recognizing the effects and experiences of impairment as being "real" can miss the true cost of what it means to be disabled.[58] Regardless of stigma associated with disability in a local context, disability marks individuals as being inherently different and in many contexts "less" than their peers.[59] This focus does not ignore empirical data on disability as it is collected through surveys but makes a concerted effort to better understand what causes relative poverty or a relative depravation of a disabled population. It resists the turn toward "critical" disability studies that is infused in much of the human rights discourse surrounding disability both in scholarship and policy.

Structural violence, defined as "the violence of everyday life that causes social suffering, as well as the extraordinary violence of war and other disasters that are beyond the control of the individual person with a disability and [their] family,"[60] is a concept familiar to feminist international relations scholars. Structural violence factors into Jacqui True's arguments on the political economy of violence against women, where violence is perpetrated not only by direct state action but also "through the structured relations of production and reproduction that govern the distribution and use of resources, benefits, privileges and authority."[61] Similar forces that cause the gendered relations of power that work to structurally devalue nonmasculinized forms of labor, or financial institutions, are at work in further disabling those who are viewed as automatically less productive due to their physical embodiment.[62]

The UN Decade of the Disabled Person from 1983 to 1992 was meant to raise awareness for many of the issues the convention and other work reviewed was intended to address, mainly the issues of education and employment of disabled persons. These macroeconomic issues, though made explicit in the CRPD, do not contain concrete plans for implementation, deadlines, or the promise of resources with which to accomplish the stated goals of the convention. The article on Freedom from Exploitation, Violence, and Abuse (Article 16) will be the explicit focus of this section. The paradox of human rights presents itself, where states are both responsible for interpreting and violating human rights, as well as the constructions of the articles themselves, which take imported meanings and interpretations of concepts and normative goals.[63]

The convention, which more than 165 states and the European Union have signed and more than 130 have ratified, reflects a certain disability experience. One born in the United States, the United Kingdom, or Germany. One where the most pressing problems for people with disabilities revolved around access, employment discrimination, and education. Based on a technological rationalism, and western Enlightenment epistemology, the notion that the West is "including" the rest is also problematic.[64] Normative goals of including disabled people are expressed in neoliberal terms, like Lamichhane's suggestions for inclusion, which focus on the education-employment nexus as a means for disabled people to become relatively less impoverished.[65] What purpose does a workplace being accessible serve those who live in a state where 90 percent of people do not work in the formal economy (as Lamichhane's case study of Cambodia showed)? These measures, explicitly directed toward getting disabled people to be productive, working members of society, do not attempt to actually include them with their corporeal trappings; they attempt to make them more like everyone else. Capitalism and the push from hegemonic capitalist states toward this type of ideal neoliberal subject has helped push a possibly emancipatory politics for people with disabilities into one co-opted and mainstreamed by wealthy states.[66]

Article 16 of the CRPD is an example of how disability rights in their current form do not take into consideration issues of structural violence, whether the source is the state, other states, or a global financial institution. The article reads, "1. States Parties shall take all appropriate legislative, administrative, social, educational and other measures to protect persons with disabilities, both within and outside the home, from all forms of exploitation, violence and abuse, including their gender-based aspects."[67] Section 2 of Article 16 deals with the responsibilities of caregivers and provision of resources for recognizing and reporting abuse. Section 3 ensures state parties will monitor programs and services for the disabled. Section 4 compels states to "promote the physical, cognitive and psychological recovery, rehabilitation and social reintegration of persons with disabilities who become victims of any form of exploitation, violence or abuse," and Section 5 maintains the need for these rights to be properly legislated.[68] There is no question that states should take these steps to protect citizens who have historically and systematically been subject to harsh confinement, torture, and generally inhumane treatment since the invention of the modern nation-state. Returning to the recurrent question of who counts can be extremely problematic when an external monitor examines whether a state followed the CRPD.

Institutionalization of physically disabled people in Jordan, a practice maligned in popular opinion and disability studies scholarship produced in the United States or the United Kingdom, is viewed as a privileged position in the local context. People in institutions have government-guaranteed sources of shelter, food, and medical treatment.[69] Section 4's goal of reintegration is one that takes a medicalized view of a concept that is inherently social: suffering. Like the psychosocial conditions created by the normalization of rape in conflict and postconflict settings, the view that somehow medical experts and the bureaucratic arm of the state can fix the problem of the effects of abuse is problematic. Baaz and Stern[70] critique the position of rape as being a defensible, natural by-product of conflict and the normalization of these processes of gender-based violence as being emblematic of a broad acceptance that these acts are a consequence of heterosexualized masculinity. Notions that the state should aspire to reintegrate the disabled into society after suffering from violence, exploitation, or abuse is emblematic of a larger problem of trying to bring disabled people up to the desired "normate" of human behavior.[71]

The normalization of violence against bodies in the Global South is not a new concept in feminist and postcolonial scholarship. Structural violence exists in multiple and intersecting forms. Connell[72] points to imperial and neocolonial violence, global capitalism, and global patriarchy as three potential sources of this kind of power over the bodies of those positioned as "victims" in the majority world who have impairments. The way in which disabled bodies are postulated in scholarship, like Lamichhane's[73] view of disability in developing countries as possibly moving "from charity to investment," and Eide and Ingstad's[74] view of poverty and disability as a "global challenge," end up positioning disabled bodies in the majority world as objects of minority world pity, as victims, as objects. Like the way in which the rise of the modern welfare state has been largely in response to the inequalities caused by the expansion of capitalism, so, too, are approaches to human rights in the minority world.[75]

While the CRPD can work to raise a disability rights consciousness that is critical for changing how individuals interact with the law, its terms are often incommensurable with the experiences of most disabled people in the world. Studies of disability rights consciousness have shown not only that these changes are slow in taking effect[76] but also that there is a discrete need for government commitments to promote these campaigns.[77] Holding nation-states accountable to these terms may prove increasingly difficult, as the push in states like Argentina, India, and Sierra Leone came from local mobilization on governments to ratify the Convention and implement laws to do so.[78] It is still too early to know what impact the CRPD will have on improving the lives of disabled people, but a radical reconceptualization of whose emancipatory politics are being promoted must be undertaken by individuals from the majority world, not imposed from above.

Resisting Ableism in Locating an Emancipatory Politics of Disability

This chapter has established the ways in which a politics of disability rooted in rights, established in the minority world, has pronounced shortcomings in affecting change in the majority world, where most disabled people live. Any approach to environmentalism and environmental justice rooted in the language of rights must first recognize and contend with the legacies of colonial violence enacted over centuries on those living in the majority world. Resisting ableism, in all its facets, is the key to finding an emancipatory politics of disability that is not simply a replication of a rights-based approach developed in the minority world of rich states.

Ableism was popularly defined by Fiona Kumari Campbell in 2001 as "a network of beliefs, processes and practices that produces a particular kind of self and body (the corporeal standard) that is projected as perfect, species-typical and therefore essential and fully human."[79] Ableism works to reinforce, and is reinforced by, the ideal body type valued by society. These neoliberal materializations of the "good" corporeal body are present in official policies, as well as in the ways of thinking and knowing what disability is in a global context. An explicit goal of the UNCRPD, like other policies enacted in the United States (1990), Australia (1992), and the United Kingdom (1995), among others, was to explicitly address these pervasive negative attitudes concerning the value and role of disabled people in society.

Campbell's updated definition of *ableism* both broadens and sharpens its focus and theoretical utility:

> A system of causal relations about the order of life that produces processes and systems of entitlement and exclusion. This causality fosters conditions of microaggression, internalized ableism and, in their jostling, notions of (un)encumbrance. A system of dividing practices, ableism institutes the reification and classification of populations. Ableist systems involve the differentiation, ranking, negation, notification and prioritization of sentient life.[80]

This updated definition helps us draw a more direct connection between concepts like disability and living in a neo- or postcolonial context. The same reification and classification of populations that were essential to the colonial project also define disability and the disabled condition. Not only do these conditions exist *within* the state, but more importantly, they are so often enacted on those living in the majority world by those in the minority world.

Raewyn Connell provides a useful frame for thinking outside of disability, impairments, masculinities, race, and other social characteristics as static and understanding them as being relational in time and space.[81] Knowledge claims of what/who counts are not even made in comparable terms when looking to measurement of disability globally, so how could rights addressing some universal set of needs possibly be comparable in this way? Extending Karel Kosik's concept of "ontoformativity" of social practice,

Connell urges us to recognize the ways in which practices bring a social order into existence over time.[82] The ways in which these processes work to gender institutions has been well studied; they can also work to reinforce stylized understandings of disability into institutions. Using a grassroots framework and ethnographic methods for better understanding disability, like those used in studies of disability and poverty, researchers can uncover the extent to which neocolonial interpretations of disability are transferred to the social relations of groups over time. While disability experience with diabetes by Indigenous Australians, for example, has become more positive in orientation and decoupled from stigma, disparities between cultural and government accepted standards of care can be problematic.[83] Cognizant of the ontoformativity of disability, which like masculinity, is not a product of corporeal embodiment but rather, a product of the social value associated with those embodiments; activists, advocates, and researchers can better understand how a universalized notion of disability must be abandoned if a truly emancipatory politics of disability is to be of use as a platform for rights claiming.

Soldatic[84] provides two examples of the ways in which "global" rights discourses like those in the CRPD exclude people with disabilities in a prima facie manner. First, language of the CRPD frames the commitments from states in terms of the modern territorial state and its citizenship requirements. Refugees fleeing war and persecution are not explicitly guaranteed these rights. The issue of political citizenship is not as problematic in places like the United States, where large numbers of noncitizens are publicly discriminated against, or Canada, which extends its constitutional human rights provisions to all people in the country, not just citizens. Second, there is no transnational justice mechanism in the CRPD, and statist terms dictate that the state be the catalyst in changing its own policies and punishing itself when it does not comply.[85] Furthermore, these violations of human rights by global governance organizations, like the World Bank not addressing disability in its policies, are unable to be prosecuted. Soldatic[86] argues that this structural violence remains the cause of impairment and disability not only through direct action like the aftereffects of Agent Orange in Southeast Asia from the Vietnam War but also through indirect action like the decision of how aid dollars are allocated. By not addressing these transnational justice concerns, documents like the CRPD do little to address the causes of the conditions that disable in the majority world.

The notion that disability is a "problem" in need of fixing has been problematized by post-structuralist critical disability studies scholarship produced in the minority world:

> Experiencing disability as a problem that some people have and simultaneously a problem that everyone has represents the dominant

ideological frame through which disability experience is mediated. Some of us are a problem to the society, its institutions and settings. That disabled people experience their lives in this way is crucial, if not essential, for the ways in which society and its institutions develop solutions to the problem of disability. Any solution developed within this framework, of course, serves to sustain the cultural conception of disability politically and socially as a problem and thus to make it disappear, to drown it, in the single social whole that contains the inevitability of problems as an integral feature of its social organization. It is important that we phenomenologically uncover the problem to which the conception "disability is a problem in need of a solution" is itself a solution.[87]

Michalko and Titchkosky's suggestion that the methodology used to uncover the problem that disability is a problem provides a promising avenue for rejecting the universality of human rights discourses on disability that promote a concept of disability, is disconnected with bodies in the majority world. Just as feminist and postcolonial scholarship has looked to social suffering and the causes and impacts of structural violence, so, too, must disability studies.

This chapter does not seek to echo the work of others who have worked to clarify the human-based threats that far outweigh those that occur "naturally" in the environment,[88] nor does it attempt to forge a disability-inclusive climate justice paradigm.[89] Rather, its aim is to set the stage for the chapters that follow by establishing two important realities. One, human rights are neither going to address the problems disabled people experience related to climate change nor allow the marriage of disability and environmental justice, which is still the predominant tack taken by states and international organizations. Two, "disability" is fundamentally different in the postcolonial context, particularly due to the legacies of ableism. These internalized legacies not only continue to be perpetuated on to disabled people around the world today, especially in postcolonial contexts in the majority world, but they are also evident in the hegemony of rights-based solutions to the problems disabled people face in relation to the environment.

NOTES

1. Shaun Grech, "Disability and the Majority World: A Neocolonial Approach," in *Disability and Social Theory*, ed. Dan Goodley, Bill Hughes, and Lennard Davis (London: Palgrave Macmillan, 2012), 52–69.

2. I am not intentionally conflating the terms *Global South*, *minority world*, and *postcolonial states* in this paper. However, it is true that much of the majority world is made up of postcolonial states, and the overlap between low- and most mid-income states that

currently make up the majority world and states that can be classified as postcolonial is not an insignificant truism.

3. Helen Meekosha and Karen Soldatic, "Human Rights and the Global South: The Case of Disability," *Third World Quarterly* 32, no. 8 (2011): 1383–97, https://doi.org/10.1 080/01436597.2011.614800.

4. Meekosha and Soldatic.

5. Sara Ahmed, "You End up Doing the Document Rather Than Doing the Doing: Diversity, Race Equality and the Politics of Documentation," *Ethnic and Racial Studies* 30, no. 4 (2007): 590–609, https://doi.org/10.1080/01419870701356015.

6. Karen Soldatic, "The Transnational Sphere of Justice: Disability Praxis and the Politics of Impairment," *Disability & Society* 28, no. 6 (2013): 744–55, https://doi.org/10 .1080/09687599.2013.802218.

7. Katharina Heyer, *Rights Enabled: The Disability Revolution, from the US, to Germany and Japan, to the United Nations* (Ann Arbor: University of Michigan Press, 2015), 4.

8. Andrew B. Jenks and Kelsey M. Obringer, "The Poverty of Plastics Bans: Environmentalism's Win Is a Loss for Disabled People," *Critical Social Policy* 40, no. 1 (2020).

9. Michael Oliver and Colin Barnes, *The New Politics of Disablement* (London: Palgrave Macmillan, 2012), 16.

10. Henri-Jacques Stiker, *A History of Disability* (Ann Arbor: University of Michigan Press, 1999).

11. Wendy Brown, *Undoing the Demos: Neoliberalism's Stealth Revolution* (Cambridge, MA: MIT Press, 2015).

12. Bill Hughes, "Civilising Modernity and the Ontological Invalidation of Disabled People," in *Disability and Social Theory*, ed. Dan Goodley, Bill Hughes, and Lennard Davis (London: Palgrave Macmillan, 2012), 17–32.

13. T. Shakespeare and N. Watson, "Defending the Social Model," *Disability & Society* 12, no. 2 (1997): 293–300. https://doi.org/10.1080/09687599727380.

14. Michael Oliver, *Social Work with Disabled People*, Practical Social Work (Houndmills, Basingstoke, Hampshire: Macmillan, 1983).

15. E. B. Jenks, "Explaining Disability: Parents' Stories of Raising Children with Visual Impairments in a Sighted World," *Journal of Contemporary Ethnography* 34, no. 2 (2005): 152, https://doi.org/10.1177/0891241604272064.

16. UN General Assembly, "United Nations Conventions on the Rights of Persons with Disabilities" (2007).

17. Jerome E. Bickenbach et al., "Models of Disablement, Universalism and the International Classification of Impairments, Disabilities and Handicaps," *Social Science & Medicine* 48, no. 9 (1999): 1173–87.

18. Michael Oliver, *The Politics of Disablement* (Basingstoke: Palgrave Macmillan, 1990); Oliver and Barnes, *New Politics of Disablement*.

19. Diane Driedger, *The Last Civil Rights Movement : Disabled Peoples' International* (London: Hurst, 1989).

20. Oliver and Barnes, *New Politics of Disablement*.

21. Stiker, *History of Disability*.

22. Jay Timothy Dolmage, *Disabled Upon Arrival: Eugenics, Immigration, and the Construction of Race and Disability* (Columbus: Ohio State University Press, 2018).

23. David Cameron and Fraser Valentine, *Disability and Federalism: Comparing Different Approaches to Full Participation*, vol. 62 (Montreal: McGill Queen's University Press, 2001).

24. Sharon N. Barnartt and Richard K. Scotch, *Disability Protests: Contentious Politics 1970–1999* (Washington, DC: Gallaudet University Press, 2001).

25. Heyer, *Rights Enabled*.

26. Susan S. Silbey, "Legal Consciousness," in *The New Oxford Companion to Law*, Oxford Companions (Oxford: Oxford University Press, 2008).

27. Émile Durkheim, *The Division of Labour* (New York: Macmillan, 1984), 39.

28. Silbey, "Legal Consciousness."

29. Heyer, *Rights Enabled*.

30. Martha Finnemore and Kathryn Sikkink, "International Norm Dynamics and Political Change," *International Organization* 52, no. 4 (1998): 887–917.

31. Oliver and Barnes, *New Politics of Disablement*; Barnartt and Scotch, *Disability Protests*.

32. Arlene S. Kanter, *The Development of Disability Rights under International Law: From Charity to Human Rights* (London: Routledge, 2014).

33. Tanya Titchkosky, "Monitoring Disability: The Question of the 'Human' in Human Rights Projects," in *Disability, Human Rights and the Limits of Humanitarianism*, ed. M. Gill and C. J. Schlund-Vials (New York: Routledge, 2014), 119–35; Meekosha and Soldatic, "Human Rights and the Global South."

34. Angela Me and Margaret Mbogoni, "Review of Practices in Less Developed Countries on the Collection of Disability Data," in *International Views on Disability Measures: Moving toward Comparative Measurement* (Bingley, UK: Emerald, 2006), 63–87.

35. Me and Mbogoni, "Review of Practices," 86.

36. Nora Groce, "Cultural Beliefs and Practices That Influence the Type and Nature of Data Collected on Individuals with Disability through National Census," in *International Views on Disability Measures: Moving toward Comparative Measurement*, ed. B. M. Altman and S. N. Barnartt, (Bingley, UK: Emerald, 2006), 43.

37. Groce, "Cultural Beliefs," 51.

38. Me and Mbogoni, "Review of Practices," 68.

39. Groce, "Cultural Beliefs."

40. Me and Mbogoni, "Review of Practices."

41. Me and Mbogoni, "Review of Practices."

42. Me and Mbogoni, "Review of Practices."

43. UN General Assembly, United Nations Conventions on the Rights of Persons with Disabilities.

44. Rebecca Yeo and Karen Moore, "Including Disabled People in Poverty Reduction Work: 'Nothing about Us, without Us,'" *World Development* 31, no. 3 (2003): 571–90.

45. Benedicte Ingstad and Arne Eide, *Disability and Poverty: A Global Challenge* (Bristol: Policy, 2011), 4.

46. Majid Turmusani, *Disabled People and Economic Needs in the Developing World: A Political Perspective from Jordan* (London: Routledge, 2018).

47. Turmusani, *Disabled People*.

48. World Health Organization, "Onchocerciasis (River Blindness)—Disease Information," Prevention of Blindness and Visual Impairment (World Health Organization, 2017).

49. World Health Organization, "Visual Impairment and Blindness" (World Health Organization, 2014), http://www.who.int/mediacentre/factsheets/fs282/en/.

50. Me and Mbogoni, "Review of Practices."

51. Kamal Lamichhane, *Disability, Education and Employment in Developing Countries* (Cambridge: Cambridge University Press, 2015), 27.

52. Lamichhane, *Disability, Education and Employment in Developing Countries.*

53. Hans Husum and Odd Edvardsen, "Poverty as Trauma: Methodological Problems When Reality Gets Ugly," in *Disability and Poverty: A Global Challenge*, ed. A. Eide and B. Ingstad (Bristol: Policy Press, 2011), 207–24.

54. Husum and Edvardsen, "Poverty as Trauma," 221.

55. Rod Michalko, *The Difference That Disability Makes* (Philadelphia: Temple University Press, 2002).

56. Michalko, *Difference That Disability Makes*, 54.

57. Ingstad and Eide, *Disability and Poverty*, 10.

58. Andrew B. Jenks, "Crip Theory and the Disabled Identity: Why Disability Politics Needs Impairment," *Disability & Society*, 2019, https://doi.org/10.1080/09687599.2018.1 545116; S. Vehmas and P. Mäkelä, "A Realist Account of the Ontology of Impairment," *Journal of Medical Ethics* 34, no. 2 (February 2008): 93–95, https://doi.org/10.1136/jme .2006.019042.

59. Husum and Edvardsen, "Poverty as Trauma," 211.

60. Ingstad and Eide, *Disability and Poverty*, 10.

61. Jacqui True, *The Political Economy of Violence against Women* (Oxford: Oxford University Press, 2012).

62. Spike V. Peterson, "How (the Meaning of) Gender Matters in Political Economy," *New Political Economy* 10, no. 4 (2005): 499–521, https://doi.org/10.1080/13563460500 344468; True, *Political Economy of Violence against Women.*

63. Meekosha and Soldatic, "Human Rights and the Global South"; Titchkosky, "Monitoring Disability."

64. Maria Berghs, *War and Embodied Memory: Becoming Disabled in Sierra Leone* (London: Routledge, 2016); Maria Berghs, "Radicalising 'Disability' in Conflict and Post-Conflict Situations," *Disability & Society* 30, no. 5 (2015): 743–58.

65. Lamichhane, *Disability, Education and Employment in Developing Countries.*

66. Meekosha and Soldatic, "Human Rights and the Global South"; Raewyn Connell, "Southern Bodies and Disability: Re-Thinking Concepts," *Third World Quarterly* 32, no. 8 (2011): 1369–81, https://doi.org/10.1080/01436597.2011.614799.

67. UN General Assembly, United Nations Conventions on the Rights of Persons with Disabilities.

68. UN General Assembly.

69. Turmusani, *Disabled People.*

70. Maria Eriksson Baaz and Maria Stern, *Sexual Violence as a Weapon of War? Perceptions, Prescriptions, Problems in the Congo and Beyond* (New York: Zed, 2013).

71. Michael Gill and Cathy J. Schlund-Vials, *Disability, Human Rights and the Limits of Humanitarianism* (London: Routledge, 2016); Rosemarie Garland-Thomson, "Integrating Disability, Transforming Feminist Theory," *NWSA Journal* 14, no. 3 (2002): 1–32, https://doi.org/10.2979/NWS.2002.14.3.1.

72. Connell, "Southern Bodies and Disability."

73. Kamal Lamichhane, *Disability, Education and Employment in Developing Countries.*

74. Ingstad and Eide, *Disability and Poverty.*

75. Mark Sherry, "The Disarticulate: Language, Disability, and the Narratives of Modernity," *Disability & Society* 30, no. 1 (2014): 166–68, https://doi.org/10.1080/09687 599.2014.964510; Mark Sherry, *Disability, Human Rights and the Limits of Humanitarianism* (Farnham: Ashgate, 2014).

76. David M. Engel and Frank W. Munger, *Rights of Inclusion: Law and Identity in the Life Stories of Americans with Disabilities* (Chicago: University of Chicago Press, 2003).

77. Meekosha and Soldatic, "Human Rights and the Global South."

78. Meekosha and Soldatic, "Human Rights and the Global South," 1386.

79. F. Campbell, *Contours of Ableism: The Production of Disability and Abledness* (London: Palgrave Macmillan, 2009), 4.

80. Fiona Kumari Campbell, "Precision Ableism: A Studies in Ableism Approach to Developing Histories of Disability and Abledment," *Rethinking History* 23, no. 2 (April 3, 2019): 138–56, https://doi.org/10.1080/13642529.2019.1607475.

81. Connell, "Southern Bodies and Disability"; Raewyn Connell, "A Thousand Miles from Kind: Men, Masculinities and Modern Institutions," *Journal of Men's Studies* 16, no. 3 (2008): 237–52, https://doi.org/10.3149/jms.1603.237.

82. Connell, "Thousand Miles from Kind," 245.

83. J. A. King, M. Brough, and M. Knox, "Negotiating Disability and Colonisation: The Lived Experience of Indigenous Australians with a Disability," *Disability & Society* 29, no. 5 (December 2013): 738–50, https://doi.org/10.1080/09687599.2013.864257.

84. Soldatic, "Transnational Sphere of Justice."

85. Soldatic, "Transnational Sphere of Justice," 746.

86. Soldatic, "Transnational Sphere of Justice."

87. Tanya Titchkosky and Rod Michalko, "The Body as the Problem of Individuality: A Phenomenological Disability Studies Approach," in *Disability and Social Theory*, ed. D. Goodley, B. Hughes, and L. Davis (London: Palgrave Macmillan, 2012), 135.

88. Julia Watts Belser, "Disability, Climate Change, and Environmental Violence: The Politics of Invisibility and the Horizon of Hope," *Disability Studies Quarterly* 40, no. 4 (December 7, 2020), https://doi.org/10.18061/dsq.v40i4.6959.

89. Penelope J. S. Stein and Michael Ashley Stein, "Disability, Human Rights, and Climate Justice," *Human Rights Quarterly* 44, no. 1 (2022): 81–110, https://doi.org/10.1353/hrq.2022.0003.

2

Disability, Colonialism, and Environmental Theory

A Political Theory Perspective

Nancy J. Hirschmann

The intersection of disability, environmentalism, and colonialism is a complicated one to which my own discipline of political science pays extremely little attention.[1] In my particular subfield of political theory, environmentalism is growing in popularity but generally ignores disability. Disability may be on the verge of a political theory breakthrough with a very small but mostly junior cohort of emerging scholars, yet environmentalism is not a prominent theme in their work either.[2] Putting these two together, then, yields an extremely small overlap. For instance, *The Oxford Handbook of Environmental Political Theory* contains one article that mentions disability.[3] By contrast, colonialism and postcolonial theory are important subsets of the field of political theory and the discipline of political science, with thousands of articles and books published. Yet disability is hardly mentioned, except perhaps in passing references to the damage done by landmines and wars to the bodies of the colonized (or postcolonized) peoples.[4] And most of it fails to attend to either disability or environmentalism. Yet bringing these three together can produce interesting new ways of thinking. This essay is an attempt to develop such an intersection.

It is by no means only political science or political theory that encounters a lack of attention to the intersections of these different vectors of power. Disability is rarely mentioned, much less engaged, by environmental theory in any discipline. Valerie Johnson notes that the environmental movement itself is marked by the absence of "voices and perspectives from those who self-identify or are identified as disabled."[5] Theory about this movement is thus not surprisingly different. In a parallel vein, the field of postcolonial studies has not often attended to disability, and this is true as well of state policies and political organizations of the North and West. As Helen Meekosha and Karen Soldatic have suggested,

> The development agenda often places the global North as more knowledgeable of human rights and therefore offers aid to "developing" countries so that they might embark on a programme [*sic*] of rights implementation. Yet this is usually done without acknowledgement of the fact that imperialism and colonialism stand as root causes of massive violations of human rights, famines, malnutrition and the ecological degradation of indigenous land and as the root cause of growing impairment in the global South.[6]

Mark Sherry has noted, and indeed documented with multiple examples, that postcolonialism has been *compared to* disability by various scholars (which is still a small subset of the literature on postcolonialism) in reductive and simplistic ways, with one often treated as a metaphor for the other.[7] Parallels and analogies, such as arguments that being a person of color in a white-dominant society or a woman in a patriarchal society constitutes a disability, generally do so in broad and sweeping terms that display considerable ignorance of the specificities of disability.[8] At the same time, Meekosha has accused disability theorists of "scholarly colonialism" in their lack of attention to "the transnational dimension of disability (in)justice."[9] And just as environmental theory and political theory have not paid much attention to disability, disability theory has not engaged much with environmentalism any more than it has with postcolonial studies. Specifically, most accounts of "the environment" in disability scholarship do not have much to do with climate change, pollution, recycling, species extinction, rising sea levels, or the vast variety of other specific topics that environmental political theory attends to. Tom Shakespeare, in fact, can be taken to imply that environmentalism and disability are separate and distinct, at times even opposed, when he observes that certain aspects of nature cannot be made accessible, such as rugged cliffs that able-bodied persons can climb but persons with certain mobility impairments cannot. Similarly, he notes, snow can create mobility issues in northern countries that get a lot of it; sandy beaches are difficult for wheelchairs to navigate unless they are specially equipped with the right kind of wheels; and hills make some cities like San Francisco less accessible than flat cities like Berlin or Philadelphia. While some of these things can be ameliorated by human action, many cannot. "It is hard to blame the natural environment on social arrangements," he maintains. Such natural barriers prove that "people with impairments will always be disadvantaged by their bodies."[10]

The view articulated by Shakespeare, a leading disability studies scholar, ironically dovetails with ableist views expressed by environmentalists about an inevitable tension between disability and environmentalism. Disabled people are often characterized as "greedy consumers" of energy and resources, since technology is frequently so central to adaptive devices and because demands for accessibility in "natural" surroundings is viewed as anti-environmental.[11] There is often intense hostility expressed toward making hiking trails accessible, for instance; yet such objections ignore the ways in which nondisabled hikers harm the environment as well, simply by their presence.[12] A glaring example of this is the long lines of hikers queuing up to reach the summit of Mount Everest, but there are many less spectacular examples, such as overcrowded national and state parks and litter along many hiking trails; on the lower portions of Mount Rainier, I have observed people going off trail to slide on snowy slopes in summer. The fact that disabled persons tend to be categorized as "vulnerable" often means society does not expect them to exhibit agency—indeed, may not see disabled persons as capable of agency—as Jacobus tenBroek noted sixty years ago, thus justifying their exclusion from environmentalist discussions and planning.[13]

These shifting variables make the intertwining of the concepts extremely challenging. The fault lines are multiple and divergent, the sheer variety of the moving parts makes it a daunting project to seek to bring them together, and the results are often counterproductive. Nevertheless, the intersection of global capitalism, racism, and sexism with colonialism and postcolonialism constructs a complex network of concepts and social forces that deeply involve disability. Considering disability could help us formulate good environmental political theory in a postcolonial world where political power always operates within the framework of global capitalism and is often controlled by it. This essay attempts to engage that process for and from my own discipline. Yet in making my argument, I will of necessity draw on a broader range of environmental writings and disability scholarship to identify points of tension and complementarity as well as connections and the contributions. I particularly argue that a postcolonial perspective can reveal the often-ignored ways in which disability is produced and treated as well as the ways that environmentalism colonizes disability. More generally, I want to suggest that environmentalism and environmental theory more broadly tend to be ableist, that postcolonial considerations can further enhance our understanding of this ableism, and that attending to disability experience can open up new ways of thinking about solutions to our current environmental crisis and about how to imagine and promote a more sustainable future.

Rethinking "Environment" and "Nature"

The concept of "the environment" has almost always been an important concept to disability studies, most centrally "the built environment." Under the so-called social model of disability, for instance, it is maintained that disability is not a condition of bodies themselves; that would be a mark of the "medical model," the idea that disability is a medical disorder, a biological or physical defect that must be treated or cured. Rather, on the social model, disability is the result of how human-made environments are structured to favor certain kinds of bodies and abilities and disfavor others to which it is unreceptive, even hostile.[14] For instance, consider architecture that incorporates stairs instead of slopes or ramps; it disables bodies that use wheelchairs for their mobility. Sidewalks with curbs similarly hamper wheelchair mobility and other kinds of mobility impairments. Visible crosswalks without auditory display put vision-impaired persons at a severe disadvantage in navigating public spaces. Academic conferences, where the panelists sit at a distance from the audience and there is no textual translation of what they are saying, much less sign language, turn hearing impairment into a disability. Disability, in this view, is not a condition of a body per se—not, for instance, the inability of a body to walk or see or hear. Rather, it is produced by the way that others have structured the environment. On this model, if we changed the environment to be more universally accessible, "disability" would disappear; bodily difference in terms of numbers of limbs or the workings of the central nervous system or the level of vision or hearing would be simply differences, like race and gender, that have no intrinsically structurally disadvantageous implications and no negative moral ones.

The social model of disability seems to provide a clean and easy connection to environmental theory: pollution is something that humans have created; it is a result and constituting part of the built environment; it is "disabling" the planet and its inhabitants, who are impeded in their ability to breathe, drink, eat, and live. This is a global phenomenon due to Western capitalist exploitation of so-called Third World economies and particularly the people living in those economies whose traditional modes of subsistence are disrupted, if not destroyed, and who are forced to participate in exploitive employment practices. These practices often produce disabilities, generally in ways that compound the effects of Western racism and patriarchalism. These causative relationships range from wars that result in lost limbs in citizens of invaded territories, to injuries sustained directly in the processes of production themselves, to the destruction of subsistence means through economic "development" and industrial pollution. Meekosha and Soldatic note that "colonial projects led to increasing rates of impairment for populations of the global South, including those indigenous populations within white-settler societies."[15] As Sherry succinctly puts it, "The history of colonialism is the poverty of the majority world, which has created large numbers of impairments."[16]

These scholars do not link much of this damage to environmental damage, aside from a brief mention of natural ecological catastrophes in Meekosha and Soldatic's call for disability scholars to attend to postcolonial issues: "Imperialism and colonialism stand as root causes of massive violations of human rights, famines, malnutrition and the ecological degradation of indigenous land and as the root cause of growing impairment in the global South."[17] But some have noted that corporate practices such as uranium mining and dumping of toxic waste on aboriginal lands in Australia, the movement of waste from "the metropole to the periphery, including the export of waste to so-called 'C havens' like China and India entail different versions of colonial appropriation of land, the original purpose of the colonial impulse."[18] Similarly, "sweatshops in Indonesia, Bangladesh, Thailand, China, Burma, Peru all offer cheaper wages, little or no trade union protection, and poor health protection," which Western corporations use to outsource labor production. Yet these practices all deploy harmful chemicals that poison workers and generate pollution in surrounding areas.[19] Studies of sweatshops in Southeast Asia and Latin America have documented muscular-skeletal disorders, eyesight injuries, stress and fatigue, skin complaints, and reproductive hazards.[20] Outsourced labor to developing countries manufactures not just goods for Western markets but disabilities for their host populations.[21] More directly, "land appropriation, resource extraction, forced removal, erasure, and devastation by settlers are all forms of land disablement that invariably wreak havoc on the land, spirit, livestock, and bodies of Indigenous people."[22]

The social model was formed in reaction to a "medical model" that viewed disability as an individual problem resulting from "defects" in individual bodies, a negative feature that must be cured or treated. The social model sought to situate impairments in a context of hostility and inaccessibility that is created through designing the world for certain kinds of bodies and not others. But it has come under attack by increasing numbers of disability theorists who point out that the extreme view of the social model seems to leave out the body itself.[23] They (and I include myself in this group) want us to recognize the ways in which the body must be included in our understanding of disability.[24] It is not always possible to accommodate disabilities out of existence, as Shakespeare suggested—all things considered equal, for instance, it will take someone with no arms longer to get dressed in the morning than it takes someone with two arms. Cognitive impairment may prevent me from being able to learn to read. Granted, those two examples have social aspects to them—the kinds of clothing that are acceptable to wear, and the role literacy plays in modernity—but the point is that some, if not most, disability qualities can be attached to the physicality of bodies in a wide variety of environments.

The relationship of disability theory to environmental theory is more complicated than what the social model might lead us to conclude. But even granting the objections to the social model, the environment as it is currently built and structured almost always makes all disabilities worse, more "disabling." Similarly, the human-made environment can cause disabling impairments in bodies, bringing disability into existence. This can happen directly, such as when landmines blow off limbs or when a car accident on a high-speed interstate highway causes spinal injury that results in paraplegia. But it can also happen indirectly or secondarily, such as when too many years of too much stress at work makes a person vulnerable to an autoimmune virus that will lead the person to develop diabetes, Crohn's disease, celiac, or other disabling conditions.[25] Inadequate health care and nutrition caused by poverty yields a variety of other vulnerabilities to disabilities and disabling illnesses.

A postcolonial perspective adds a further dimension to both the limits and the insights of the social model. For if "settler-colonialism is the foundational structure in nation-states where the discipline of disability studies is most prominent," then the social model will reflect the perspectives and ideals of settler colonialism.[26] "Colonialism was not only an economic process, but also one of imposing Eurocentric knowledge on the colonized," an imposition that disability scholars should be attuned to but often are not.[27] In Third World countries plagued by neocolonial exploitations' poverty and war, even conceptualizing disability is a colonial effect of what appears abnormal from the colonizer's context; for in the colonized countries themselves, "the notion of normalcy explodes given the almost normalised extra stress of living with inter-ethnic conflict and war."[28] Drawing on Jasbir Puar's work, Laura Jaffee and Kelsey John note that "disability is not an identity that easily or unproblematically traverses national boundaries, and for settler states to promote it as such among peoples of colonized and occupied nations, perpetuates a colonial savior logic invoked to justify forced removal, dispossession, and disavowal of Indigenous nationhood."[29]

Yet the social model's notion of "environment," as centered on the built environment, while seeming to ignore the objection that Shakespeare raises, offers an important contribution to environmental theory. Humans live in the natural world and have shaped it to such an extent that anthropologists claim that we occupy a new age, the "Anthropocene." As Steven Vogel argues, the "natural" environment is always already "built"—shaped, determined, and defined by human action. Disability's conceptualization of and recognition of the environment and how it impacts, interacts with, and forms bodies can help us formulate a set of questions and inquiries into environmental political theory. Most directly, the notion of the built environment plugs directly into the notion of the Anthropocene and the argument that humans have now shaped the "natural" environment to such an extent that Vogel and other scholars suggest that "nature" does not actually exist anymore and that we must develop "an environmentalism for the built environment."[30]

Bill McKibben suggests that humans are always "post-nature."[31] Political theorists and philosophers, particularly feminist ones, have long engaged a critique of the concept of nature and the natural, especially the association of women with nature and men with culture. Indeed, this was once a dominant theme in ecofeminism, which argued that the planet is "raped" by global corporations who exploit its resources and then claim that they are ameliorating rather than creating problems—for instance, by creating jobs, when instead they are destroying traditional modes of subsistence and exploiting now-dependent workers.[32] Disability analysis contributes to this. For instance, some of the examples I have offered of disability conditions raise questions about naturalness; it may be natural for the body's immune system to go into overdrive in response to industrial pollution, malnutrition, and stress created by exploitative labor conditions and inadequate wages, or for internal organs to become damaged because one must carry drinking water farther distances due to climate change altering the course of a river, but if the originary cause is based in social relations that are the product of late industrial and now global capitalism, then what is the "nature" of this "natural" response? It may be a function of the natural way that the body works to lose feeling in one's legs when the spinal cord is injured in a land mine explosion or from a bullet wound, but we generally balk at calling paraplegia a "natural" condition; it seems more accurate to say that it was produced by human activity. Does this mean that nature is gone, that there is no such thing? Is McKibben correct that "nature" has been destroyed?[33] Is every aspect of our planet's environment "built" one way or another?

Catriona Mortimer Sandilands argues that the very concept of nature has from the beginning incorporated a variety of anthropocentric biases. The struggle to maintain "pristine wilderness" that sat at the heart of the environmental movement in the United States, for instance, entailed an ideology of escape from the increasingly industrialized and densely populated urban centers. Such discourse is evident in the work of Enlightenment philosophers such as Jean-Jacques Rousseau, who believed that cities were hotbeds of corruption and that the countryside was the location of virtuous simplicity.[34] But in the twentieth century, for environmentalists like John Muir, national parks like Yellowstone and Banff were not just places to preserve species diversity and atmospheric cleanliness but "were understood as destinations for recreational travelers, places where the elite could partake in the healthy and morally uplifting activities of hiking and mountain climbing."[35] Sandilands notes that although Muir was largely motivated by the pollution created by urban industrial centers, his understanding of "pollution" included the influx of "foreign" (that is, European) immigrant labor and dense crowding in the cities. She notes that this period also saw the entry of significant numbers of women into the industrial labor force.[36] She argues that this "class-, race- and gender-specific view of nature being imposed on the landscape" also required the removal of persons living there, specifically Native Americans and First Nations people.[37] Though one might argue that national parks in the United States are less "elitist" than might have been the case when Muir was active, the educational levels for park visitors is still considerably higher than the national average—and 95 percent of visitors are white.[38] This all suggests that the notion of "nature" as a "pure" entity is a fiction and that it is not just a result of human action but of racist, classist, imperialist, ableist human action.

Colonialization of Disability within Environmentalism

Whether such claims are completely true is a matter of debate, of course. As disability scholar Alison Kafer remarks, "Although I agree with environmental critics in their deconstruction of the nature experience and their insistence that there is no bright line between nature and culture, I cannot deny that I feel different outside, away from traffic and exhaust pipes and crowds of people. That I have been conditioned to feel this way does not change the fact that I feel more at peace in my body when perched on the side of a cliff, or gazing over a meadow, or surrounded by sequoias."[39] Multiple studies have confirmed that spending time out of doors in nature has multiple beneficial health effects, particularly related to reducing stress and strengthening the immune system. Such information was popularized during the COVID-19 pandemic lockdowns.[40]

But the challenge to the meaning of "nature" suggests that disability and anti-colonialist insights into the complexities of how the built environment is built are relevant. It is important to note that the built environment must always contend with what most think of as "nature"; for instance, hurricanes and other storms cause flooding and structural damage, even if these are in part a result of climate change that humans have brought about through carbon emissions. In such "natural" disasters, disabled persons are forgotten or left for last in cases of evacuation and are otherwise neglected, as David Abbott and Sue Porter have noted.[41] Hurricane Katrina and superstorm Sandy in the United States offer two examples of persons with disabilities being virtually abandoned. Racism has been highlighted in the former, and many victims of both storms still have not had their homes restored—we know this because some media attention is paid to racial environmental injustice. But we hear extremely little about disability. Heat waves are another example, as disabled people make up a disproportionate number of related fatalities but are rarely recognized as such (though some may be included in the category of the elderly, whose danger is often stressed in the popular press).[42]

Moreover, the ways in which climate change produces disability are unacknowledged, often because the link between disability and climate damage is not always visible, obvious, or direct. As Paul Mohai, David Pellow, and J. Timmons Roberts argue, "mainstream" (and therefore generally Western) environmental movements ignore social justice and equality issues; yet there is documentation of a disproportionate impact of environmental issues on people of color and poorer populations, not to mention women. Such damage and its link to environmental damage is difficult to see and measure at times because environmental injustices are not immediately obvious.[43] Brooke Ackerly and Katy Attanasi, for instance, argue that deforestation, a global phenomenon, has forced Bangladeshi women to walk farther to gather the family's supply of water, which they carry back balanced on their heads. Such heavy head-loading for such long distances causes physiological problems, including prolapsed uteruses in these women—an "invisible disability" until they become pregnant and are thereby more likely to die in childbirth.[44] Similarly, Aurora Morales notes the ways that international development, in exploiting new markets, will promote products that might not pass safety standards in other countries or segments of society where oversight and regulation are more serious, resulting in disability. Work in Indigenous environmentalism and disability studies has shown the ways that settler colonialism has produced and promoted both environmental destruction and disability.[45] Disability thus intersects with environment, gender, race, ethnicity, and global capital, and theoretical analyses must strive to take account of them all at once.

The civil war in Rwanda, perhaps more accurately called a genocidal war, is a clear and heartrending example of the intersection of colonialism, environmental destruction, and disability. Though fighting was conducted by the "native" population, the war's origins are generally attributed to Belgian colonialism, which resulted in new forms of racism. Existing tribal groupings of Rwandan people—Tutsi, Hutu, and Twa—were separated into racially "superior" and "inferior" categories, with Tutsi being seen as more "European" and "intelligent" than others and Hutu being seen as "dumb [sic], but good-natured and loyal subjects." All Rwandans were given corresponding "identification cards" that were used to regulate these different classifications. This had concrete effects on the access of categorized Rwandans to higher education and positions in governmental administration. Accordingly, "not only did a great ethnic chasm emerge but a hatred of Tutsi by Hutu." In the genocidal violence that occurred in the 1990s after the Belgians had departed, these categories "told Hutu extremists who to kill and who to reprieve." Indeed, the Hutu viewed the Tutsi as colonizers who had invaded from Ethiopia.[46]

In addition to the horrific and brutal killing that ensued, this war produced environmental devastation. Rwanda previously had "the most complex savannah ecosystem in eastern Africa"; "more than 12% of the territory was covered by national parks and natural reserves," much of which was the site of the large-scale military conflict. This resulted in the loss of many animals, some killed directly (such as a "silver back mountain gorilla" whose "autopsy revealed that six bullets had been shot at him"). Others died through displacement and destruction of food and habitat.[47] Rwanda's first major conflict happened in Agakara National Park and resulted in the loss of "90% of its big mammals, with important loss and changes in habitats."[48] Human corpses thrown into rivers produced profound changes in biodiversity in the Nile River basin.[49] Neighboring countries to which Rwandan refugees escaped suffered from "deforestation, soil degradation, local pollution and poaching" due to the resulting "high demand" of desperate refugee populations.[50]

Not surprisingly, it was also the case that genocidal war "resulted in increased disability, not only as a direct result of the violence but also because of the breakdown of health, vaccination, and rehabilitation services." Since "most of the killing was done by machete, many of those who did not die were left with disabilities—limbs amputated and widespread trauma, both physical and psychological."[51] Disability was not a prominent feature of Western perceptions of the war, however; as one Rwandan put it, "When you watch TV and see caravans of refugees you hardly ever see PWDs. That is because most of the time they were left behind and most probably their loved ones perished with them."[52] More generally, due to relative poverty in Rwanda, "proportionally more disabilities are caused by untreated health problems and environmental pollution."[53] One study demonstrated that the trauma of genocide has "long-term and intergenerational effects," measuring negative effects on height growth of children exposed to genocide "from exposure in utero through adolescence," most likely attributable to nutrition deficits and the effects of forced labor and post-traumatic stress disorder.[54]

Thus, the relationship between disability, environmental degradation, and colonialism is not merely coincidental or parallel but intertwined and causal. Yet disabled people and disability scholars are generally not included in major international conferences on climate change and other policy-oriented discussion pertaining to environmental damage—arguably a different form of "colonial paternalism" where disabled persons are seen as subordinate to and under the "protection" of the "able bodies" who are supposedly more "capable." There is a certain unwillingness or at least a lack of attention to the need to accommodate disabled people in climate discourse and policy-making, what Gregor Wolbring calls a form of "adaptation apartheid." He maintains that ableism is a major problem in the environmental movement; society expects the disabled to cope with certain forms of climate change on their own and does not incorporate such considerations into its approaches.[55] Such attitudes suggest that colonialism and postcolonialism are not exclusively relevant to nations and communities who experienced actual historical colonization by Western imperial forces and continue to experience the exploitation of Western global capital. Rather, they are relevant to privileged Western societies in the ways that disabled persons experience their own colonization within those societies.

The forms that such apartheid or colonization take certainly include obvious and active resistance to and exclusion of disability concerns; this is a significant reason for ableist environmental policies. As Kafer points out, when arguments are made about the links between environmental harm and human bodies, too frequently "illness and disability appear . . . as tragic mistakes caused by unnatural incursions into or disruptions of the natural body and the natural environment."[56] This negative view of disability feeds too often into environmental advocacy.

A clear example is recent furor over asthma inhalers, deemed to have a greater carbon footprint than eating meat or driving a car, which targeted asthmatics as if they had a choice over their condition.[57] Many directed their rage at asthmatics themselves for using their inhalers "improperly" and for failing to switch to "greener" inhalers. Not only were such attacks completely ignorant of disability perspectives—as one blogger put it, "My technique may not always be the best, but thinking clearly is difficult to do when you are not getting enough oxygen to the brain." Completely missing was an attack on the corporations that make huge profits by manufacturing the inhalers with the propellant hydrofluoroalkane that emits greenhouse gases.[58] Even more significant was the failure to recognize that air pollution—a major contributor to which is corporate manufacturing, both directly (through production) and indirectly (through production of trucks and SUVs, for instance)—contributes heavily to asthma and is the most frequent trigger of an asthma attack, which causes a person to need the inhaler in the first place. The focus on individual asthmatics, like the mania about recycling in schools, shifts attention away from the real source of the problem of climate change. Disability scholars and advocates want a critical perspective of climate change that does not demonize illness and disability.

As Abbott and Porter note, "Discourse around energy consumption and 'right behaviour' makes a number of ableist assumptions."[59] Indeed, the degree to which disability is viewed almost exclusively negatively by those attending to environmental concerns could make one quite skeptical of the collaboration I am aiming at. It begs the question: Can efforts toward sustainability and disability accommodation be reconciled? Are the two inevitably at odds? Is environmentalism in the twenty-first century inevitably ableist? The overall utilitarian bent of much environmentalist theory is concerning to minority populations; in dealing with large-scale environmental questions such as species preservation, it is difficult not to think of how particular changes that an ethical environmental policy requires must appeal to the needs of the many in preserving the health of the planet. As Sarah Jaquette Ray asserts, "Disability is the category of 'otherness' against which both environmentalism and adventure have been shaped."[60] So will disabled persons be sacrificed on the altar of consequentialism—as often happens in political theories of justice—in the face of global disaster?[61] Answers to these questions depend on the theoretical values and principles underlying our approach to environmental problems, which are largely ableist.

Just as we find in the built environment, in so-called natural settings like mountain trails, access is generally conceived to be a special accommodation to those with disabilities. But this ignores the ways in which access for nondisabled bodies is similarly constructed. The very existence of a trail, for instance, is premised on a human body that hikes on two legs (often carrying a large backpack). Thus, instead of critiquing the building of ramps on a trailside hut where hikers spend the night, we could just as easily critique the building of stairs into the hut: as one respondent to quite vicious harangues of disabled hikers asked, "Why bother putting steps on the hut at all? Why not drag yourself in through a window?"[62] Hiking trails are created and maintained; so why are further modifications to make such trails disability accessible seen as so much more "artificial"? As Kafer adds, in relating a hiking experience of her own in which she proceeded on a trail quite successfully despite official warnings not to, who determines how much modification is needed to make a trail accessible?[63] As Sandra Lambert recounts of her numerous kayaking trips to national and state parks, nondisabled people generally assume that disability access requires either much more than is really needed or far less.[64] These assumptions arise from the failure to include disabled persons in planning discussions from the start: disability apartheid or colonization.

It is not just actively negative attitudes toward persons with disability that creates disability as a colonial outpost of environmental theory and public policy, however. Political theory can reveal that ableism also results from sincere environmentalist efforts at sustainability that simply do not think about disability—that is, rather than actively hostile exclusion, disability just never occurs to them. Neil Adger argues that "increases in income inequality concentrate resources in fewer hands and in particular places. It has been shown both theoretically and by wide observation that such concentration leads to decisions on environment being made by groups who can insulate themselves from its consequences."[65] Charles Mills calls this phenomenon the epistemology of ignorance, which entails the building of a body of knowledge that fails to attend to the experiences of colonized people, whether literal settler-states or metaphorical, such as women, people of color, and disabled people.[66] A prominent example in the United States is community and commercial efforts at sustainability that involved the elimination of plastic straws, which cause significant pollution problems and threats to marine life. But straws are also extremely helpful to people with upper-body impairments in drinking fluids. Such policy enactments completely left out disability perspectives. The resulting controversy produced a "compromise" whereby disabled persons could request straws, but that policy continues the stigmatizing and singling out of disabled persons who need "special" accommodation and who must justify their requirement, thus reinforcing their colonized status, marking them as deviants who appear to put their selfish needs above the planet's.

Epistemological ignorance is not simply about knowledge; it is about power. Unless disabled persons have access to positions in the discussion from which they can point out these issues in a way that has political force, their perspective will not be heard. What Miranda Fricker identified as "epistemic injustice" involves the exclusion of certain voices and the failure to attend to the knowledge that their experiences reveal, either through disbelief and dismissal, willful ignorance, or active hostile exclusion. I would add to that what might be called "innocent ignorance," which is the unconscious failure to understand that what looks "normal" from the perspective of privilege—because a person has never encountered disability—is actually oppressive. Disabled persons experience all these forms of epistemological exclusion on a regular basis, but this "innocent ignorance" is just as pernicious as more hostile and malicious forms of ignorance. Both kinds of epistemic injustice and exclusion create the framework for hostility and antagonism and make it not only possible but seemingly justifiable to those who exhibit it.[67]

Moreover, when such injustice comes from *within* progressive movements, it may be even harder to see. For instance, feminism clearly threatens white patriarchal assumptions about how the world works, and since these assumptions translate into material relations of power, it also thereby threatens actual male power. But middle-class white feminism has at various times also been unwelcoming to feminism of color and lesbian feminism, and such exclusions have been harder for white feminists to recognize and address, not necessarily because they are willfully racist or homophobic (though some may be) but because they are not self-consciously aware of their privilege and how that leads to oppressive behavior. Similarly, environmentalists *should* be more in tune to exploitation, exclusion, and domination since those concepts sit at the heart of their critique of Western neoliberalism and capitalist production. Yet they are often ignorant of their own ableism. By including a disability perspective into our considerations of the environment, our epistemic framework for understanding the environment and our responses to environmental degradation can be enhanced, enlarged, and more nuanced.

A Disability Perspective on Colonialist Environmentalism

There are several contributions that a disability perspective can make to environmental theory. As mentioned, the importance of the "built environment" to disability theory has the potential to open up important arguments in environmental political theory. Insofar as Vogel is correct that the natural is always already built, then the insights of disability studies can make important contributions to environmental discussions. The central connection between disability and environmentalism must center on the changes that humans have made to the "natural environment" and not just the built environment as if it has no relation to the "natural," as it currently appears in much disability theory when we talk about stairs and ramps and elevators, curb cuts and crosswalk signals, trains, planes, and buses.

The connections between the social model and this no-longer-truly-natural environment are potentially profound, in both the direct and indirect senses: for instance, flooding caused by rising sea levels and more intense storms make wheelchair mobility more difficult, if not impossible; air pollution to which a baby is exposed in utero could produce a neural tube defect, a disability with which both the baby and parents must contend; epigeneticists have maintained that a variety of environmental factors, even some related to the season and month in which a baby is born, can produce illness and disability ranging from asthma and cardiovascular conditions such as hypertension to colitis, myopia and other "eye conditions," and attention deficit hyperactivity disorder.[68] When talking in terms of postcolonial contexts, this connection becomes even more pronounced, as global capitalist production, outsourcing, and irresponsible pollution create disabilities among economically vulnerable populations. A disability perspective can thus help

us see the harms that occur to human bodies through environmental degradation caused by the built environment, deepened by postcolonial capital
and by disablist policies that are supposedly designed to respond to it.

A disability perspective can help us attend more to the complex ways in
which disability is produced by negative forces; its inclusion is also key to
reminding us that this negativity is not everything about disability experience, and it is not inconsistent with leading a good life.[69] Indeed, this perspective can help environmentalists and environmental political theorists
understand that disability is not *just* nonnegative. It can also help us see that
disabilities can bring positive experiences and make valuable contributions
to understanding the environment and how humans can and should interact with it; and that persons with disabilities lead meaningful lives not just
despite their disabilities but also because of them. Including these perspectives can promote different ways of thinking about attempts to ameliorate
the disabling effects of specific impairments, which can appear to harm the
"natural" environment, such as when hardscape surfaces are built in natural
spaces like beaches or forests to enhance mobility access.[70] As Kafer points
out, many such efforts can be done in such a way that they do not harm the
environment any more than the alternatives that are assumed to be better.
For instance, might paved trails be more likely to discourage people from
walking off trail? And is paving the only way to create access?

Such questions reflect a kind of "epistemic inclusion" where the perspectives of disabled persons and their lived experiences and their relation to the
environment is needed and valued in the construction of environmental
policies and practices. There are several ways in which a disability perspective can further environmentalism and environmental political theory. The
first might be to follow the feminist metaphorical route, particularly the
critique of the alignment of women with nature. But such connection is also
material, with environmental damage to women's bodies during pregnancy
producing fetal impairments that endanger the health of the mother and
present more after-birth challenges to her as the (usual) primary caretaker,
as gender is linked to the negative narrative of disability.[71] It can directly
impact women's health and mortality as well, such as in the example mentioned earlier of Bangladeshi women experiencing prolapsed uteruses due
to heavy head-loading. On a parallel track, we could discuss the ways the
planet is being impaired and disabled by a variety of human behaviors and
point to the kinds of real damage that pollution does to human bodies as
well as animals and flora.[72] Obviously, such an approach is worrisome and
problematic for reasons I have discussed, particularly the danger that the
negative aspects of disability will overwhelm the concept and that the value
of disability experience will be suppressed. But with the participation of
disability scholars and advocates who adopt a more self-critical perspective,

a route can be developed to carefully recognize the real harm that is being done to bodies without creating a totalizing discourse about disability as lives-not-worth-living.

A second model might be the growing literature on environmental justice, which importantly documents the disproportionate impact and greater vulnerability of the poor, racial and ethnic minorities, and exploited "third world" labor forces to the immediate effects of environmental pollution and degradation but has not generally extended to include disability as a category of analysis or disabled persons as a group so affected.[73] Environmental racism, for instance, operates geographically: class and racial segregation may group racial minorities and poor persons in particular regions or neighborhoods where hazardous waste sites, incinerators, and toxic dumping from factories are particularly acute. Thus, to take a U.S.-based example, if an incinerator for toxic waste is proposed to be located near a community inhabited primarily by African Americans or Latinos without adequate notification or an opportunity for popular input—or, even allowing for such input, it is ignored or rejected under apparently race-neutral rationalizations—then it becomes a bit more straightforward to identify ways in which environmental hazards such as incinerators or toxic waste sites are targeted at specific racial and ethnic populations.[74]

For disability environmental theory, neither of these models is directly applicable; disabled persons, like women, are dispersed and spread out across class, race, ethnicity, nation, and other determinants of geographical distribution. Disabled persons live everywhere and belong to every race, gender, ethnicity, religion, and class (though the generally higher rates of poverty among disabled persons sets some parameters). Similarly, they do not demand an absolute end to pollution because they recognize the need for continued technology for assistive devices ranging from electronic wheelchairs to asthma inhalers; instead, they can advocate for cleaner and greener technology as well as an end to corporate practices that produce impairments and create disabilities.[75]

Perhaps the most important contribution that disability can make to environmentalism lies in perspective. Sandilands points out that how people experience nature is shaped by gender, race, sexuality, and ability. One might argue that ecofeminists, environmental justice theorists, and queer theorists have shown us the first three, and that disability theory can show the last. Yet even here the divisions are rather forced: Sandilands comes to her recognition of a "queer ecology" by considering AIDS, a condition that is also highly relevant to a disability perspective; indeed, a disability perspective could be superior, since not all queer persons, nor only queer persons, develop AIDS.[76] Kafer suggests that a disability perspective can help us toward "recognizing our interdependence" on each other as humans, and between humans and nature, and that this perspective of interdependence "disrupt[s] the ableist ideology that everyone interacts with nature in the same way."[77] But it also creates space for pausing and thinking about what that interaction is and how it occurs. For instance, staying on a trail that is itself a threat and a harm to "nature" is better than going off the trail and creating a new line of destruction, but we respect the trail only if we understand that we are as dependent on nature as it is on our not abusing it.

Along these lines, Abbott and Porter similarly note that disabled persons have vast experience with overcoming barriers and responding to risk, all of which make their insights valuable and useful to environmentalist debates. Persons with disabilities are skilled at adapting to environments, because they have to be in order to survive, rather than making their environments adapt to their bodies, because they are often powerless to do that. But this skill and attention to adaptation allows them to develop, as David Mitchell and Sharon Snyder put it, "alternative strategies of nonnormative living."[78] The daily requirements of negotiating a physical environment, whether "natural" or "built," tends to produce a skillful set of problem-solving abilities and provides useful insights about the value of interdependency and scarcity as well as the importance of human relatedness.[79] Disabled people have had to develop the skill of understanding and appreciating the limits of things rather than insisting on limitlessness. Such a perspective, Abbott and Porter maintain, can help yield progressive solutions "that would benefit all," in keeping with the universal access ideology, "as opposed to being seen as a specialist or marginal viewpoint."[80] The perspective of disability also gives many disabled persons insight into the very idea of what constitutes our "environment," as discussed earlier in this essay, and may help broaden our understanding of what an environmental political theory should be thinking about.

These various shifts in perspective would be in keeping with, and could help further develop, what Julian Agyeman calls a "just sustainability paradigm," which gives priority to ideals and values of justice and equality while keeping in mind the importance of the environment and its continued protection—for instance, promoting "pedestrian-friendly" streetscapes while working within sustainability principles.[81] Though Agyeman does not discuss disability, his principle could easily be extended to "wheelchair friendly." For instance, he notes that there is a tension between present and future generations but that it can be resolved through thinking over the long-term consequences of present action. For instance, could the United States have closed coal mines without pushing West Virginia and Kentucky voters into the arms of Donald Trump if the Obama administration encouraged the construction of green energy businesses in those states through aggressive incentives? Such a measure could have helped both the current generation of workers by providing new jobs rather than threatening unemployment and future generations who will suffer the most from current coal use. Though this is not Agyeman's example but my own, tensions between generations have parallels to supposed tensions between persons with disabilities and those without, or even among persons with different kinds of disabilities.

Kafer makes a similar point, providing examples of such negotiations between groups who do not share an experiential perspective but can be said to share a roughly common goal if they view the goal more broadly. For instance, feminists who are worried about the retrenchment of women's reproductive rights are often hostile to arguments that women should carry any fetus to term if they do not want to, including when the fetus is impaired. As such, they are at odds with disability advocates who are aware of a long history of eugenics, including abortion, against persons with disabilities, as well as prenatal testing and "genetic counseling" pressure to abort fetuses with Down syndrome and other "birth defects." Yet pro-choice feminists and disability advocates could come together over legislation that provided more detailed information and economic and social supports to the raising of children with impairments without mandating that a woman carry a given fetus to term.[82] This kind of thinking is similarly needed to reconcile the needs of disabled persons and environmentalists without stimulating the irrational and ableist fears of the latter. As Kafer asks, "Can we imagine a crip interaction with nature, a crip engagement with wilderness, that doesn't rely on either ignoring the limitations of the body or triumphing over them?" She advocates for disabled persons "to write [ourselves] back into nature even as [we] unpack the binary of nature and self, nature and human."[83]

Obviously, these recommendations I offer are abstract, at best analogous, and not made in the context of specific environmental dilemmas, which have only served as examples to illustrate my theoretical points; the disability contribution to environmentalism is still working toward an identity. The point I am trying to make is that a disability perspective can contribute to a more complicated way of thinking about the relationship between human bodies and the environments in which we are located that we are seeing in some environmental theory, the ways that we shape and affect them, and the ways in which they shape and affect us; attending to disability would be useful for disability political theory. We must end the silencing of knowledge that subordinate groups like disabled persons possess and include them in the construction of policy decisions and normative judgments about environmental welfare.

NOTES

1. This essay was written under the auspices of the Stanley I. Sheerr Term Chair in the Social Sciences and the Roberta R. Segal Professorship in American Social Thought at the University of Pennsylvania. It was presented at the American Political Science Associa-

tion annual meeting, the Southern Political Science Association annual meeting, and the European Conference on Politics and Gender. Thanks to participants for comments and suggestions.

2. See, for instance, Barbara Arneil and Nancy J. Hirschmann, eds., *Disability and Political Theory* (Cambridge: Cambridge University Press, 2017); Lorraine Krall McCrary, "The Politics of Community: Care and Agency in People with Intellectual Disabilities at L'Arche," *Politics, Groups, and Identities* 9, no. 2 (2021): 409–22; Claire McKinney, "Biopluralism, Disability, and Democratic Politics," *Politics, Groups, and Identities* 9, no. 2 (2021): 423–37; Stacy Clifford Simplican, *The Capacity Contract: Intellectual Disability and the Question of Citizenship* (Minneapolis: University of Minnesota Press, 2015); Amber Knight and Joshua Miller, *Prenatal Genetic Testing, Abortion, and Disability Justice* (New York: Oxford University Press, 2023).

3. Teena Gabrielson, "Bodies, Environments, and Agency," in *The Oxford Handbook of Environmental Political Theory*, ed. Teena Gabrielson, Cheryl Hall, John M. Meyer, and David Schlosberg (New York: Oxford University Press, 2016), 399–400; Rosemarie Garland-Thomson, "Misfits: A Feminist Materialist Disability Concept," *Hypatia: A Journal of Feminist Philosophy* 26, no. 3 (2011): 591–609; Nancy J. Hirschmann, "Feminist Thoughts on Freedom and Disability" (corrected title from "Feminist Thoughts on Freedom and Rights," errata in vol. 8, no. 3), *Politics & Gender* 8, no. 2 (2012): 216–22.

4. See, for instance, Duncan Ivison, *Postcolonial Liberalism* (Cambridge: Cambridge University Press, 2002); Margaret Kohn and Keally McBride, *Political Theories of Decolonization: Postcolonialism and the Problem of Foundations* (New York: Oxford University Press, 2011); *Postcolonialism and Political Theory*, ed. Nalini Persram (Lanham, MD: Lexington, 2007).

5. Valerie Ann Johnson, "Bringing Together Feminist Disability Studies and Environmental Justice," in *Disability Studies and the Environmental Humanities: Toward an Eco-Crip Theory*, ed. Sarah Jaquette Ray and Jay Sibara (Lincoln: University of Nebraska Press, 2017), 76.

6. Helen Meekosha and Karen Soldatic, "Human Rights and the Global South: The Case of Disability," *Third World Quarterly* 32, no. 8 (2011): 1394.

7. Mark Sherry, "(Post)colonizing Disability," *Wagadu* 4 (Summer 2007): 10–22, esp. 11–14.

8. Alice Domurat Dreger, *One of Us: Conjoined Twins and the Future of Normal* (Cambridge, MA: Harvard University Press, 2004); Iris Young, *On Female Body Experience: Throwing Like a Girl and Other Essays* (New York: Oxford University Press, 2005).

9. Helen Meekosha, "Decolonising Disability: Thinking and Acting Globally," *Disability & Society* 26, no. 6 (October 2011): 666–82, at 668 and 676; Teodor Mladenov, "Disability and Social Justice," *Disability & Society* 31, no. 9 (2016): 1226–41, at 1230.

10. Tom Shakespeare, *Disability Rights and Wrongs* (London: Routledge, 2006), 45, 46. See also Alison Kafer, "Bodies of Nature: The Environmental Politics of Disability," in *Disability Studies and the Environmental Humanities*, 202.

11. David Abbott and Sue Porter, "Environmental Hazard and Disabled People: From Vulnerable to Expert to Interconnected," *Disability & Society* 28, no. 6 (2013): 839–52, at 840, 843, 847. See also Paul Pepper, "It's Not Easy Being Green," *Disability Now*, 2007, accessed December 1, 2008, http://www.disabilitynow.org.uk/living/style/its-not-easy-being-green (however, this website is no longer active).

12. Jennie Bricker, "Wheelchair Accessibility in Wilderness Areas: The Nexus between the ADA and the Wilderness Act," *Environmental Law* 25, no. 4 (1995): 1243–70.

13. Jacobus tenBroek, "The Right to Live in the World: The Disabled in the Law of Torts," *California Law Review* 54, no. 2 (May 1966): 841–919. See also Jacobus tenBroek, "The Disabled in the Law of Welfare," *California Law Review* 54, no. 2 (May 1966): 809–40.

14. On the medical and social models, see Barbara Arneil and Nancy J. Hirschmann, "Disability and Political Theory: An Introduction," in *Disability and Political Theory*, ed. Arneil and Hirschmann.

15. Meekosha and Soldatic, "Human Rights and the Global South," 1394.

16. Sherry, "(Post)colonizing Disability," 16.

17. Meekosha and Soldatic, "Human Rights and the Global South," 1394.

18. Meekosha, "Decolonising Disability," 676.

19. Ibid., 677.

20. Ibid., 676.

21. Claire Mayhew and Michael Quinlan, "The Effects of Outsourcing on Occupational Health and Safety: A Comparative Study of Factory-Based Workers and Outworkers in the Australian Clothing Industry," *International Journal of Health Services* 29, no. 1 (1999): 83–107; Rafael Moure-Eraso, Meg Wilcox, Laura Punnet, Leslie MacDonald, and Charles Levenstein, "Back to the Future: Sweatshop Conditions on the Mexico–U.S. Border: Occupational Health Impact of Maquiladora Industrial Activity," *American Journal of Industrial Medicine* 31, no. 5 (1997): 587–99.

22. Laura Jaffee and Kelsey John, "Disabling Bodies of/and Land: Reframing Disability Justice in Conversation with Indigenous Theory and Activism," *Disability and the Global South* 5, no. 2 (2018): 1407–29, at 1408.

23. See, for instance, Nirmala Erevelles, *Disability and Difference in Global Contexts: Enabling a Transformative Body Politic* (New York: Palgrave Macmillan, 2011); Shaun Grech, *Disability and Poverty in the Global South* (New York: Palgrave Macmillan, 2015); Helen Meekosha and Russell Shuttleworth, "What's So 'Critical' about Critical Disability Studies?" *Australian Journal of Human Rights* 15 (2009); Chris Bell, "Introducing White Disability Studies: A Modest Proposal," in *The Disability Studies Reader*, ed. Lennard J. Davis (Taylor & Francis, 2006); Tom Shakespeare, *Disability Rights and Wrongs* (London: Routledge, 2006); Dimitris Anastasiou and James M. Kauffman, "The Social Model of Disability: Dichotomy between Impairment and Disability," *Journal of Medicine and Philosophy* 38, no. 4 (August 2013): 441–59.

24. See, for instance, Erevelles, *Disability and Difference*; Elizabeth Barnes, *The Minority Body: A Theory of Disability* (Oxford: Oxford University Press, 2016); Nancy J. Hirschmann, "Invisible Disability: Seeing, Being, Power," in *Civil Disabilities: Citizenship, Membership, and Belonging*, ed. Nancy J. Hirschmann and Beth Linker (Philadelphia: University of Pennsylvania Press, 2015), 204–22.

25. Huan Song, Fang Fang, Gunnar Tomasson, Filip K. Arnberg, David Mataix-Cols, Lorena Fernández de la Cruz, Catarina Almqvist, Katja Fall, and Unnur A. Valdimarsdóttir, "Association of Stress-Related Disorders with Subsequent Autoimmune Disease," *Journal of the American Medical Information Association* 319, no. 23 (2018): 2388–2400.

26. Jaffee and John, "Disabling Bodies," 1408.

27. Meekosha, "Decolonising Disability," 677.

28. Fiona Kumari Campbell, "Geodisability Knowledge Production and International Norms: A Sri Lankan Case Study," *Third World Quarterly* 32, no. 8 (2011): 1455–74, at 1467.

29. Jaffee and John, "Disabling Bodies," 1412.

30. Steven Vogel, *Thinking Like a Mall: Environmental Philosophy after the End of Nature?* (Cambridge, MA: MIT Press, 2015), 7.

31. Bill McKibben, *The End of Nature* (New York: Random House, 1989).

32. Susan Griffin, *Women and Nature: The Roaring Inside Her* (New York: Harper and Row, 1980), 3.

33. McKibben, *End of Nature*. See also Vogel, *Thinking Like a Mall*, 16, for a similar notion of nature that he calls "biological," which I do not really accept, since we tend to think of biology as pertaining to fauna (including humans), not flora, despite David George Haskell's argument in *The Song of Trees: Stories from Nature's Great Connectors* (New York: Penguin Random House, 2017).

34. Jean-Jacques Rousseau, *Emile: Or, On Education*, trans. Allan Bloom (New York: Basic, 1979), 59.

35. Catriona Mortimer Sandilands, "Unnatural Passions? Notes toward a Queer Ecology," *Invisible Culture: An Electronic Journal for Visual Culture*, no. 9 (2005): 5.

36. Ibid.; see also Nancy J. Hirschmann, *Gender, Class and Freedom in Modern Political Theory* (Princeton, NJ: Princeton University Press, 2008).

37. Sandilands, "Unnatural Passions?," 5.

38. J. J. Vaske and K. M. Lyon, *Linking the 2010 Census to National Park Visitors*, Natural Resource Technical Report, Fort Collins, CO: National Park Service, 2014. The authors note, for instance, that although one-third of Americans have a college BA or higher degree, two-thirds of national park visitors have such degrees. The percentage of visitors over age sixty-four mirrors that of the general population but includes many more white people than persons of color.

39. Kafer, "Bodies of Nature," 220.

40. Lisa Anderson, Sus Sola Corazon, and Ulrika Karlsonn Stigsdottir, "Nature Exposure and Its Effects on Immune System Functioning: A Systematic Review," *International Journal of Environmental Research and Public Health* 18 (2021): 18, 1416–64; Masashi Sog, Maldwyn J. Evans, Kazuaki Tsuchiya, Yuya Fukano, "A Room with a Green View: The Importance of Nearby Nature for Mental Health during the COVID-19 Pandemic," *Ecological Applications* 31, no. 2 (2021): 1–10; Alisha Haridasani Gupta, "The Mental Health Benefits of an Inclusive Outdoor Escape: Amid Pandemic Stress and Racial Violence, Many Communities of Color Have Turned to Wilderness Areas for Healing," *New York Times*, July 7, 2022, accessed February 6, 2023, https://www.nytimes.com/2022/07/07/well/mind/ecotherapy-mental-health-diversity.html?searchResultPosition=5.

41. Abbott and Porter, "Environmental Hazard," 842.

42. Gregor Wolbring, "A Culture of Neglect: Climate Discourse and Disabled People," *M/C Journal* 12, no. 4 (2009).

43. Paul Mohai, David Pellow, and J. Timmons Roberts, "Environmental Justice," *Annual Review of Environment and Resources* 34 (2009): 405–30. I fully recognize the oxymoron of "mainstream environmentalism," given how much the "mainstream" of world politics tends to ignore environmental issues.

44. Brooke Ackerly and Katy Attenasi, "Global Feminisms: Theory and Ethics for Studying Gendered Injustice," *New Political Science* 31, no. 4 (2009): 544; Hirschmann, "Invisible Disability."

45. Aurora L. Morales, *Kindling: Writings on the Body* (Cambridge, MA: Palabrera, 2013); Jaffee and John, "Disabling Bodies."

46. Troy Riemer, "How Colonialism Affected the Rwandan Genocide," *Umuvigizi: Telling the Truth about the Genocide and Fighting the Denial*, accessed January 11, 2023, https://umuvugizi.wordpress.com/2011/08/16/how-colonialism-affected-the-rwandan-genocide/.

47. Samuel Kanyamibwa, "Impact of War on Conservation: Rwandan Environment and Wildlife in Agony," *Biodiversity and Conservation* 7 (1998): 1403.

48. Ibid., 1401–2. See also Nancy J. Hirschmann, "Environmentalism and the Marvel Cinematic Universe: *Spider-Man Far from Home* as a Cautionary Tale" in *The Politics of the Marvel Cinematic Universe*, ed. Nicholas Carnes and Lillian J. Goren (Topeka: University of Kansas Press, 2022), 174.

49. Kanyamibwa, "Impact of War on Conservation," 1403.

50. Ibid., 1404. Restoration efforts began in 2010, motivated significantly by the need for tourism dollars. See Benedict Moran, "Rwanda's War Nearly Destroyed this Park. Now It's Coming Back," *National Geographic* online newsletter, May 7, 2019, https://www.nationalgeographic.com/environment/article/akagera-national-park-rwanda-conservation?loggedin=true&rnd=1701262706817 (login required). See also Callixte Gatali and Kjell Wallin, "Bird Diversity in the Savanna Habitats of Akagera National Park, Rwanda, in the Post-war Recovery Period," *Ostrich* 86, no. 3 (2015): 267–76 on the critical importance of Akagera to the biodiversity of the African continent.

51. Vyvienne R. P. M'kumbuzi, J. B. Sagahutu, J. Kagwiza, G. Urimubenshi, and K. Mostert-Wentzel, "The Emerging Pattern of Disability in Rwanda," *Disability and Rehabilitation* 36, no. 6 (2014): 476.

52. Art Blaser, "People with Disabilities (PWDs) and Genocide: The Case of Rwanda," *Disability Studies Quarterly* 22, no. 3 (Summer 2002): 53, quoting from a personal email from Ben Ruwumbara on October 12, 2002.

53. Ibid., 54.

54. AnnaMaria Milazzo and Jose Cuesta, "Long-Term Well-Being among Survivors of the Rwandan and Cambodian Genocides," *Journal of Development Studies* 57, no. 8 (2021): 1413–27, at 1414.

55. Wolbring, "Culture of Neglect."

56. Alison Kafer, *Feminist, Queer, Crip* (Bloomington: Indiana University Press, 2013), 157–58.

57. Michelle Roberts, "Asthma Carbon Footprint 'As Big as Eating Meat,'" *BBC Online*, October 30, 2019, accessed January 25, 2020, https://www.bbc.com/news/health-50215011.

58. Whitney Lee, "People Who Use Inhalers Aren't Responsible for the Climate Crisis. Corporations and Governments Are," *Rooted in Rights*, November 12, 2019, accessed January 25, 2020, https://rootedinrights.org/people-who-use-inhalers-arent-responsible-for-the-climate-crisis-corporations-and-governments-are/.

59. Abbott and Porter, "Environmental Hazard," 847.

60. Sarah Jaquette Ray, "Risking Bodies in the Wild: The 'Corporeal Unconscious' of American Adventure Culture," *Journal of Sport and Social Issues* 33, no. 3 (August 2009): 257.

61. For instance, Peter Singer, whose work on animal rights has recently connected with environmental issues, believes persons with "severe" disabilities should not be permitted to exist. See also Abbott and Porter, "Environmental Hazard," 843–44.

62. Kafer, *Feminist, Queer, Crip*, 138, quoting Joseph Huber, "Trailblazing in a Wheelchair: An Oxymoron?" *Palestra: Forum of Sport, Physical Education, and Recreation for Those with Disabilities* 17, no. 4 (2001): 52.

63. Kafer, *Feminist, Queer, Crip*, 136–39; see also Sandra Gail Lambert, *A Certain Loneliness: A Memoir* (Lincoln: University of Nebraska Press, 2018), regarding kayaking trips that nondisabled persons, particularly park rangers, tried to stop her from taking.

64. Lambert, *Certain Loneliness*.

65. W. Neil Adger, "Inequality, Environment, and Planning," *Environment and Planning A: Economy and Space* 34, no. 10 (2002): 1717.

66. Charles Mills, *The Racial Contract* (Ithaca, NY: Cornell University Press, 1999); see also Carole Pateman and Charles Mills, *Contract and Domination* (Cambridge, UK: Polity, 2007), for "the settler contract."

67. Miranda Fricker, *Epistemic Injustice: Power and the Ethics of Knowing* (New York: Oxford University Press, 2007).

68. Mary Regina Boland, Zachary Shahn, David Madigan, George Hripcsak, and Nicholas P. Tatonetti, "Birth Month Affects Lifetime Disease Risk: A Phenome-Wide Method," *Journal of the American Medical Information Association* 22, no. 5 (2015): 1042–53, at 1052.

69. For more on my view on this issue, see Nancy J. Hirschmann and Rogers M. Smith, "Rethinking 'Cure' and 'Accommodation,'" in *Disability and Political Theory.*

70. Kafer, "Bodies of Nature," 215–16; Bricker, "Wheelchair Accessibility."

71. Robert R. M. Verchick, "Feminist Theory and Environmental Justice" in *New Perspectives on Environmental Justice: Gender, Sexuality and Activism*, ed. Rachel Stein (New Brunswick, NJ: Rutgers University Press, 2004), 70.

72. Greta Gaard, "Toward a Queer Ecofeminism," *Hypatia* 12, no. 1 (1997): 114–37.

73. I use the older term "third world" here rather than the more popular "global south" to include the fact that such exploitation happens among poorer populations and populations of color throughout the world, as the following example in the text shows.

74. On environmental racism, see Kimberly P. Fields, "Beyond Protest: The Effects of Grassroots Activism on Maryland and Pennsylvania's Responses to Environmental Justice," *Environmental Justice* 11, no. 1 (2018): 15–28.

75. My use of "they" should not be taken to imply my lack of membership in disability community; rather, it refers specifically to the disability advocates who engage with environmental issues. Since my disabilities are predominantly invisible, however, I recognize that my membership in the disability community may be questioned by some. See Hirschmann, "Invisible Disability."

76. Sandilands, "Unnatural Passions?," 4.

77. Kafer, *Feminist, Queer, Crip*, 144.

78. See David T. Mitchell and Sharon L. Snyder's notion of "cripistemologies" in *Biopolitics of Disability* (Ann Arbor: University of Michigan Press, 2015), 77.

79. Abbott and Porter, "Environmental Hazard," 841.

80. Ibid., 840.

81. Julian Agyeman, "Toward a 'Just' Sustainability?" *Continuum* 22, no. 6 (2008): 751–56.

82. Kafer, *Feminist, Queer, Crip*, 161–68.

83. Kafer, *Feminist, Queer, Crip*, 142.

3

(Post)Colonialism, Eco-Ableism, and the Production of Knowledge

Memona Hossain

Disability is not simply an objective fact created by attaching a prefix to the word *ability*. As the linguistic philosopher Jacques Derrida identified, the journey that moves from the signifier to the signified is in fact a messy relationship.[1] Signifiers hold positions of power that give meaning to something that otherwise remains unidentified. Words represent meaning for what they are trying to represent, and words in fact represent a once-removed meaning because the signifier itself is never precisely *the* thing it is signifying.[2] Where disability is the signifier and people with disabilities are the signified, how do the intricacies of lived experiences travel on the path toward meaning that is conveyed through words? What happens when that journey is further complicated by the nuances of a climate change crisis? Which version of the multitude of possible permutations of signifier to signified journey gains the greatest voice when we use the word *disability*? When one version becomes the dominant placeholder in representing that journey to create meaning, it doesn't mean all other versions cease to exist. However, it does mean that those journeys are not accounted for. Those narratives become extinguished and perhaps forgotten. Erasure happens, and it happens through a defined process.

Emily Nusbaim and Maya Steinborn define *erasure* as the process whereby societal norms indicate that certain "disabled people cannot possibly be sources of knowledge because they lack, fundamentally, the ability to possess knowledge about themselves or the world . . . they are viewed as . . . non-entities incapable of taking on or producing information."[3] This essay explores the phenomenon of erasure as it pertains to knowledge production of disability as a lived experience. It will then look at erasure once again as in the realm of environmental activism by people of disability—namely, eco-ableism. Some specific cases of eco-ableism will be presented in exploring how it interacts with poverty, aspects of plastic bans, transportation usage, and electricity usage. The essay will end by looking at some concepts in ecopsychology that can provide answers to the issue of eco-ableism.

As an author who has been professionally involved in the field premised on the lived experiences of developmental disabilities, mental health, and medically fragile individuals for over fifteen years, I've consciously developed this essay through the voices of persons with disabilities and those from diverse backgrounds. Drawing from authentic voices that interrogate the interconnective relationship between disability, colonialism, and environmentalism, this essay attempts to bring voices of scholars who live with disabilities as well as those who identify as people of color. It is important that concepts such as eco-justice and disability studies are nuanced, and multiple dimensions of disability experiences must be explored to genuinely delve into a deconstructive exploration of colonial impacts in these spheres.

The Knowledge Production of Disability

The term *disability* is a socially constructed identity premised within a cultural context[4] that encompasses certain experiences and ways of knowledge at the cost of excluding others. Hilary Weaver explains that "abnormalcy and normalcy work to produce one another."[5] Paul van Trigt and Susan Legene explored the writing of disability in colonial history and the development of disability as a "dichotomy of active (Western) helpers acting on behalf of (non-Western) sufferers."[6] When Western helpers seek to find and enable the agency of the non-Western "other," the intentional implication is that the non-Westerner is the one that is not normal.[7] For the concept of disability to exist in this way, a series of embedded actors within a network of relations are important to validating and upholding the role of one another. The group that can find and enable agency within the other can only do so when disability and the otherizing exist to enable the enabling. According to van Trigt and Legene, such a network of relationships implies "a dominant image of people with disabilities as marginalized people who suffer silently and have no agency."[8] However, as Helen Meekosha has critiqued and written extensively on the context of disabilities studies, "disability studies was constructed as a field of knowledge without reference to the theorists, or the social experience, of the global South. There has been a one-way transfer of ideas and knowledge from the North to the South in this field."[9] Such a one-way transfer further perpetuates the colonial agenda that must be disrupted. She continues to address the issue of how impairment has been produced in the Global South through processes of colonization, and she critiques how the *Sage Encyclopedia of Disability* (Albrecht 2005) is a five-volume publication that has absolutely no reference to Indigenous peoples or "the imperialistic, militaristic and colonial processes responsible for disabling millions of people across the globe."[10] Meekosha labels this as a process of "grand erasure" and critiques the central role colonialism plays in structural, cultural, economic, and political knowledge production.[11] Meekosha and Soldatic write about grand erasure, which ignores how colonialism and imperialism have acted as major causes of "human rights violations, famines, malnutrition and the ecological degradation of indigenous land and as the root cause of growing impairment in the global south."[12] Disabled lives of the south, when seldomly recognized, tend to be simplified, generalized, and homogenized and are often decontextualized and dehistoricized.[13] Disability studies and scholarship is often void and neglectful of the underlying structures that contribute to the production of disabilities.[14] Dominant models of disability studies and scholarship tend to overlook the very structures through which humans are brought into being. It is parochial to claim scholarship in this field without simultaneously acknowledging the oppressive systems that have produced disablement.[15]

Disability scholarship has dominantly been developed by white people.[16] There has been a historical noninclusive and narrow focus on a monolithic understanding of disability that does not pay attention to the implications of power and privilege. There has been a focus on the white experience and, as the article "Skin, Tooth and Bone: The Basis of a Movement Is Our People" claims, an "invisibiliz[ing] the lives of people who live at intersecting junctures of oppression."[17] The result of erasure and the upholding of a certain narrative become widely accepted truths when repeated often enough and when perspectives are normalized through societal practices. What happens is that societal language, policies, infrastructure, institutions, processes, and movements reinforce erasure. Erasure of people with disabilities is the product of colonial impact.

Research shows intersections between colonization and ableism.[18] A normative framework governs the differential valuing and classification of bodies and the perceived distance from the dominant, idealized identity categories; this influences the likelihood of experiencing prejudice and discrimination and exclusion.[19] Karen Calder-Dawe claims that categories including "ablebodied, white, Anglo-Saxon, upper middle class, adult, male and heterosexual"[20] enable citizens of society to perform their social roles with a high degree of success. Social roles are a combination of behaviors, functions, relationships, privileges, duties, and responsibilities that are widely understood and positively valued.[21] Ableism is the reflection of sentiments held by social groups and social structures that value and promote specific abilities and a preference for certain abilities over others. Ableism generates a perceived deviation when there is a lack of "essential" abilities creating a diminished state of being.[22]

According to Linda Williams and Monica Slabaugh, "Ableism silences, dismisses, misrepresents and oppresses the disabled."[23] In the context of everyday interactions, the capacity and character of people with disabilities are provoked with ableist assumptions.[24] As Gregor Wolbring states, "Ableism is one of the most societally entrenched and accepted isms and one of the biggest enabler for other isms."[25] Ableism penetrates through ideas, practices, institutions, and social relations that presume able-bodied-ness and that marginalize people with disabilities to become invisible "others."[26] Ableism confirms that there is a societal knowledge production model that assumes a single point of departure and accepted norm from which other discourses and models are defined.

The convergence of ableism and colonialism resides in the historical privileging of ability as it served colonial tools of interest.[27] Professor Jay Dolmage, of the University of Waterloo in Canada, researches disability rights and speaks about how ableism has been sustained through academic institutions like universities as spaces of knowledge construction and development. Dolmage speaks about how people with disability "have been the object of study and not purveyors of the knowledge base of disability."[28] He speaks about how psychiatric institutions and universities have historically worked together to provide spaces for research that furthered eugenics and that universities have been "both arbiter of ability, and creators/enforcers of disability, . . . and thus delineated and disciplined the border between abled and disabled."[29] The current environmental activism discourse is one area where the border of ableism pervades strongly.

Eco-Ableism

"We declare clearly and unequivocally that planet Earth is facing a climate emergency"[30] reads the World Scientists' Warning of a Climate Emergency signed by over eleven thousand scientists from 153 countries around the world, published in *BioScience Journal* on November 5, 2019. The statement proposes that "to secure a sustainable future; we must change how we live. . . . [This] entails major transformations in the ways our global society functions and interacts with natural ecosystems."[31] The environmental activism discourse on responding to climate change and the sustainability movement is a social response. Some common themes include a concern for the environment, a focus on one's personal responsibilities, and the impact of actions and behaviors on the environment.[32] According to Deborah Fenney Salkeld, the imaginings of environmental citizens are strongly tied to "assumption[s] of a white, male, non-disabled norm . . . the unequal participation of anyone diverging from this norm is obscured and often ignored."[33] People with disabilities face (multiple) barriers in the commonly identified pro-environmental activities within the environmental citizenship discourse. What results is eco-ableism.

When environmental engagement excludes people with disabilities, it is an erasure of their presence. As the Simon Fraser University's sustainability project has identified, "Efforts to improve sustainability that ignore the existence of disabled people, is not environmentalism, but eco-ableism."[34] Discussions on how individuals can reduce their ecological footprints ought to include the realities of people living with disabilities.[35] A single-dimensional acknowledgment of people with disabilities that depicts them as vulnerable or incapable of contributing further deepens the impact of eco-ableism.

While environmental activism presumes that a collective commitment to lifestyle changes is required to address the global crisis, it simultaneously excludes the distinct parts that comprise the collective. Andrew Dobson and Derek Bell have noted that a common theoretical framework that underlies environmental activism is "clear moral or justice-based rationale actions, implying active awareness."[36] There is also a disembodiment that happens when linking this to personal lived experiences. Where embodiment is not acknowledged, a natural default state of able-bodied and able-minded citizens is assumed, while individuals with disabilities are made to be excluded and unable to perform the conceptualized environmental activism duties in which the *normal* society engages. To better understand the process of erasure and implications on lives, let's focus on a few specific examples.

Disability, Poverty, and Eco-Ableism

Jeanine Braithwaite and Daniel Mond write that disability and poverty are "both a cause and consequence of each other."[37] In addition to compromised access to employment and income opportunities, households comprising people with disabilities may spend more on items such as transportation, heating, medical services, and special equipment, thus increasing the general standard-of-living costs.[38] The 2019 Annual Report on People with Disabilities in America shows a disparity of over 40 percent between people with disabilities and their counterpart of people without disabilities who are employed.[39] The study shows that people with disabilities who live below the poverty line is 14 percent higher than those who do not have disabilities.[40] Spanish economist Joan Martinez-Alier has shown in his research that poor people are unable to focus on being green "either because they lack awareness (they have no taste for environmental amenities because they have more immediate necessities) or they have not enough money to invest in the environment, or both reasons simultaneously."[41]

There is a belief that environmental activism is a social product of prosperity, and there is a positive correlation between income level and environmental activism. Some economists argue that economic growth is good because as income increases and a middle class emerges, there is a growing level of attention to the quality of life that promotes environmental activism behaviors.[42] Here we see the impact of eco-ableism on people with disabilities. If an individual with disability is predisposed to economic inequalities, the person's ability to engage in environmentally conscious behavior is also likely to be compromised.

People with Disabilities and Plastic Bans

If you live in Europe, North America, or parts of India, chances are you have come across bans on single-use plastic straws. Other single-use plastic items are also being targeted as major contributors to massive amounts of plastic consumption that contribute to environmental degradation.[43] However, these quick-adoption and wide-sweeping policies overlook the impact this has on one-fifth of the world's population—namely, people with disabilities.[44] In 2015, a video went viral that showed researchers in Costa Rica pulling a plastic straw out of an endangered sea turtle's nose.[45] In January 2018, Eco-Cycle reported that Americans use (and waste) 500 million straws a day. This gained public attention. Eco-Cycle later reported that the figure was a miscalculation.[46] The actual number is estimated to be closer to 175 million straws.[47] There is no doubt that this amount of plastic consumption has a negative impact on the environment and must be addressed. However, what kind of responsible action can be taken to mitigate these issues, and where does accountability truly lie? According to Andrew Jenks and Kelsey Obringer, "There is no readily identifiable scientific data or analysis which claims straw bans will address the omnipresence of plastics in the world's oceans."[48] Oceanographer Kara Lavender, who has done extensive research on plastics in the ocean, has said, "We are not going to solve the problem by banning straws."[49] Research by Jenna Jambeck and her colleagues suggests that for dramatic change to occur, the state is the primary stakeholder that must be held accountable.[50] Facts are conflated, assigned value without strong or verified evidence, and done so at the cost of individuals with disabilities. When plastic and straw bans are implemented, where do the stakes of marginalized people get considered? How can environmental solutions be deemed successful or a normative public good when this leads to disadvantaging groups of the population?[51]

Precut, premade, and prepackaged single-use plastic items are not a luxury but often a necessity for individuals who are visually impaired and unable to use a knife, who are physically unable to lift heavy pots, or who participate in every aspect of preparing a meal from beginning to end. These items and modern food developments have "provided an avenue for people previously institutionalized, home-bound, and care-taker reliant to live more independently,"[52] according to Jenks and Obringer. Modern innovations make it possible for parents to care for children at home who may have otherwise been institutionalized.

Furthermore, plastic and straw bans make certain presuppositions about individuals who can abstain from their use. They presume that other alternatives are as easy to adopt in terms of usability without much interruption to daily living and that the cost of their adoption is not problematic. As writer and activist sb. Smith, a disability advocate and individual living with multiple disabilities, writes, there are multiple barriers to straw bans and plastic alternatives, such as injury risks from harder materials like bamboo, glass, and metal; the inability to position less malleable material straws; the additional cost of other straws; and the fact that certain straws are not adaptable to high temperature liquids.[53]

Eco-ableism assumes an exclusionary erasure of people with disabilities in single-use plastic and straw bans. Placing the onus on people with disabilities to find an alternative to single-use plastic is at the heart of the problem, which is the search for retroactive solutions to a problem that was initially created by the process of erasure and noncollaborative and inclusive discussions of defining environmental activism behaviors.[54]

Green Travel and Eco-Ableism

Over the past decade, reducing gasoline consumption and its impact on curtailing greenhouse gas emissions has been a major focus of action.[55] Walking, biking, and carpooling as well as micromobility options and public transportation have all been adopted as positive alternatives by city planners and city dwellers alike. Green travel behavior is associated with people living in high-density communities that are closer to city centers.[56] As a means to having access to employment, education, health care, shopping, social outings, and recreational activities, transportation is essential to complete participation in a community.[57] Individuals with disabilities may have several health care and social service–related appointments that may be important to their well-being. In 2011, Y. Zhang highlighted a four-phase process that inculcates the accessible journey chain.[58] This includes the set off from origin through every mode of movement required, including walking right up to or through the door of the destination. According to Jun Park and Subeh Chowdhury, "The link between every element must be seamless for the whole journey to be completed by the user."[59] Every element of the chain also feeds back to the cycle, enabling continuity. Seemingly simple issues like cracks or uneven surfaces on footpaths can increase the risk of falls and injuries for those with visual impairments or who are trying to maneuver equipment.[60]

Additionally, lack of lighting, audio announcements at crossings, traffic signs with poor visibility, construction blockages, and lack of alternate routes pose barriers for people with disabilities. From an environmental activist perspective, the "immediate and obvious" solutions to reducing greenhouse gas emission is the greening of the transport sector. In his proposed Green Transportation Hierarchy in 1994, Canadian Chris Bradshaw ordered the priority of green transportation as walking, bicycling, shared vehicle, and single-driving.[61] Green transportation emphasizes a "decrease in private motor cars and an increase in walking, bicycling and public transport systems, thus creating low-cost, pollution-free, land resource and space saving transportation system suitable for all kinds of travelers."[62] But is it really for all kinds of travelers? Consider some of the statistics around transportation usage and people with disabilities. The U.S. Bureau of Transportation Statistics reports the following:

- 54 percent of the total number of people who are homebound (never leave their homes) in the United States are people with disabilities.
- 40 percent of the people who have difficulty getting appropriate transportation are people with disabilities.
- People with disabilities are four times more likely than people without disabilities to face difficulty accessing appropriate transportation.
- Approximately 55 percent of air travelers with disabilities experience problems at airports.[63]

Common issues that people with disabilities face when trying to get from one place to another in their communities include nonexistent or inoperable lifts and ramps; steep slopes; nonexistent or malfunctioning automatic doors; problems with reservations; nonexistent or inoperable elevators; issues with eligibility for use; lack of communication accessibility (i.e., for the deaf or hard of hearing); lack of door-to-door services when necessary; attitudinal barriers among drivers; ability to carry any additional equipment(s); and nonexistent or blocked specialized lanes and spaces.[64] As the green transportation movement toots its horn on decreasing the use of private vehicles, it may be diminishing conveniences for the majority of people—who were taken into consideration as this movement was developed—but how about the marginalized group of people whose entire ability to move around is being extinguished? Was the green transportation aspect of environmental activism developed in consideration of the fact that some people's everyday transportation needs depend on multiple complicating factors and that some may not be able to live without access to personal and specialized vehicles? Elizabeth Wright, a writer, Paralympic medalist, and disability activist, posted a reflection on her need for her own vehicle:

> My car may be a blue, zippy little thing, but it is my very big symbol of complete independence. Without my car—modified to enable me to drive—I wouldn't be able to work, socialize, or generally enjoy life to the extent that I do. Frankly I couldn't live without my car.[65]

It can be argued that people with disabilities may opt to reduce some aspects of their transportation activities or choose other modes of engaging in environmentally conscious behaviors if transportation is not a reasonable option. However, the problem is that the green transportation movement has been created and bolstered by a specified body and set of abilities. Others have been left to bear the guilty burden of being active contributors to greenhouse gas emissions. Victoria Broadus explains that "disability can be considered an interaction between an individual and a non-inclusive society in that it only exists as a disability when the environment and circumstances create disabling experiences."[66] For individuals whose ability to move through society and be visible in public spaces is already compromised, the green movement does little to resolve this erasure.

Electricity Use and Equipment

Inaugurated in Sydney, Australia, in 2007, the Worldwide Fund for Nature introduced the Earth Hour campaign, whereby people around the world "switch from passive bystanders to active participants in global efforts to fight climate change."[67] Participation involves suspending light usage for a specified hour in each country. This is an expression of collective commitment to Earth, and the campaign has spread to more than 188 countries.[68] Hoi-Wing Chan, Vivien Pong, and Kim-Pong Tam have studied the identity perspective of Earth Hour participation and have identified that group belonging is strongly attached to the roles, expectation, and prescribed courses of action that are predefined for membership to such identity groups.[69] Therefore, to validate and maintain a social identity of pro-environmentalism, participation in events such as Earth Hour is required.[70] It is also part of a wider movement to reduce electricity and energy consumption as environmentally friendly behaviors. However, individuals with disabilities may have electricity-dependent equipment needs for their daily functioning. Some examples include oxygen concentrators, ventilators, electrically charged wheelchairs, feeding equipment, regular dialysis, medical equipment, lift and transfer equipment, communication equipment for individuals that may not be able to speak otherwise, and therapy equipment, among others. As identified in the 2010 U.S. Census, 4 percent of the noninstitutionalized population is dependent on electricity-based technology for one or more activities of daily living.[71] Aside from potentially being unable to participate in events like Earth Hour and to change their electricity consumption, such populations are also at risk of negative life impacts when natural disasters cause power outages. Noelle Molinari and colleagues point out that while "a power outage, however brief, may be considered a nuisance to many, for [some] it has the potential to cause an acute decompensation that, depending on the severity and duration, may become life threatening."[72] As Sarah Olexsak and Alan Meier have shown in their study of the impact of Earth Hour, "in order to create the enduring behavior needed to reduce energy consumption, pro-environmental behavior must last beyond the duration of the intervention."[73] Thus, this becomes another form of eco-ableism to which persons of disabilities are exposed. When people are erased from participation opportunities as part of an entire humanity, it has an impact on their self-identity. According to Sam Mcfarland, Matthew Webb, and Derek Brown, "People with a strong humanity identity consider themselves as part of the all-inclusive community of humans and are committed to contributing to the welfare of humanity as a whole."[74] Both environmental self-identity and humanity identity are important to supporting and participating in environmental behaviors.[75] When environmentally friendly behaviors are adapted as part of wider movements such as decreasing electricity consumption, if the point of departure is an all-encompassing identification of humanity that welcomes participation, then it neither compromises the participation of individuals with disabilities nor excludes them from identifying with all of humanity.

Eco-Ableism, Embodiment, and Social Exclusion

Through the specific examples of eco-ableism explored, we can see that the embodiment of environmental activism is identified within a specified body type, which divorces from bodies that fall outside of its category. Salkeld explains that the "neglect of the body leads to structures and spaces—both physical and social—that are subconsciously designed around the embodiments of a dominant group who fail to recognize the specificity of their own group features."[76] A lack of recognition of embodiment has implications for people with disabilities.[77] Research shows that embodiment is implicated largely in white, educated, middle-class citizens, who are also by implication child-free and free of other caring responsibilities.[78] Salkeld further claims that the starting point for developing green practices within the environmental movement should "be a balance between a universalism that values disabled people equally, and an acknowledgement of different embodiments with differing needs."[79] Self-identity and social identity are interrelated, and studies show they have an interconnection in which one enhances behavior toward the other.[80] A study conducted by J. Semeijn and colleagues found that "disabled people highly value the opinion of people in their surroundings when considering [the] purchase of environmentally friendly cars."[81] This research asserts that attitude and social norms directly affect the intentions of people with disabilities and their environmental choices. People with disabilities should be recognized as potential contributors to the environmental movement. This requires "a recognition of different embodiments and acknowledgment of potential barriers to contribution,"[82] says Salkeld.

There are steps that must be "taken at the institutional level to lessen colonial harm, as imparted through academic spaces,"[83] says Dolmage. "All of the myths about education have us believe that it's effort, not privilege; it's intellect, not external forces, that allow us to move up and down those steps,"[84] says Will Sloan. Such beliefs must be challenged at their crux. Solutions require balancing notions of enabling factors and the self-identified needs of persons with disabilities.[85] According to R. T. Goins et al., seeking the perspectives of people with disabilities is important "to ensur[ing] policies and community efforts effectively address the needs expressed by individuals themselves."[86] According to Cameron Greensmith, the "present absences and absent presences of disability"[87] evoke an understanding of normalcy and an erasure through eco-ableism. A decolonization of the erasure in eco-ableism needs to happen.

For the purposes of this essay, a definition of decolonization can be taken from W. A. Wilson and M. Yellow Bird's work *For Indigenous Eyes Only: A Decolonizing Handbook* as "the intelligent, calculated, and active resistance to forces of colonialism that perpetuate the subjugation and/or exploitation of our minds, bodies, and lands, and it is engaged for the ultimate purpose of overturning the colonial structure and realizing [Indigenous] liberation."[88] As critical disabilities researcher Xuan Thuy Nguyen emphasizes, "It is important to question who produces theory . . . neo-colonial discourses have gestured towards exclusion by embodying theories and produc[ing] knowledge through former colonial spaces."[89] Nguyen asserts that we need to understand disability differently and challenge the forms of power and those modes of interpretation that are embedded in Northern epistemologies and that we need to "create spaces for [other] voices to 'speak back.'"[90]

We must be aware of the ways colonial and neocolonial ideologies inform our interpretations of the Other and require scholars to challenge privileges as "knowledge producers" about disability.[91] Nguyen further asserts that it may require us to reconsider how disability has been depicted as a truth "within transnational spaces and temporality" and how our intellectual work has produced "particular meanings, discourses, representations, and social relations."[92] This may lead to new forms of knowledge, power, and subjectivities.[93] In this context, it is helpful to explore the movement from shallow environmentalism to deep ecology.

Shallow environmentalism is the reaction to the current ecologically destructive patterns by emphasizing immediate physical symptoms such as fuel-efficient vehicles and other such immediate actions.[94] By contrast, a deep ecology movement is one that requires deeper root cause changes to address ecological destruction, including cultural and political changes.[95] This type of movement is pluralistic and draws inspiration from nature-centered wisdom, recognizing the intrinsic worth of all natural phenomena.[96] Deep ecology comes from the framework of ecopsychology, and I want to move toward an exploration of ecopsychology as a possible point of departure for knowledge production as it pertains to environmental activism and for decolonizing the erasure embedded in eco-ableism.

What Is Ecopsychology?

"*Ecopsychology* began as a countercultural conversation between psychotherapists, environmentalists, activists, writers, and educators about what might happen if ecology and psychology intersected."[97] Ecopsychology is premised on the interconnection of human beings with a web of intimate connections binding all living beings.[98] Ecopsychology studies the relationship between human beings and the natural world through ecological and psychological principles. The field seeks to develop ways of deepening the emotional connection between individuals and the natural world in ways that can nurture sustainable lifestyles and remedying alienation from nature.

This understanding is based on a rational, emotional logic derived through the human relationship with the natural world. As ecopsychologist Michael Cohen describes in his book *Well Mind, Well Earth*, "The key to sustainable personal and global wellness in balance is to obtain consent to exist from all parties, including other species and the mineral kingdom."[99] Estrangement from nature's ability to balance produces apathy, resistance to change, and prejudices.[100] Intrinsically, "ecopsychology cannot be the exclusive purview of the economically and educationally privileged . . . nor can nature . . . be something only available to a privileged few."[101] In fact, the deteriorated state of Earth's natural environment infers that our models of knowledge are not effective.

Knowledge Production through the Lens of Ecopsychology

From the perspective of ecopsychology, environmental activism is a personal journey defined by the Earth connection each individual experiences. Wide-sweeping actions do not become the basis for defining environmental activism. Rather, individualistic narratives define those responses. Each participant becomes a valued contributor to a wider movement rather than becoming socially isolated and vulnerable due to an inability to participate. Each of us can begin making contributions to personal and global wellness. In this model, nature becomes the guide and mediator for environmental activism. When the point of departure for knowledge development is the nature–human connection and relationship, then the point of departure for developing knowledge is one that is premised on an individual's experience and personal relationship with nature.

Rather than the external influences of colonialism, Global North–developed knowledge, or able-bodied perspectives building a knowledge base, this enables an organic knowledge production system where all bodies have an equal access starting point. There is not a predetermined language of knowledge production that is presumed—be it English or any other spoken language, or vertically in terms of academic language. When nature–human interaction is the starting point, this presumes a non-language-based point of departure.

Toward a Holistic, Inclusive Understanding of Environmental Activism

Michelle Nario-Redmond et al. point out that people with disabilities are "often at a disadvantage, not because of their impairments, but because of the way society views them."[102] Individuals' ecological behavior is impacted by more than just their opinions and willingness to engage; it is also impacted by economic, social, and cultural conditions.[103] As their 2019 study results suggest, we still know very little about how to effectively shift the public narrative on social determinants of disability.[104] However, we do see that the normative window of change is opening to question the elements of ableism—that is, "what insults, what harms, what failures of policy are now being called into question as ableist,"[105] though they may have been acceptable years ago. The current model of environmental activism carries a status and insinuations of agency. As Salkeld says, if there is "status to be gained in being identified as an environmental [activist], this should be available to disabled people *and* non-disabled people [alike]."[106] What is needed is a reimagining of environmental activists in a way that facilitates the emergence of more contributions and less disabling consequences and avoids their potential categorization of what Salkeld coins "failed citizens."[107] As ecopsychology suggests, "The fragmentations in ourselves, between each other and between us and nature has the opportunity to be overcome . . . by diving deep in our own stories and . . . moving our green psychology to a sense of the self as embodied in the [Earth], [thus] reclaim[ing] parts of ourselves and parts of our history that have been disowned and fragmented."[108] In moving to see the land and community around us as part of ourselves and not removed from us, we can find and step into a meaningful responsibility for caring for what is our collective home.

Every part of the global life community is part of a web and consists of relationships that hold this together; this must be acknowledged. Ecopsychology emphasizes the feeling and connection and sees the "needs of the planet and the person as a continuum."[109] As Paloma Pavel and Carl Anthony put it, "Our reckless and unsustainable relationship to the Earth has a history that is intertwined with the history of racial and social injustice."[110] We need to deconstruct the culture of denial and separation because this prevents us from "claiming all of our planet, our human community, and all of ourselves as worthy of care and protection."[111] We must look at the destructive and divisive paradigms shaping our current narrative to then clearly identify a path toward cohesion and a holistic narrative of environmental activism.

NOTES

1. Charles W. Bingham, "Derrida on Teaching: The Economy of Erasure," *Studies in Philosophy and Education* (Springer Science and Business) 27, no. 1 (2008): 17.

2. Bingham, "Derrida on Teaching," 17.

3. Emily A. Nusbaim and Maya L. Steinborn, "A 'Visibilizing' Project: 'Seeing' the Ontological Erasure of Disability in Teacher Education and Social Studies Curricula," *Journal of Curriculum Theorizing* 34, no. 1 (2019): 26.

4. Tom Shakespeare, "Disability, Identity and Difference," in *Exploring the Divide: Illness and Disability,* ed. Colin Barnes and Geoff Mercer (Leeds: Disability, 1996), 94.

5. Hilary N. Weaver, "Disability through a Native American Lens: Examining Influences of Culture and Colonization," in *All My Relations: Understanding the Experiences of Native Americans with Disabilities,* ed. Hilary Weaver and Francis K. O. Yuen (New York: Routledge, 2018), 19.

6. Paul van Trigt and Susan Legene, "Writing Disability into Colonial Histories of Humanitarianism," *Social Inclusion* 4, no. 4 (2016): 194.

7. Ricardo Roque and Kim A. Wagner, "Introduction," in *Engaging Colonial Knowledge: Reading European Archives in World History*, ed. Ricardo Roque and Kim A. Wagner (UK: Palgrave Macmillan, 2012), 18.

8. Paul van Trigt and Susan Legene, "Writing Disability into Colonial Histories of Humanitarianism," *Social Inclusion* 4, no. 4 (2016): 194.

9. Helen Meekosha, "Decolonising Disability: Thinking and Acting Globally," *Disability & Society* 26, no. 6 (2011): 668.

10. Meekosha, "Decolonising Disability," 671.

11. Meekosha, "Decolonising Disability," 671.

12. Helen Meekosha and K. Soldatic, "Human Rights and the Global South: The Case of Disability," *Third World Quarterly* 32, no. 8 (2011): 1394.

13. Shaun Grech, "Decolonising Eurocentric Disability Studies: Why Colonialism Matters in the Disability and Global South Debate," *Social Identities* 21, no. 1 (2015): 6.

14. Laura Jordan Jaffee, "Disrupting Global Disability Frameworks: Settler-Colonialism and the Geopolitics of Disability in Palestine/Israe," *Disability & Society* 31, no. 1 (2016): 126.

15. Jaffee, "Disrupting Global Disability Frameworks," 127.

16. C. Bell, "Is Disability Studies Actually White Disability Studies," in *The Disability Studies Reader*, ed. L. J. Davis (New York: Taylor & Francis, 2010), 374–82.

17. "Skin, Tooth and Bone: The Basis of a Movement Is Our People," in *Reproductive Health Matters*, 2016, 11–12.

18. David Mitchell and Sharon I. Snyder, "Disability as Multitude: Re-Working Non-Reproductive Labor Power," *Journal of Literary & Cultural Disability Studies* 4, no. 2 (2010): 179–83.

19. Karen Witten, Penelope Carroll, and Octavia Calder-Dawe, "Being the Body in Question: Young People's Accounts of Everyday Ableism, Visibility and Disability," *Disability & Society* 35, no. 1 (2020): 133.

20. Witten, Carroll, and Calder-Dawe, "Being the Body in Question," 132–33.

21. Daniel C. Lustig and David R. Strauser, "Causal Relationships between Poverty and Disability," *Rehabilitation Counselling Bulletin* 50, no. 4 (2007): 196.

22. Gregor Wolbring, "The Politics of Ableism," *Society for International Development* 51, (2008): 252–53.

23. Linda Williams and Monica Slabaugh, "Ableism and Erasure," https://www.invisibledisabilityproject.org/unseen-zine/2017/6/5/ableism-and-erasure.

24. Witten, Carroll, and Calder-Dawe, "Being the Body in Question," 132–34

25. Wolbring, "Politics of Ableism," 255.

26. Vera Chouinard, "Making Space for Disabling Differences: Challenging Ableist Geographies," *Environment and Planning D Abstract* 15 (1997): 380.

27. Emily J. Hutcheon and Bonnie Lashewicz, "Tracing and Troubling Continuities between Ableism and Colonialism in Canada," *Disability & Society* 35, no. 5 (2020): 695–714

28. Will Sloan, "Reckoning with Ableism and Colonialism: Scholars Interrogate Harmful Legacies and Discuss Possible Futures," July 2018. School of Disability Studies' Annual Activist Lecture, Toronto, Canada, https://www.ryerson.ca/news-events/news/2018/07/reckoning-with-ableism-and-colonialism/.

29. Sloan, "Reckoning with Ableism and Colonialism."

30. W. J. Ripple et al., "World Scientists' Warning of a Climate Emergency," *Bioscience* 70, no. 1 (2019): 8–12.

31. Ripple et al., "World Scientists' Warning of a Climate Emergency," 8–12.

32. Derek Bell, "Environmental Citizenship: Global, Local and Individual," in *Routledge Handbook of Global Environmental Politics*, ed. P. Harris (London: Routledge, 2013), 347–58.

33. Deborah Fenney Salkeld, "Environmental Citizenship and Disability Equality: The Need for an Inclusive Approach," *Environmental Politics* 28, no. 7 (2019): 1259.

34. Simon Fraser University, *Sustainability Projects: Re-Use for Good*, accessed February 3, 2020, https://www.sfu.ca/sustainability/projects/reuse.html#accessibility.

35. Salkeld, "Environmental Citizenship and Disability Equality," 1260.

36. Andrew Dobson and Derek Bell, "Introduction" in *Environmental Citizenship*, ed. Andrew Dobson and Derek Bell (Cambridge, MA: MIT Press, 2006), 127–50.

37. Jeanine Braithwaite and Daniel Mont, "Disability and Poverty: A Survey of World Bank Poverty Assessments and Implications," *European Journal of Disability* 3 (2009): 219–30.

38. Braithwaite, "Disability and Poverty," 228.

39. A. Houtenville and S. Bouge, "Annual Report on People with Disabilities in America," University of New Hampshire Report, Institute on Disability, 2019.

40. Houtenville and Bouge, "Annual Report on People with Disabilities in America."

41. Jean Martinez-Alier, "The Environment as a Luxury Good or 'Too Poor to Be Green?'" *Ecological Economics* 13, no. 1 (1995): 8.

42. Martinez-Alier, "Environment as a Luxury Good," 9.

43. Andrew B. Jenks and Kelsey M. Obringer, "The Poverty of Plastics Bans: Environmentalism's Win as a Loss for Disabled People," *Critical Social Policy* 40, no. 1 (2020): 152.

44. Jenks, "Poverty of Plastics Bans," 152.

45. Jane J. Lee, "How Did a Sea Turtle Get a Straw up Its Nose?" *National Geographic*, August 15, 2017.

46. Christian Britschgi, "Another City Cites Bogus Stats from 9-Year-Old to Justify Straw Ban," *Reason*, May 18, 2018.

47. David M. Perry, "Banning Straws Won't Save the Oceans," *Pacific Standard*, June 5, 2018.

48. Jenks, "Poverty of Plastics Bans," 153.

49. Setch Borenstein, "Science Says: Amount of Straws, Pollution Is Huge," *Skanner, Seattle and Portland Combined Edition*, April 8, 2018.

50. Jenna R. Jambeck et al., "Plastic Waste Inputs from Land into the Ocean," *Science* 347, (2015): 768–71.

51. Jenks, "Poverty of Plastics Bans," 155.

52. Jenks, "Poverty of Plastics Bans," 157.

53. Sb. Smith, *Infographic: Response to Straw Bans from Disability Perspective*, 2018, https://sb-smith.com/activism/.

54. Jenks, "Poverty of Plastics Bans," 158–59.

55. Matthew Kahn and Eric A. Morris, "Walking the Walk: The Association between Community Environmentalisms and Green Travel Behaviour," *Journal of the American Planning Association* 75, no. 4 (2009): 389.

56. Kahn, "Walking the Walk," 389.

57. S. Jansuwan, K. M. Christensen, and A. Chen, "Assessing the Transportation Needs of Low-Mobility Individuals: Case Study of a Small Urban Community in Utah," *Journal of Urban Planning and Development* 139, no. 2 (2013): 104–14.

58. Y. Zhang, "Barrier-Free Transport Facilities in Shanghai: Current Practice and Future Challenges," in *Bridging Urbanities: Reflections on Urban Design in Shanghai and Berlin*, ed. Bettina Bauerfeind and Josefine Fokdal (Berlin: Lit Verlag, 2011), 135.

59. Jun Park and Subeh Chowdhury, "Investigating the Barriers in a Typical Journey by Public Transport Users with Disabilities," *Journal of Transport & Health* 10 (2018): 362.

60. Park, "Investivating the Barriers," 361.

61. Han-Ru Li, "Study on Green Transportation System of International Metropolises," *Science Direct* 137 (2016): 762.

62. Li, "Study on Green Transportation System," 763.

63. U.S. Department of Transportation, *Bureau of Transportation Statistics*, 2017, accessed February 22, 2020, https://www.bts.gov/archive/publications/freedom_to _travel/data_analysis.

64. Jill L. Bezyak, Scott A. Sabella, and Robert H. Gattis, "Public Transportation: An Investigation of Barriers for People with Disabilities," *Journal of Disability Policy Studies* 28, no. 1 (2017): 52–60.

65. Elizabeth Wright, "Climate Change, Disability and Eco-Ableism: Why We Need to Be Inclusive to Save the Planet," *UX Collective*, February 19, 2020, accessed February 20, 2020, https://uxdesign.cc/climate-change-disability-and-eco-ableism-why-we-need -to-be-inclusive-when-trying-to-save-the-88bb61e82e4e.

66. Victoria Broadus, "Access for All: Transport for the Disabled Poor," *City Fix*, August 2, 2010, accessed February 22, 2020, https://thecityfix.com/blog/access-for-all -transport-for-the-disabled-poor/.

67. Hoi-Wing Chan, Vivien Pong, and Kim-Pong Tam, "Explaining Participation in Earth Hour: The Identity Perspective and the Theory of Planned Behaviour," *Climate Change* 158, (2019): 309.

68. Chan, Pong, and Tam, "Explaining Participation in Earth Hour," 310.

69. Chan, Pong, and Tam, "Explaining Participation in Earth Hour," 314.

70. Chan, Pong, and Tam, "Explaining Participation in Earth Hour," 315.

71. M. W. Brault, *Americans with Disabilities: 2010* (Washington, DC: U.S. Census Bureau).

72. Noelle Angelique Molinari et al., "Who's at Risk When the Power Goes Out? The At-Home Elecricity Dependent Population in the United States, 2012," *Journal of Public Health Management and Practice* 23, no. 2 (2012): 152.

73. Sarah J. Olexsak and Alan Meier, "The Electricity Impacts of Earth Hour: An International Comparative Analysis of Energy-Saving Behaviour," *Energy Research & Social Science* 2, (2020): 159.

74. Sam Mcfarland, Matthew Webb, and Derek Brown, "All Humanity Is My Ingroup: A Measure and Studies of Identification with All Humanity," *Journal of Personality and Social Psychology* 103, no. 5 (2012): 830–53.

75. Chan, Pong, and Tam, "Explaining Participation in Earth Hour," 322.

76. Salkeld, "Environmental Citizenship and Disability Equality," 1263.

77. Salkeld, "Environmental Citizenship and Disability Equality," 1263.

78. Dobson and Bell, "Introduction," 127–50.

79. Salkeld, "Environmental Citizenship and Disability Equality," 1271.

80. Chan, Pong, and Tam, "Explaining Participation in Earth Hour," 309.

81. J. Semeijn et al., "Disability and Pro Environmental Behavior—An Investigation of the Social Determinants of Purchasing Environmentally Friendly Cars by Disabled Consumers," *Transportation Research Part D* 67 (2019): 204.

82. Salkeld, "Environmental Citizenship and Disability Equality," 1274.

83. Sloan, "Reckoning with Ableism and Colonialism."

84. Sloan, "Reckoning with Ableism and Colonialism."

85. Lisa I. Iezzoni, Mary B. Killeen, and Bonnie L. O'Day, "Rural Residents with Disabilities Confront Substantial Barriers to Obtaining Primary Care," *Health Services Research* 41 (2014): 1258–75.

86. R. T. Goins et al., "Perceived Barriers to Health Care Access among Rural Older Adults: A Qualitative Study," *Rural Health* 21, no. 3 (2005): 207.

87. Greensmith, "Pathologizing Indigeneity," 31.

88. W. A. Wilson and M. Yellow Bird, *For Indigenous Eyes Only: A Decolonizing Handbook* (Santa Fe, NM: School of American Research, 2005), 2.

89. Xuan Thuy Nguyen, "Critical Disability Studies at the Edge of Global Development: Why Do We Need to Engage with Southern Theory," *Canadian Journal of Disability Studies* 7, no. 1 (2005): 18.

90. Nguyen, "Critical Disability Studies at the Edge of Global Develoment," 20.

91. Nguyen, "Critical Disability Studies at the Edge of Global Develoment," 22.

92. Nguyen, "Critical Disability Studies at the Edge of Global Develoment," 22.

93. Nguyen, "Critical Disability Studies at the Edge of Global Develoment," 22.

94. Arran Stibbe, "Environmental Education across Cultures: Beyond the Discourse of Shallow Environmentalism," *Language and Intercultural Communication* 4, no. 4 (2004): 243.

95. Arne Naess, *Ecology, Community and Lifestyle: Outline of an Ecosophy* (Cambridge: Cambridge University Press, 1990).

96. C. Manes, *Green Rage: Radical Environmentalism and the Unmaking of Civilisation* (New York: Little, Brown, 1990), 148.

97. Linda Buzzell and Craig Chalquist, "Ecopsychology and the Long Emergency: Fostering Sanity as the World Goes Crazy," *Ecopsychology* 7, no. 4 (2015): 184.

98. Christie M. Manning and Elise L. Amel, "No Human Left Behind: Making a Place for Social and Environmental Justice within the Field of Ecopsychology," *Ecopsychology* 6, no. 1 (2015): 14.

99. Michael J. Cohen, *Well Mind, Well Earth* (Washington: Project Nature Connect—Institute of Global Education, 1997), 20.

100. Cohen, *Well Mind, Well Earth*, 20.

101. Manning, "No Human Left Behind," 15.

102. Michelle R. Nario-Redmond, Alexia A. Kemerling, and Arielle Silverman, "Hostile, Benevolent, and Ambivalent Ableism: Contemporary Manifestations," *Journal of Social Issues* 75, no. 3 (2019).

103. Brent Lovelock, "Disability and Going Green: A Comparison of the Environmental Values and Behaviours of Persons with and without Disability," *Disability & Society* 25, no. 4 (2014): 468.

104. Nario-Redmond, "Hostile, Benevolent, and Ambivalent Ableism."

105. Nario-Redmond, "Hostile, Benevolent, and Ambivalent Ableism."

106. Salkeld, "Environmental Citizenship and Disability Equality," 1275.

107. Salkeld, "Environmental Citizenship and Disability Equality," 1274.

108. Paloma M. Pavel and Carl Anthony, "Building Just and Resilient Communities: New Foundations for Ecopsychology," *Ecopsychology* 7, no. 4 (2015): 257.

109. Theodor Roszak, *The Voice of the Earth: An Exploration of Ecopsychology* (New York: Touchstone, 2015), 14.

110. Pavel and Anthony, "Building Just and Resilient Communities," 256.

111. Pavel and Anthony, "Building Just and Resilient Communities," 256.

4

Rights and Responsibilities in Australia

Debility and Dispossession in Settler Colonialism

ALICE WEXLER

In this chapter I will "un-bifurcate" person and environment, body and land in an attempt to describe the Indigenous worldview, albeit through the non-Indigenous eyes of a white woman from a colonialist country.[1] Therefore, I forefront the voices of First Nations peoples of Australia, particularly Indigenous scholar, politician, and attorney Noel Pearson, who is the focus of the latter part of this chapter.

Kombu-merri and Waka Waka philosopher Mary Graham explains that land is the primary matter in Indigenous life: "The land, and how we treat it, is what determines our human-ness."[2] Land, or "country," cannot be decoupled from Indigenous self, identity, and physical and mental well-being: "disablement of the Earth . . . is inextricable from the disablement of Indigenous ontology, bodies, and communities."[3] From this standpoint, disability studies does not sufficiently embrace the daily trauma of dispossessed land, culture, kinship, and ancestral history. The colonialist Australian fiction of terra nullius, or devoid of civilization, legally evaporated Indigenous knowledges of land as invalid.

The trauma of colonialism in Australia is the story of the violence of first contact, historically narrated in the language and knowledge system of the conqueror. Therefore, generations of conquered people inherited a fractured time and place of "unspeakable things."[4] Terra nullius was the totalizing expression of the colonists, removing Australian Indigenous peoples' meaning and traces of culture from the land, which now exists as common law "positioning us as trespassers."[5] Goenpul scholar Aileen Moreton-Robinson uses the term *postcolonizing* as the current condition of Australia in which white was and continues to be intentionally constructed as the national identity through which the non-white Other was configured. The erasure of historical processes of Indigenous Australian peoples' knowing perpetuates the myth of terra nullius through white domination of Indigenous representation and possession.[6]

The term *debility*, introduced by Jasbir K. Puar, is therefore more relevant in this context: the debility of social and economic disempowerment and the dispossession of country.[7] Additionally, colonized populations considered disposable are usually more likely to *become* disabled, and the admission of a bodily disability invites the violence of an additional marginalized identity in a fusion of disability, race, and colonialism.[8] Spaces in the so-called Global South are iconic in revealing how disability has been constructed by white male ableism and its perpetuation of the ideal body. The collision of debility and land (or home) is thus experienced in a heightened and qualitatively different way in colonized countries such as Australia. Individuality as an ideal in "racial capitalism and colonialism"[9] separates and marginalizes Others who historically operated in interdependent and mutual societies. The making of outsiders is thus inherent in capitalist systems, who are not only different but have less value and thus "occupy multiple marginalized locations," such as in health care, education, economic access, and a healthy environment.[10]

Within the white/heteronormative patriarchy is embedded the violence of assigning the nonnormative categories of race, gender, and embodiment. As Moreton-Robinson wrote, all Australian citizens have equal rights, but not all citizens have equal access to resources and opportunities. "Race, class, gender, sexuality, and ableness are markers that circumscribe the privileges conferred by patriarchal white sovereignty within Australian society."[11] She employs the concept of "possessive logic" to reveal the underlying cause of the government's system of rationalization leading to the "inevitable answer, that is underpinned by an excessive desire to invest in reproducing and reaffirming the nation-state's ownership, control, and domination."[12] This logic promotes the notion that the government is race-neutral, democratic, and egalitarian, which perpetuates Australia's invisible patriarchal white sovereignty.

Thus, the term *debility* is useful as a way of framing disability studies within settler colonial studies, postcolonial theory, environmental studies, and critical race theory. Illuminating what is lacking in disability discourse, Puar explains, "Debility addresses injury and bodily exclusion that are endemic rather than epidemic or exceptional" and so invites thought about the exclusion embedded in living that cannot be resolved through accommodations.[13] Puar's project is to unmoor disability from its hegemonic roots and reestablish it as a product of imperialistic violence, settler colonialism, and the inequality of resources. Most disabled people live in occupied and developing countries. Puar continues, "My project refuses to reify racialization as defect but rather asks what other conceptual alternatives are available besides being relegated to defect or its dichotomous counterpart, embracing pride."[14] Empowerment discourse, the core of disability studies, therefore, is not useful in a discussion of global injustice, war, colonialism, and occupation.[15] Debility lies neither within defect nor pride but rather invites alternative concepts and insights. Although disability and debility overlap and interact in various ways, debility calls attention to the too-often-overlooked areas in disability studies: transgressions toward humanity by Western colonial imperialists acted on non-Western Others.

More precisely, Indigenous curator Brenda Croft (Gurindji, Malgnin, and Mudpurra) calls this biopolitical phenomena in Australia *colonial stress disorder*,[16] a compounding of intergenerational trauma endured by the government policy known as the *Stolen Generations* in the twentieth century, which makes debility a heightened experience. The forceful removal of children, typically with Indigenous mothers and non-Indigenous fathers, who were pejoratively called "half-castes," were placed in missions or settlements. This government policy was ostensibly to give children the opportunity to live in a white society, but its darker purpose was to eviscerate any remnants of their culture and language through assimilation.

Not all areas of Australia were occupied equally in the early twentieth century. The coastal regions were desirable while the center of Australia was considered an endless desert. Also known as the Wheat Belt, the south-west of Western Australia was one of the most colonized areas on the continent because of its fertile soil. In this region, white incursion was most damaging and complete, and therefore I will focus on this area. The loss of natural vegetation because of clearing the bush, and the "anglicizing" of the landscape with pastures, cows, and sheep, meant the loss of medicine, food, and ancestral heritage. Against this backdrop I highlight critical events and government policies that impacted Indigenous lives. Later in the chapter I shift to the Northern Territory and the contentious philosophy and politics of Noel Pearson,[17] a brutal realist who was tired of losing. The core of Pearson's pragmatic philosophy is that rights and responsibilities are inseparable. While the underlying reason for the overwhelming substance abuse and domestic violence that haunts the Stolen Generations is ostensibly dispossession, racism, unemployment, and trauma, Pearson risks the ire of Indigenous peoples by recommending that the current generation take responsibility for these injustices. Hence, the categorization *disability* as an effect of colonization is a slippery matter, such that it has negative connotations for some Indigenous peoples. In this context, *debility* has more political and social leverage. In the following section I turn to the historical event of the British occupation of the First Nations peoples of Australia.

Background

Unlike the United States, Canada, and New Zealand, Indigenous Australians are the only First Nations peoples colonized by the British Crown who have not been offered a treaty. The story of Black and white coexistence in Australia began in 1788 with the willful forgetfulness of Governor Arthur Phillip, who settled in New South Wales, and other British explorers who were officially ordered to establish friendship and trust among the inhabitants of New Holland. Nor was it legal for private settlers to dispossess and disperse Indigenous people to clear the land by designating the continent terra nullius. This designation made the Indigenous peoples nomads without rights to land and disrupted their philosophical understanding of one natural world that encompassed the human and more-than-human.[18]

The Consciousness of Land

Generalizing Indigenous consciousness is problematic because of the differential in impact made by uneven colonization: pervasive settlement in fertile regions, such as the Wheat Belt in the south-west of Western Australia; the relatively untouched land in the desert; and urbanization on the coastline.[19] The paradoxical phenomenon of dispossessed Indigenous peoples in metropolitan locations positioned as outside the zone of authentic geographical identity without sustained connections to traditions added another traumatic layer of dislocation. Other forms of forced dispossession were cattle stations, reserves, settlements, and adoption of children into white families.

> In effect, colonization produced multiple contexts that shaped the construction of Indigenous subjectivities that were and are positioned within discursive formations of history relative to a particular space, country, and time. These subjectivities are tied to our ontological relationship to the land and serve to ground our political as well as our cultural identities.[20]

Tim Rowse divides the history of the Australian occupation between the north and the south, the south being enveloped in "White Australian nationalism," while the north (Northern Territory) was mostly untouched by public or private investment until mining opportunities changed the plan of operation.[21] While Indigenous peoples in the south were herded into missions and settlements, Indigenous peoples in the north were left to live in loosely designated reserves. Assimilation and eugenicist ideology, as it was practiced in the south, failed in the north, and its lack of political and economic investment led to the welfare state, its inhabitants embedded in precolonial traditions and marginalized from the cultural capital of the south. The lack of organized control in the north eventually resulted in the government's military intervention known as the Northern Territory Emergency Response (NTER), regarded by Indigenous peoples as a recolonization of the Northern Territory.

Sustainable Land Development

Western Australia grows twelve thousand of the twenty-four thousand plant species in Australia; nine thousand species exist in the southwest of Australia—six thousand of which are not found anywhere else in the world—second only to the Amazon jungle in biological diversity. Because of its extraordinary biodiversity, the Sterling Ranges have been claimed as a site for resource management, conservation, and cultural heritage, which resulted in a park management plan. The Ranges are also one of the spiritual centers in the south-west. The intersection of the spiritual meaning of land and economic development, and the integration of vocation with social, emotional, and cultural support, are the primary points for sustainable economics and quality of life in the south-west. Thus, because of the difference in social and political marginalization between remote, rural, and metropolitan Australian Indigenous peoples, each region developed unequal access to resources.[22]

The clearing of the land removed vital resources on which Indigenous people depended, especially in the richly biodiverse areas. Their physical removal from the land meant that their asset base was lost, not in the Western notion of asset but as a range of physical, emotional, and metaphysical resources, from food and clothing to totems. Interconnection with the land thus meant not only survival in terms of food and medicine but also the perpetuation of their connection with ancestry, history, and knowledges. From this vantage point, says Puar, disability is everywhere and yet is not claimed as disability because academic research is not usually drawn from Indigenous ontologies and epistemologies. Disability caused by the capitalist, colonial exploitation of the environment produces the debility of precarious living.

Indigenous care for land is qualitatively different than Western concepts of land ownership and management. Indigenous peoples are not conceived as the center of the world but part of an interdependent ecosystem in which plants, and animals created by ancestral beings have the same rights to exist on the land.[23]

Our ontological relationship to land, the ways that country is constitutive of us, and therefore the inalienable nature of our relation to land, marks a radical, indeed incommensurable, difference between us and the non-Indigenous. This ontological relation to land constitutes a subject position that we do not share, that cannot be shared, with the postcolonial subject, whose sense of belonging in this place is tied to migrancy. Indigenous people may have been incorporated in and seduced by the cultural forms of the colonizer, but this has not diminished the ontological relationship to land.[24]

Indigenous belonging is ontologically tied to the Dreaming originating with ancestral beings that designates one's land of origin.[25]

Indigenous peoples from other countries describe the disconnection from land as a physically disabling experience, not unlike vertigo, "a spinning of the head and a simultaneous nausea as if flung by a world which seemed to have gone off its bearings. There was no more terrible part of our 19th century story than the herding together of broken tribes, under authority, and yoked by new regulations, into settlements and institutions as substitute homes."[26] Displaced from land and herded to country in which they had no connection, they were dependent on the paternalistic policies that deepened and entrenched them in a cycle of poverty. Language groups that had never identified with the religions, totems, and ceremonies of other cultural groups have come together in the recent past to forge their rights to land and resources.

In her report for UNESCO, Bidjara scholar Marcia Langton describes how the disabling loss of resources since contact has not abated and has in fact worsened. While the Indigenous populations grow exponentially, the essential infrastructure becomes insufficient for life, leading to a "social and health catastrophe far worse than current problems, which governments seem unable to ameliorate."[27] Langton refers to a speech in Canberra in 1997 given by the governor-general of Australia, Sir William Deane, at the launch of *The Health and Welfare of Australia's Aboriginal and Torres Strait Islander People*, in which he warned that the gap in health levels between Indigenous and other Australians was widening. An Indigenous man, he noted, was three times more likely to die between the ages of fifteen and twenty-four than his non-Indigenous peers. An Indigenous man of thirty-five was more than eight times more likely to die before his forty-fourth year than a non-Indigenous man. The mortality rates of Indigenous children also follow the same disparity.

In subsequent sections I cite important landmarks in Indigenous government policy since 1967, especially land rights acts that, although promising, were not sufficient or committed in their willingness to make definitive changes toward Indigenous autonomy and securing their economic future.

Indigenous futures depended on the ability to use the land and its resources while maintaining cultural obligations and ecological sustainability.

Post-1967 Referendum Australia: From Assimilation to Self-Determination

The 1967 Citizen Rights Referendum was meant to be the most significant referendum in the history of Indigenous and white coexistence since 1788. It stands as the demarcation where assimilationist notions and policies turned toward Indigenous self-determination. Nevertheless, it was a sleight of hand by the federal government to assume control of Indigenous peoples from the states. The referendum was overwhelmingly voted by Australians who thought they were endorsing full citizenship rights to Indigenous peoples, thereby alleviating chronic and systemic poverty. "Instead, the Constitution was changed to give the federal government the power to make laws on behalf of any race, and Indigenous people could be counted in the census."[28] It was only during the 1990s that these changes to the constitution were revealed by academics. Since the referendum, Indigenous peoples have been accorded civil and political rights incrementally only through removal of discriminatory policies. And Indigenous peoples still live in chronic and systemic poverty.[29]

Two controversial figures emerged to dominate the Black and white conversation at the end of the twentieth century and the beginning of the twenty-first. H. C. (Nugget) Coombs, a white public servant for Indigenous affairs, presided over Indigenous-specific structures and programs and was considered the architect of self-determination, while Guugu Yimithirr attorney and scholar Noel Pearson became identified with welfare reform. Both Coombs and Pearson have been maligned and caricatured. But as the conversation progresses, more leverage has been afforded these intellectual leaders by recasting the recent history of successes and missteps of Indigenous policies as an ongoing *experiment*.

The first thirty years after the landmark referendum were dominated by Coombs's ideology; the decades that followed (the 1990s through the present) have been dominated by Pearson's infamous welfare reform and radical reversal of passive Indigenous economies. The ideological differences between the two phases are that in the first lies the more mainstream notion that policy should reflect the equality and sameness of Indigenous and non-Indigenous peoples. The second notion, which has carried the struggle for Indigenous land rights, is that while Indigenous peoples have equal political, social, and economic rights, they maintain their historical and cultural differences and, therefore, policy must reflect those differences. *Difference* here must be understood as privilege rather than as weakness.

Whitlam's Government Impact on Western Australia

During its short three-year tenure (1972–1975), the Whitlam Labor government was the most innovative and pro-Indigenous government following the previous two decades of Liberal governance, most notable for its passage of the Racial Discrimination Act (RDA). The dismissal of the Whitlam government in 1975 caused an uproar, yet Whitlam left a legacy that would transform social consciousness.[30] Although racist ideology and policy did not end, nor would Indigenous affairs be a high priority, a new direction was in the air. Noel Pearson[31] noted that Whitlam took a risk that no other prime minister had before by applying the international perspective on the Liberal Party's nationalist "white Australian" rhetoric as not only racist but also an economic rationalization for greed that could not be easily overturned.

The government in Western Australia following Whitlam in the late 1970s and early 1980s, however, was one of the most conservative under the leadership of Sir Charles Court. As a partial antidote, the Aboriginal Legal Services (ALS) was formed in 1973 as a voluntary legal service for Indigenous peoples in Perth, with its main purpose and priority to provide legal advice for Indigenous peoples in custody who were disadvantaged in court and overrepresented in prison. In 1979, its focus was the escalation of negative and often brutal encounters between the police and Indigenous peoples and the policy of mass incarceration based on "zero tolerance" for public drunkenness and other offensive social behavior that often spiraled into more serious charges. Police racism and violence against Indigenous peoples in Western Australia was tacitly accepted, which was alleviated by ALS representation in court. When ALS turned toward protecting Australian Indigenous peoples from mining company infringement, Charles Court incited a fear campaign in the media suggesting that they were being manipulated by "white political agitators, Labor supporters, left wingers, even communists."[32] Known as pro-development ideology that had dominated Western Australian politics since the 1890s, massive pastoral land clearing of the early to mid-twentieth century was giving way to minerals. This legacy, argues Quentin Beresford,[33] formed the highly conservative frame of mind in the state that, when combined with its geographic isolation, encouraged a frontier mentality. Court's uncompromising authoritarian personality completed the picture. Although having a solid conservative base, he was characterized by progressives and activists, particularly Indigenous peoples, environmentalists, feminists, and unionists, as "one of the most polarizing of Western Australia's political leaders . . . oppressive on issues of political rights generally and 'colonial' in his response to Aborigines."[34] Court marginalized Indigenous peoples from the democratic process through intimidation, such as depriving illiterate people the right to vote and, most conspicuously, by changing the 1977 Western Australian Electoral Act, claiming that the fate of the government should not depend on uneducated people.[35] In reality, Court was making way for the mining industry's intrusion into Indigenous reserves. His proposed change to the 1979 Western Australia Mining Act permitted mining companies to enter Indigenous reserves without negotiating with the Aboriginal Lands Trust.[36] These incursions prompted the people at Noonkanbah Station to form the Kimberley Land Council (KLC).

Noonkanbah Station

The Noonkanbah community in a remote area of the Kimberley in the northwest of Western Australia became the racial and political flashpoint for the conflicting interests between Indigenous land rights and the nascent multinational mining industry. Premier Court's argument was typical of the conservative effort to protect Australian land for white interests by challenging the lineage of Indigenous cultural and spiritual connection to the land. Individual Indigenous Australian activists and groups, such as Robert Bropho and the ALS, joined the community from all over the country for a peaceful standoff with the police and the American Amax mining company. It was a dramatic episode in Indigenous politics for the nation—the first time an Indigenous community demanded its inherent rights to land and the protection of sacred sites. Although its members ultimately lost the battle, they ushered in the land rights movement.

The Noonkanbah Station was leased as pastoral land in 1976 by the Aboriginal Land Fund Commission in order "to maintain its own culture, free from European influence."[37] Until the Aboriginal Heritage Act of 1972, sacred sites had no legal protection. The bill was prompted by the mining industry's desecration of these sites in the late 1960s and early 1970s in which sacred stone was mined in the Western Desert. The act was a sign of progress, but as with all legislation that claimed to "protect" Indigenous interests, it came with a hitch: the minister for Aboriginal Affairs had the power to override decisions. The Noonkanbah Station tested whether the government would uphold the new legislation. Fear struck when in 1979 Amax notified the community that it intended to drill an exploratory hole in the middle of a sacred site.

> Thus, Noonkanbah became a political line in the sand for right-wing politicians in Western Australia and elsewhere in the country. As one unsourced "senior Liberal" told the *Daily News* [March 28, 1980], "the fight for the north has begun. If we don't hold on, the blacks could take over right through the Territory and Queensland."[38]

The conflict heated up when the government granted land to mine at the site after the Western Australian Museum's survey reported that the area should be protected under the Aboriginal Heritage Act. ALS prepared a brief that stopped exploration, but mining rights were restored within a month. For the first time, a unified Indigenous community defied the white Australian legal order and set up camp at the site, intimidating miners to leave. Yet no one, including Prime Minister Malcolm Fraser, was willing to defy Charles Court, "one of the fiercest defenders of states' rights in the country."[39] Further amendments to the act made it less reliable for Indigenous cultural interests—for example,

> the government of the day can decide in the interests of the broader community what Aboriginal sites should be destroyed or damaged, no matter how sacred or important or special their significance to Aboriginal people may be. Aboriginal people have no right to be heard on the topic, although private property owners may appeal to the Supreme Court if the Minister will not authorize a disturbance.[40]

By August 1980, a convoy of forty-five trucks and ancillary vehicles embarked from Perth and traveled north. ALS was threatened with disbandment for allegedly inciting Indigenous people rather than providing them with legal assistance. Public attention was now focused on the impending crisis. The first and most critical decision was made about the location for the "last stand," which would be in a dry creek bed at Mickey's Pool. Sixty people with their vehicles camped out for the night, prepared for nonviolent resistance the following day.

"The next morning 'all hell broke loose.' At 8:15 A.M., overseen by a big police contingent, a front-end loader and a grader started dragging the vehicles aside."[41] The police dragged elders and churchmen into paddy wagons as ALS monitored their treatment. The aftermath was devastating for everyone involved in the protest, particularly the community, which never fully recovered. However, ALS made land rights a unified cause for all Indigenous peoples, expanding the new Kimberley Land Council into a network that crossed the nation. The parameters of the battle ahead were drawn and continued until the landmark 1992 *Mabo* decision, although deeply flawed,[42] would recognize native title.

Searching for a Treaty

Negotiating a treaty between Indigenous and non-Indigenous Australians has had both symbolic and real importance as a recognition of prior ownership of land and the protection of those rights going forward into the future. A treaty as a priority, however, has invited debate within Indigenous Australia—one side emphasizing its symbolic importance and the other, the changes that a treaty would introduce. In *What Condition a Treaty*, the authors debate whether a treaty is a good investment of resources when conditions on the ground are in need. For many, to fight for a treaty is to attack systemic injustice: debilitating economic and educational resources, poverty, violence, and drug abuse. No less important, writes Eualeyai/Kamillaroi law scholar Larissa Behrendt,[43] is the notion of nation-building; a treaty invites both Indigenous and non-Indigenous Australians to reflect on the kind of nation they want to live in. The Australian government was prepared to recognize Indigenous ownership but not willing to support Indigenous separation as a legal status, even though a precedent was set[44] by the domestic treaty negotiated between North America and New Zealand's Indigenous peoples and their governments.

The first Indigenous senator, Neville Bonner, was unimpressed with shallow symbolic gestures that lacked the will to be implemented. "It's all very well to say, 'Aborigines are entitled to Land Rights.' That's a great statement. A profound statement. Aborigines are entitled to land rights. But implementing them is the basis of everything."[45] The most widespread response from Indigenous informants was the distraction caused by pursuing grand gestures such as treaties and land rights. "After its signing, Aborigines would still have to fight just as hard for land and for housing, against unemployment and against discrimination,"[46] since treaties are not legislative documents. The term *practical reconciliation* grew from such concerns as housing, infrastructure, education, and health services.[47] By 1983, the notion of a treaty was rejected by the Senate Standing Committee on Constitutional and Legal Affairs, conveniently holding onto the traditional meaning of a treaty as a compact between autonomous nations.

Eddie Mabo Jr., whose father was the plaintiff in the landmark *Mabo* decision, perceived the inherent contradiction in calling for Indigenous sovereignty from the Commonwealth and at the same time calling out the same government for not fulfilling its obligations to deliver services. Finally, he asked, how can talk of an Aboriginal treaty exist under a colonial government?

> If the basis of those to obligation are based on us being the same, and not on the basis of being Indigenous people whose legal rights are based on platforms of prior occupation and ownership of land, then we contradict the central arguments within the calls for a treaty. . . . How can we continue to ignore that we are captives of a colonizing government and delude ourselves and pretend to take up a position outside the barbed wire fences of government legislation and policy and call for our own release? The mind boggles.[48]

How might a treaty achieve its original purpose of recognizing the unambiguous rights of Indigenous peoples as original occupants rather than as an assimilated ethnic minority if they depended on the legal, political, and moral obligations of government?[49] The models that had evolved during the 1980s, Mabo argued, would not provide Indigenous self-representation under the framework of a colonized people. Interference from non-Indigenous people, no matter how well intended, could not help them answer questions they must ask themselves.

The *Mabo* Decision and Native Title Act[50]

Eddie Mabo lived in Townsville in the Torres Strait Islands, which had a distinct history from the mainland because its First Nations peoples had not been forced from their land. As original inhabitants, many assumed that the land belonged to them. Mabo was under this assumption until historian Henry Reynolds told him that the land he lived on was owned by the Crown.[51] This revelation late in life drove him to seek justice for the Islanders and, ultimately, Indigenous peoples on the mainland. In 1982, Mabo and four other plaintiffs began proceedings in the High Court asserting their traditional rights of ownership on the Murray Islands.[52] The 1975 Racial Discrimination Act (RDA) would play a critical role by prohibiting discriminatory treatment by the government on the basis of race. After the first Mabo case was struck down in 1988, it went before the High Court and passed with a majority of six to one on June 3, 1992, four months after Eddie Mabo died. Robert Tickner called it "one of the most important decisions the High Court of Australia will ever deliver and elevated the process of reconciliation."[53] However, its symbolic and practical consequences would be debated for decades. Moreton-Robinson argues that the rule of extinguishment used by the High Court in the Mabo decision transgressed the rule of common law whereby the Crown is meant to protect the interests of its subjects.

The decision protects the property interests of patriarchal whiteness by reinscribing the legitimacy of the sovereignty of the white patriarchal nation-state. The decision affirms white identity by creating in law a hybrid of settlement that diminishes but does not erase terra nullius.[54]

The *Mabo* decision did not threaten the land rights of non-Indigenous Australians but rather acknowledged the potential for native title to exist in Aboriginal-occupied traditional lands with historical connections. Pearson elucidates the meaning of special rights for Indigenous people, which are both symbolic and real but do not threaten the law of the land. Nonetheless, this assertion of Crown sovereignty is based on the unjust fallacy of European superiority "*by the mere act of settlement.*"[55] *Mabo*, therefore, would remain primarily a symbolic correction of terra nullius.[56]

At this moment of heated conflict, Paul Keating would give his renowned Redfern Park speech on December 10, 1992, in recognition of the UN International Year of the World's Indigenous People. Many historians, scholars, and politicians believe it to be one of the most important and eloquent speeches given by an Australian prime minister. The following is a small section.

> The starting point might be to recognise that the problem starts with us non-Aboriginal Australians. It begins, I think, with that act of recognition. Recognition that it was we who did the dispossessing. We took the traditional lands and smashed the traditional way of life. We brought the diseases. The alcohol. We committed the murders. We took the children from their mothers. We practiced discrimination and exclusion. It was our ignorance and our prejudice. And our failure to imagine these things being done to us. With some noble exceptions, we failed to make the most basic human response and enter into their hearts and minds. We failed to ask—how would I feel if this were done to me?[57]

Keating acknowledged *Mabo* as the beginning of an admission of injustices and a recognition of Indigenous peoples as original owners of the continent. Opponents of *Mabo* called such sentiments artifacts of the "guilt industry," claiming Indigenous Australians were treated preferentially, which gained credibility and eventually dominated the debate. Pearson wrote presciently that such responses are a reminder that

> Mabo has put to rest two gross fantasies. Firstly, it has put to rest the fantasy that the blacks were not and are still not here. The fantasy of terra and homo nullius. Secondly, Mabo also puts to rest the fantasy

that the whites are somehow going to pack up and leave. Coexistence remains our lot.[58]

Keating won the 1993 election, and the continuation of native title discussion was secured. Meanwhile, the states refused the right of consent for Indigenous peoples, ignoring the history of dispossession and their relationship as title holders.[59] As the Keating government began to bend, Pearson and Yawuru attorney and academic activist Mick Dodson accused the government of treating *Mabo* as a land management proposition, ignoring its cultural significance to Indigenous peoples.

Finally, a Senate majority was achieved and "Australia had its Native Title Act unambiguously recognising, protecting and enhancing the High Court's decision in the Mabo case."[60] But Indigenous leaders, such as Pearson, and non-Indigenous civil rights experts believed that *Mabo* did not go far enough to secure the civil rights of Indigenous peoples. The High Court failed to clarify that the Commonwealth had a fiduciary (honor of the Crown) duty to protect their rights and interests. This omission still prevents the High Court today from its compatibility with the Crown as a fiduciary. Nevertheless, for Indigenous peoples, *Mabo* represented a greater cause than land rights alone. It sought to conform legal principles to international human rights—in other words, democracy's embrace of its obligation to protect marginalized peoples and to make right past injustices.

Competing Ideologies

Australian governance has historically embedded white masculine power, racism, and ableism into its laws, evident in the overt subjugation of Indigeneity in political and social processes. Aligned with this ideology was the government policy of prohibiting disabled Others to cross its borders. The 1901 Immigration Restriction Act excluded "any idiot or insane person . . . any person suffering from an infectious or contagious disease of a loathsome or dangerous character."[61] The policy of removing children was purposely designed to whiten and thus disable the Indigenous identity by erasing Indigenous meaning and traces of culture from the land. From this perspective, disability has unwanted connotations for Indigenous peoples who are reclaiming their autonomous culture in a white nation-state. As Pearson wrote, disablement of the Indigenous peoples was the plan to which he refused to succumb, even at the cost of disapproval within Indigenous society. Pearson was particularly affected by the "second wave" of colonialism as a leader in the Cape York Peninsula in the Northern Territory (NT), where alcoholism and domestic abuse were escalating. Federal intervention in the form of the NTER (commonly referred to as "The Intervention") of 2007 introduced by the Howard government, which occupied Indigenous communities in the NT, was meant to "protect" a degenerate and childish people. In violation of the UN Declaration of Human Rights and of Rights of Indigenous Peoples, the Australian government disrupted the right of self-determination of Indigenous communities, reviving the trauma of the Stolen Generations. In 2012 when the act expired, the intervention was reinstated and renamed Stronger Futures in Northern Territory Act.

Competing ideologies continued between the Labor and Liberal governments, between the so-called radical and moderate Indigenous leaders, and between settlers and Indigenous peoples. Noel Pearson cuts through these competing or opposing philosophies as artifacts of white law and culture. No matter how illegitimate, artificial, or revisionist colonial law might be, since 1788 it has been the Indigenous reality. "It determines our ability to exercise our law, enjoy our rights and maintain our identities."[62] *Mabo* and native title created an in-between space for Indigenous peoples, a gesture toward acknowledging that First Nations peoples have laws but that they are subsumed under the Commonwealth. Pearson, the realist, asked, "What strategies can we pursue to make Aboriginal law have consequence for our colonial condition?"[63] The first step, as he conceived it, would be to extinguish the binary politics that keep ideologies spinning in different and unequal orbits. Although *Mabo* had been the best outcome possible, Pearson knew what many Indigenous people failed to accept: the liminal space *Mabo* and native title inhabited, a law recognizing human rights rather than land rights.

What relevance can the Indigenous body have on the white body? Pearson often looked toward the civil rights movement in the United States as a mirror of Indigenous struggle. Uncle Tom and Malcom X represented two polarities in the white dualistic mind, a conveniently constructed reality that controlled the narrative "as moderate or radical, conservative or activist, to suit themselves, and we have internalised these characterisations and made them our own."[64] This critique provided Pearson with his controversial notions that upended the white narrative of Indigenous people as helpless, dependent, and victimized. Others, such as Moreton-Robinson, claimed he fell into the racist, patriarchal, neoliberalist trope of the Howard government and its ongoing race war. Nor was there mention from Pearson about government silence when such issues as domestic violence and sexual abuse were reported by the NT Indigenous peoples with recommendations. Federal funds allocated for the Northern Territory were instead funneled to wealthy white electorates. In 1991, the National Inquiry into Racist Violence revealed the media's pathologizing of Indigenous peoples in the Northern Territory. Morten-Robinson calls these acts by the federal government and the media evidence of the race war that must be acknowledged as part of the social failures of the Northern Territory.

Nevertheless, Pearson held Indigenous people responsible for their fail-ings, especially for domestic and alcohol abuse. Victim politics would only go so far, he cautioned; eventually, white Australians would repel their char-acterization as villains, a prophetic statement given the long jurisdiction of the Howard government. He feared the backlash of *Mabo* and the Native Title Act, given that Aboriginal affairs meant political death to the Labor Party. Such was the implication of the Liberal Party slogan, *For All of Us*. "If this was going to be the government for all of us, for whom had Paul Keating been governing?"[65] Almost no one, Pearson concluded. He thought that *Mabo* and native title would be objectionable to most Australian citizens. The subtle phrasing of the Liberal Party's slogan woke the unconscious and conscious fears of non-Indigenous people as well as their hidden and overt racism. Meanwhile, Keating was cast as appealing to the multicultural *Mabo* crowd and other fringe-interest groups the Liberal Party blamed for the economic, social, and psychological failings of Australia. The subliminal message was a brilliant political and psychological strategy that accom-plished its intent to uncover undefined resentment: that the people in "Mid-dle Australia" weren't getting what they were entitled.[66]

Pearson saw an opportunity to unite with the Right in politics and life by finding like causes. "The only way to get wide support for Indigenous Aus-tralians' aspirations is to first get support from the most conservative people among decent Australians. If you first get the support of the Left, it will be-come a Left-versus-Right issue."[67] He argued that the welfare check was the primary motivator in maintaining the status quo and, thus, he suggested that the passive welfare mentality was the cause of the debilitating cycle of addiction and social and economic decline. Pearson makes the important distinction between passive welfare and welfare proper. The latter "involves working taxpayers collectively financing systems aimed at their own and their families' security and development. The immersion of a whole region into dependence on passive welfare is different from the mainstream experi-ence of welfare."[68]

The term *self-determination* also undergoes scrupulous analysis from Pearson, who suggests its meaning has been restricted to political rhetoric. The right to power and autonomy must coexist with responsibility and ac-countability. "The right to self-determination is ultimately the right to take responsibility. Our traditional economy was a real economy and demanded responsibility (you don't work, you starve). The whitefella market economy is real (you don't work, you don't get paid)."[69] Pearson argued that since becoming citizens with the right to welfare, the Indigenous economy not only stalled but also debilitated Indigenous traditional values and relation-ships: the values of responsibility and sharing were corrupted by the obliga-tion to share and buy alcohol with welfare checks. According to Pearson, the paradigm itself invites destructive behavior in both the recipient and the provider. The cycle is exacerbated by both Indigenous and non-Indigenous exploitation of store owners, check cashers, and drug dealers who profit in abuse and debility. And possibly more insidious, passive welfare in this context is a political power construct in which half of the partnership becomes increasingly powerless while the powerful maintain an appearance of benevolence and superiority, a fiction without a lasting solution. The mentality of victimhood is nurtured in this paradigm, justifying one's right to assistance without reciprocity, while the government reflects the image of a people incapable of contributing to society. Pearson's detractors, however, noticed his use of the terminology of the Howard government to pathologize Indigenous rights activists as incompetent and naive, while connecting Indigenous citizenship rights to the ultimate failure of welfare.[70]

The Radical Centre

Perhaps Pearson's most lucid theory about the vagaries of both the Right and the Left is his search for a synthesis, which he calls the "radical centre."[71] He was inspired by the election of Barack Obama, whom he considers the closest example of a union between W. E. B. DuBois and Booker T. Washington. The disunion between the two ideologies have divided and shaped the race debate in the United States. The problem, Pearson argues, is the self-sustaining disadvantage and disengagement from real economy, perpetuated no matter who is in power because it has gone under the radar. Shelby Steele, Pearson's counterpart in the United States, also raises unpopular issues that challenge the radical Left by critiquing progressive orthodoxy.

Steele's explanation of how white guilt for past injustices imposes a challenge to moral authority in the United States parallels white Australia's questionable moral position. Like the United States, Australians have disassociated themselves with the past while acknowledging its existence in order to maintain the moral high ground. To resolve systemic racism, the United States has legislated bills that make systemic changes. Since the 2016 presidential election, however, the United States has seen an abrupt psychological reversal, a backlash to a thirty-year attempt to equalize opportunity.

The following quote is essential in understanding how Pearson's ideology was influenced by Steele:

Few who live in liberal democracies today would contest the idea that freedom is crucial to a decent life. A related—although perhaps more frequently debated—assertion is that only by being responsible for one's life can one assume agency for it. Agency, Steele believes, is what makes us fully human. With the rise of black consciousness, however, the idea that black Americans must take personal responsibility to get ahead was subverted by the idea that responsibility was a tool of oppression and white America was responsible for black American advancement.[72]

Steele, in turn, was influenced by his father's sense of responsibility, although it was a responsibility without possibility. No possibility existed if he was prohibited from joining the unions and, therefore, maintaining a living wage. Because the heavy responsibility of African Americans was mostly fruitless, it came to represent "the primary experience of oppression . . . the condition of oppression itself."[73] This scenario illuminates the historical repressive nature with which responsibility was foisted onto Black Americans. Responsibility without possibility is an untenable position that set up white America (and Australia) to take on the burden of responsibility as compensation for its historical oppression while demonstrating its new social morality. This redistribution of responsibility led inexorably to the unintended effect of infantilizing and debilitating Black Americans. The fallacy of decoupling social justice from individual responsibility lies in an inherent lack of equity. It is also an admission of defeat, "and it can also literally kill."[74] Pearson quotes a segment from Steele's 1999 essay in *Harper's Magazine* that elucidates this hard pill to swallow.

> We allowed ourselves to see a greater power in America's liability for our oppression than we saw in ourselves. Thus, we were faithless with ourselves just when we had given ourselves reason to have such faith. We couldn't have made a worse mistake. We have not been the same since.[75]

According to Steele and Pearson, the aftermath of both U.S. and Australian civil rights victories was the misstep of using them to promote the politics of victimhood, which relied on the two faces of "*white guilt and moral vanity.*"[76] Eventually, race becomes an expedient tool for political gain while losing its humane purpose: "Pragmatism and a remorseless Kissingeresque grasp of power make winning and survival the main prize every time."[77] Even after the first programs to alleviate Indigenous poverty and lack of access didn't work and, in fact, caused debility and secondary problems, the welfare-state mentality dug in.

Pearson's theories have galvanized fierce opposition. Like Selby Steele's in the United States, Pearson's ideology has been used to justify the Right's compassionless policies. And while Pearson's logic is a welcome alternative to failed ideologies and policies, he sometimes misses the balanced radical centre, which is his theoretical and practical goal. For example, his analysis of Indigenous legal aid, which he submits as an example of a skewed system, seems itself to be skewed. Pearson faults legal aid for pointing to the criminal justice system rather than Aboriginal behavior as the primary problem of the Indigenous broken social order and overrepresentation in custody. While the Royal Commission into Aboriginal Deaths in Custody acknowledges alcoholism as a significant problem, Pearson believes that drugs and alcohol have been underestimated as the primary problem, particularly its connection with child abuse. Yet evidence has shown that the criminal justice system is riddled with racist policies. To this point Pearson argues that Black progress cannot be conditional on the decline of racism or it will never arrive—an expectation Steele calls "social determinism," the structural social problems that become excuses. Considering the shootings of unarmed Black men in the United States and the unveiling of an entrenched racism in the police force, Pearson's point is unfounded and even destructive. Nevertheless, Indigenous people have not solved the relatively recent problem of alcoholism. The "old" Indigenous law did not encounter alcoholism, gambling, money, and property rights. These are the new disabling challenges in Indigenous culture that must be wrestled within Indigenous law.

Final Thoughts

In the Boyer Lectures, *The Quiet Revolution: Indigenous People and the Resources Boom*, Marcia Langton[78] begins by correcting contemporary fictions and misconceptions that might have inadvertently gained currency. For example, in *After the Dreaming*, W. E. H. Stanner[79] unintentionally supported the widespread view that the Australian economy and Indigenous life were incompatible. Further, it has been assumed that Indigenous peoples were categorically opposed to mining. Misconceptions are also reflected in government legislation, such as the fifty-year-old work-for-the-dole model called the Community Development Employment Program (CDEP), which ended in 2015. Legislation such as this, which Pearson calls passive welfare, were based on the exceptionalist ideology that Aboriginal people are "incapable of joining the Australian polity and society."[80] Notwithstanding the decolonizing attempts of such key figures as Whitlam, Coombs, and Stanner, Langton claims that the 1960s and 1970s were rife with such misconceptions and erroneous legislation based on stereotypes such as the "new noble savage" romanticized by the "wilderness" rhetoric of the environmental movement, creating the perfect storm for delayed economic development. She blames this segment of the political Left for envisioning the "cultural Aborigine" while excluding the notion of "a thriving, educated, economically engaged Aboriginal population."[81] Langton explains that Indigenous people object to the term *wilderness* because "the term, particularly as it is popularized, has the effect of denying the very existence of Aboriginal biogeography."[82] This argument is not an objection to protecting the environment; rather, it highlights the need to recognize the interdependency between cultural and natural values. The term *wilderness* ignores the notion that land is a human artifact: "It is land constructed by us over tens of thousands of years—through our ceremonies and ties of kinship, through fire, and through hunting over countless generations."[83] Wilderness is a modern notion of terra nullius. According to Indigenous peoples, wild country means country that has been neglected or abused. Indigenous peoples know how to see the signs of responsible, quiet, human interaction with country.[84]

Enter the mining industry's intrusion into this changing landscape. Mining marked the beginning of the struggle for Indigenous land rights and the preservation of sacred Indigenous land that the industry assumed as lease holders. To make matters worse, environmentalists who purported to advocate for Indigenous rights instead staged a campaign by using their support to preserve nature and biodiversity. This was not a bad premise, but the real concerns of Indigenous peoples about a sustainable economy was never part of this picture, which exemplifies the importance of centering Indigenous intersectional interests. For the next three decades Indigenous groups would protest and petition for self-management; national land; civil, economic, and social justice; and compensation for loss of land.[85]

The policies in the previous section and throughout this essay are founded on the objectives of the Global North that do not include Indigenous aspirations. The history of enforced dependency of Indigenous Australians has caused intergenerational disablement and cannot be compared with the concerns of (Northern) disability studies. Paul Abberley[86] called the violence of the Global North an *impairment as social product* at the intersection of colonization and disability. When resources are not available for survival, the core issues of disability studies lose their relevancy.[87] "Social suffering does not equate with the concept of personal tragedy as critiqued by disability scholars"[88] and must be understood as the aftermath of genocide: the destruction of, or the attempt to destroy, a group of people.

NOTES

1. Laura Jaffee and Kelsey John, "Disabling Bodies of/and Land: Reframing Disability Justice in Conversation with Indigenous Theory and Activism," *Disability and the Global South* 5, no. 2 (2018): 1419.

2. Mary Graham, "Some Thoughts about the Philosophical Underpinnings of Aboriginal World Views," *Australian Humanities Review* 45 (2008): 181–82.

3. Jaffee and John, "Disabling Bodies of/and Land," 1408.

4. Elaine Coburn et al., "Unspeakable Things: Indigenous Research and Social Science," *Socio: La nouvelle revue des sciences sociales* 2 (2013).

5. Aileen Moreton-Robinson, *The White Possessive: Property, Power, and Indigenous Sovereignty* ([Kindle DXversion]. Retrieved from Amazon.com, 2012), loc. 650.

6. Aileen Moreton-Robinson, "Introduction: Resistance, Recovery and Revitalization," in *Blacklines: Contemporary Critical Writing by Indigenous Australians*, ed. Michelle Grossman (Melbourne: Melbourne University Press, 2003), 127–31.

7. Jasbir K. Puar, *The Right to Maim: Debility/Capacity/Disability* (Durham, NC: Duke University Press, 2017). Puar explains the relationship between disability and debility as follows: "I mobilize the term 'debility' as a needed disruption (but also expose it as a collaborator) of the category of disability and as a triangulation of the ability/disability binary, noting that while some bodies may not be recognized as or identify as disabled, they may well be debilitated, in part by being foreclosed access to legibility and resources as disabled . . . and that debilitation is a necessary component that both exposes and sutures the non-disabled/disabled binary" (xv).

8. According to Puar, four-fifths of disabled people live in the Global South, or developing countries (xvii); Karen Soldatic, "*Post*colonial *R*eproductions: Disability, Indigeneity and the Formation of the White Masculine Settler State of Australia," *Social Identities* 21, no. 1 (2015): 57; Shaun Grech, "Decolonising Eurocentric Disability Studies: Why Colonialism Matters in the Disability and Global South Debate," *Social Identities: Journal for the Study of Race, Nation and Culture* 21, no. 1 (2015): 8.

9. Malini Ranganathan, "Thinking with Flint: Racial Liberalism and the Roots of an American Water Tragedy," *Capitalism Nature Socialism* 27, no. 3 (2016): 3.

10. Catherine Jampel, "Intersections of Disability Justice, Racial Justice and Environmental Justice," *Environmental Sociology* 4 (2018): 6.

11. Moreton-Robinson, *The White Possessive: Property, Power, and Indigenous Sovereignty*, loc. 7888.

12. Ibid., loc. 1797.

13. Ibid., xvii.

14. Puar, *Right to Maim*, xx.

15. Ibid., xvii.

16. Brenda Croft, Interview with Alice Wexler, April 21, 2019.

17. Noel Pearson, *Up from the Mission: Selected Writings* (Melbourne: Black, 2009).

18. Irene Watson, "Re-Centering First Nations Knowledge and Places in a Terra Nullius Space," *Alternative* 10, no. 5 (2014).

19. Alice Wexler, *Art and Resistance in Settler Colonial Australia* (forthcoming).

20. Moreton-Robinson, *White Possessive*, loc. 562.

21. Tim Rowse, *Indigenous and Other Australians since 1901* (Australia: UNSW Press, 2017).

22. Wexler, *Art and Resistance*.

23. Moreton-Robinson, *White Possessive*.

24. Ibid., *White Possessive*, loc. 511.

25. Ibid., *White Possessive*, loc. 545.

26. W. E. H. Stanner, *The Dreaming and Other Essays* (Victoria, NSW: Black), 257.

27. Marcia Langton, "Emerging Environmental Issues," "Emerging Environmental Issues for Indigenous Peoples in Northern Australia," UNESCO and EOLSS, 2009, 89.

28. Moreton-Robinson, *White Possessive*, loc. 3191.

29. There are still large gaps in outcomes between Indigenous people and other Australian citizens on all social indicators. Our life expectancy rates are seventeen years less than the rest of the population, our health is the worst in the country, we live in overcrowded houses, we have the highest unemployment rates, we are overrepresented in the

criminal justice system, and our education outcomes are well below the Australian average. Ibid., loc. 3201.

30. Robert Tickner, *Taking a Stand: Land Rights to Reconciliation* (New South Wales: Allen & Unwin, 2001), 16.

31. Pearson, *Up from the Mission*, loc. 805.

32. Quentin Beresford, *Rob Riley: An Aboriginal Leader's Quest for Justice* (Canberra: Aboriginal Studies, 2006), 88.

33. Ibid., 88.

34. Ibid., 89.

35. Ibid., 90.

36. Ibid.

37. Ibid., 104.

38. Ibid., 106.

39. Ibid., 110.

40. Ibid.

41. Ibid., 116.

42. See Moreton-Robinson, *The White Possessive*, chap. 5.

43. Larissa Behrendt, "Foreword," in *What Good Condition: Reflections on an Australian Aboriginal Treaty*, ed. Peter Read, Gary Meyers, and Bob Reece (Canberra: ANU Press, 2006), xi–xii.

44. Pearson, *Up from the Mission*, loc. 5773.

45. Peter Read, Gary Meyers, and Bob Reece, eds., *What Good Condition: Reflections on an Australian Aboriginal Treaty* (Canberra: ANU Press, 2006), 34.

46. Ibid., 37.

47. Tim Rowse, "From Enforceability to Feel-Good: Notes on the Prehistory of the Recent Treaty Debate," in *What Good Condition: Reflections on an Australian Aboriginal Treaty*, ed. Peter Read, Gary Meyers, and Bob Reece (Canberra: ANU Press, 2006), 75.

48. Eddie Mabo Jr., "A Treaty for Whom?" in *What Good Condition: Reflections on an Australian Aboriginal Treaty*, ed. Peter Read, Gary Meyers, and Bob Reece (Canberra: ANU Press, 2006), 101.

49. Mabo Jr. also questioned ATSIC's right "to negotiate a treaty on behalf of all Indigenous people in this country," 102.

50. *Mabo* and the Native Title Act are extremely complex legislation. A thorough and insightful explanation of their meanings can be found in Noel Pearson's *Up from the Mission: Selected Writings*, in the chapter "Land Is Susceptible of Ownership," loc. 642.

51. When Reynolds received a grant to research "Black oral history," he appointed Mabo as his research assistant. Damien Short, *Reconciliation and Colonial Power: Indigenous Rights in Australia* (Hampshire: Ashgate, 2008), 37.

52. Tickner, *Taking a Stand*, 85.

53. Ibid., 86.

54. Moreton-Robinson, *White Possessive*, loc. 1555.

55. Ibid.

56. Terra nullius was the totalizing expression of removing Australian Indigenous peoples' meaning and traces of culture from the land.

57. Tickner, *Taking a Stand*, 95.

58. Marcia Langton, *The Quiet Revolution: Indigenous People and the Resources Boom. Boyer Lectures* ([Kindle DX version]. Retrieved from Amazon.com, 2012), loc. 1196.

59. Tickner, *Taking a Stand*, 190.

60. Ibid., 192.

61. Soldatic, "*Post*colonial *Re*productions," 60.

62. Ibid., 573.

63. Ibid., 580.

64. Ibid., 588.

65. Ibid., 1335.

66. Australian politics of the late 1990s to mid-2000s is uncomfortably like U.S. politics today, especially with Pearson's (2009) astute commentary. "So poor Middle Australia, the Great Mainstream of Australia . . . had lived through thirteen long years of neglect and misery at the hands of an uncaring federal government" (para. 10). *For all of us* can also be equated with the *all lives matter* response to Black Lives Matter.

67. Pearson, *Up from the Mission*, loc. 1528.

68. Ibid., loc. 3042.

69. Ibid., loc. 2296.

70. Moreton-Robinson, *White Possessive*.

71. "The 'radical centre' may be defined as the intense resolution of the tensions between opposing principles—a resolution that produces the synthesis of optimum policy. The radical centre is not to be found simply by splitting the difference between the stark and weak tensions from either side of popularly conceived discourse, but rather where the dialectical tension is most intense, and the policy positions much closer and more carefully calibrated than most people imagine" (Pearson, *Up from the Mission*, loc. 4000).

72. Pearson, *Up from the Mission*, loc. 3693.

73. Ibid., loc. 3693.

74. Ibid., loc. 3864.

75. Ibid., loc. 3725.

76. Ibid., loc. 3741.

77. Ibid., loc. 4048.

78. Langton, *Quiet Revolution*.

79. Stanner, *After the Dreaming*.

80. Langton, *Quiet Revolution*, loc. 224.

81. Ibid., loc. 510.

82. Ibid., loc. 1066.

83. Langton, "Emerging Environmental Issues," 92.

84. Langton, *Quiet Revolution*, loc. 1066.

85. See the Bark Petition, the first and only petition to Parliament, and the 1998 Barunga Statement, which still exists in Parliament.

86. Paul Abberley, "The Concept of Oppression and the Development of a Social Theory of Disability," in *Disability Studies: Past Present and Future*, ed. Len Barton and Mike Oliver (Leeds: Disability, 1997), 173–74.

87. Helen Meekosha, "Decolonising Disability: Thinking and Acting Globally," *Disability and Society* 26, no. 6 (2010): 667–82.

88. Ibid., 671.

II

Redefining Blindness and Deafness through (Dis)Ability, Colonialism, and the Environment

5

Blind Horizons

The Worlds of People with Sight Loss during
Scotland's Long Nineteenth Century

IAIN HUTCHISON

B y the dawn of the nineteenth century, blindness and sight loss were disabling conditions that had increasingly attracted attention from the likes
of philanthropists, educators, improvers, and religious missionaries. This
essay explores sight loss within a historical context in the late nineteenth and
early twentieth centuries, and the geographical scope is Scotland, notably
its capital city, Edinburgh, and the surrounding rural hinterland.[1] It uses the
archival records of two, sometimes complementary but sometimes competing, entities that endeavored to support and to direct the lives of people with
sight loss. One of these, the Royal Blind Asylum (RBA), Edinburgh, functioned within both a residential and nonresidential framework, catering for
what it saw as the able-bodied blind and therefore operating through the
provision of both work for adults and, from 1876, education for children and
young people. The other, the "Edinburgh Society for Promoting Reading
amongst the Blind on Moon's System" (ESPRB) focused on the "outdoor"
blind—that is, blind people who mostly lived in their own homes rather than
in or near institutional settings and who were generally considered unable,
often through old age or infirmity, to work to support themselves.[2]

For this essay, the concept of "environment" is given a broad interpretation and from several perspectives: geographical environment (urban/rural);
familial versus institutional environments; and top-down cultural environments often emanating from well-meaning but agenda-driven interventionists such as religious evangelists, philanthropists, and benefactors. The essay
also considers blind peoples' perspectives on outside interventions into their

lives, lives where environments expecting of gratitude toward outside benevolence were created by interventionists, but where there were also environments of rejection and rebellion against well-intended external patronage
and direction. The term *disability*, which collectivizes a wide range of impairing conditions and circumstances, is a relatively modern one. For example, Henri-Jacques Stiker has questioned whether "disability and handicap [are] one and the same thing."[3] In his original discourse on disability's
history, he wrestled with "how . . . to classify and divide the disabled" until
deciding "to focus on the tendency toward fusion into a generic 'disabled
person,'" a process enabled "on the level of social treatment," a progression
facilitated by the rise of the social model.[4] *Blindness* is another collective
term for a range of degrees and experiences of impaired vision.[5] "Blind society" within the context of this essay was remote from the British colonial
project across a global empire but was subject to the elite gaze that was often
nurtured by the spoils of colonialism. "Blind society" was othered in a manner similar to that experienced by Indigenous people in colonized lands and
whose sense of otherness was influenced by eugenic ideas of the time.[6] Environmental influences were pervasive, affecting those with sight loss by
placing boundaries to their worlds in industrial, urban complexes or in rural idylls where the presence of family and neighbors provided some elasticity
to otherwise confining parameters. Yet in the contrasting urban/rural landscapes, external efforts were being made to create a social environment shaped
by paternalistic intervention. These overtures were absorbed by blind people
who felt helpless to resist, were used to advantage when it suited them, or were
deflected or rejected by them with various degrees of success and failure.

While this is a localized study in a national context, historical records present opportunities for the essay to highlight elements of colonial, imperial,
and international connections. These connections are explored and interpreted in several ways, such as by consideration of interchange of ideas that
occurred between Scottish benefactors and supporters of the blind and their
counterparts in Europe, North America, and other parts of the globe, and
through examples of blind people with empire-connected families or associations. While the environments that predominated were a variety of
institutional settings, there were also environments without institutional
impact and where it was often domestic and familial environments that were
highly influential. The essay is based primarily on original source records
for blind organizations, notably the Royal Blind Asylum and School, Edinburgh,[7] and on the activities of outdoor blind missionaries working for the
Edinburgh Society for Promoting Reading amongst the Blind, which served
outdoor blind people across southeast Scotland while various sister societies
were gradually established in other regions to create a national network
"whose field of operations embraced all Scotland, including the Orkney and

Shetland islands."[8] A register of outdoor blind people in Edinburgh and south-east Scotland, in use between c. 1903 and c. 1910, provides interesting insight to blind lives because the incomplete nature of many entries on its pages indicates that the society's outreach was spurned by many blind people.[9]

Environment, Geography, and Family

"Blind" people in late nineteenth- and early twentieth-century Scotland were by no means a homogenous group. Individual life experiences were shaped by when their sight loss occurred and the degree of vision impairment, by their day-to-day living environment, their networks of family and friends, their material and physiological circumstances, and numerous other factors. In an exploration of the lives of outdoor blind people living at the beginning of the twentieth century in Edinburgh and its neighboring counties, research has shown that "every one of them was an individual and their life courses embraced varied experiences of dependence and independence, vigour and ill-health, assertive willpower or deteriorating mental well-being."[10] Through individuals' life journeys, circumstances and their living environments were subject to change, this also affecting their practical and their physiological needs.

Charles Warren writes that "it is easy to imagine that the climate and the environment exist simply as an unchanging, passive backdrop to human history. The reality, of course, is that neither is ever static; human histories have been played out in concert with complex environmental histories."[11] Certainly this was true of nineteenth-century Scotland when agricultural innovation and industrialization made a massive impact on the rural and urban landscapes. Historian T. M. Devine highlights this when he writes that in the 1830s, "just over one-third of the Scottish population lived in towns of over 5,000 inhabitants, [but] by 1911 this proportion had risen to nearly 60 per cent."[12] These changes were complex and the environments experienced by blind people affiliated to the RBA were in stark contrast to those falling under the paternal, evangelizing visits of the outdoor blind missionaries. While many blind handicraft workers—who were engaged in manufacturing with rope, cane, hessian, and similar commodities provided by the RBA—lived in their own homes, usually in proximity to the asylum workshops, their status as "able-bodied" blind was often dependent on the benevolence of the RBA.[13] This was highlighted in instances where individuals transgressed the RBA's regulations, which were often moralistic in nature, and they were consequently ejected from continued RBA patronage. An example of this and its consequences is found in the case of Thomas Manderson, who, as a young man, was an RBA outworker, employed as a weaver, but who had originally been admitted as a ten-year-old inmate in 1825.[14] In

1846, he requested permission to marry Agnes Miller, a partially sighted day worker in the RBA Female Department.[15] The institution expected compliance with a protocol where blind people under its protection requested RBA approval of their wish to marry. This requirement was an assault on the independent agency of Manderson and Miller, but blind people under the RBA's patronage had little option other than to comply. The couple nonetheless followed this edict, but trouble ensued when it was learned that Miller was pregnant and that Manderson was the father. Rather than being credited for proposing to do the "honorable thing," both were dismissed from the institution.[16] They duly married, but three weeks after their dismissal, it was learned that the couple were in "great want"; consequently, Manderson was reluctantly readmitted.[17] Manderson's able-bodiedness, defined through his ability to perform a skilled handicraft and earn a living wage, was ultimately dependent on the RBA's magnanimity and to his agreeing to conform to rules that would not be applied in the same way to sighted people, or indeed to the disabled outdoor blind. Of the blind school pupils, historian Olive Checkland has noted that "those who could become financially independent after leaving were regarded as prize pupils," an observation that shows that Manderson, who as a child attended blind school, was typical of the vast majority of blind adults in that no matter how productive a worker he was under blind workshop patronage, he was found to struggle when independence was thrust on him.[18]

The outdoor blind were generally classified as "disabled" blind because they were unable to work. Some did work—in occupations that included basket- and net-making, wheel turning, sheephead-singeing, hair and oakum teasing, beehive making, dealing in victuals, selling newspapers and tea, and performing or teaching music.[19] However, these working outdoor blind often did not earn enough to survive without the support of family members, friends, charity, or poor relief. Nonetheless, as outdoor blind they lived in an environment that offered them significant independence and control. The ESPRB gave welfare support to a few of the people on its register, notably after its receipt of a generous bequest in 1905.[20] Ultimately, the ESPRB's name was suggestive of providing training to read embossed print, but the underlying agenda of its missionaries was religious evangelism. The missionaries were counseled that "to be useful in this work, union to Jesus Christ is indispensable. [You are to] read chiefly select portions from the Scriptures . . . [ensure that] no trashy light reading [is] allowed . . . [and] above all, seek the glory of God in the salvation of the people visited, never forgetting the words of our Lord—'Lo, I am with you alway [sic], even unto the end of the world.'"[21] This approach was not unique to the ESPRB; other outdoor blind societies followed a similar ethos. For example, the Mission to Outdoor Blind for Glasgow and the West of Scotland, which promoted reading with the Alston system of raised type, instructed its officers that "while it is not desired that secular subjects should be altogether avoided, you are expected as much as possible to lead the conversation on to religious subjects, so as to promote their temporal and eternal welfare."[22] This strategy was what Checkland saw as a "programme of piety" where the Scottish churches sought "to stay the tide of secularism and to recall the nation to God and his worship" in which "the philanthropists . . . were the driving force."[23] Furthermore, historical geographer Hazel McFarlane identifies particular concern on the part of RBA directors that women inmates should undergo "a purifying process of strict adherence to religious regimes" and that "Christianity and expressions of Christian beliefs indicated the taming of a savage, animal-like group, and cleansing females of their immoral, depraved, dirty origins was crucial in the purification process."[24]

However, many blind people rejected proselytizing strategies, with one of the ESPRB missionaries recording, seemingly with some despair, that "sometimes in the country we are at first looked upon with suspicion, and several visits are necessary to convince our new friends that we have come all the way from the city to see them and interest ourselves in their welfare."[25] These words were written in 1910, a decade after John Brown, the founding missionary, had retired, and after those following in his wake, while committed to the religious ethos, conducted their work with perhaps a slightly softer touch. Nonetheless, a significant number of the outdoor blind, who the ESPRB's missionaries endeavored to befriend, continued to give them short shrift, as they had more pressing concerns than learning how to read scriptures with their fingers. It may therefore be argued that, in some ways, the "disabled" outdoor blind could exercise greater agency and live in an environment that offered them greater freedom and independence than the "able-bodied" blind who were dependent on the RBA and had to bow to its demand for godliness and respectability in return for its provision of employment and the opportunity to earn a living. Outdoor blind resistance eventually resulted in the ESPRB's embossed book-lending service adjusting its diet of biblical texts of the 1860s to a more varied literary catalog by the Edwardian period, and its accommodation of Braille books as well as those in Moon.[26]

Toward the end of John Brown's four-decade tenure as head missionary of ESPRB, his antagonism toward the RBA was suggested by his comments in the 1896 Annual Report:

Let me, as in former years, emphasise the fact that this Society is in no way connected with the "Edinburgh Royal Blind Asylum." That institution, I believe, is doing good work on its own lines.[27]

While distancing the ESPRB from the RBA in this manner, Brown was none-theless aware of what the RBA practiced. The two organizations were well acquainted with each other's activities, as demonstrated three years later, when fifty volumes of scripture in Moon type were gifted to the ESPRB by the RBA (which used Braille).[28] Furthermore, in 1901, Brown's successor, Charles Ness, expressed his view "that to provide work is the sphere of the Blind Asylum."[29] Ultimately, both organizations aspired to encourage religious virtue in the blind people under their influence, ESPRB in teaching reading of Moon script and the RBA in laying down its expectations when providing employ-ment to the "able-bodied" blind. They had similar goals but operated in differ-ent environments, and blind people embraced these competing institutional environments at different stages of their lives as their individual circumstances made expedient.[30]

As is demonstrated later in this essay, the RBA garnered international interest, notably through its school. The ESPRB's activities were more local-ized, occasional forays to the Orkney and Shetland islands, which lie beyond the north coast of Scotland, being its prime claim to "overseas" activity and beginning in 1869.[31] However, the ESPRB did have a small measure of inter-national engagement. For example, it received a £500 legacy from expatriate Scottish merchants in New York in 1871,[32] and sent religious books in Moon type to New Zealand in 1879. Speakers addressing the Society's annual gen-eral "Tea Meeting" addressed audiences on their experiences in other parts of the world, an example being the Reverend Dr. J. H. Wilson, who waxed lyrical about Egypt. He told his audience:

> The land was covered with blind people, and the number was grow-ing. One reason of this was the terrible heat of the sun, and another was the sand. A snow storm here [Scotland] was not to be compared with a sand storm in Egypt. The sand got into the eyes, and so did the flies, and as the people had a superstition which prevent them removing the flies, these insects carried disease from one person to another. The poor people there longed to have skilled professional treatment, and he hoped they would see the day when Edinburgh would send out a medical missionary, who would be received with open arms, and by none more gladly than the Blind.[33]

The ESPRB's adherence and commitment to the Moon system of em-bossed type did not stop at the purchase and promotion of William Moon's books but actively echoed the publisher's declaration that his was a "Chris-tian work . . . work that has been carried on with prayer and faith."[34] Moon traveled extensively and the missionary nature of his raised-type publishing took the parochial reach of the ESPRB and similar outdoor blind societies on to a truly colonial, imperial, and global stage—as periodically publicized in the Edinburgh society's annual reports. An ESPRB overview in 1883 gave a long list of languages embraced by Moon type. Languages in the Moon catalog included Arabic, Armenian, Bengali, Danish, Dutch, French, German, Hindustani, Irish, Japanese, Malayalam, Norse, Tahitian, Tamil, and Turkish, while Moon's linguistic scope embraced several Chinese dialects, and claimed that the Lord's Prayer and "tester sheets" were provided in 194 tongues.[35] So, although the ESPRB was a regional body, it could claim affiliation to a world-wide, multilanguage corpus through its devotion to Moon type.

Interventionist Networks

By the second half of the nineteenth century, the sailing ship had increasingly given way to the steamship; international travel required commitment of time and money, so, apart from emigrant voyages, it was primarily a privilege reserved for the comfortable classes with freedom to absent themselves from business cares for long periods. It was people of this social status who were at the forefront of funding and directing bodies designed to "organize" the lives of people marginalized by impairing circumstances such as sight loss. Edinburgh's Royal Blind Asylum was an important port of call for worldwide patrons of and contributors to blind philanthropy, as is demonstrated by visitor book entries, notably for the RBA's school at West Craigmillar between 1876 and 1948.

Developments in transport by sea and by rail were also accompanied by ever-expanding and efficient postal services. Correspondence between blind organizations became commonplace; this included the exchange of annual reports produced by asylums, workshops, schools, and missions—to which notes were frequently attached requesting reciprocation. The RBA was very much part of these exchanges, and it received printed reports from throughout the United Kingdom and from abroad. For example, publications received in the late 1870s include several reports from Europe such as *Wirksamkeit des Preussuschen Provinzial-Vereins für Blinden-Unterricht zu Königsberg*, the Prussian provincial organization for blind teaching in what is now Kaliningrad, Russia; *Kriftiania Blindeinftitut*, the Blind Institution of Oslo, Norway; *Instituut tot Onderwijs van Blinden et van her Gesticht voor Volwassen Blinden te Amsterdam*, the Institute for the Education of the Blind and of the Blind Adult Asylum at Amsterdam; and *Institut des Sourds-Muets et des Aveugles de Varsovie*, The Deaf-Dumb and Blind Institute of Warsaw. Presented in beautiful Gothic script—𝕯𝖎𝖊 𝕭𝖊𝖌𝖊𝖌𝖓𝖎𝖋𝖋𝖊 𝖚𝖓𝖉 𝕭𝖊𝖗𝖒ö𝖌𝖊𝖓𝖘𝖌𝖊-𝖇𝖆𝖍𝖗𝖚𝖓𝖌 𝖉𝖊𝖗 𝖁𝖊𝖗𝖋𝖔𝖗𝖌𝖚𝖓𝖌𝖘- 𝖚. 𝕭𝖊𝖑𝖈𝖍ä𝖋𝖙𝖎𝖌𝖚𝖓𝖌𝖘𝖆𝖓𝖙𝖆𝖑𝖙 𝖋ü𝖗 𝖊𝖗𝖜𝖆𝖈𝖍𝖋𝖊𝖓𝖊 𝕭𝖑𝖎𝖓𝖉𝖊 𝖎𝖓 𝕽ö𝖍𝖒𝖊𝖓—was a report from Röhmen in Baden-Württemberg, and the same style is used by Copenhagen's Royal Blind Institute—𝕯𝖊𝖙 𝕶𝖔𝖓𝖌𝖊𝖑𝖎𝖌𝖊

𝕭𝖑𝖎𝖓𝖉𝖊-𝕴𝖓𝖘𝖙𝖎𝖙𝖚𝖙. American reports are suggestive of some institutions, such as New York Institution for the Blind, being all-embracing in their outreach to people with sight loss, but there is diversity of focus by other institutions specializing in such spheres as education, work and shelter, hearing loss as well as sight loss, gendered provision, and racial segregation. Those "specializations" are often emphasized in their names, such as Arkansas Institute for the Education of the Blind; Wisconsin Institution for the Education of the Blind; Maryland Institution for the Instruction of the Blind; Institution for Education of the Blind and the Industrial Home for the Blind [Louisiana]; Pennsylvania Working Home for Blind Men; Virginia Institution for the Education of the Deaf and Dumb and the Blind; and the Institution of the Colored Blind and Deaf-mutes [Maryland].[36]

Edinburgh's Royal Blind Asylum opened in 1793. The city's blind school, a separate enterprise from the asylum and its workshops, opened in 1835.[37] In 1876, the two institutions combined to form the Royal Edinburgh Blind Asylum and School; this heralded relocation of the school from the original building in Gayfield Square to a new residential school a few miles from the city center at West Craigmillar. Here it occupied an ornate three-story edifice, described in a report of the elaborate opening ceremony as embracing "a light French style of architecture."[38] The inauguration of the school at West Craigmillar, to be occupied by both girls and boys as well as some female blind adult residents, was a flamboyant occasion marked by a procession of, for example, Masonic Lodge delegates from across Scotland and a military band, and the event was attended by aristocratic and civic dignitaries and philanthropic supporters.[39] To record attendance at this august celebration, a Visitors Book was provided, and this continued in use to varying degrees for the next seven decades.[40]

The Visitors Book carries remarks by its many signatories, but these have limited value for gauging impressions garnered by this voyeuristic procession, it not being polite to their hosts to express observations that were anything other than complimentary. However, the Visitors Book does have value in recording for posterity the types of people who graced the school with their fleeting and chaperoned presence—and in indicating the international, colonial, and imperial as well as local/national domicile of individuals and groups. The Visitors Book reveals guests that included patrons and improvers, elites and clergy, and those with a professional interest in sensory impairment—hearing loss as well as sight loss.

The ritual of recording and signing at the conclusion of each visitation was often with brief and repetitive comments such as "much pleased," "much delighted," "much interested" that were ascribed constantly during the mid-1880s.[41] However, while what most guests said in the book may not offer particular insight to the school's lived environment, their identities show how elites gravitated to this and other institutions that they saw as offering succor and hope to "the suffering and helpless"—the words used by overseas missionary William McGregor in expressing his personal perception of life with sight loss.[42] Elites included landed aristocracy, such as the earls of Tweeddale, Breadalbane, Stair, Glenconner, and Leven and Melville, whose signatures were often accompanied by colorful hand-drawn representations of family crests highlighting their places at the heart of the British imperial establishment and their personal lived environments of country estates that were far removed from mainstream urban and rural life and were markedly very different from those of blind people under varying degrees of institutional control.

The international pull of West Craigmillar is conspicuous, and the affiliations of the blind school's guests show the institution to be on the front line of British imperial patronage and interest, attracting visitors from colonial outposts in Australia, Canada, India, New Zealand, and South Africa. Visitors also arrived from Argentina, China, Denmark, Egypt, Germany, Japan, Manchuria, Norway, Spain, Switzerland, Syria, Turkey, and the United States, these countries providing visitors to the RBA from a range of cities, provinces, or colonies. As might be expected, many of the international visitors to the RBA included the likes of religious missionaries or colonial careerists such as W. R. G. Moir, who described himself as "HM's Indian Civil Service" and who was a District and Sessions judge in Lucknow.[43] The Reverend R. Henderson "of Edinburgh and late of Victoria, Australia," writing in the third person, declared his passion for such visits:

> He has in different countries visited Asylums for the blind and had occasion to note the benefits their inmates gained from the industrial, educational, and religious privileges they engaged. He has to renew this testimony in regard to the Edinburgh Royal Blind Asylum and School after repeated visits. Having today had . . . opportunity for examining the Institution, he has been favourably impressed with the attainments of the children in all the branches of their education, and the success of the industrial department. The good order that prevails, and in evident cheerfulness and happiness of the inmates reflects the greatest credit to Mr and Mrs MacCulloch [the superintendent and his wife].[44]

There was also a particular interest from representatives of institutions across the world similarly established for people with sight loss—and hearing loss—and from others with associated professional interest in sensory impairment. These were in addition to a procession of representatives from English and Irish institutions to the RBA. In 1888, a representative of the Royal Institution for the Blind, Copenhagen, declared "very much interested," while a decade later the Inspector of Schools for the Blind from Kristiania (Oslo) was marginally more expansive when he recorded his appreciation "for looking of [sic] this excellent and well conducted institution."[45] In 1903, an American consular report lauded the founding by Branco Rodrigues of a blind school in Lisbon, Portugal, with "a new kind of industry" consisting of "unraveling or 'picking' vegetable fibers used as stuffing material for furniture, beds, etc."[46] Rodrigues founded two schools, the other being in the northern Portuguese city of Porto, and in this capacity he visited the Edinburgh blind school in 1909.[47] As ocean voyages became easier, more distant visitors included the manager of the Institute for the Blind, New South Wales, Australia, while from the United States the RBA hosted the superintendent of the Missouri School for the Blind, St. Louis, and two ladies representing the School for the Blind, New York City.[48] The Institute for the Blind at Overbrook, Pennsylvania, was established in 1832 and published the first volume of raised type in the United States; this early American institution was also represented when Miss Sadie Smyth arrived at West Craigmillar in 1902.[49]

The school Visitors Book shows an interesting interface between blindness and deafness. Florence Swainson, Church of England Zenana missionary, founded a deaf school, initially under the umbrella of the Sarah Tucker Institute for blind children, at Palamcotta (Palayamkottai) in the south of India in 1895.[50] Swainson visited West Craigmillar in 1909 when her school's focus was on industrial training, but around this time her school turned its attention to communication development and education, perhaps suggesting the influence of her observations from Edinburgh and elsewhere during her "tour." In the Edwardian period, Condi di Montornés, vice president of the Colegio di Sordo-Mudos y Ciegos di Valencia, arrived with a small delegation.[51] This Spanish institution was founded in 1887 to provide education for deaf children but soon after also began receiving scholars with sight loss.[52] It is apparent from the backgrounds of several visitors that those with an interest in hearing loss had an interest in practices used for sight loss, while combination of the two forms of sensory impairment in some locations was dictated by both need and availability of provision. Two years after Condi di Montornés's visit, T. C. Forrester arrived at West Craigmillar, describing himself as "previously of the School of Blind and Deaf, Overlea" (in Maryland). Later, his interest focused on hearing loss when he became superintendent at Maryland State School for the Deaf.[53]

In addition to those involved with institutions, there were individuals who had other professional or personal interests in sensory impairment, such as H. Gekmezian, professor of the deaf and dumb from Constantinople (Istanbul), Turkey.[54] Others of note included Adelaide Moon (1845–1914), who had worked closely with her father, Dr. William Moon (1818–1894), in the creation and promotion of the Moon system of raised type (favored by ESPRB),[55] while one of the later entries was that of the high-profile deaf-blind American, Helen Keller (1880–1968), who visited during the interwar years in the company of her secretary, Scotland native Polly Thomson (1885–1960), and her teacher, Anne Sullivan Macy (1866–1936).[56] The primary purpose of Keller's 1932 visit to Scotland was to receive an honorary Doctor of Laws degree from the University of Glasgow, but she wrote that her wider travels were "tremendously enriched" by "*The Holywood* [sic] *Collection of Scottish Verse*, which was presented to me at the Craigmillar School for the Blind,"[57] a volume that was reported as being "an anthology of modern Scottish Verse . . . a Braille book recently printed at the [Royal Blind Asylum]."[58]

The diverse international appeal of the RBA's school to visitors is further suggested by interesting signatories writing in the scripts of their native tongues.[59] While, in 1880, Elias al-Hawi signed solely in Arabic, other visitors inscribed bilingual entries that combined Roman script beside scripts of their native languages.[60] These were Kumar Gajendra Narayan from Koch Behar in India, who signed in Bengali; Liu Chuen Yao from Moukden (Shenyang) in Manchuria, who signed in beautiful Chinese script; and Hariprasad Bhagwanji Joshi, whose signature appeared in Hindi.[61] However, the motivation for Ji Duo-na, of "Wu-king-fu, South China" to sign in Chinese in 1895 may have been the signatory's way of emphasizing his having spent the last two decades in the east as a missionary and self-professed linguist.[62] "Duo-na" is a corruption of Donald (or "Dòmhnall" in Gaelic), and this was Reverend Donald Maciver (1852–1910), originally from the Scottish Highland parish of Foddarty. Soon after graduating from the University of Aberdeen, Maciver departed to Wukingfu (Wujing) on the Longjiang River in Guangdong province to work for the English Presbyterian Mission, and in 1905 he published an English-Hakka dictionary that ran to nearly fourteen hundred pages.[63] While there may have been an element of showmanship in some of these linguistically diverse entries, they further emphasize the global interchange that the institution was able to nurture.

Elias al-Hawi, full name Phadlallah Elias al-Hawi (1864–1933), was sixteen years of age when, newly arrived from Shweir, near Beirut (then in Syria), he visited West Craigmillar. Phadlallah Elias al-Hawi later embarked on medical training at the University of Edinburgh and subsequently became general practitioner in the parish of Strathdon, Aberdeenshire, where he lived for the remainder of his life.[64] Assimilating himself to permanent settlement in Scotland, the sixteen-year-old who signed his name in Arabic in the Visitors Book as al-Hawi also used the Scottish surname of Howie; this is how he appears in many official records. He married Jane Edith Fleming in 1902 and they had three daughters.[65] When he died in 1933, his contribution to the Strathdon community was lauded as "a fidelity that won the hearts and affection of the people," and his funeral was noted as "one of the largest in the district for many years."[66] Of the many overseas career imperialists and religious missionaries to appear in the RBA visitors book, Elias al-Hawi was an interesting exception; as a Syrian youth newly arrived from Beirut, he was embarking on a journey that changed his life course and resulted in his complete assimilation within the Highland community where he settled and gave medical succor for four decades. However, the records reveal that he shared some of his journey with a relative. Their exact relationship is not immediately clear, but Ghosn al-Hawi or Howie (1853–1916), who had sight loss due to adherent cataract, preceded Elias to Edinburgh, arriving in 1874 to join the blind asylum as a knitter and remaining until the following year.[67] Ghosn then studied at the University of Edinburgh until 1877, after which he returned to Syria for three years to run an industrial school for the blind.[68] He was back in Edinburgh in 1880, coinciding with Elias's visit and providing an interesting interface with the ESPRB in that he addressed the society's annual general meeting about his work in Beirut.[69] It is likely that his return to Edinburgh was also to chaperone his young relative; in 1881, they were both in lodgings in the city as "students."[70] While Elias ultimately spent his adult life in Scotland as a medical doctor, Ghosn went on to practice as a clergyman in Canada and then in his native Syria.[71]

The religious/moral ethos that guided institutions such as the RBA also presents itself in the Visitors Book, such as in 1879 when Reverend J. M. Eppstein wrote that he was "very much gratified and pleased, and wish[ed] the establishment success and God's abundant blessing."[72] Eppstein had been a Christian missionary to the Jews in Smyrna since 1867, where, three years later, he opened a mission house "which included a chapel, a dispensary, a reading-room and a Wanderers' home."[73] In 1881, William McGregor, a missionary visiting from Amoy, China (and mentioned earlier), exhibited candidly how he saw his religious convictions interface with society's "unfortunate." He, like many others, perceived people with sight loss to be "victims" without hope when he wrote that he "was very much impressed with the thought of what the suffering and helpless owe to Christ and Christianity."[74] A decade later, McGregor was to be found in Amoy "giving instructions to the students of the seminary" where it was noted that "many of the native helpers and unordained evangelists have spent one or two years under a special course of training."[75] These men were part of expanding Scottish nineteenth-century missionary outreach in a range of spheres that Esther Breitenbach notes reached a hiatus during "the period between 1880 and 1920 [that] was both the 'high imperial era' and the 'high missionary era.'"[76]

The West Craigmillar Visitors Book is not a source that provides critique by those making inspection tours, over a seven-decade period, of the blind school's conduct or care of its pupils. It does, however, provide evidence of the stream of people who made visits, including wealthy lay people from throughout the United Kingdom and from across the world, whose numbers included people with a professional interest in children and young people with sensory impairments. The Visitors Book places the RBA in the mainstream of a colonial, imperial, and international environment of elites with freedom to travel the world and to engage in periodic displays of philanthropic, professional, and religious patronage. However, to gauge how blind people thought about their personal situations and living environments, we must look elsewhere.

Experiences of the Blind Population

In sharp contrast to the cosmopolitan flow of visitors surveying the RBA workshops and especially the school, the people falling under the benevolent care of the institution originated almost totally from Scotland. There were small numbers from England and Wales. Likewise, those from Ireland were also few, with ten people identified, mostly from the early nineteenth century before the introduction of the poor law to Ireland in 1838 and before reform of church poor law provision in Scotland to civic provision in 1845.[77]

The small number of Irish cases shows the diversity of circumstances of those coming under the paternalism of the RBA from beyond Scotland. Although Ireland became an integral part of the United Kingdom in 1800, to many in Ireland this development was viewed as colonization, a view that did not diminish as the century progressed. As a question that continues to be debated, it is worth considering that those cases designated as belonging to Ireland might include some who may have lived in Scotland for many years.[78] Seven cases were admitted during the time when poor law provision was made by parish churches at a local level, while three would have fallen under the civil relief provisions of the Poor Law (Scotland) Act of 1845, also known as the New Poor Law, and which was often diligent in weeding out paupers who did not have a strong claim to aid from a Scottish parish.[79] All Irish blind falling under the RBA were adult males except for Catherine McArthur, a sixteen-year-old who had been blind from infancy and who undertook some sewing and spinning. She had been recommended to the RBA by the minister and heritors (i.e., ratepayers) of the Scottish parish of Ayr. Cause or nature of sight loss is given for seven of the nine men, showing some diversity including amaurosis, inflammation, ophthalmia, accident, and explosion of gunpowder. The record for the ophthalmia case, twenty-two-year-old Henry McWhinney, admitted in 1816, shows that he had been in military service in Egypt.[80] Four, one of whom was Catherine McArthur, were ultimately dismissed by the RBA.[81] These dismissals occurred several years after they had been placed on the RBA register and provide interesting insights to the tensions that might occur in institutional environments. One dismissal by the RBA directors was Peter Cunningham, expelled after a stay of seven years because, with another man, he "had absconded from the Asylum . . . and . . . had been detained at Dunbar by the Chief Magistrate and sent back to Edinburgh"; consequently, it was recorded that, "considering the evil consequences, of such an example, the [directors'] meeting approved of these parties being refused admission to the House."[82] The other six all died while still at the RBA, highlighting significant lifelong affiliation once under the institution's benevolence and control.[83]

Besides Ghosn al-Hawi, there are only three cases identified in the admission register of the RBA who were designated as coming from the wider reach of the British Empire, and one of those is spurious—that of ten-year-old Loisa Paradies of Durban, South Africa. It may have been overenthusiasm on the part of the RBA for her to have been entered into the register as being admitted on January 22, 1902—only for this to have subsequently been countermanded by the remark "Did not enter. Schedule not returned."[84] If Loisa was an anticipated catch from good colonial stock, the RBA had to wait more than two decades before a similar opportunity arose with the arrival of Lily Eleanor Burke. Lily was born c. 1900 and was a member of what might be termed a typical Raj family. Her father was Miles Aloysius Burke, a racehorse trainer from Assam; her mother was Lily Christiana Burke (née Towers) (1862–1927), widow of Robert Clint Chill (b. 1853 in Agra, d. 1898 in Penang)—a family with deep roots in India and Burma.[85] It was in the aftermath of her mother's death in Malaya in 1927 that, on October 19, 1928, Lily Eleanor was admitted to the RBA, age twenty-eight, as a parlor boarder at an annual fee of £50.[86] Lily spent two decades with the RBA, until February 1949, when she was transferred from its Thomas Burns residential home for ladies in Edinburgh to the town of Hawick in the Scottish Borders.[87] This move was occasioned by her admission to St. Andrews Convent, where Augustinian nuns managed a care home. Lily's removal had, it seems, come about by the onset of "acute mania with confusion," which was later compounded by acute lobar pneumonia. At age forty-eight, her death occurred after only a few weeks in Hawick, her modest affairs being administered by a brother on his arrival from London to register her demise.[88]

The other "colonial" admission to the RBA arrived earlier than these cases and was of humbler stock. Michael George James was registered on September 8, 1894, as a fifteen-year-old, denoted as being from Kyzabad (Faizabad), India, and under the sponsorship of Edinburgh School Board at £15 per session. However, eighteen months later he was reclassified as an adult, and responsibility for his referral to the RBA passed to Edinburgh Parish Council, in effect identifying him as a destitute pauper.[89] However, the Parish Council's financial responsibility for him was brief, as he died on

October 16, 1896, age seventeen, his death registration revealing that he was then living close to the blind asylum workshops, where he was employed as a brush maker.[90] Both parents were deceased, and his father, also named Michael, had not been a beneficiary of imperial wealth exploitation but had been a sergeant in the King's Own Scottish Borderers who then worked as a laborer after his discharge from the military with a small army pension. Michael (Senior) died on January 22, 1894, at Edinburgh's Longmore Hospital, a long-stay institution for "incurables"; his wife, Elizabeth, had predeceased him, so their son Michael's ultimate need for material support had fallen on the blind school later that year.[91]

In 1915, as military personnel experienced traumatic sight loss during the Great War, RBA set up a sister organization called Scottish War Blinded (SWB), which catered to soldiers and sailors with foreign experience. SWB was to have an enduring role that has now lasted for more than a century.[92] Alec MacKenzie had two decades of working in the Far East after the Great War. This came to an end for him in 1941, when Japan occupied Singapore and Malaya, and he is an example of the continuity of the Great War–inspired SWB organization, under the auspices of RBA, where conflict inevitably gives an international flavor even as the British colonial period was gradually ending.[93]

If there are few "international" blind people appearing in the registers and records for the blind asylum and school, it might be expected that people appearing on the Register for the Outdoor Blind, generally noted for their poverty and dependency, would be even less likely to exhibit cosmopolitanism. They had broad experience of town and rural environments, not least because they were not institutionalized but rather living their lives in various local contexts. However, there was one exception, Sir Alexander Hope, 15th Baronet, who resided in a forty-one-room mansion, Pinkie House, near the town of Musselburgh. His inclusion in the Outdoor Blind Register was probably no more than a bit of name dropping that alluded to the reality that no matter one's station in life, everyone is vulnerable to sight loss. Hope (1824–1918) had served in the Bengal Civil Service from 1845 to 1875; when his name was entered on the register, he was at an advanced age, which was probably why he was declared "blind." While he may have been a colorful character, the minimalist entry for Alexander Hope in the outdoor blind register suggests that he was one of those who declined to engage with the missionaries and their evangelizing efforts among the outdoor blind.[94]

Conclusion

In a collection that focuses on environment and colonialism, the study of blind experience in a region of one country, Scotland, offered by this essay may seem to be micro and even peripheral to the wider concepts under investigation. However, I argue that, in this case, there were wide divisions and contrasts in international and colonial experience depending on not just whether people lived with sight loss but where they were positioned within the social milieu of Scottish society. Breadth or constraint of environmental experience depended on whether, as an "able-bodied" blind person, one was dependent on the blind asylum for work, education, and sustenance or whether as one of the "disabled" outdoor blind, one "benefited" from the relative freedom that was offered from the loose nature of philanthropic direction and intervention emanating from the ESPRB.

This investigation shows that moral ethics and religion played a particularly important role in Victorian and Edwardian Scotland. Those who aided, supported, and rallied blind people under the umbrellas of philanthropic organizations, such as the RBA and ESPRB, came from the respectable classes, people who adhered to religiously motivated philanthropy and patronage and who exercised, to quote historian Callum Brown, their "bourgeois values and separateness through the power of mission work to improve society."[95] Numbers of these wealthy patrons enjoyed links with far-flung parts of the world; this is reflected in the visits made to the blind school at West Craigmillar but also demonstrates networks of people who had involvement with European, North American, and colonial society and who endeavored to engage with the lives of children and adults with sensory impairments. Notable among these were religious missionaries and evangelists who held the belief that blind people needed to be "saved" because their deprivation of sight meant that they were denied access to the Bible and Christian teachings. In Scotland, this belief was the motivation for the formation of outdoor blind societies headed by missionaries whose objectives of inviting blind people to learn to read various styles of embossed print was firmly focused on teaching that skill using scriptural texts. Some blind people responded positively to such overtures, learning to read the scriptures and welcoming the insights and comfort they felt these texts offered them in their darkened worlds. However, there were others, both those classed as outdoor blind and those affiliated to the RBA, who had little time for well-meaning people who wished to save their souls.

Very few blind people had opportunity to stray beyond either the city streets around the RBA or the environment of their local parish. The closest they ever got to the exotic places of empire occurred through the embossed pages of the occasional raised-type book that romanticized these far-off places through verbal images of native peoples with flamboyant costumes and unfamiliar customs, jungle wildlife both beautiful and dangerous, palaces, temples, and fragrant bazaars.[96] These readers' own environments were the noisy streets of Edinburgh close to the blind workshops, the strict and structured classrooms of West Craigmillar, and, for outdoor blind, their networks of family and friends in city and countryside.

Investigation of the experience of living with sight loss in Edinburgh and its hinterland of small towns, villages, and agricultural smallholdings, accompanied by research of the benefactors of blind people, brings together the three themes of this collection—disability, colonialism, and environment. The blind residents of Edinburgh and nearby counties inhabited diverse environments. They were participants in urban workshops and rural husbandry; they variously lived in both community settings and in the regulatory environments of the RBA's residential, employment, or educational facilities. Notably, their worlds were in sharp contrast to environments experienced by many of their patrons and supporters. The fruits of colonial exploitation permeated Scottish society, and the wealthy classes especially benefited from these and from careers that often placed them in positions of commercial, evangelistic, or humanitarian influence and power, self-justified by their belief that they were part of a "civilizing" mission in territories across the world. Disability, in the form of sight loss in this particular study, created a dynamic that brought together people from diverse environments—namely, the blind population of the southeast of Scotland and the philanthropically motivated moneyed classes whose comfortable lives and wealth had been aided, directly or indirectly, by the power dynamic of colonization.

NOTES

1. I would like to express my gratitude to the Strathmartine Trust for an award that aided the research for this essay.

2. Works that provide historical context for the RBA and the Scottish outdoor blind societies include the following: R. Meldrum, *Light on Dark Paths: A Handbook* (Edinburgh: John Menzies, 1883); Gordon Phillips, *The Blind in British Society: Charity, State and Community* (Aldershot: Ashgate, 2004); Helen Dunbar, *History of the Society for the Blind in Glasgow and the West of Scotland* (Glasgow: Glasgow and West of Scotland Society for the Blind, 1989); Iain Hutchison, *Feeling Our History: The Experience of Blindness and Sight Loss in Edwardian Edinburgh, The Lothians and The Borders* (Edinburgh: RNIB, 2015); and Hazel MacFarlane, "Out of Sight, Out of Mind: Blind Asylums and Missions in Scotland," in *The Routledge History of Disability*, ed. Roy Hanes, Ivan Brown, and Nancy E. Hansen (London: Routledge, 2017), 273–98. H. J. Wagg and Mary G. Thomas provide a comprehensive overview of the early blind organizations in Scotland in *A Chronological Survey of Work for the Blind* (London: Pitman, 1932).

3. Henri-Jacques Stiker, *A History of Disability* (Ann Arbor: Michigan Press, 1999), 121, translated by William Sayers from *Corps infirmes et sociétiés* (Paris: Éditions Dunod, 1997), revised from original text published by Éditions Aubier Montaigne, 1982.

4. Ibid., 186.

5. From 1851, the decennial Scottish census asked, in a manner that left discretion as to interpretation of the individual members of each household, "Whether blind or deaf-and-dumb." In 1911, the census administrators decided that blindness meant being "totally blind." Consequently, in the world of official statistics, blind people with some residual vision therefore became sighted again, including some of those who might be residents of institutions for blind children or adults.

6. The term *eugenics* was coined by Francis Galton (1822–1911) in 1883 when he wrote of "the science of improving the human stock through selective breeding" in *Inquiries into the Human Faculty and Its Development* (London: Dent, 1883), 24–25.

7. From 2021, known as "Sight Scotland."

8. Lothian Health Service Archive (LHSA), Edinburgh Society for Promoting Reading amongst the Blind (ESRPB), 1886 Annual Report, GD52/1/1/1, 5.

9. Iain Hutchison, "The Value of a Flawed Source: The Register of the Missions to Outdoor Blind for Edinburgh, the Borders and the Lothians, c. 1903–10," *Scottish Archives* 22 (2016): 98–117.

10. Hutchison, *Feeling Our History*, 98.

11. Charles Warren, *Managing Scotland's Environment*, 2nd ed. (Edinburgh: Edinburgh University Press, 2009), 8.

12. T. M. Devine, *The Scottish Nation 1700–2000* (London: Penguin, 1999), 253.

13. See William Auchincloss (*A Few Statistics in Connection with the Blind in Scotland* [Glasgow, 1886], 16), who lists making baskets, mattresses, palliases, mats, sacks, and brushes as activities providing notable employment to blind workers. Auchincloss was one of the commissioners on the Royal Commission on the Blind, 1889.

14. Royal Blind Asylum and School (RBAS), Register of Admissions 1793–1963 (RA), Thomas Manderson, No. 164; Decennial census for St. Cuthberts, Edinburgh, 1851.

15. RBAS, Minute Book 1835–49, August 10, 1846, 370.

16. Ibid.

17. Ibid., August 31, 1846, 372.

18. Olive Checkland, *Philanthropy in Victorian Scotland: Social Welfare and the Voluntary Principle* (Edinburgh: John Donald, 1980), 273.

19. LHSA, ESPRB, 1868 Annual Report, GD52/1/1/1, 4.

20. LHSA, ESPRB, 1906 Annual Report, GD52/1/1/3, 1.

21. LHSA, ESPRB, 1897 Annual Report, GD52/1/1/2, 15.

22. LHSA, Outdoor Blind Society for Glasgow and the West of Scotland, 1862 Annual Report, GD52/1/1/1, 4.

23. Checkland, *Philanthropy in Victorian Scotland*, 30.

24. McFarlane, "Out of Sight, Out of Mind," 279.

25. LHSA, ESPRB, 1910 Annual Report, GD52/1/1/4, 5.

26. LHSA, ESPRB, 1863 Annual Report, GD52/1/1/1, 3; 1870 Annual Report, GD52/1/1/1, 5; 1903 Annual Report, GD52/1/1/3, 4.

27. LHSA, ESPRB, 1896 Annual Report, GD52/1/1/2, 3.

28. LHSA, ESPRB, 1900 Annual Report, GD52/1/1/3, 5.

29. LHSA, ESPRB, 1901 Annual Report, GD52/1/1/3, 5.

30. Hutchison, *Feeling Our History*, 3.

31. LHSA, ESPRB, 1870 Annual Report, GD52/1/1/1, 4.

32. LHSA, ESPRB, 1872 Annual Report, GD52/1/1/1, 1.

33. LHSA, ESPRB, 1885 Annual Report, GD52/1/1/1, 7.

34. William Moon, *Light for the Blind: A History of the Origin and Success of Moon's System of Reading for the Blind* (London: Longman, 1875), vii.

35. LHSA, ESPRB, 1883 Annual Report, GD52/1/1/1, 12; John Rutherford, *William Moon LLD FRGS FSA and His Work for the Blind* (London: Hodder and Stoughton, 1898), 241.

36. RBAS, External Institution Reports.

37. "West Craigmillar Institution for the Blind," *Daily Review,* May 22, 1877.

38. "Edinburgh Royal Blind Asylum and School," *The Scotsman,* May 16, 1876.

39. "Royal Blind Asylum and School at West Craigmillar," *The Scotsman,* May 23, 1876.

40. The RBA archive also holds visitor books for the workshops in Edinburgh's Nicolson Street, but these lack the richness of the West Craigmillar School Visitors Book (WCSVB).

41. RBAS, West Craigmillar School Visitors Book (WCSVB), August 1884–May 1885.

42. WCSVB, 1881.

43. WCSVB, October 8, 1904; *The India List and India Office List for 1905* (London: Harrison and Sons, 1905), 54.

44. WCSVB, June 17, 1881.

45. WCSVB, July 13, 1888, and c. 1897/8.

46. "Consular Reports: Commerce, Manufactures, Etc.," 71, no. 269 (United States Bureau of Foreign Commerce, 1903): 611.

47. WCSVB, September 13, 1909.

48. WCSVB, July 10, 1902; August 18, 1902; 1903.

49. Edith Willoughby, *Overbrook School for the Blind* (Charleston, SC: Acadia, 2007); WCSVB, 1902.

50. WCSVB, September 23, 1909; M. Miles, *Disability Care & Education in 19th-Century India: Dates, Places & Documentation* (Birmingham, England: Miles, May 1997), 31–34.

51. WCSVB, c. 1905/6.

52. Amparo Casado Melo, "Antecendentes de la Educación de Ciegos y Sordos en España," *Papeles Salmantinos de Educación* 12 (2009): 139.

53. WCSVB, c. 1911/12; Bulletin, 1917, No. 43, *Educational Directory, 1917–18* (Washington: Government Printing Office, 1917), 136.

54. WCSVB, November 8, 1895.

55. WCSVB, June 17, 1901, and June 21, 1905.

56. WCSVB, June 20, 1932.

57. Helen Keller, *Helen Keller in Scotland* (London: Methuen, 1933), 126. The presentation book would appear to be W. H. Hamilton, ed., *Holyrood: A Garland of Modern Scots Poems,* (London: J. M. Dent, 1929) and subsequently published (2 vols.) in Braille. I thank Rod Hunt of the Scottish Poetry Library for this information.

58. "Helen Keller in Edinburgh, Visit to the Blind Children," *Edinburgh Evening News,* June 20, 1932.

59. For linguistic insights, I would like to thank friends and colleagues Lin Shi, Nasser Smiley, Pegah Shahbaz, and Suchitra Choudhury for their assistance with the WCSVB entries discussed in this section.

60. WCSVB, October 9, 1880.

61. WCSVB, September 1879, undated 1897, and April 18, 1899.

62. WCSVB, December 16, 1895.

63. Zhijun Tian, "A Chinese-English Dictionary: Hakka Dialects Spoken in Kwangtung Province and Its Writers" (in Chinese at www.sinoss.net). D. MacIver, *A Chinese-English Dictionary: Hakka Dialect as Spoken in Kwang-tung Province* (Shanghai: Presbyterian Missionary Society, 1905).

64. For assistance in pursuing the paper trail for Phadlallah Elias al-Hawi, I am grateful to Peter Duffus, administrator of the Glenbuchat Heritage website.

65. Registration of Marriage, Edinburgh, 1902; Decennial Census for Strathdon, 1911.

66. "Death of Dr. P. E. Howie," *Aberdeen Press and Journal*, April 24, 1933; "Highland Honours in Strathdon," *Aberdeen Press and Journal*, April 26, 1933.

67. RBAS, RA, 14, No. 561.

68. Amanda Burstein, "The Significance of Costume in the Howie Family Portrait" at http://canadianportraits.concordia.ca/analysis/2_BURSTEIN-NPG3-FINAL_DV .pdf, accessed March 23, 2020; LHSA, ESPRB, 1881 Annual Report, GD52/1/1/1, 7.

69. LHSA, ESPRB, 1881 Annual Report, GD52/1/1/1, 7.

70. Decennial census for St. Leonards, Edinburgh, 1881.

71. *The Canada Presbyterian*, December 7, 1892, 3; Burstein, "Significance of Costume."

72. WCSVB, July 7, 1879.

73. Gidney William Thomas, *A History of the London Society for Promoting Christianity amongst the Jews* (London: Society for Promoting Christianity amongst the Jews, 1908), 383.

74. WCSVB, c. October 1881.

75. P. W. Pitcher, *Fifty Years in Amoy or, a History of the Amoy Mission, China* (New York: Reformed Church in America, 1893), 177–78.

76. Esther Breitenbach, *Empire and Scottish Society: The Impact of Foreign Missionaries at Home, c. 1790 to c. 1914* (Edinburgh: Edinburgh University Press, 2009), 57.

77. Donnacha Seán Lucey, *The End of the Irish Poor Law: Welfare and Healthcare Reform in Revolutionary and Independent Ireland* (Manchester: Manchester University Press, 2015); Rosalind Mitchison, *The Old Poor Law in Scotland: The Experience of Poverty, 1574–1845* (Edinburgh: Edinburgh University Press, 2000).

78. Terence McDonough, ed., *Was Ireland a Colony? Economics, Politics and Culture in Nineteenth-Century Ireland* (Dublin: Irish Academic Press, 2005).

79. More than two decades passed between the admission of Peter Cunningham in 1826 and William Paterson in 1848, which is perhaps explained by a response from the RBA to an inquiry from Dublin in 1933. The RBA declined to receive this Irish case because "funds do not permit [the RBA] to receive all the Applicants from Scotland, [therefore] it would be impossible to listen to those from Ireland." RBAS, Minute Book 1825–35, June 17, 1833, 288. Following the 1845 Act, Irish paupers would frequently be returned to Ireland, such as J. C., who, in 1869, was given lessons in reading by Moon's System by the outdoor missionary until "he was ordered to leave for his own parish in Ireland." LHSA, ESPRB, 1870 Annual Report, GD52/1/1/1, 4.

80. RBAS, RA, Henry McWhinney, No. 76.

81. RBAS, RA, Catherine McArthur, No. 114.

82. RBAS, Minute Book 1825–35, June 17, 1833, 288–89.

83. RBAS, RA—the others were Peter Brodie, No. 81; John Brown, No. 116; Joseph Short, No. 118; William Smith, No. 129; Peter Cunningham, No. 179; William Paterson, No. 309; Michael Rowley, No. 402; and Joseph Jackson, No. 496.

84. RBAS, RA, Loisa Paradies, No. 1059.

85. "Towers and Chill Families in India, Burma and Penang," accessed February 24, 2020, https://www.ancestry.co.uk/boards/localities.asia.burma.general/268/mb.ashx.

86. RBAS, RA, Lily Eleanor Burke, No. 1872.

87. Leyla Kerlaff, *Royal Blind 225 Years, 1793–2018* (Edinburgh: Royal Blind, 2018), 6.

88. Registration of Death, March 3, 1949, Hawick.

89. RBAS, RA, Michael George James, Nos. 932 and 958.

90. Registration of Death, October 16, 1896, Edinburgh.

91. Registration of Death, January 22, 1894, Edinburgh.

92. In 2021, the Scottish War Blinded organization was renamed "Sight Scotland Veterans."

93. Scottish War Blinded, *1915–2015 Scottish War Blinded: A Century of Expanding Horizons* (Edinburgh: Scottish War Blinded, 2015), 36–37.

94. LHSA, "Register of the Outdoor Blind" of the Edinburgh Society for Promoting Reading amongst the Outdoor Blind, GHD/19, entry nos. 380 and 986, Sir Alexander Hope; https://www.geni.com/people/Sir-Alexander-Hope-of-Pinkie-15th-Baronet /6000000018438051410, accessed March 3, 2020.

95. Callum G. Brown, *Religion and Society in Scotland since 1707* (Edinburgh: Edinburgh University Press, 1997), 107.

96. Such an example was a Moon volume on explorer Captain James Cook, a memoir offered to outdoor blind readers by ESPRB. LHSA, ESPRB, 1870 Annual Report, GD52/ 1/1/1, 5.

6

Curing a "Toxic Condition"

Deafness and Public Health Policy during the Porfiriato

Holly Caldwell

In 1904, Mexico participated in the World's Fair, which took place in St. Louis, Missouri. The report *Mexico Ayer y Hoy 1876–1904* discussed the nation's economic strides and was distributed at the event as part of exhibiting Mexico's progress and modernization during the late nineteenth century. Prepared under the authorization of the Mexican government, Bernardo Mallén's report detailed the significant improvements that occurred under the regime of Porfirio Díaz, particularly in the field of public education. The report described the final third of the century in reformist language: "A great nation can only be formed of educated citizens. . . . To attempt to found a great nation without forming citizens who would be competent to exercise their civil rights and duties, would be as absurd as to build the heavy walls of a great palace on a foundation of quicksand."[1] One decade earlier, Trinidad García reflected on the enormous responsibility he was about to undertake by accepting the post as the newly appointed director of Mexico's first school for the D/deaf—the Escuela Nacional de Sordomudos (National School for Deaf-Mutes; hereafter ENSM):

> When the Head of the Republic honored me with the appointment as Director of the National School for Deaf-Mutes, I was about to renounce this high and undeserved honor, because I realized the enormous weight of responsibility that the government was about to contract, with Society [*sic*] and the poor students, who are as pitiable as they are in need of education.[2]

While seemingly unconnected, these two events juxtapose two important national concerns of the Mexican government during the late nineteenth century. Policymakers believed that educating the masses would help to advance some of the government's other vital initiatives regarding public health, civilization, and progress. Deafness was associated with immoral behaviors, disease, and unsavory marital unions, and those "afflicted" with the condition were viewed as an obstacle to creating a fit and healthy nation. Drawing on Kelly Fritsch's discussion of how disabilities—or conditions labeled as "disabilities"—have historically been viewed as "individually economically quantifiable toxic conditions," this essay examines both how Porfirian policymakers enacted a multifold mission to restructure Mexico City in the interest of civilizing what they perceived as their "backward populations" and the ways in which their goal to rid the urban environment of "degenerate" characteristics that caused deafness introduced a series of failed sanitation reforms at the ENSM.[3] I argue that deafness and its perceived associated causes were framed as an individual health problem as well as a threat to the nation's health, which was believed to have resulted from a toxic urban environment.

Mexico's time line of understanding and defining deafness is not unlike that of the United States and Europe, in that for centuries, deafness was viewed as a disorder warranting charity and piety. There are two key widely accepted turning points in the history of the D/deaf in North America, both of which were spurred by reformers, many of whom were not D/deaf. The first took place in 1817, when Thomas H. Gallaudet and Laurent Clerc established the American Asylum for the Deaf in Hartford, Connecticut, where students were encouraged to take part in a vibrant cultural community.[4] Through their interactions with hearing and nonhearing individuals, students and teachers alike inspired the creation of a D/deaf community. The second began in the late nineteenth and continued through the twentieth century when a group of oralist reformers sought to overturn this cultural community by eliminating the use of sign language in deaf schools. Such reformers insisted that the "English vernacular must be made the vernacular of the deaf if they are not to become a class unto themselves—foreigners among their own countrymen."[5] Despite being a proponent of the combined method, which drew on both the manual (sign) and oral methods, Trinidad García expressed a preference for the latter, describing the manual method as "a very embarassing and delayed" form of communication.[6] His words echoed the sentiments that had circulated at the Milan Congress of 1880 and that had since taken root in many Western nations and began influencing policy at the ENSM.[7] Although responses to oralism from the D/deaf community were varied, Deaf scholar Paddy Ladd has aptly described the deliberate suppression of sign language and forced adoption of oralism as *linguis-*

tic colonialism, a phenomenon where Deaf cultures and patterns were "shaped by both acquiescience to and resistance against that cultural domination by majority cultures."[8] For policymakers, oralism was considered the progressive approach to "normalize" the D/deaf and incorporate them into mainstream society because it provided a solution to the issues plaguing late nineteenth-century society, such as urbanization, growing linguistic and cultural diversity, and industrialization.

The creation of Mexico's first school for the deaf in 1866 was grounded in broader social reforms to prevent impoverished deaf children (often orphaned or abandoned) who were housed in Mexico City's Foundling Home from becoming social parasites that would threaten the national order.[9] In response to such concerns, Mexican elites began to implement tools to reform and regulate their populations, a form of institutionalized care that, in many ways, was a double-edged sword. Although they served to protect vulnerable children and were designed as part of a progressive economic and social model, such programs were part of a mechanism of controlling populations and thus sanctioned in the interests of social control.[10] This state-directed campaign coincided with the advent of the professionalization of medicine and public health in the late nineteenth century, which caused a shift in how the Deaf were viewed. As a modernizing Latin American state, Mexican policymakers subscribed to the precepts of positivism, a philosophy in which individuals were valued and judged primarily by their economic usefulness to the nation; those who were categorized as "defective" or "abnormal" were often defined as lacking such usefulness.[11] Deafness thus came to be viewed as the by-product of poverty, disease, and immorality, which led elite reformers to consider it one of the most significant obstacles to creating a fit and healthy nation. Although deafness itself is not a disability but rather a communicative difference, within the context of the modernizing and industrializing state, Deaf individuals were categorized as "undesirable" due to their perceived lack of usefulness.[12] To borrow Beth Linker's definition, disability, disease, and illness are slippery concepts that change over time and are shaped by time and place.[13] Thus, policies enacted under modernizing states ensured that deafness *became* classified as a disability by imposing social and economic requirements (through the establishment of "norms" and labor) as well as physical barriers (such as the educational system) that alienated or limited the D/deaf from achieving their full potential. Several factors have been proposed as causes for this shift in perception—industrialization coupled with economic rationalism, the development of notions of "normality" and "abnormality," and the increasing medical surveillance of "deviant" bodies.[14] Ladd's concept of *linguistic colonialism*, coupled with the work of disabilities scholar Helen Meekosha—in which she challenges us to better understand the complex ways in which colonialism and postcolonial powers have impacted disability (and the ways in which it is framed) within colonized environments—provides a foundation to discuss the link between poverty and disability in the Global South.[15] Historically, there has been a direct correlation between poverty and the prevalence of disabilities, mental disorders, and conditions such as deafness and blindness in Latin American societies, a phenomenon that scholars have referred to as "poverty within poverty."[16] As targets of a state-directed campaign, Mexico's D/deaf populations became subject to what can be characterized as a form of "colonialism within colonialism" as they faced what Ladd has described as "social and cultural colonization in the paternalistic endeavors to civilize them."[17]

Throughout history, Mexico's Deaf were, and to some extent remain, characterized and categorized *by* their "disability" despite the fact that Deaf individuals typically do not view themselves as disabled.[18] Mexico has historically conceptualized disability under the medical paradigm grounded in part on Talcott Parsons's illness model, which proposes that a person defined as sick enters "the role of sanctioned deviance" and that medical interventions are needed to modify the condition.[19] Though there have been significant strides in constructing a social model that resists the medicalization of disability in recent decades, the medical model—or the notion that disability is a shameful and undesirable condition that should be remedied and policed by the medical profession—has persisted in various forms since the late nineteenth century.[20] From a medical standpoint, deafness was not only considered an illness that stemmed from a toxic environment—either contracted from undesirable familial traits or localized geographic exposure—but was stigmatized as socially backward because it posed an impediment to the positivist project of nation-building. For decades, physicians and policymakers struggled with how to tap into this potential workforce and transform the Deaf into "useful," economically viable citizens.

Since language concerning D/deafness and the D/deaf has evolved over time, this essay will use two sets of language. In recent years, scholars have acknowledged that deafness is a cultural construction as well as a physical phenomenon.[21] In simple terms, there are two constructions of deafness that now dominate—Deafness as designating a member of a cultural and linguistic minority and deafness as a disability or hearing impairment.[22] The culturally Deaf do not view themselves as disabled but rather as a linguistic minority who embrace the cultural norms, beliefs, and values of the Deaf community. Their use of sign language signifies that they share a common communication difference from hearing members of society, but that these barriers disappear once they are part of a signing community. The lowercase version of the term refers simply to the condition of having a hearing and communicative difference. In the interest of respecting the values and identity of the Deaf community, I have elected to not employ the Mexican government's recently devised terms *personas con discapacidad* or *personas con capacidades diferentes* and have opted instead to use *Deaf* or *deaf* when offering my analysis of the historical material in this essay.[23]

Positivism, Public Health, and Deafness

When Porfirio Díaz assumed power, he initiated a series of changes that significantly impacted life in the nation's capital during a period of dictatorial rule collectively known as the Porfiriato (1876–1911). In order to create a modern, civilized, and progressive society, the Díaz regime followed the tenets of positivism, a scientific philosophy that had recently begun to shape the political and social discourse in Mexico.[24] Adopting the Comtean motto of "Order and Progress," Díaz followed this model of European-derived positivism with the intent of creating a quintessential positivist technocracy.[25] As Mexican policymakers envisioned their modernized society, they drew on the European colonizing model to diagnose and cure their own population of perceived backwardness to achieve their vision of "health," which resembled what Sharon Betcher has described as "a structure of exclusion, a new, even morally loaded biologism," a form of health that included categorizing or classifying populations through the use of scientific methods to determine those individuals as possessing or lacking worth.[26] Although Mexico itself was not a colonial power, Díaz's elite inner circle of government officials, prominent citizens, and urban professionals—collectively known as *científicos*—implemented a series of aggressive measures and reforms as part of the nation's overarching goal to achieve progress, growth, and civilization. As part of this process, they implemented methods that mirrored the European colonial project of controlling, monitoring, and regulating those categorized as unruly and wayward.

Drawing on the principles of positivism, Porfirian policymakers understood and implemented progressive ideals to promote modernizing agendas that influenced public health policy. In their view, this public health reform would include introducing sanitation programs, reorganizing the urban environment of the capital city, and restricting what elites perceived to be the unseemly behaviors of the lower class. They viewed deafness and its perceived causes—poverty, toxic environments, disease, and immorality—as symptoms that called for both diagnosis and cure as part of a broader national civilizing project, which reinforced the notion that "disability" was considered "an individually economically quantifiable toxic condition."[27]

Those who subscribed to positivist ideas maintained that a fusion of "order and progress" would provide Mexican society with elite-driven control to reform the population as well as the nation's disordered landscape.

Part of this reform included a twofold mission to improve public health conditions.[28] First, officials believed that the city could be regenerated through sanitary and hygienic knowledge, essential to urban design and planning. Second, they worked to transform habits of the urban population through the inculcation of European customs. Mexican physicians and hygienists opined that transforming the city and its inhabitants required a thorough scientific diagnosis before solutions could be applied. This agenda mirrored what Ellen Samuels has described as Western modernity's "crisis of identification—driven by colonialism, urbanization, class and geographic mobility, and the rise of the welfare state—that led to a drive for incontrovertible evidence to biologically certify, capture, and control identity," a phenomenon that, according to disabilities scholar and activist Alice Andrews, enforces and produces biological normalcy, resulting in disablement.[29] It was within this context of biological classification and categorization and distinguishing the "normal" from the "abnormal," the "able-bodied" from the "dis-abled," that the construct of dis-ablement often formed.[30] As the Porfirian elite sought to reinvent and remold their nation and its inhabitants into a new, modern Mexico, they worked in collaboration with científicos. Together they adopted and employed European notions of hierarchical social order to specify how society should be organized, how social hierarchies should be constituted and maintained, and what it meant to be "civilized" and modern.

In the eyes of the contemporary elite, an urbanized and sanitary metropolis signified everything that was "modern," "cultured," and "civilized."[31] Alejandra Osorio and Jay Kinsbruner have established that there was an inextricable link between colonialism, modernity, and patriarchy in many Latin American urban environments, as Spanish colonial authorities constructed cities with centralization of power to establish order, improve sanitation, and defend their empire from both internal and external threats.[32] While nineteenth-century Mexico City represented the center of the nation's political, cultural, and intellectual life, Pablo Piccato has noted that the urban environment also elicited images of disease, crime, and poverty.[33] As Díaz implemented a comprehensive and aggressive campaign to transform the Mexican nation into a modern state, the capital and its "backward and degenerate" populace were at the forefront of these goals. Education, public health, and moral hygiene became crucial components of the government's initiatives to promote the idea that the nation's capital was a showcase of modernism. Many of these reforms, which included developing the mining and textile industries, increasing the export agricultural economy, and constructing a modernized railway system, were implemented during the first three decades of the Díaz regime and reflected how elites sought to reinvent a capital that paralleled the sophistication found in European and North

American cities, particularly Paris, London, and New York.[34] Officials understood that improving the capital city's moral cleanliness and sanitation of both its landscape and residents was essential to building a civilized and progressive society that reflected European standards. For científicos, the nation's body politic and economy had to be sanitized—and maintain a prescribed measure of good health—to achieve this ideal.[35]

European ideals of controlling, reforming, and sanitizing urban populations as well as restructuring urban environments were designed to fit the needs of elites. The transformation of the nation's poor and "disabled" was a significant part of this endeavor. Such reform-minded thinking impacted how disease was understood and treated. Historically, deafness was medically defined, understood, and analyzed in terms of deviance. From the seventeenth through the nineteenth centuries, medical practitioners and social scientists alike commonly viewed the occurrence of deafness as divine judgment for immoral or unseemly behavior. Deafness was considered one of the most severe "disabilities," particularly due to its potentially socially isolating nature. The difficulty in communicating in a traditional sense with the Deaf, coupled with ignorance and misinformation about deafness, as well as preoccupation with what caused it and how it could be "treated," exacerbated negative public perception about the hearing difference. Deviations from what was perceived as "normal," Lennard Davis argues, were rarely tolerated, with R. A. R. Edwards arguing that sign language made the D/deaf "foreigners in their own land," since the use of sign language physically and visibly marked them as abnormal.[36] In the British Empire, attitudes toward disability (which included deafness) as well as biological registers of expressing other forms of colonial difference, such as race, ethnicity, and gender, spurred concerns about the "health" of the "imperial race."[37] Similarly, as científicos were working to establish a set of norms in Mexican society in the latter half of the nineteenth century, fears of individuals who could potentially disrupt that agenda created a context in which individuals labeled mad, mentally disabled, or insane were "increasingly perceived as a threat to social harmony and stability and the nation's progress and prosperity."[38] Since deafness was categorized as a sickness and a disorder that could (and should) be cured through medical intervention, the Deaf were categorized as mentally incapable and classified in the same legal category as the insane. Such medical classifications not only resulted in the denial of rights and privileges of the Deaf but effectively made them targets for the government's civilizing project.[39]

Drawing on the colonial model, científicos created a domestic social policy that turned inward to solve the problem of marginalized populations.[40] They used both covert and overt methods to study deafness and the Deaf, with the expressed interest to reform these individuals and rid society and the nation at large of this affliction. Ignacio Trigueros, statesman and director of the ENSM, drew attention to the plight of his city's deaf population in 1867. It was believed that by improving the lives of the deaf—and by ensuring them happy and productive futures—society at large would improve.[41] Trigueros insisted that the ENSM provided a social and educational haven for its students who otherwise could not communicate. In his view, the institute afforded these young people a place where they could gain awareness of a variety of subjects, such as language, science, and morality. By instituting a mandated educational system for the masses, including those with communicative "disabilities," the Mexican government believed it would improve the character of the body politic, which was essential to creating a modern and progressive state.[42]

"Civilizing" the Capital

By forging close links between ideals of order, cleanliness, and hygiene, científicos created a discourse that encompassed society as a whole. They viewed moral education as inherently linked to physical and intellectual education.[43] Ensuring the health of its population was not only essential for Mexico's well-being; it was also important in terms of economic development and national defense, as healthy citizens were the reflection of a healthy state.[44] By linking health with moral virtue and economic vitality, Sharon Betcher argues, we yoke health with "the agenda of biopolitics and its multiplication of pathologies to increase corrective desire, its aggravation of the yearning to belong by way of normalization."[45] In classifying and categorizing marginalized groups, científicos devised terms of normality and abnormality, spurring fears that "degenerate" characteristics would ultimately infect the nation's health and gene pool.[46] Such fears would inspire a host of urban renewal projects and, ultimately, a series of failed sanitation reforms at the ENSM.

In keeping with the country's economic growth, the Díaz administration developed extensive projects to reshape the urban geography of the capital.[47] As the authority of science gained precedence over the authority of religion in providing a set of concrete principles for the proper ordering of a modern capitalist society, public health matters, social welfare reform, and education became issues of profound political importance.[48] Drawing on the central tenets of positivism, engineers, physicians, and other municipal officials were at the forefront of creating policies, a trend that promoted these figures into positions of unprecedented power and influence. Mexican engineers became "physicians" of the city and were esteemed as agents of civilization and modernity, whereas physicians emerged as key shapers of public health policy and were the driving force behind such reforms. The government financed public works that paved and widened streets, erected new monuments and public buildings, and installed new sewage systems and public lighting.[49] Areas such as the Alameda were adorned with city services and lush, public spaces and became an upper-class place of leisure. Tree-lined boulevards, such as the Paseo de la Reforma, were modeled on the grand avenues of Europe.[50] The modernization and urbanization project also changed the aesthetics and overall feel of the capital, signifying to Mexican elites that they embraced the refinement and modernity commonly found in major European cities while also encouraging further development.[51] Not all areas of the capital experienced this level of growth. Lower-class *colonías* had become a haven for crime and posed a particular source of conflict for authorities and developers as they reorganized the city.[52] Elites commonly referred to the streets of these areas as "morally bad" and its residents as "indigent, drunk, or sinister looking," which ran counter to the nation's goal of achieving order and progress.[53] The poor, in their view, had to be removed from the capital's more luxurious spaces and physically moved to colonías located on the outskirts of the city. Porfirian elites labeled the poor who lived in such dilapidated areas as morally corrupt and degenerate while simultaneously naming themselves as superior arbiters of morality and modernity.

The cleanliness of the capital was paramount to maintaining the moral integrity, fitness, and productivity of the nation, a notion that resembles Sarah Jaquette Ray's analysis of environmentalism, which "evolv[ed] in tandem with social Darwinism, [and] portrayed life as a contest for both genetic and national survival. Those who were fit, both individuals and races, 'naturally' dominated those who were weaker."[54] Physicians, hygienists, and other Porfirian officials, Claudia Agostoni contends, created a "linguistic barrier" that separated those who had the knowledge and the scientific authority to inspect the city and recommend solutions to urban health problems from those who did not.[55] Their authority was rooted in their command of scientific and medical language and was buttressed by burgeoning knowledge about the human body and the origins of diseases. The Díaz administration widely advertised the benefits that would be delivered through its urban renewal project through the removal of sources of vagrancy and vice from city streets.[56] In particular, Mexican civil engineer and political economist Alberto J. Pani highlighted the importance of improving public sanitation in *La Higiene en Mexico*, stating, "The issue of personal hygiene is of paramount importance in a nation where the long-standing practice of uncleanliness of the lower classes, who rarely wash or bathe or change clothes, who spit, urinate, and throw garbage wherever they please, has been noted as a serious cause of morbidity."[57] Medical professionals held that miasmas and unclean living conditions caused and contributed to the spread of deafness, and it was commonly believed that contracting the "illness" either could be prevented or was within the control of the sufferer.[58] Those who subscribed to miasma theory believed that bad or "night air" caused most diseases such as cholera and deafness, and that walls and cesspools preserved smells and transmitted the odors of bodily tissues.[59] By framing disability as an individual health problem resulting from a toxic environment, this belief system perpetuated a cultural preoccupation with problematizing the origin of disability and preventing its reproduction.[60]

Sanitation Codes and the ENSM

Improvements in the medical understanding of deafness worldwide, coupled with growing technologies and therapies to treat the ailment, collided with the proliferation in positivist ideals that pervaded this period. If technological advancements in medical science could prevent or cure deafness, then this reinforced social stigma that would be attached to individuals who were either born deaf or contracted an illness that rendered them deaf.[61] Rapid urbanization and population growth in the capital presented a new host of concerns. As Asunción Lavrin points out, "Desirable as this growth was, it was plagued by alarming health problems that reflected badly on nations wishing to join the mainstream of Western 'progress.'"[62] As public health and welfare reform influenced policies at schools, hospitals, and other institutions, the ENSM was no exception in that one of its primary goals was to fulfill the requirements for national hygiene. In addition to lacking basic instructional supplies, many schools in Mexico City were rife with pollution, poor sanitation, and diseases such as smallpox, typhus, malaria, Spanish influenza, and tuberculosis. The *American Annals of the Deaf and Dumb* differentiated between "normal" students and "abnormal" students and highlighted the fact that "deaf-mutes" suffered from more health problems than their non-deaf counterparts:

> One has only to go into any large institution for the deaf to see how sad, painful, and marked are the signs of this dread disease. And when it has been stated that the majority of the deaf and dumb die from strumous complaints and consumption, enough will have been said on this head for the present purpose.[63]

Deafness was thus considered a condition that was to blame for the deaf individual's ill health—and not exposure and vulnerability to conditions such as crime, poverty, disease, and hunger, to which many found themselves subjected in rapidly changing urban environments. Neither municipal authorities nor school administrators considered these extraneous factors that were beyond the control of the urban poor when assigning blame to "vice-ridden" agents. However, this does not appear to be the case with the ENSM, whose directors and health inspectors were openly concerned with the institution's dilapidated facilities and advocated for better conditions for their students. When referring to the Deaf pupils under his charge, sanitation inspector Luis Jiménez described them as "quite unfortunate beings who were certainly worthy of better care."[64] Casting aside what is likely a condescending description of the Deaf students, Jiménez's report reveals a degree of progressive thinking when he advocates that these individuals were "worthy of better care."

For centuries, writers like Dr. Luis Ruiz had tried to draw some correlation between deafness and the environment. As one of the most important hygienists of nineteenth-century Mexico, Dr. Ruiz served as the scientific editor of the *La Libertad* throughout the tenure of the positivist journal's publication. He argued that administrative and economic policies were inextricably linked to hygienic issues and that the capital's public health was negatively impacted by its surrounding environment. Since there existed a perceived link between odors and death, the development of public health policy was based on analysis of air, the struggle against putrid miasmas, and the increased value placed on aromatics. Medical officials and sanitary reformers called for a sanitary code that would establish regulative norms, such as paving walkways, plastering walls, and draining swamps to sanitize public spaces and confront the challenge of crowding. Many científicos, as well as Alexander Graham Bell, believed that environment, climate, and geography might be the ultimate cause of deafness. The Volta Bureau highlighted the difference between the various types of deafness and the ways in which it was contracted: "It is very important to carefully to distinguish between those born deaf and those who have lost their hearing from illness or other abuse; these two classes are generally called 'congenital' and 'accidental.'"[65] García noted that "unfortunately, there are numerous diseases that cause accidental deaf-muteness of children in early childhood, among them are listed first, eruptive fevers, particularly scarlet fever and smallpox, pneumonia, rheumatism and diphtheria." García also attributed deafness, and the difficulties in teaching those lacking hearing and speech, to "a sluggish lymphatic constitution."[66] Other Mexican physicians supported these ideas, such as those published in *Diario del Hogar*, where a medical researcher on deafness maintained,

> At least three quarters of the cases of deafness originate in catarrhal disease of the nose and throat involving the Eustachian tube and middle ear and mastoid cells. Such individuals typically have weak vitals, are neurotic, anemic, with sensitive skin and bad digestive organs, and in particular, the cervical spine is especially weak and

contributes to visceral sickness from a fluxion of blood to the head. Therefore the condition of such individuals always worsens with the cold, as there is not enough vitality to get rid of the mucous quickly.[67]

This practitioner claimed that determining the cause of deafness was urgent, in that "Each day deafness becomes more and more common, with treatment often failing, thus making it necessary to pay more systematic attention to the conditions that can influence the persistence of this condition."[68] To avoid aggravating the symptoms of those suffering from accidental deafness, the ENSM formally proposed and enacted a series of architectural remedies.

ENSM staff drew on the different models of schools for the Deaf that existed in France and Belgium, and in its annual review, the school's director debated whether the institution should be located within the city limits or on the outskirts of town. The National School for the Deaf in Paris was in the heart of the city and was deemed undesirable in terms of its living conditions and sanitation, whereas one of the best schools in Belgium was on the outskirts of Brussels. Research uncovered that the Flemish school was located on high ground, surrounded by large and beautiful gardens, with impeccable sanitary facilities. As a result of these findings, it was determined that "the school building should be located outside the city and in an elevated location."[69] These specifications were set to avoid excess moisture and to encourage renewal of fresh air and water drainage, recommendations that were published in medical journals.[70] According to the guidelines presented by the Superior Board of Health, without a license issued by the county government "no hotel, inn, guest house, or public room" could be made available or open to the public.[71] All schools, both public and private, remained subject to hygienic and medical inspection pursuant to the provisions of this code, according to the law on compulsory education and the respective regulations.[72] In his 1898 institutional report, Francisco Vázquez Gómez, a Porfirian doctor who researched the relationship between deafness and health in the nation's capital, evaluated the moral health of the institution and attributed good hygiene to one's ability to receive a good education.[73] To reap the "maximum benefits of sunlight" and "to avoid moisture," reports on the school disclosed that "bedrooms should be located on the top floor of the building."[74] The building lacked adequate space to accommodate the number of enrolled students, so the school's administration sought to remedy this issue. The ENSM took measures to protect its students from miasmatic emanations by redesigning the building in such a way that encouraged the movement of air, coupled with desiccating walls, bathrooms, and bedrooms. Moral and sanitation codes were instituted so that schools, including the ENSM, could be properly monitored and evaluated according to the government's prescribed standards.

Hygiene was thus used as a tool to distinguish clean and civilized bodies from dirty and backward ones; it served as one of the most visible markers of respectability. In his internationally esteemed work, *Compendio del Manual de Urbanidad y Buenas maneras*, Manuel Antonio Carreño defined cleanliness as a natural marker of a "civilized body" and illustrated how the use of proper hygiene could protect against threats of contamination.[75] Yet, Mexico City's limited supply and distribution of potable water made cleanliness a challenge.[76] Medical specialists had recommended that due to their "sluggish lymphatic systems," Deaf students required a regular supply of cold water not only for cleanliness but also as a "powerful restorative aid."[77] Severe shortages of clean water significantly compromised the health and sanitation of students, faculty, and staff at the school. The director of the ENSM and health inspectors alike expressed concern for the welfare of both faculty and students; they followed specific guidelines to ensure that its student body would remain healthy. Windows were to remain open during the day "in order to clean the air in the building."[78] Since it was feared that students would catch a chill in the evening following their washing routines, toilets and sinks were installed in proximity to the bedrooms. However, they needed to be ventilated to prevent noxious emanations from entering the sleeping quarters. Based on his observations at the deaf school in Paris, Vázquez Gómez argued that frequent usage of the toilet facilities would cause high humidity and moisture in the air that would emanate to the bedrooms, so toilet seats were specially designed in a convex form to prevent this occurrence.[79] Despite these measures, toilet and bathing facilities were substandard due to the water shortage.

Issues with drainage, contaminated water, and "prevalence of miasmas" were not the only concerns. Subjects pertinent to the school's curriculum were also put at risk. Horticulture was a primary field of study at the ENSM, because it provided male students with a valuable skill with which they could support themselves following graduation. A study conducted by Antonio Peñafiel in 1884 revealed that drinking water conveyed in aqueducts and distributed to public sources was "highly unfavorable for public health and consumption."[80] His analysis concluded that sewage containing human excrement was regularly flushed into the river, which served as the city's drinking water. The combination of human feces, flies, and an insufficient water supply shared by over three hundred thousand people, according to Peñafiel, was the primary contributing factor to the extraordinarily poor health and high death rate of the capital.[81] In his letter to the secretary of the interior, ENSM director Trinidad García reported that since the founding of the school, there had been five sources designated for drinking water that were absolutely necessary to maintain the gardens, bathrooms, laundries, and general housing facilities. In the previous year, only one of these sources had received water and even then the source was not without interruptions.[82] An analysis conducted by the Public Office of Health and Sanitation revealed that the institute's water supply contained unhealthy levels of salts and large proportions of animal matter, and it was advised that it only be used to water the plants.[83] Due to the insufficient quality and quantity of water, plants were withering and the garden was in unsatisfactory condition. García stressed that the school's gardens were essential, not only for decorative purposes and hygienic reasons but to provide Deaf students (in most cases, boys) with a vocational education in horticulture so they could contribute to the domestic economy.[84] Several years later in 1900, García once again petitioned the *Ayuntamiento* to enlist its assistance, stating that it had been "two or three weeks since water had been delivered through its source to the institute" and that the school was not receiving even the daily amount needed for household consumption. He requested that the *Ayuntamiento* grant a more substantial supply of water to the institute at the earliest opportunity.[85] Despite numerous complaints to the *Ayuntamiento*, little action was taken to remedy the situation.[86] School officials petitioned to the local and federal governments over several decades to remedy the lack of potable water supply and expressed concern over the school's ability to care for its daily needs. According to letters written by the school's directors, this matter remained unaddressed and one of heightened concern well into the 1930s.

Conclusion

During the Porfiriato, medicine and science were emblems of power and modernity that contributed to a "civilizing project" that targeted marginalized populations, such as the poor and the "disabled." Elites drew on discourses of disease coupled with the Comtean positivist ideals of "order and progress" to reform what they perceived to be "backward" populations and renovate their capital city.[87] Municipal officials introduced sanitation programs, reorganized the capital's city space, and worked to reform the "backward" masses into their version of a modern and ideal citizen. Though positivist ideals of creating a progressive society made up of citizens that adhered to specific standards of morality and cleanliness helped to create a more progressive society, it also caused significant difficulties in many aspects of life for D/deaf individuals.

The Porfirian goal of achieving progress and creating a modern and "civilized" populace fell short of its ideals. Díaz and his government were widely praised in the international press for implementing modernization projects and encouraging industrial progress that helped Mexico to realize its "potential" and put the nation on the world stage. While this growth created a façade that pleased elites and earned Díaz international recognition, it became apparent that he prioritized economic growth over other issues, particularly the needs of his people. This was perhaps nowhere more apparent than in the nation's capital, which despite significant restructuring, suffered from a variety of serious health concerns and disease outbreaks. Concerned for the welfare of the students who lived at the institute, school administrators enacted a series of reforms in the hopes of protecting their pupils from aggravating what was believed to be an already "weak disposition."[88] Although their efforts were largely unsuccessful because they were not scientifically sound, hygiene inspectors and administrators instituted architectural changes and introduced their own measures to prevent the proliferation of miasmas. For decades, the ENSM continued to advocate on behalf of its students to improve conditions at the school. The struggle for D/deaf students enrolled at the ENSM to achieve basic recognition and necessities from their government represents a revealing case that contributes to a long-standing historical debate maintaining that those categorized as "disabled" did not find that the Porfirian ideal applied to them or enhanced their everyday lives.

Despite the rise in the study of deafness in the nineteenth century, the D/deaf faced discrimination and struggled to obtain employment, education, and civil rights. When differences like deafness were categorized as "disabilities" stemming from toxic environments, they came to be viewed under the modernizing agenda as toxic conditions that threatened the health and order of the nation at large. As Porfirian policymakers enacted their plan to restructure the capital in the interest of civilizing "backward" populations and ridding the urban environment of "degenerate" characteristics, they exacerbated existing health and sanitation concerns at the ENSM. By framing deafness as an individual health problem, one could argue that they also unwittingly undermined their own agenda.

NOTES

1. Bernardo Mallén, *México Ayer y Hoy 1876–1904* (México: [s.n.], 1904), 48.

2. Trinidad García, *Discurso Pronunciado por el director de la Escuela Nacional de Sordo Mudos* (México: Tipografía "El Lapiz del Aguila," 1898) 3.

3. Kelly Fritsch, "Toxic Pregnancies: Speculative Futures, Disabling Environments, and Neoliberal Biocapital" in *Disability Studies and the Environmental Humanities: Toward an Eco-Crip Theory*, ed. Sarah Jaquette Ray and Jay Sibara (Lincoln: University of Nebraska Press, 2017), 376.

4. Douglas C. Baynton, *Forbidden Signs: American Culture and the Campaign against Sign Language* (Chicago: University of Chicago Press, 1996), 3–5. The school was originally called the Connecticut Asylum at Hartford for the Instruction of Deaf and Dumb Persons.

5. Baynton, *Forbidden Signs*, 27.

6. García, *Discurso Escuela Sordo-Mudos*, 13.

7. For example, in 1894, the Mexican medical journal *La Medicina Científica* published the initial findings by Dr. James Kerr Love of Glasgow, who argued that [deafness]

was worsened by using finger spelling or sign language. See *La Medicina Científica*, September 1, 1894, 269–70. Such views mirrored those presented at the Milan Congress of 1880, where it was determined that oralism was a more effective means of educating and thus communicating with the deaf. It should be noted that the controversial adoption of oralism was likely due to the disparate number of hearing and nonhearing delegates in attendance, 160 to 4, respectively. See Arthur A. Kinsey, *Report Congress on the Education of the Deaf, Held at Milan, September 6th–11th, 1880* (London: W. H. Allen, 1880), vol. 26, 105.

8. Paddy Ladd, *Understanding Deaf Culture: In Search of Deafhood* (Clevedon, UK: Multilingual Matters, 2003) 17, 79.

9. El Archivo Mexicano, *Colección de leyes, decretos, circulares y otros documentos: Tomo V* (Imprenta de Vicente García Torres: Mexico, 1861), 736–59. This document provides supporting evidence that Mexican president Benito Juárez first initiated the creation of a school for the D/deaf as early as 1861. See also *Ley Reglamamentaria de la instrucción en el Distrito Federal y Territorios de Tepie y la Baja California* (México: Distrito Federal, 1890).

10. See María Cristina Salazar, *Los Esclavos Invisibles: Autoritarismo, explotación y derechos de los niños en América Latina* (Tunja, Boyacá, Colombia: Universidad Pedagogica y Tecnologica de Colombia Facultad de Ciencias de la Educacion, 2006).

11. For a discussion of the role of positivist philosophy in nineteenth-century Mexican society, see Charles A. Hale, *The Transformation of Liberalism in Late Nineteenth-Century Mexico* (Princeton, NJ: Princeton University Press, 1989).

12. It is perhaps due to this line of thinking that records documenting the lives of D/deaf individuals from this period have not been preserved, as I have only been able to locate records and testimony from hearing individuals to reconstruct this history. Other historians on Mexico's D/deaf population have also documented their struggles with this issue. See Johan Cristian Cruz Cruz and Miroslava Cruz-Aldrete, "Integración social del sordo en la Ciudad de México: enfoques médicos y pedagógicos (1867–1900)," *Cuicuilco* 56 (2013): 173–201; Christian Giorgio Jullian Montañés, "Genesis de la Comunidad Silente de Mexico: La Escuela Nacional de Sordomudos (1867–1886)" (unpublished undergraduate thesis, UNAM, 2001). Jullian Montañés has published work on Mexico's school for the blind, which was founded in 1871 and merged with the school for the deaf in 1928. See Christian Giorgio Jullian Montañés, "Educación especial y ciencias médicas frente a la ceguera en la ciudad de México, 1870–1928," in *Curar, sanar y educar: enfermedad y sociedad en México*: siglos XIX y XX, ed. Claudia Agostoni (México, D.F.: Universidad Nacional Autónoma de México, 2008): 43–70.

13. Beth Linker, "On the Borderland of Medical and Disability History: A Survey of the Fields," *Bulletin of the History of Medicine* 87, no. 4 (2013): 499–535. https://www.jstor.org/stable/26305957.

14. See Lennard J. Davis, "Constructing Normalcy: The Bell Curve, the Novel, and the Invention of the Disabled Body in the Nineteenth Century," in *The Disability Studies Reader*, ed. Lennard J. Davis (New York: Routledge, 1997), 3–16; David M. Turner, "Introduction: Approaching Anomalous Bodies," in *Social Histories of Disability and Deformity*, ed. David M. Turner and Kevin Stagg (London: Routledge, 2006); David Landes, *The Unbound Prometheus: Technological Change and Industrial Development in Western Europe from 1750 to the Present* (New York: Cambridge University Press, 1969).

15. Helen Meekosha, "Decolonising Disability: Thinking and Acting Globally," *Disability & Society* 26, no. 6 (2011): 667–82.

16. Researchers note that historically, individuals with disabilities (and their families) living in underdeveloped nations have struggled with the problem of "poverty within

poverty," as they are often at risk of becoming invisible within their own societies and lack the means (or are presented with logistical barriers) to negotiate hospital care, garner food with which to feed their families, or secure uniforms and appropriate footwear to attend school, which further contributes to their invisibility and dehumanization. See Secretaría de Educación Pública, *Memorias y actualidad en la Educación Especial de México: Una visión histórica de sus Modelos de Atención* (México, D.F.: Dirección de Educación Especial, 2010), 27, 46, 77, 176, 225. See also Alice Andrews, "Autoimmune Actions in the Ableist Academy," in *Ableism in Academia: Theorizing Experiences of Disabilities and Chronic Illnesses in Higher Education*, ed. Nicole Brown and Jennifer Leigh (London: UCL Press, 2020), 108; Susan Burch, *Signs of Resistance: American Deaf Cultural History, 1900 to World War II* (New York: New York University Press, 2002); Arne E. Eide and Benedicte Ingstad, eds., *Disability and Poverty: A Global Challenge* (Bristol, UK: Policy, 2011); Julie Sadler, "War Contaminant and Environmental Justice: The Case of Congenital Heart Defects in Iraq," in *Disability Studies and the Environmental Humanities: Toward an Eco-Crip Theory*, ed. Sarah Jaquette Ray and Jay Sibara (Lincoln: University of Nebraska Press, 2017), 338–57.

17. Quoted in Esme Cleall, "Orientalising Deafness: Race and Disability in Imperial Britain," *Social Identities* 21, no. 1 (2015): 24.

18. Though Mexico adopted a national disabilities law in 1995 under the regulations of the United Nations, it does not have widespread laws protecting the individual rights of *personas con discapacidad*, or "people with disabilities." The Persons with Disabilities Act of the State of Mexico uses the phrase "personas con capacidades diferentes" (people with different abilities). The definition states that these are persons "suffering from a loss, impairment or reduction of an organ or physical, sensory or intellectual function, which restricts daily life activities and prevents their individual and social development." See International Disability Rights Monitor (IDRM), *Regional Report on the Americas 2004* (Chicago: International Disability Network, 2004), 260–89. According to the National Institute of Statistics and Geography's (INEGI) 2010 census, 35 percent of Deaf individuals in minority communities in Mexico lack education, with only 5.4 percent and 4.1 percent reporting having attended any middle or high education level, respectively. These figures are reported in Miroslava Cruz-Aldrete and Miguel Ángel Villa-Rodríguez, "Middle School Deaf Education in Mexico: A Postponed Issue," in *Change and Promise: Bilingual Deaf Education and Deaf Culture in Latin America*, ed. Barbara Gerner de García and Lodenir Becker Karnopp (Washington, DC: Gallaudet University Press, 2016), 107.

19. Guillermo Flores Briseño, "Disability Policy (Mexico)," in *Encyclopedia of Social Welfare in North America*, ed. John M. Herrick and Paul H. Stuart (Thousand Oaks, CA: Sage, 2005), 80–83. See also Andrews, "Autoimmune Actions in the Ableist Academy"; Tobin Siebers, *Disability Theory* (Ann Arbor, MI: University of Michigan Press, 2008); Susan Wendell, "Unhealthy Disabled: Treating Chronic Illness as Disabilities," *Hypatia* 16, no. 4 (2001): 17–33.

20. See Flores Briseño, "Disability Policy (Mexico)," 80–83; Sarah F. Rose, *No Right to Be Idle: The Invention of Disability, 1840s–1930s* (Chapel Hill: University of North Carolina Press, 2017); Tobin Siebers, "Disability in Theory: From Social Constructionism to the New Realism of the Body," in *The Disability Studies Reader*, ed. Lennard J. Davis (New York: Routledge, 1997), 173–84; Jaipreet Virdi, *Hearing Happiness: Deafness Cures in History* (Chicago: University of Chicago, 2020).

21. See Baynton, *Forbidden Signs*; Susan Plann, *A Silent Minority: Deaf Education in Spain, 1550–1835* (Berkeley: University of California Press, 1997); Christian Cuxac, *Le*

langage des sourds (Paris: Payot, 1983); Nicholas Mirzoeff, *Silent Poetry: Deafness, Sign, and Visual Culture in Modern France* (Princeton, NJ: Princeton University Press, 1995); Susan Plann, *The Spanish National Deaf School: Portraits from the Nineteenth Century* (Washington, DC: Gallaudet University Press, 2007); Anne Quartararo, *Deaf Identity and Social Images in Nineteenth-Century France* (Washington, DC: Gallaudet University Press, 2008).

22. Scholar and applied linguist Boris Fridman-Mintz has recently proposed expanding this definition, suggesting that Mexican Deaf individuals fall into one of three fundamental Deaf identities: Spanish-speaking Deaf individuals (whom he identifies as the speaking Deaf), Deaf individuals who are socially isolated and linguistically undefined (the semilingual Deaf), and members of the Mexican Deaf community (the signing Deaf). See Boris Fridman-Mintz, "Inclusive Education in Mexico: De Facto Segregation of the Signing Deaf," in *Change and Promise: Bilingual Deaf Education and Deaf Culture in Latin America*, ed. Barbara Gerner de García and Lodenir Becker Karnopp (Washington, DC: Gallaudet University Press, 2016), 123. See also Sarah Chinn, "Gender, Sex, and Disability from Helen Keller to Tiny Tim," *Radical History Review* 94 (2006): 240–48; Cleall, "Orientalising Deafness"; Catherine J. Kudlick, "Disability History: Why We Need Another 'Other,'" *American Historical Review* 108, no. 3 (2003): 763–93; Harlan Lane, "Hearing Agenda: Eradicating the Deaf-World," in *Deaf World: A Historical Reader and Primary Sourcebook*, ed. Lois Bragg (New York: New York University Press, 2001); Doris Zames Fleischer and Frieda Zames, *The Disability Rights Movement: From Charity to Confrontation* (Philadelphia: Temple University Press, 2011); Virdi, *Hearing Happiness*.

23. The Persons with Disabilities Act of the State of Mexico uses the phrase "*personas con capacidades diferentes*" (people with different abilities), which states that these individuals "suffer from a loss, impairment or reduction of an organ or physical, sensory or intellectual function, which restricts daily life activities and prevents their individual and social development." I acknowledge that the terms deaf and deaf-mute are offensive to many in the Deaf community; thus, these terms as well as their Spanish translations *sordo* or *sordomudo* will only be used when referring to the hearing and communicative difference of deafness or in the direct translation of historical documents in order to preserve the integrity of the original texts. See International Disability Rights Monitor (IDRM), *Regional Report on the Americas 2004* (Chicago: International Disability Network, 2004), 260–89.

24. Israel Katzman, *La arquitectura del siglo XIX en México* (México: Centro de Investigaciones Arquitectónicas, Universidad Nacional Autónoma de México, 1973), 19; see also Pablo Piccato, "Urbanistas, Ambulantes, and Mendigos: The Dispute for Urban Space in Mexico City, 1890–1930," in *Reconstructing Criminality in Latin America*, ed. Carlos Aguire and Robert Buffington (Wilmington, DE: Scholarly Resources, 2000), 113–48.

25. August Comte, *System of Positive Polity* (Paris: Carilian-Goeury and Vor Dalmont, 1852); Auguste Comte and John Henry Bridges, *A General View of Positivism* (Paris: [s.n.], 1848). See also Pablo Piccato, *City of Suspects: Crime in Mexico City, 1900–1931* (Durham, NC: Duke University Press, 2001).

26. Sharon V. Betcher, "The Picture of Health: 'Nature' at the Intersection of Disability, Religion and Ecology," *Worldviews* 19, no. 1 (2015): 16. http://www.jstor.org/stable/43809763.

27. Fritsch, "Toxic Pregnancies," 376.

28. Claudia Agostoni, *Monuments of Progress: Modernization and Public Health in Mexico City, 1876–1910* (Calgary: University of Calgary Press, 2004), 25.

29. Quoted in Andrews, 110. See also Davis, "Constructing Normalcy."

Holly Caldwell

30. For a discussion of disability as a social, political, and cultural construct, see Lennard Davis, *The End of Normal: Identity in a Biocultural Era* (Ann Arbor: University of Michigan Press, 2013).

31. Moisés González Navarro, *Población y sociedad en México, 1900–1970*, vol. 1 (México: UNAM, 1974), 396–97.

32. See Jay Kinsbruner, *The Colonial Spanish-American City: Urban Life in the Age of Atlantic Capitalism* (Austin: University of Texas Press, 2005); Alejandra B. Osorio, *Inventing Lima: Baroque Modernity in Peru's South Sea Metropolis* (New York: Palgrave Macmillan, 2008).

33. See Piccato, *City of Suspects*.

34. Mallén, *México Ayer y Hoy 1876–1904*, 7.

35. Carlos Welti, "Instituciones y sobrevivencia: De la independencia al México actual" in *México en tres momentos, 1810–1910–2010: hacia la conmemoración del bicentenario de la Independencia y del centenario de la Revolución Mexicana: retos y perspectivas*, ed. Alicia Mayer (México, D. F.: Universidad Nacional Autónoma de México Instituto, 2007), 148–62.

36. See Davis, "Constructing Normalcy," 3–16; R. A. R. Edwards, *Words Made Flesh: Nineteenth-Century Deaf Education and the Growth of Deaf Culture* (New York: New York University Press, 2012), 5.

37. Cleall, "Orientalising Deafness," 25, 32.

38. Stephanie Sharon Ballenger, "Modernizing Madness: Doctors, Patients and Asylums in Nineteenth-Century Mexico City," (PhD diss., University of California, Berkeley, 2009), 5, ProQuest (AAT 3382834).

39. Dublan and Lozano, eds. *Legislation Mexicana*, vol. 11, chap. 10, Title 9, 238.

40. For a discussion of "home colonialism" and the ways in which Britain implemented social domestic programs to reform its idle and poor communities, see Barbara Arneil, "The Failure of Planned Happiness: The Rise and Fall of British Home Colonies," in *Happiness and Utility: Essays Presented to Frederick Rosen*, ed. Georgios Varouxakis and Mark Philip (London: UCL Press, 2019), 269–88.

41. Ignacio Trigueros, *Memoria de los Ramos Municipales* (México: Imprenta Económica, 1867) 69–70.

42. Antonio García Cubas, *Mexico: Its Trade, Industries, and Resources* (Mexico: s.n., 1893), xix.

43. *Memorias del Primer Congreso Higiénico-Pedagógico reunido en la Ciudad de México el Ano de 1882* (México: Imprenta del Gobierno, 1882); *Memorias del Segundo Congreso Médico Pan-Americano verificado en la ciudad de México* (México: Hoeck y Compañía Impresores y Editores, 1898).

44. See George Rosen, *History of Public Health* (New York: MD, 1958), which has suggested that the notion of protecting, strengthening, and promoting the welfare of its citizens was one of the most important functions of the modern state.

45. Betcher, "Picture of Health," 12.

46. Mexican policymakers viewed their populations as backward and unfit, and they devised ways to reform them. Mexican criminologists linked vices and behaviors such as ignorance, alcoholism, gambling, prostitution, and idleness to crime, and recommended education, prison reform, and rationalized criminal laws to combat vagrancy and crime. See Robert M. Buffington, *Criminal and Citizen in Modern Mexico* (Lincoln: University of Nebraska Press, 2000); James Alex Garza, *The Imagined Underworld: Sex, Crime, and Vice in Porfirian Mexico City* (Lincoln: University of Nebraska Press, 2007); Nancy Leys Stepan, *The Hour of Eugenics: Race, Gender and Nation in Latin America* (Itha-

ca, NY: Cornell University Press, 1991); Laura Suárez y López Guazo, *Eugenesia y racismo en México* (México: UNAM, 2005).

47. Katzman, *La arquitectura del siglo XIX en México*, 19.

48. Agostoni, *Monuments of Progress*, 77.

49. Barbara Tenenbaum, "Streetwise History: The Paseo de la Reforma and the Porfirian State, 1876–1910," in *Rituals of Rule, Rituals of Resistance: Public Celebrations and Popular Culture in Mexico*, ed. William Beezley et al. (Wilmington, DE: Scholarly Resources, 1994), 127–50.

50. The Paseo de la Reforma was first laid out under Emperor Maximilian's rule between 1864 and 1867 and later inaugurated in 1877.

51. Piccato, *City of Suspects*, 17–18; Garza, *Imagined Underworld*, 20–22; Tenenbaum, 145–46.

52. See Miguel S. Macedo, *La criminalidad en México: medios de combatirla* (México: Oficina Tipografia de la Secretaría de Fomento, 1897); Jesús M. Rábago, *Historia del gran crimen* (México: Tipografia de "El Partido Liberal," 1897); Carlos Roumagnac, *Los Criminales en México: ensayo de psicología criminal* (México: Tipografía El Fénix, 1904); Carlos Roumagnac, *La estadística criminal en Mexico* (México: Imprenta de Arturo García Cubas Sucessores Hermanos, 1907).

53. Julio Guerrero, *La génesis del crimen en México: estudio de psiquiatría social* (México: Librería de la Vda de Ch. Bouret, 1901).

54. Sarah Jaquette Ray, "Risking Bodies in the Wild: The 'Corporeal Unconscious' of American Adventure Culture," in *Disability Studies and the Environmental Humanities: Toward an Eco-Crip Theory*, ed. Sarah Jaquette Ray and Jay Sibara (Lincoln: University of Nebraska Press, 2017), 30.

55. Agostoni, *Monuments of Progress*, 15.

56. Antonio Peñafiel, *Memoria sobre las aguas de la capital de México* (México: Oficina Tip. De la Secretaría de Fomento, 1884), 5–6, 53. See also Ayuntamiento Constitucional de Mexico, *Documentos Relativos al Drenaje de la Ciudad de México* (Mexico: Tipografa de la Oficina Impresora del Timbre, 1897), 8; Roberto Gayol, *Projecto de Desagüe y Saneamiento para la Cuidad de México* (México: Oficina Tip de la Secretaría de Fomento, 1892); Luis Ruiz, *Maladies Endémiques Observées dans la République Mexicaine* (México: s.n., 1892).

57. José Ángel Ceniceros, *El Problema Social* (México: Ediciones Botas, 1935), 35.

58. Miasma theory prevailed from ancient times through the nineteenth century, when germ theory became more widely accepted.

59. Peñafiel, *Memoria sobre las aguas de la capital de México*, 15. Dr. Manuel de la Fuente held that the discoveries made by Koch were not unquestionable truths for science.

60. See Fritsch, "Toxic Pregnancies," 365–66.

61. See deaf historian Jaipreet Virdi's book, *Hearing Happiness*, an excellent work that examines the endless search for deafness cures in American history.

62. Cited in Nichole Sanders, "Protecting Mothers in Order to Protect Children: Maternalism and the 1935 Pan-American Child Congress," in *Maternalism Reconsidered: Motherhood, Welfare and Social Policy in the Twentieth Century*, ed. Marian van der Klein, Rebecca Jo Plant, Nichole Sanders, and Lori R. Weintrob (New York: Berghahn, 2012), 149.

63. Edward Allen Fay, ed., *American Annals of the Deaf and Dumb* (Washington, DC: Gibson Brothers, 1878), 12.

64. Report from hygiene inspector Luis Jiménez, AHSSA, BP, EE, ENSM, Archivo Historico de Secretaría de Salubridad y Assistencia, México, D.F., Beneficencia Pública,

Establecimientos Educativos, Escuela Nacional de Sordo Mudos, folder 1, file 40, August 22, 1878. Hereafter referenced as AHSSA, BP, EE, ENSM.

65. Department of Commerce and Labor Bureau of the Census, *Special Reports: The Blind and the Deaf 1900* (Washington, DC: Government Printing Office, 1900), 73. See also "Los sordo mudos y su instrucción," *El Eco de Ambos Mundos*, December 16, 1874; Fay, *American Annals of the Deaf and Dumb*, 10; Joseph Claybaugh Gordon, *Notes and Observations upon the Education of the Deaf* (Washington, DC: Volta Bureau, 1892), xi.

66. García, *Discurso Escuela Sordo-Mudos*, 7–8.

67. *Diario del Hogar*, October 1, 1902. See also *Periódico de la Academia de Medicina en México*, July 15, 1836. Articles such as these illustrate that these concerns were published in medical journals since the early nineteenth century.

68. *Diario del Hogar*, October 1, 1902.

69. Francisco Vázquez Gómez, *Informe rendido por el professor de la Escuela Nacional de Sordo-Mudos de México* (México: La Europea de J. Aguilar Vera y C, 1898), 23.

70. See *El Instructor*, November 1, 1893.

71. Baranda, *Codificación Tomo VII*, 27, 29–30.

72. Baranda, *Codificación Tomo VII*, 35.

73. Vázquez Gómez, *Informe rendido por el professor*, 5.

74. Vázquez Gómez, *Informe rendido por el professor*, 25.

75. Manuel Antonio Carreño, *Compendio del Manual de Urbanidad y Buenas maneras* (Lima: Benito Gil: Editor, 1874), 32–34.

76. ACN, *Documentos Relativos al Drenaje*, 8. OJD, *Memoria del desague*; Ruiz, *Maladies Endemiques*; Gayol, *Projecto de Desague*; Anonymous, *Drainage Works*.

77. Report, AHSSA, BP, EE, ENSM, folder 4, file 10, March 1897.

78. Vázquez Gómez, *Informe rendido por el professor*, 25–26.

79. Vázquez Gómez, *Informe rendido por el professor*, 25–26.

80. Peñafiel, *Memoria sobre las aguas de la capital de México*, 155.

81. Peñafiel, *Memoria sobre las aguas de la capital de México*, 128–31, 156–58.

82. Letter from Trinidad García to the Secretaría de Gobernación, AHSSA, BP, EE, ENSM, folder 4, file 3, March 1897.

83. Letter from Trinidad García to the Secretaría de Gobernación, AHSSA, BP, EE, ENSM, folder 4, file 3, March 1897; Ceniceros, *El Problema Social*, 31–32.

84. Letter from Trinidad García to the Secretaría de Gobernación, AHSSA, BP, EE, ENSM, folder 4, file 3, March 1897; Vázquez Gómez, *Informe rendido ENSM*, 27.

85. Letter from Trinidad García to the Ayuntamiento, AHSSA, BP, EE, ENSM, folder 4, file 28, May 5, 1900.

86. Report, AHSSA, BP, EE, ENSM, folder 4, file 10, March 1897.

87. See Agostoni, *Monuments of Progress*.

88. See *Diario del Hogar*, October 1, 1902. See also *Periódico de la Academia de Medicina en México*, July 15, 1836.

7

The Blindness of Colonial Modernity

A Blind Man's Remembrance of Things Past

AUBREY TANG

This essay investigates how colonial modernity privileges the sense of sight. It examines the 1976 operatic song *Yiwang/Yik Wong* (A Blind Man's Remembrance of Things Past), written and performed by Du Huan/Dou Wun (1910–1979), the most acclaimed blind Cantonese musician of the *dishui nanyin/deiseoi naamyam* (tunes of the southern blind people) tradition. The song chronicles Dou's life not only as a legendary musician but also as a blind man who lived under British rule in colonial Hong Kong between 1926 and 1975. This essay draws on Dou's song and his life experiences to call into question the modernity of Hong Kong's environmental shift from a preindustrial southern Chinese city to an international financial center, during which blind Cantonese people suffered a process of exclusion thanks to various colonial capitalist governing approaches. As the ensuing discussion will demonstrate, in the premodern/early modern Cantonese environment blind people could enjoy a high degree of mobility and autonomy, but when the former colony was transformed into a center of capitalist modernity, the blind were increasingly restricted and marginalized in Hong Kong society. This thesis shows the need for an expansive conceptualization of the "colonial." Although (post)modern Hong Kong is often trivialized as part of the Global North, the relatively nonocularist tradition from premodern/early modern Cantonese culture, which is the scope of this study, should be compared to other marginalized cultural practices due to colonialism. The paradoxical colonial identity of Hong Kong explains why the available research on Dou was not conducted by scholars from the Global

South. It also reveals that the current Global North/South bifurcation, some-times helpful for understanding other colonial histories, is counterproduc-tive for hearing the voices of Hong Kong's colonial subaltern. Hong Kong has an unconventional colonial historical trajectory that cannot be understood in terms of the Global North–South divide, so this essay employs the more applicable concept of colonial subalternity as opposed to the Global South.

Methodologically speaking, this essay uses a sensory studies approach to illustrate how colonialists relegated blind people to the margins in modern life. It also uses a historical approach to explain colonial Hong Kong's ecology of disease. Drawing on the critical theory of Walter Benjamin, Michel Fou-cault, Oskar Negt, and Alexander Kluge as well as the cultural historical stud-ies of Constance Classen, this essay first acknowledges a cultural history of blindness before turning to a critical discussion regarding the position of the blind in a colonial capitalist economy. It aims to illustrate certain key aspects of the cultural logic of colonial capitalism in order to identify the ableism that was necessarily embedded within it.

A Blind Man's Remembrance was published in 2008 as a six-hour edited version of Dou's performances of the song from June 19–26, 1975, at the Fu-long/Fulung Tea House (Sheung Wan, Hong Kong) as well as from March 6–13, 1976, at the University of Hong Kong.[1] As in the term for the *deiseoi naamyam* genre, *deiseoi* is the name of a sign of Chinese divination. Because it was historically offered by blind people, the sign became an epithet for the blind. *Naamyam* means southern tunes, referring to a type of Cantonese op-eratic music. A short naamyam song typically has a duration of ten to thir-ty minutes and is usually backed with one or two instruments. Compared with that of other Cantonese operatic genres, the musical structure of naam-yam songs is relatively minimal and repetitive. Written in colloquial lan-guage, deiseoi naamyam was a style of rapping/narrative singing performed by blind musicians in Hong Kong and the Pearl River Delta, where Canton-ese was spoken as the main language. Before the 1920s, deiseoi naamyam was typically sung in teahouses, bars, private parties, and brothels.[2] Accord-ing to *A Blind Man's Remembrance*, its primary audience in Hong Kong was the poor. Although there is no equivalent of deiseoi naamyam in other cul-tures, Hong Kong fans have commonly compared it to Delta/Texas/Pied-mont Blues, given the similarities between the two genres in terms of their minimalist setups, idiosyncratic singing voices, and themes of personal hard-ship, war, death, lost love, sex, humor, hope, and so on. The autobiographical theme of *A Blind Man's Remembrance* is unusual, given that autobiography was never a feature of the deiseoi naamyam tradition, yet the song was writ-ten at the request of musicologist Bell Yung. At the start of his performanc-es of the song at Fulung Tea House, Dou would always politely inform his audience that he was aware that the autobiographical convention was not traditionally part of operatic music, and he would humbly ask his audience to give his experimental efforts a chance.

A Blind Man's Remembrance outlines Dou's life up to the moment of his performances. He was born in 1910 in the rural village of Zhaoqing, Guangdong, and lost his eyesight as an infant. At the age of seven, he was sent as an apprentice to a blind fortune teller; three years later, at the age of ten, he was taken to Henan, Guangzhou. After learning to sing, he moved to Hong Kong when he was sixteen. He had great success singing in brothels in Yau Ma Tei, Hong Kong, and soon married an opera songstress. Together they had three children, but all three died when they were very young. Dou then lost his livelihood when the organized sex trade was criminalized. The couple had another child, but the child and Dou's wife and his mother all died within three years. After enduring World War II, he enjoyed some success, but his business was soon hurt by the effects of radio technologies and new infrastructure. He briefly tried singing in Macau, but his efforts did not come to fruition. After returning to Hong Kong, he was taken in by some friends and later hired to sing for a local radio station, which he did for fifteen years, a period that represented the most stable employment in his life. As opera fell out of popularity in 1970s Hong Kong, he lost his job and was forced to return to the streets to sing. By the time he reached his sixties, there were times he could not even pay rent or afford warm clothes in the winter. After a period of instability, he began living on disability allowances. However, the payments were insufficient, and Dou continued to struggle, frequently returning to singing in the streets. Sometimes he was invited to sing for audiences of remote villagers, academics, culturati, and other groups. He died four years after recording A Blind Man's Remembrance, still in poverty, at the age of seventy-nine, when few remembered him.[3]

In the first part of the ensuing discussion, I focus on Dou's early life, which transpired during a premodern/early modern era of high mobility and autonomy. In the second part of the essay, I argue that when Dou moved to Hong Kong he was repeatedly inhibited and marginalized as a disabled musician despite the colony's development as a cosmopolitan center. I describe three approaches of colonial governance that reveal the regulationist logic of Hong Kong's colonial capitalism. The first of these approaches was the regulation of sexuality, which preluded a larger colonial logic that sought to control all auratic expressions historically practiced by the disabled due to their extremely unique and irreproducible historical positions in Hong Kong society. By imposing controls on the sex trade and implementing disease control measures, the colonizers normalized a Eurocentric idea about nature based on Western natural history, one that viewed hygiene as the natural disposition of life; the colony therefore had to avoid diseases and discontinue any non-Western culture of sex or any nonregulationist sexual practices. In the capitalist colony, I argue, the control over sexual practices served as a prelude to the control of all auratic expressions—a case in point being the music performed by the blind at brothels. Since both (nonvirtual) sex and deiseoi naamyam were highly irreproducible cultural expressions, they went against the logic of the capitalist mode of production. As Hong Kong became groomed as a model bourgeois colony, the auratic practices in question were aborted by the logic of colonial capitalism. The second approach—the regulation of space—further corroborated how auratic practices were spatially regulated in midcentury Hong Kong. Through the utilization of radio technologies and new infrastructure, it undermined the inherent subversive essence in Dou's music. This musical expression challenged technology, bourgeois ideals, and scientism, thereby rebelling against colonial capitalism. In this manner, the music conspicuously flaunted its rebellious character, defiantly opposing both technological and spatial regulations. Finally, the third approach of Hong Kong's logic of governance was the regulation of time, an example of which was the frequent imposition of power blackouts and curfews in the colony, both of which revealed a similar underlying colonial violence: that of the imposition of a homogeneous consciousness. This stage of my argument will also address an underlying issue with bourgeois consciousness in the colonial context: its limited awareness of the bodily agency of the colonial population.

A Mobile Blind Man before Colonial Modernity

From the song, one hears that Dou's visual impairment started in 1913 when he was three months old. There was a tradition whereby all newborns were taken to the town hall where their mothers prepared a snack of "tea eggs" for the villagers. Dou's eyes were accidentally damaged when the adults were cooking. With no access to health care in his village, he began to lose his clarity of vision. When he was a young child, his family's thirty acres of farmland and three houses were also inundated by floods.[4] After his father died, his mother was unable to care for Dou and his four siblings, so she sent her seven-year-old son to a famed local blind healer/fortune teller named Huang Fen/Wong Fan. Under the arrangement, Dou was to receive low-cost room and board as well as an apprenticeship for blind children under Wong's tutelage. As it turned out, Dou was more useful to Wong than vice versa. Wong's business began to do poorly, and he failed to teach Dou any skills. When his business went bust, he decided to use Dou—who at the time still had partial vision—as a guide on his escape route. The two of them moved to Henan, where Wong continued to deprive Dou of any education. Fortunately, Dou managed to make a decent living by going door to door and singing simple songs. Although he was never properly trained as a singer, people would give him a pittance for his efforts, considering he was only ten.

While singing in the streets, Dou would also hang out with other blind musicians on a nearby bridge, the Huanzhu Bridge, a meeting place where blind musicians would rest, wait for calls, and socialize at night. It was through this community of other blind musicians that he met his guru Sun Sheng/ Suen Sang, who taught him singing and the zither every day for two years before Dou finally moved to Hong Kong at the age of sixteen.

Dou migrated to Hong Kong following a recommendation from two older blind musician friends, Blind Fat and Ah Choi, who had left Hong Kong and sought refuge in Guangzhou during the 1925 Canton–Hong Kong workers' strike. Once the strike was over, these two veterans offered to take Dou and another young musician back with them to Hong Kong to help them seek a better life. The four musicians took a riverboat to Shiqi, Guangdong, and then a ferry to Qianshan, Macau. The older musicians had offered to pay the travel costs for their two young companions, but they were given free passage for being "*jianghu zidi*"—that is, fraternal strong men with special skills on the go. Not only did they receive special treatment from the boatmen but they also made money by singing for the other passengers.

Hong Kong was where Dou would finally meet success, although he kick-started his career while passing through Macau, where he sang at a brothel following Ah Choi's advice and easily made some money. At that point, Ah Choi offered to take Dou in, thinking Dou could do just fine in Macau without going to Hong Kong. However, Dou turned down the offer because he had promised his young companion that they would go to Hong Kong together. In Hong Kong, Dou began singing in the streets during the day and at the brothels at night, where he sang naanyam. Soon he earned a lucrative income for a seventeen-year-old. When Dou started out working at the brothels, the highest wages of "ordinary competent mechanics" were only $1.35 to $3.10 per day.[5] Duo was making $2.00 per night by singing for only a few hours.

Dou's travel experience shows that talented blind people had a high degree of mobility, independence, and autonomy in the premodern/early modern Cantonese environment. Despite his impaired vision, he had managed to move from his hometown in Zhaoqing to Henan with a blind man at the age of ten. Later, as an adolescent, he traveled to Hong Kong via Shiqi, Guangdong, and Qianshan, Macau, in the company of three blind friends. Even with today's infrastructure, for a traveler with regular vision it still takes about seventy-five minutes by train to travel from Zhaoqing to Henan, seventy minutes from Henan to Shiqi, a little over an hour by bus from Shiqi to Macau, and forty-five minutes by bus from Macau to Hong Kong. Yet in *A Blind Man's Remembrance*, with his delightful lyrics and playful, colloquial Cantonese,

Dou's voice radiates positive energy when he sings about his long trip from almost a century ago:

> We four, aye, we four in 1926, sallied forth on the night of the 13th, on the third month of the Chinese calendar. We headed down the waterway aboard a Shiqi floral-stern riverboat. The evening was as uneventful as the day that followed, and by the afternoon, we had arrived at our midway point, Shiqi. There, we spent the night, only to discover the next day that our trusty Shiqi riverboat would take us no farther. So, on the 14th, we boarded a ferry to Qianshan, eventually making our way to Macau. Aboard that ship, with nothing better to do, we sang and played music, earning money along the way.[6]

The lyrics depict a young blind man in control of his life. It was unclear whether it was only he or his entire group of friends who did not expect the necessity of boarding a second watercraft. Regardless, he does not express doubt or fear even though there was uncertainty on his journey. Instead, he engaged with the moment, even making some money while waiting around. For this hopeful, courageous young blind man, the sky was the limit.

Not only was Dou autonomous; he was also a dignified musician. In *A Blind Man's Remembrance*, although at times he would remind the audience that he was "the unlucky one" (meaning he was disabled), his story strongly suggests that he had a certain status as a musician. On the ship, he identified as a person with mobility and special skills ("*jianghu zidi*") who therefore got a free trip. Even as a child, he had the confidence to sing door to door when no one had taught him how to sing. When he began singing professionally, he bumped up his income by moving his performances from the streets to the brothels, revealing his progressive outlook on life. The Cantonese opera historian Meibao Cheng made a similar observation about Dou's 1975 performance of the operatic song "Making a Fuss with the Provincial Officer Mei." In his performance, Dou introduced himself and referenced some places where he had sung, including Sixian Island (Guangdong), Henan, and West Point (Hong Kong). Although these locations sound remote to today's young audience, especially to residents of Hong Kong, it sounds like, for the blind man, they all belonged to one world:[7]

> Well, it's like this. When I first broke into the opera scene, I sang the "dragon boat" music genre. You know Sixian Island? That's where I used to sing dragon boat songs. And then I went to Henan and started singing naamyam. That's how I got into naamyam. As for singing dragon boat songs at the restaurants, I've done that many times. I've been singing dragon boat with Blind Wah at the teahouse [Jianyuan/]

Ginjyun in West Point. Yeah, that's where I sing dragon boat. Very well.[8]

Both examples indicate that distance and blindness did not deter Dou from engaging with the world to an extent that younger and culturally conditioned generations today might find difficult to fathom. His high degree of mobility shows that in the premodern/early modern Cantonese environment, even if a blind person had minimal financial or other types of support from family, they could nonetheless function as relatively self-sufficient and powerful participants of society by exchanging information, moral support, and resources with other blind people in a tightly knit community of the disabled.

The story of this premodern/early modern man uninhibited by his visual impairment firmly attests to Constance Classen's 1990s theory of sensory hierarchy. Classen argues that the senses are determined not only biologically but also culturally and that the importance of each sense depends on cultural traditions and values.[9] For example, in a Western environment, olfaction was emphasized and formalized in classical and medieval times, devalued since the Enlightenment, and eventually relegated to the realms of sentiments and sexuality by the nineteenth century.[10] Likewise, in a Cantonese environment, although the historical trajectory of sensory hierarchization is different from that of the West, *A Blind Man's Remembrance* testifies to a destabilization of the supremacy of visual sensation, the highest-ranked sense in modern life, during the premodern/early modern period of Cantonese cultural history. *A Blind Man's Remembrance* suggests an era before sight became the most privileged sense in the high modern/postmodern age and when an underprivileged blind man could still attain a high degree of autonomy.

Colonial Regulationism

One might assume that a positive and talented musician would enjoy a good life in British colonial Hong Kong, a supposedly modern and liberal city. However, that did not happen. Colonial capitalism had transformed Hong Kong from preindustrial village to cosmopolitan urban environments, but it failed the blind. Instead of focusing on blatantly discriminatory policies that favor the nondisabled, I will outline three governing approaches in colonial Hong Kong that systematically normalized a nondisabled bourgeois lifestyle and marginalized all bodies that did not or could not assimilate into its underlying ableist capitalist culture.

The Regulation of Sexuality

The first colonial approach was that of regulating sexuality by criminalizing the organized sex trade. We hear Dou singing about losing his livelihood in

1935 when the colonial government shut down all the brothels. That was also the year his wife gave birth to their fourth child after their three other children had all died when they were very young. In addition, Dou had to support his mother after moving her to Hong Kong from Zhaoqing. To top it off, he also struggled with opium addiction, a habit he had naively picked up at the brothels. He tried taking care of his family, especially his precious fourth child, who he hoped would not die like his other children. Unfortunately, after Dou had spent years of singing in the streets for meager amounts of money, his son passed away at the age of five. Dou's mother died the following year. Soon after, Imperial Japan invaded and occupied Hong Kong during World War II, and one year later, Dou's wife also passed away from an illness.

The 1935 banning of the organized sex trade directly contributed to Dou's later misfortunes prior to the Japanese occupation. His entire family relied on his income, and he was unable to make ends meet after the ban was imposed. To understand how colonial policies subscribed to a Eurocentric idea of nature that affected the livelihood of the blind in 1930s Hong Kong, we must first understand the interdependence of the sex industry and the blind community. The lives of sex workers and blind people were interconnected during the premodern/early modern period in Guangdong and Hong Kong because of blind people's limited work choices and sex workers' business model. Since the late nineteenth century, blindness was prevalent in China and Hong Kong. The disabled Scottish missionary Reverend William. H. Murray described the 1870s "densely crowded streets of Chinese cities,"

> where an extraordinary number of blind men [mingled] in every crowd, some going about alone, or guided by the man in front of him, while the leader [felt] his way with a long stick—a most literal illustration of the blind leading the blind. A gentleman assured me that he had on one occasion seen no less than 600 miserable blind beggars all assembled to share a gratuitous distribution of rice![11]

Murray estimated that one in six hundred people in China during that time was blind.[12] Assuming his estimate was correct, there would have been 3.2 times more blind people in China than in the United States at that time.[13] To make a living, blind children would learn skills, including fortune-telling and musical performance. These trades sometimes could bring in an income higher than those made by sighted people:

> I have been told by medical missionaries that they have sometimes offered to treat curable cases of defective sight in young children and the parents have refused to allow them to do so, because as the children

grew up they would not be able to earn so much, and consequently they would themselves have to work harder.[14]

Dou's music went far beyond his fortune-telling. His guru stopped him from learning anything but singing and playing the zither, not wanting him to become an instrumentalist, a profession that would not earn him a living as high as that of a *shiniang/sinoeng* (female master) [also called *guji/gugei* (blind female musician)]. Since the 1860s, disadvantaged blind daughters, like visually impaired boys, were sent to or adopted by entertainment businesses, musicians, or unmarried women, who would raise and train them as musicians for profit.[15] Between 1916 and the mid-1920s, these blind song-stresses became trendsetters, performing in teahouses, at concerts, and for private parties. They also toured and released music albums in Guangzhou, Hong Kong, and Macau. Against his fierce competitors of the opposite sex, Dou was advised by his guru to never play instruments for others but to instead establish himself as a singer, because a singer would have a better life. That was good advice. A month after checking into a building in Mong-kok, Hong Kong, inhabited entirely by blind people, he coincidentally reunited with a friend from Henan who knew the brothels and subsequently introduced him to the brothel scene in Yau Ma Tei. At only seventeen, Dou was performing at brothels and private parties for a stable clientele of sex workers and their customers.

Unfortunately, despite Dou's extraordinary musical talents, the organized sex trade that provided an audience for his performances was systematically regulated and eventually criminalized. Prior to British colonial rule, the organized sex trade was legal in Hong Kong, in accordance with the law of the Great Qing empire[16] that ceded Hong Kong to Great Britain. After the British empire took over in 1857, colonial rulers began to impose licensing requirements on brothels and subject sex workers to medical examinations. Brothels were geographically segregated to serve their designated racial groups (European, Chinese, Japanese, and Indian, through the decades). Female sex workers who infected their European clients with venereal disease were punished and medically incarcerated. Those serving European men were inspected more rigorously compared to those serving Chinese men, and they were reportedly subjected to demeaning weekly examinations. The police and medical authorities could enter all brothels at any time. New sex workers had to be approved by the Registrar General. Unlicensed brothels, or those with zoning issues, were shut down. Even after London directed the colonial government to cease its demeaning physical examinations in 1886, the colonial government continued to conduct them until 1890. In 1923, all sex workers were (re)investigated and licensed and were required to keep accurate records of all men they served, and police and military authorities could look up the men's personal information at any time.[17] By 1935, London decided to close all brothels in Hong Kong, even though half of the city's tax revenue over the three prior decades had been paid by sex workers.[18] The primary rationale for these colonial control measures was the alleged spread of venereal disease.

As Michel Foucault explains, sex is repressed in capitalist environments because it plays a role opposite to that of power in Western culture. "[Sex] produces . . . absences and gaps; it overlooks elements, introduces discontinuities, separates what is joined, and marks off boundaries."[19] Sexuality has the potential to subvert the coherent structure of power in capitalist societies, so it is always surveilled and regulated. In addition, according to Western natural history, hygiene is an innate disposition, not only of human life but of animal life as well. In Christian and Hellenic thought, cleanliness is associated with purity and innocence; being unclean and foul is associated with guilt and sin. A fundamental belief held from the inception of Western culture is that the behavior of the entire human race is hygienic by nature and that disease avoidance behaviors are natural among all living creatures.[20] Likewise, during colonial times, hygiene was conceived as the natural form of life in modern society. Anything "unhygienic," such as sexual practices that disrupted the "natural" hygienic state, was censored by the regulationist regime. Conflating the idea of sexuality as a threat for the colonial capitalist environment and the idea of diseases as disturbances of the natural state of life, the colonial government was determined to combat the issue of venereal disease. Sex disrupted the colonial government's normalized notion of "social hygiene" and was a source of great preoccupation in London.[21]

Consequently, in the name of hygiene (and its association with "nature"), the colonizer mandated exclusive and disciplined practices of sexuality. Its racist regulations significantly modified Hong Kong's infectious disease environment and suppressed the culture of sexuality that Hong Kong had retained from Imperial China. For the British Parliament, venereal disease constituted a threatening anomaly, and sex was therefore medicalized. Not only was venereal disease pathologized but it was stigmatized by culture and by race. The colonial government believed that sex workers, especially those serving Chinese men, were the source of infection in Hong Kong.[22] However, as historians have discovered, the number of infected people among the European community drastically decreased because of the colonial government's medical concern for only European soldiers, sailors, and policemen, making the native Chinese community seem more disease ridden. In reality, Hong Kong's ecology of disease was affected by the colonizer. Before the British occupied Hong Kong in 1839 during the First Opium War with the

Great Qing empire, Hong Kong was primarily a small fishing village with a few thousand farmers and fishermen. There was no evidence showing that venereal disease was a significant character of Hong Kong's epidemiology any more than it was in other parts of the Pearl River Delta. Within three years after British colonialism, new patrons, including the British nationals and Chinese merchants, arrived. Hong Kong became "a bustling town" "forthwith invaded by brothel keepers and prostitutes from the adjoining districts of the mainland of China."[23] The colonial government promoted "the incalculable benefit" of its Victorian venereal disease control, but its navy was remembered as arriving with an astonishingly high number of sexually transmitted disease infections.[24] This is not to blame troops deployed overseas, who in general have been threatened by STDs—that is, to "slut-shame" them—but to understand the racist modification and representation of Hong Kong's ecology of venereal disease during early British colonialism.

One might ask, what was the role of the blind musicians in this situation of colonial regulation of sexuality? Within the mutualistic relationship between blind musicians and sex workers, the two groups shared several commonalities and particularities. First, they were both marginalized sectors of the population. Many deiseoi naamyam songs are about disappointments and sufferings in life, such as lost love, death, deceit, distant love, and so on—themes with which both marginalized groups could relate. Second, the blind musicians' irreplaceable nature of existence was conjugated with the socially subversive position of the sex workers, as previously explained. Deiseoi naamyam performances in brothels, like (nonvirtual) sex, were largely irreproducible, being spatiotemporally exclusive. In other words, these performances had what Walter Benjamin called "aura"—"originally, the embeddedness of an artwork in the context of tradition found expression in a cult."[25] As a musical tradition, deiseoi naamyam performances were embedded with the unique, anti-ableist identities of their blind Cantonese performers. In ritual terms, the spirit of the blind was embedded in the ritual musical sounds they performed. Their music therefore constituted the uncompromising expression of an "auratic mode of existence . . . never entirely severed from its ritual function."[26] Just like (nonvirtual) sex, the ritualistic music of these blind performers could only be produced at a singular historical location by singular historical actors. Authentic deiseoi naamyam could be played only at the historically specific venues where this generation of blind Cantonese musicians performed and nowhere else and by no one else. This kind of auratic "presence" apparently contradicted the modern technologism to which the colony aspired. As Benjamin observed in the 1930s, mechanically reproduced images, such as film, would shatter aura, tradition, and cultural heritage. Auratic expressions would be forcefully displaced by mass-produced images in a fascist modern mode of production.[27] Along with the 1935 ban on the organized sex trade in Hong Kong, the highly irreproducible tradition of deiseoi naamyam was therefore predictably displaced.

The Regulation of Space

The second colonial approach to governance was the regulation of space through mass media communication technology and land-use planning. It modified Hong Kong's preindustrial environment through the physical displacement of the impoverished bodies. As we learn in *A Blind Man's Remembrance*, in 1950 when Dou's career had picked up, media technology replaced his singing in the lives of opera fans. As he put it in his song lyrics, "Oy vey, you know, good times never last long. Time was 1950, and suddenly there popped up *a monster*, one that killed by way of technology. What was it? It was called Radio Rediffusion" (emphasis added). Radio Rediffusion was a British company that offered a wired radio broadcasting service.[28] Other radio broadcasts predated Radio Rediffusion, but the company's transmissions were more accessible to the working class in terms of installation and power supply. Because Kowloon, where Dou sang, was the area where workers resided, they could either install Radio Rediffusion or piggyback on their neighbors' installation for free. Moreover, transistor radios, another accessible technology, also emerged during this time. As a result, Dou's live audience drastically shrank. His friends suggested that he try singing in King George V Memorial Park in Jordan, a park where many people cooled off every evening. Once again Dou followed their advice and subsequently enjoyed huge success in the park, due to his ability to charm his audiences. Fans would crowd the park every evening. When it rained, they set up a covered space in the adjacent wet market to hear him sing. For two years, Dou thought he had secured his future. Yet one day, the colonial government rolled out an extension project. The park was fenced in, and the crowds disappeared. Dou tried to sing behind the wet market but there was little traffic. He could earn only a quarter of his average income and once again fell into poverty.

Just as Dou was displaced from the sex industry, he was now likewise displaced from the streets by the colonial control of space via the mechanical reproduction of sound and the bourgeois development of infrastructure. Radio Rediffusion's broadcast of reproduced sound images enticed an economically disadvantaged community—Dou's mostly working-class fans—away from traditional performance venues, and thanks to the increasing availability of radios, poor people no longer had to leave their homes for entertainment. Even when some still went out for fresh air and music, as seen in King George V Memorial Park, public space was regulated in the name of land-use planning. Parks played an important role in Hong Kong as spaces of leisure for the low-income population. They were where members of the working class found refuge from the heat at a time when temperature control was expensive. They were also places where people without access to the press could learn the latest news, socialize (when the colonial bourgeoisie rejected them in other spaces), network, find love and work, purchase medicines that were elsewhere inaccessible, and so forth. King George V Memorial Park had a particular historical resonance for the people who congregated there, since it was rumored to have had sightings of ghosts from World War II. The park was therefore a space for those who had suffered the trauma of the war, where survivors would bring offerings and mourn on festive occasions.[29] In such an anti-technology, anti-bourgeois, anti-scientist space, Dou's park concerts were practically "the working-class's defense organization."[30] For two years, he had organized a "proletarian public sphere" with a unique Yau Ma Tei experience that posed a contradiction to Hong Kong's capitalist modernity. As a result, the space was shut down and he was expelled.

The Regulation of Time

The third colonial approach to governance was the regulating of time via power blackouts and curfews. During World War II, Hong Kong was under Japanese occupation between 1941 and 1945. Working at the time as a poor street musician with a sick wife to care for, Dou lived in an adverse environment with inflation, food shortages, looting, and massive deaths due to famine. In *A Blind Man's Remembrance*, we hear Dou trying to survive by continuing to sing in the dangerous streets at night during the war, literally walking past dead bodies abandoned in the streets. He also passed by shuttered businesses, many of which were now used as morgues to house copious numbers of corpses. Even though Dou had little musical competition at the time—since most other blind musicians had either fled or perished—after his first wife passed away in 1942, he could still barely put food on the table. Worst of all, the following year Imperial Japan announced the great blackout, banning all use of lighting after midnight throughout the city. The absence of light brought Dou's nighttime performances to an end, along with his main source of income. With his food supplies depleted and with no other alternatives, he was forced to marry a blind, widowed opera songstress so that they could support each other. The marriage eventually ended over financial issues.[31]

After the war, Dou experienced a few years of ups and downs before heading to Macau in 1954. A friend situated him there and found him a gig at a teahouse. Within a week, he had found stable work at hotels and inns. He would sing for a casino restaurant that paid him a good wage to perform every night from 2 A.M. to 5 A.M. Unfortunately, as he remarks in *A Blind Man's Remembrance*, "good times never last long, really. . . . We heard an explosion—a time bomb, people said. Then the world changed." Macau had entered a border dispute with the People's Republic of China (PRC). The city was planted with time bombs and put under curfew.[32] As a result, Dou lost most of his business, and after running out of money, he returned to Hong Kong, which he considered his permanent home.

Both cases illustrate the omnipotent power of social lockdowns to regulate time and physically displace the impoverished bodies in the colonies. Dou's career and livelihood were subjected time and again to the interference of imperial powers. While Imperial Japan and Great Britain were clearly foreign powers, PRC was not Dou's home country either. PRC was a new regime that had formed in mainland China following Dou's migration to Hong Kong. Regardless of which colonizer/empire was ruling over colonies like Hong Kong and Macau, as a colonial subject Dou was always subjected to a technological control over consciousness: a homogenous time-consciousness. Critics have long agreed that time-consciousness is not unanimous, time itself being a modern technological and cultural construct. By homogenizing a shared local time, technology controls bodies in modern society, dating back to early modern Europe where "the public clock was 'an indicator of modernity.'"[33] English and Swiss legislation prohibited factory workers from bringing private timepieces to work, because everyone had to adhere to the factory clock, which by law was set by the country's official public clock.[34] To challenge a politically sanctioned clock was therefore to risk discipline and punishment. Other complicit technologies, such as the printing press and television, further reinforced a homogenous time. Modern readers read newspapers and novels to imagine a national community whose members share the same time.[35] Modern viewers follow radio and television programming to organize their private lives.[36] When it comes to history, according to Western Social Democratic theory, countries and cultures are expected to "progress" by following a prescriptive historical trajectory, because the entire world must share one single homogeneous, empty time.[37] Postcolonial cultures that defy "the ideology of progress or 'development' [imposed] from the nineteenth century" onward are therefore considered backward.[38] Over and over, time in the colonies was rendered homogenous by empires, whether for the purposes of invasions, territorial disputes, or colonial control, as seen in Dou's experience in Hong Kong and Macau.

These examples of a problematic homogeneous time-consciousness reveal that the fundamental type of colonial oppression goes beyond the usual, more predictable types of oppression—for example, ableist segregation, lack of accessibility, and so forth. The most fundamental colonial oppression is the change effected on consciousness, because consciousness determines one's experience of everything, including disability, in a colony. The imposition of a homogenized consciousness erases the subaltern's sentience and replaces it with what the colonizer considers a modern way of life. This is why colonial violence against disabled bodies is never limited to the physical, sensory, and cognitive body that the word *disability* typically connotes; it also subjects the underlying consciousness of disabled bodies. Colonial violence includes changes to underlying consciousness, as seen in colonial experiences of land uses, economic structures, language, values, aesthetics, customs, and so on—even *the mind* of the native—all of which must be decolonized, as postcolonial theorists such as Franz Fanon and Ngũgĩ wa Thiong'o have argued.[39]

The conversion of mind/consciousness is the most extreme form of colonial violence, to which those at the bottom of society are more susceptible than members of the bourgeoisie and the upper class. For instance, although in a colonial modernity such as that of Hong Kong everyone was subjected to a homogeneous time, the working class had less freedom to work around it than did the more privileged citizens. Since Dou's audiences in Yau Ma Tei were typically Cantonese working-class members with laborious jobs during the day, nighttime was usually the only moment this population had to enjoy their cultural lives. Blackouts and curfews therefore meant Dou's immediate loss of this audience. By contrast, the colonial upper class had access to labor and technology to allay some of the oppression of homogeneous time. During a later stage of Dou's career, he met a wealthy customer, He Yao Guang/Ho Iu Kwong, a Hong Kong real estate tycoon. For years, Ho would invite Dou to perform privately at his upscale residence in Happy Valley. While Ho was busy working away from home, Dou would sing at his house, and his staff would record the music so that Ho could listen to it when he returned home. This example shows how in colonial modernity, the upper class, thanks to its access to labor and technological resources, had some power to defer the imposition of homogeneous time with a minimal loss of aura via control over both the authentic and the reproduced image.

Conclusion

This study examines Dou's early life and discovers that he was highly mobile, thriving and in control of his destiny during the period of his life that coincided with premodern/early modern Cantonese culture in the Pearl River Delta. Although he lost his vision soon after he was born, and although his family was practically bankrupt, he was able to travel long distances and support himself at a young age. Meanwhile, without any communication technology, he was able to exchange labor with, receive moral support from, and cohabitate with members of the large Cantonese blind community. Through this community, he met his music guru and received proper musical training before moving to Hong Kong, the more urbanized British colony. Dou's high degree of mobility and autonomy in southern China aligns with Classen's theory in sensory studies,[40] suggesting that premodern/early modern Cantonese culture was less visualist than today.

This study then notes an overall decline in Dou's quality of life after he moved to Hong Kong. Over the various stages of his career, the talented musician would situate himself in a new setting and attract a temporary large audience before a regulationist form of colonial or military control would intervene to ruin his livelihood. The essay discusses three of these regulationist forms of control, focused on sex, space, and time. One after the other, these three approaches to regulation confirm the ideas about aura and homogeneous time put forth by Walter Benjamin, who theorized that in a capitalist mode of production, mechanically reproduced images would liquidate tradition and cultural heritage.[41]

For Hong Kong's colonial state apparatus, the first approach was to systematically censor and suspend auratic native practices. The colonizer appropriated a Eurocentric conception of nature to medicalize and pathologize sexuality in Hong Kong, which preluded the extinction of other mutualistic auratic practices such as deiseoi naamyam, an integral part of the organized sex trade. Although, technically speaking, sex and naamyam could be reproduced virtually, the loss of authenticity of these highly auratic practices was less compromising than it was in the case of other, more reproducible types of cultural expression. Brothel sex and deiseoi naamyam were extremely historically specific practices and expressions, being less reproducible than other less contextual cultural expressions or forms of mass entertainment that did not have an authentic existence—for example, film. The auratic intensities of the organized sex trade and deiseoi naamyam performance were highly subversive in the face of colonial capitalism, and they were consequently eliminated through regulation.

The second colonial approach to exclude the blind man from Hong Kong's modernity was to spatially displace his music. Radio technologies were made accessible; public space was closed. These phenomena were signs of spatial control over impoverished bodies in a colonial modernity where most of Dou's audience was made up by the working class. By dispersing poor bodies in this way, the colonizers also eliminated the "proletarian public sphere" where, as Negt and Kluge argue, the "proletarian counterpublic sphere confronts these public spheres, which are permeated by the interests of capital, and does not merely see itself as the antithesis of the classical public sphere."[42] If Hong Kong's thriving mass culture in the 1950s (mostly found in the cinema) exemplified Jürgen Habermas's notion of the traditional bourgeois public sphere,[43] then Dou's concerts were Hong Kong's quintessential proletarian counterpublic sphere, where the auditory perceptions of the working class collided with the visualism of the bourgeoisie. Following Negt and Kluge, regarding the poor it was not so much about constituting the "antithesis" of Hong Kong's mainstream bourgeoisie (because, particularly in a colonial context, these two groups might share some common interests). Rather, the proletarian counterpublic sphere that Dou's concerts created was more about marking a sharp difference between bourgeois time and the historical time lived by his audience during the 1950s, an era when Hong Kong witnessed the immigration of 2.2 million immigrants from mainland China and subsequently experienced housing shortages, food shortages, education and health care challenges, political polarization, and so on. Once again, the story about King George V Memorial Park confirms Benjamin's critique of the fallacy of colonial homogeneous, empty time,[44] when there were clearly heterogeneous historical times being shared by different classes in Hong Kong society. As we know, heterogeneity is threatening for capitalist society, and this proletarian counterpublic sphere was therefore shut down.

The third colonial approach responds even more precisely to this temporal heterogeneity. Since a different time-consciousness is a threat to the capitalist regime, time must be completely homogenized. The blackouts and curfews Dou experienced were not limited to British colonialism but were also the features of other, adjacent imperial powers. Technologized timekeeping was used as a universal governing approach to homogenize a colony's time-consciousness, regardless of who the colonizer was. This section of the essay extends the problem with homogeneous time-consciousness to other aspects of homogeneous consciousness, referencing earlier postcolonial reflections about national consciousness in order to demonstrate the importance of understanding the mind when considering issues of disability, for consciousness determines how one experiences one's physical, sensory, cognitive body and the world. In other words, colonial consciousness affects the sensation and perception of one's body and the world.

ACKNOWLEDGMENTS

My thanks to Jim Lo, who ripped the CDs of the song in a Hong Kong library (not only during the COVID-19 pandemic but also on a day when the city was hit by a typhoon), as well as to my grandparents, So Kun and Leung Mui, who, as natives of Yau Ma Tei, provided me with the most wonderful stories and childhood memories.

NOTES

1. Bell Yung, liner notes to *Piaobo Xiangjiang wu shi nian: di shui nan yin: quan ben "Shi ming ren Du Huan yi wang"* (*Blind Dou Wun remembers his past: 50 years of singing naamyam in Hong Kong*) (Hong Kong: Chinese University of Hong Kong Chinese Music Archive, 2008), CD.

2. "Nanyin (Southern Tunes)," *Hong Kong Intangible Cultural Heritage Database*, accessed March 8, 2020, https://www.hkichdb.gov.hk/zht/item.html?bb7eacf0-911a-42 6c-be23-74b47c8137ca.

3. Sonia Ng, "The Story of a Virtuoso Blind Musician: Douwun," in *The Story of A Virtuoso Blind Musician: Dou Wun (1910–1979)*, Hong Kong Memory (HKM), accessed March 8, 2020, http://hkmemory.org/douwun/.

4. Ibid.

5. *Hong Kong Blue Book* (Hong Kong: Government of Hong Kong, 1927), 365.

6. Huan Du, *Piaobo Xiangjiang wu shi nian: di shui nan yin: quan ben "Shi ming ren Du Huan yi wang"* (*Blind Dou Wun remembers his past: 50 years of singing naamyam in Hong Kong*) (Hong Kong: Chinese University of Hong Kong Chinese Music Archive, 2008), CD.

7. Meibao Cheng, *Sheng Gang Ao da zhong wen hua yu du shi bian qian* (Popular Culture and Urban Change in Guangzhou–Hong Kong–Macau) (Beijing: She hui ke xue wen xian chu ban she, 2017), 1–2.

8. Do Huan Chang Longzhou: Da Nao Mei Zhifu, "Dou Wun Sings Dragon Boat: Making a Fuss with the Provincial Officer Mei," YouTube video, 38:15, April 18, 2022, https://www.youtube.com/watch?v=oxsp8aDdAyY.

9. Constance Classen, "The Senses," *Encyclopedia.com*, Encyclopedia of European Social History (July 27, 2020), https://www.encyclopedia.com/international/encyclope dias-almanacs-transcripts-and-maps/senses.

10. Constance Classen, *Aroma: The Cultural History of Smell* (New York: Routledge, 1994), 1–92.

11. C. F. Gordon-Cumming, *The Inventor of the Numeral-Type for China by the Use of Which Illiterate Chinese Both Blind and Sighted Can Very Quickly Be Taught to Read and Write Fluently* (London: Downey, 1899), 10.

12. Ibid., 12.

13. Wilbur J. Cohen, "Security for the Blind," vol. 6. *Social Insurance*, Committee on Economic Security (CES), May 16, 1935, https://www.ssa.gov/history/reports/ces/ces 6blind.html#:~:text=The%201930%20Census%20listed%2063%2C489,per%20 100%2C000%20in%20New%20Mexico.

14. Gordon-Cumming, *Inventor of the Numeral-Type for China*, 10–12.

15. Shuping Li, Xiaona Wang, "Jindai guangzhou gu ji tanxi" (An analysis of contemporary Guangzhou blind female musicians), *Gansu Social Sciences* 4 (2014): 142. See also Shu Li, Xiaona Wang, "Guji yu Qingmo minchu Guangzhou chengshi wenhua yule shenghuo" (Blind female musicians and Guangzhou's urban entertainment cultural life during the late Qing and the early republic era), *History Teaching* 2, no. 591 (2009): 1–2.

16. Hao Wu, *Tangxi Fengyue Shi* (A History of Tangxi) (Hong Kong: Ci wen hua tang, 2010).

17. R. J. Miners, "State Regulation of Prostitution in Hong Kong, 1857 to 1941," *Journal of the Hong Kong Branch of the Royal Asiatic Society* 24 (1984): 143–49, 156, 158; John M. Carroll, *A Concise History of Hong Kong* (Lanham, MD: Rowman & Littlefield, 2007), 67–68.

18. "Yike pingyong de zitenghua" (An ordinary calamus flower), Ziteng, accessed March 8, 2020, https://web.archive.org/web/20200804003310/http://ziteng.org.hk/zht/%E4%B8%80%E9%A1%86%E5%B9%B3%E5%BA%B8%E7%9A%84%E7%B4%AB%E8%9 7%A4%E8%8A%B1.

19. Michel Foucault, *The History of Sexuality Volume 1: An Introduction*, trans. Robert Hurley (New York: Pantheon, 1978), 83. See also A. L. Stoler, *Race and the Education*

of Desire: Foucault's History of Sexuality and the Colonial Order of Things (Durham, NC: Duke University Press, 1995).

20. Valerie A. Curtis, "A Natural History of Hygiene," *Canadian Journal of Infectious Diseases and Medical Microbiology* 18, no. 1 (2007): 4–11.

21. Miners, "State Regulation of Prostitution in Hong Kong," 151.

22. See Frank Welsh, *A History of Hong Kong* (London: Harper Collins, 1997), 262–63; Carroll, *Concise History of Hong Kong*, 68; Miners, "State Regulation of Prostitution in Hong Kong," 150.

23. Carroll, *Concise History of Hong Kong*, 30; Philip Howell, "Race, Space and the Regulation of Prostitution in Colonial Hong Kong," *Urban History* 31, no. 2 (2004): 238.

24. Welsh, *History of Hong Kong*, 261.

25. Walter Benjamin, *The Work of Art in the Age of Its Technological Reproducibility and Other Writings on Media*, trans. Edmund Jephcott et al. (Cambridge, MA: Harvard University Press, 2008), 24.

26. Ibid., 24.

27. Ibid., 20, 22.

28. Xiaojue Wang, "Radio Culture in Cold War Hong Kong," *Interventions: International Journal of Postcolonial Studies* 20, no. 8 (2018): 1157–58.

29. Janet Lee Scott, *For Gods, Ghosts and Ancestors: The Chinese Tradition of Paper Offerings* (Hong Kong: Hong Kong University Press, 2007), 50.

30. Oskar Negt and Alexander Kluge, *Public Sphere and Experience: Toward an Analysis of the Bourgeois and Proletarian Public Sphere*, trans. Peter Labanyi et al. (Minneapolis: University of Minnesota Press, 1993), xliii–xliv.

31. Ng, "Story."

32. Ibid.

33. Alexis McCrossen, *Marking Modern Times: A History of Clocks, Watches, and Other Timekeepers in American Life* (Chicago: Chicago University Press, 2013), 4.

34. Gerhard Dohrn-van Rossum, "Time," in *Oxford Handbook of Early Modern European History, 1350–1750 Volume 1: People & Place* (Oxford, UK: Oxford University Press, 2015), 16.

35. Benedict Anderson, *Imagined Communities: Reflections on the Origin and Spread of Nationalism* (London: Verso, 1991), 24.

36. Lynn Spigel, *Make Room for TV: Television and the Family Ideal in Postwar America* (Chicago: Chicago University Press, 1992), 3–4.

37. Walter Benjamin, *Illuminations: Essays and Reflections*, trans. Harry Zohn (New York: Random House, 2007), 260.

38. Dipesh Chakraparty, *Provincializing Europe: Postcolonial Thought and Historical Difference* (Princeton, NJ: Princeton University Press, 2000), 7.

39. Frantz Fanon, *Les damnés de la terre* (Paris: La Découverte, 2002), 42, 44; Ngũgĩ wa Thiong'o, *Decolonising the Mind: The Politics of Language in African Literature* (Harare, Zimbabwe: Zimbabwe, 1981).

40. Classen, *Aroma*, 1–92.

41. Benjamin, *Work of Art*, 22.

42. Negt and Kluge, *Public Sphere*, xlvi.

43. Ibid., xliv.

44. Benjamin, *Illuminations*, 260.

III

Disabled Bodies, Ecologies, and
Imperialist Subjectivities

8

Dis/Enabling Spaces

Crip-Ecologies of Shakespeare's The Tempest

JOHN GULLEDGE

> It is not enough to claim that human subjects are construct-
> ed, for the construction of the human is a differential opera-
> tion that produces the more and the less "human," the
> inhuman, the humanly unthinkable. These excluded sites
> come to bound the "human" as its constitutive outside, and
> to haunt those boundaries as the persistent possibility of
> their disruption and rearticulation.
>
> —JUDITH BUTLER, *BODIES THAT MATTER*[1]

"Your tale, sir, would cure deafness."[2] A curious line, isn't it? The odd prognosis comes from a confused but attentive Miranda as she attempts to both remember and forget her past. Prospero, her father, is midway in recounting their historical narrative and his exposition of the play's prior events, however suspect and dubious the tale may be. Most interestingly, it comes after his nervous and repetitive query to his daughter, "Dost thou hear?"[3] Remembering is, if nothing else, anxiety inducing for Prospero, and what we discover as *The Tempest* unfolds is that the tales he tells do far less than cure physical impairment or social difference. They are, for a lack of better words, silencing and, in the most symbolic sense, deafening. For the drama, the "cripping" of ecologies begins with this: the linguistic usurpation of the Other's material history. Like space within which they move and live, characters are transfigured into "excluded sites," and as Judith Butler has conceptualized, these inhumans and humanly unthinkable specters point, like a paradox, to what we might conceive and know.

By constructing her history (despite her insistence that she remembers herself),[4] Prospero interjects his own ideology and biased recollections—a double invention of both memory- and meaning-making.[5] He is thus able to establish Miranda's forgetfulness and redesign her identity (as he would have it). After some protestation, she finally relents: "You have often / Begun to tell me what I am, but stopped / And left me to a bootless inquisition."[6] The odd exchange shows Prospero's paranoia of others taking command of their own histories and his compulsion to remind them of a past that serves his own notion of self. Miranda effectively becomes a material artifact of his own constructed history. Indeed, this scene frames the play with a series of similar narratives—to Miranda, to Ariel, and to Caliban—where Prospero insists that each has forgotten origins that he is somehow more capable of recalling. To Ariel, for example, he asks, "Dost thou forget / From what a torment I did free thee?" And despite Ariel's multiple assurances that he has, in fact, *not* forgotten, Prospero is unsatisfied: "Thou dost [forget]," "Thou liest," "Thou hast [forgotten]."[7] The questions he presents are meant to carve out an opening for doubt and uncertainty in the hearer, only to retract its own query and re-present it as a claim in the form of a rhetorical question. In both instances, Prospero linguistically usurps the material histories of these other characters, dislocating them from the times and places they have and continue to occupy, in order that he might "frame and re-frame" himself in the play's troubling ecology. In doing so, he can normalize his own sense of self as the new standard for the island—a standard that the others are weighed and measured against but that also requires the others to act as margins defining who and what he is and, of course, what he might be(come) by the curtain's close.

In this essay, I trace the development of Ariel and Caliban as two body-texts that both reflect and represent the island's ecology. In viewing them as embodiments of the natural elements—Caliban of water and earth; Ariel of air and fire—one may understand how in simply reducing them they become integral parts of the healthy body and the healthy city; they are in effect the early modern humors balanced. Prospero's alteration to their ecological functions and abilities frustrates their interactions with the island space, transforming it from enabling to disabling. My use of the symbolic and metaphorical (indeed, the literary) is deliberate but limited. Following Mark Sherry's charge that "neither disability nor postcolonialism should be understood as a metaphor for the other experience," I have endeavored to locate this chapter's engagement with disability and empire—in the early modern period and beyond—as sites of friction and mutual enforcement.[8] By returning to a colonial text like *The Tempest* and reading it as a postcolonial text, this chapter attempts to carry the ongoing, ever-branching effects of empire as much as its roots in the sixteenth and seventeenth centuries. *The Tempest* is a particularly rich site for feeling out the frictions between these shifting terms because it makes use of both the material and the metaphorical dimensions of disability and colonial identification. As Sherry admits, "The connections [metaphors] make between quite disparate experiences evoke meanings that shape perception, identity and experience."[9] Rather than seeing one stand in as a metaphor for discussing the other, however, I am much more interested in locating the metaphors that are forced to speak across representations of disability and postcolonialism—mutually enforcing codifications that literature helps us to negotiate. Because it is a play and thus "lives" in iterative reproductions, *The Tempest* also speaks to the aftermath of the early modern imperial project and permits new contact zones to arise, such as the intersection with natural and social ecologies, as is the case of my treatment here.

"O' Heaven, O' Earth": Fleshing Out the Island

First, consider the bodies—of flesh, of land, of text—and how the three collide in sometimes harmonious but often dissonant ways. Peter Greenaway's flamboyant 1991 film, *Propsero's Books*, is a striking and unusual adaptation of *The Tempest*. In it, Prospero serves as an even more intrusive narrator, speaking the lines of other characters as he recounts the events of the drama. Greenaway presents the text as Prospero's (re)vision and metacreation. As the panorama of mirror visuals he utters and writes down into his books come to life in image, we are reminded of the uncomfortable obsession viewers have with the human body. An adaptation that removes embodied utterance from the play's characters, it is nonetheless a film that is constantly pointing us toward the body. These figures in Prospero's library are barely clothed, if at all, and one cannot help but hear Stephano's observation of Caliban halfway through the play ("My man-monster hath drowned his tongue")[10] as each of these unusual figures move and act without ever getting a word in edgewise. They are voiceless images, operating as functions of some authorial command in a well-wrought tableau. Indeed, Greenaway himself had this to say about the island space in *The Tempest*:

> An island full of superimposed images, of shifting mirrors and mirror-images—true mirages—where pictures conjured by it can be as tantalizingly substantial as objects and facts and events, constantly framed and re-framed. This framing and re-framing becomes like the text itself—a motif—reminding the viewer that it is all an illusion constantly fitted into a rectangle . . . into a picture frame, a film frame.[11]

Greenaway's version highlights the constructed nature of text, body, and space that I argue is integral to the dramatic tensions of the play. Bodies in *The Tempest* are never what they seem and yet there is a consistent anxiety over the material and natural world that these bodies occupy. Greenaway begins and ends his adaptation the same way: with a single drop of water. The textual, symbolic production of Prospero's narration—and his paranoid obsession with re-remembering past events—is framed and reframed by natural matter, signaling us to reconsider this postcolonial play considering emerging theories in ecocriticism and disability studies.

By having the other characters remain mute until the end, Greenaway invites a consideration over the ways certain bodies and minds can construct the material histories and thus identities of others. In this sense, it is perhaps more useful to consider Prospero not as categorically "normal" but as a "normate." Coined by Rosmarie Garland-Thomson in her pioneering work on disability representation, the "normate" "designates a social figure through which people can represent themselves as definitive human beings. Normal, then, is the constructed identity of those who, by way of bodily configurations and cultural capital they assume, can step into a position of authority and wield the power it grants them."[12] Prospero's ability to manipulate language, inscribe ideology, and reconstruct identities (his own as well as the others on the island with him) enables him to "step into a position of authority" and demarcate the standard body—in this case, his version of *a* standard body. Of course, this means he can demarcate the nonstandard body, too, and so he does with the figures of Ariel and Caliban.

It is here that stigma arises not as an analytical reading of another's body but a rhetorical speaking of one's own anxieties, fears, anger, and hatred. Stigma is a heuristic for Otherness: the at-first unintelligible figure is reformed into a site of ideological meaning, rendering a body of *matter* mere objects of the symbolic. In a similar fashion, impairment and early modern constructions of deformity are socially reconstituted as disability. Like Karen Barad, I view "materiality [as] discursive" and argue that discursive practices are, quite simply, boundary-making apparatuses: "The determination of boundaries, properties, and meanings is differently enacted. . . . Apparatuses are dynamic (re)configurings of the world."[13] In this sense, the Shakespearean stage was a spectacle of entertainment but also a site of social and cultural negotiations. Displayed on the stage were a series of power dynamics (political, gendered, racial, economic, dis/ability), and this exercise of power was collective and performative. The spectator's undiscerning obedience to the hegemony that empowers the person to gaze complicates any capacity for contestation. In staged and structured seeing, the ideology-inscribing process of "enfreakment" takes place. Elsewhere, Garland-Thomson describes "enfreakment" as a systematic method of spectacular Othering as it "emerges from cultural rituals that stylize, silence, differentiate, and distance the persons whose bodies [are] colonized and commercialized."[14] The construction of social margins vis-à-vis ideology inscription—in this case, framed by non-normative bodies—relies on the spectator/spectacle relationship. What I mean, of course, is the subject/object relationship and how that relationship plays out in the act of looking. The reveries projected in spectacle, whether good or ill, are shattered and qualified by a rational awakening to earthly realities that displaces the enfreaked Ariel and Caliban to that of interactor.[15]

Early modern fascinations with the "curious" and "strange" materialized in the *Kunstkabinett/Wunderkammern*,[16] anatomy theaters, pamphlets on witchcraft and superstition, natural historical specimens, grottoes, portraits, and, of course, all things "monstrous." This artificial staging of the unknown (or unknowable) walks a fine line between affirming the Other and abjecting it toward a liminal space of nothingness. The at-first unintelligible figure is disformed into a site of ideological meaning, rendering the material body into nothing more than discourse. In a similar fashion, impairment and early modern constructions of deformity are socially reconstituted as disability.[17] If materiality is itself always discursive, as Barad suggests, it is no surprise that a *being*—take Caliban, for example—can be signified in various, meaning-making ways: "monster," "beast," "strange," "earth."[18]

So, too, does this process of resignification extend to the ecology of *The Tempest*'s island-space. Just as Caliban's figure is unintelligible to the privileged, "normate" bodies of the play, the landscape is exceedingly incomprehensible as well: it is described at different points of the play as "desolate," "uninhabitable," "inaccessible."[19] This very same unintelligible island, however, is characterized elsewhere by the same characters as "lush" and "green."[20] It is also, of course, the site of reconciliation for Prospero and his brother, leading to a long tradition of reading the play as about forgiveness. During the Renaissance, the treatment of nature and the natural world was largely imagined by analytical and thus distancing terms. Cabinets of curiosity did not fade with the Enlightenment, and their "wondrous" contents were often transplanted from one ecology to another with mercenary intentions. Miranda (taken from the Latin *mirari*, "to wonder at") is the epitomized wonderer and object of wonder, as her name suggests. Indeed, this play is constantly pulling back the curtain, as it were, to reveal the Island's many curiosities, whether they be of a natural or "intelligible" ecology or not.

By approaching the play's treatment of these two different body-texts through the lens of a "crip-ecology," one discovers how these curiosities become less spectacular and increasingly integral to the survival and existence of others. Often, discussion surrounding disability and environment rely on the social model's concern with man-made, built spaces. The stress in this case is a question over access and the ways inaccessibility disables particular minds and bodies. "Crip-ecology" includes these concerns but widens the lens to include "nature" and "the natural" world. In so doing, we might highlight the limitations of a framework that has scaffolded disability studies since the early 1990s.[21] Allying crip theory and ecocritical discourse points toward emerging scholarship that, as Robert McRuer explains, "insists that accessing (or making accessible) the 'circuit of culture' entails attending to the sites where images and identities are produced."[22] These spaces can be artificial like the early modern stage, natural like the strange island on which Prospero finds himself, or humanlike as with the "monstrous" Caliban.

However, what I want to suggest here is similar to what Allison Kafer argues in "Bodies of Nature": "Given the often exclusionary dimensions of 'nature' and 'wilderness,' it is important to explore how those considered out-of-place find ways of engaging and interacting with nature."[23] Environmental researchers describe the ways in which "social arrangements" become mapped onto "natural environments" in strikingly similar language to the ways the "monstrous" body is socially remapped (thus, material impairment or deformity becomes an ideological and symbolic disability). *The Tempest* allows us to consider and complicate Kafer's assumption that "disabled people are figured as out of place"[24] in "nature" and "environment" discourses produced within an ableist milieu. Indeed, it is the unintelligible body of Caliban that thrives in the inaccessible terrain of the island; instead, his "disability"[25] arises from an ecological rift wherein the "integrated humans-in-the-land"[26] is severed. Prospero's intrusion disrupts the habitude of the markedly—both physically and mentally—different Caliban, and I am particularly interested in the lasting effects of this intrusion into Caliban's enabling space: How might that shift signal Caliban's status as a TAB (temporarily able-body)? By what means do these performed bodies play out their varying dis/capabilities? And what is left of the play's crip-ecology once its intruders dissemble and abandon it?

"Where Is the Enchanted Island Situated? Nowhere, yet Everywhere"[27]

As Geraldo U. De Sousa observes, what is immediately striking about the setting of *The Tempest* is that "the island has no name." There is something fascinating and startling about the nameless island. It is disorienting and contradictory, "and the characters discover that their senses prove unable to convey the essence of the island."[28] Only Ariel and Caliban seem to have knowledge of specific locations. It appears they have psychologically embedded the mapped land not by place names but by circumlocutions that identify interactions they have had with that part of the island. Their "maps" are embodied topographies, less inscription and more intuition. The two are cartographers of experience rather than deployers of what has been called cartosemiotics, the symbolic renderings of cartographic representation forms. The latter, of course, was en vogue during the Renaissance, and the dramatization of the characters' voyage to, landing on, and mapping of the island-space is, in part, a reflection of Shakespeare's commercial savviness. Ariel and Caliban's ecological commitments defend them from the otherwise observation from Paul Shepard: "An environment without place names is fearful" and "landscapes without place names are disorienting."[29] In this nowhere, yet everywhere place, Caliban and Ariel fear only one thing: the intruders and what they might do to their habitat and habitude within said ecology.

Marjorie Garber identifies the common interpretation of Caliban and Ariel as two contrasting figures when she writes, "If Ariel is imagination personified, surely Caliban is something like libido (sexual desire) or id (basic human drives). If one thing is clear on Prospero's island, it is that, for all his anarchic and disruptive qualities, Caliban is *necessary*—like the body itself."[30] And indeed, Prospero and Miranda require Caliban for survival: "We cannot miss him," Prospero says, meaning of course they cannot do without him; "he does make our fire, / Fetch in our wood, and serves in offices / That profit us."[31] His material connection to the ecology of the island and its material history provides Caliban with the skills and knowledge to best access the apparently "inaccessible" space. To be clear, he and the land are one and the same, at least representationally: "Thou earth, thou: speak!"[32] commands Prospero to Caliban, begging the incomprehensible natural world to conform to the use of signs and symbols, a kind of dramatic, semiotic tyranny. In this way, the text locates both Caliban and the island as *monstrum*, the Latin origin for "omen" and giving us the English word *monster*. As a rhetorical technology, these monstrums of culture and society disclose the wide-ranging attitudes, beliefs, and ideologies that characterize their temporal and spatial renderings. Reading, in this case, is not done in a vacuum displaced from context. Likewise, the reading is both an interrogation and fabrication of the deviant body. These signifiers, when inscribed on an abject-to-be body, result in a de-monstration of ideological difference. Projected and constructed, this figure of the "abnormal" is a rhetorical site for reading (by definition, it "reveals," "warns," and "shows"). Nevertheless, what is to be read is often what culture has already inscribed on it: the anxieties and fascinations, the politics and economics—the very fabric of the normative self that can just as easily displace personhood as it might—and indeed does—scaffold and frame the ontological "subject." And so, for the play, the "deformed savage" is dramatically linked with the "desolate isle."[33]

By rereading Prospero and his relation to the island in this way, we are likewise enabled to reread the body-bound Caliban and disembodied Ariel as more than mere Others. We might be so bold as to read them as interactors with and within the spaces they inhabit, and in doing so, recognize the ecological implications of different minds and bodies in-the-land. If Caliban is bestial, a creature of the sea, then the play certainly seems to suggest capabilities his ecological commitment to the island ensures. By their own admission, it is by *his* knowledge and *his* capable body that Prospero and Miranda survive in the first place. Similarly, it is by Ariel's specific abilities that Prospero can regain his dukedom. These two native characters, who enable the others at every turn, are purposefully marked by the four natural elements because of their prescribed relationship—their interconnectedness—with the natural world. Prospero has no power here except to enslave and demand; his relationship to his surroundings puts him at a disadvantage, and so, to enable himself, he begins to alter its ecological fabric.

Allison Hobgood's discussion of Caliban as a figure of disability reminds us of how disability has often been imagined as something individual. Caliban's "character encapsulates disability's supposed, and hence stigmatizing, singularity . . . [set] against the notion that all human bodyminds are generally and inherently able."[34] Indeed, the play sets up Caliban as an oppositional figure, but to read his difference as "personal deficiency" hazards an interpretation that ignores his interaction and cooperation with not only the other characters but with the island itself. Inhumanity is only "delimiting" in this classic reading of Caliban, leaving very little room for its liberatory potentiality. What I want to suggest here is that the play's largely xenophobic treatment of Caliban opens the door to two competing but coordinated realizations: first, that "disability stigma enables racist, colonial hegemony,"[35] and second, the anxious fragility of that hegemony, especially given the spatial context of the drama's action.

Long debated in critical discourse is the time and place of *The Tempest.* Is this the "old" or "new" world? Is this play's source, as colonial readings would argue, a tale about imperialism and the colonization of Indigenous peoples?[36] How do such interpretations reconcile the clear indication that the island's location must be in the Mediterranean Sea, not far from the coast of Africa? Instead of attending to these questions of time and place, as worthwhile as such an analysis may be, I am reconsidering this island as an ecological space *elsewhere.* I do not wish to suggest that early modern as well as contemporary insights into the colonial project are lost on this reading of the play; indeed, those illuminations underpin it at every step. "What is most magical about the isle, however," argues Garber, "is that in being many places at once, geographically, culturally, and mythographically hybrid, it eludes locations and becomes a space for poetry, and for dream."[37] And so it is a sort of "green space" of possibility and potentiality, ensuring its long-lasting epithet of "romance" and mystery play. Remarkably, it points to and resists time and place simultaneously. By considering the island as a place *elsewhere*, I am emphasizing "the ambiguous and amorphous nature of Caliban's deformity" in the plays' performance and reception histories as well as its embeddedness within the text itself. In other words, the lack of speci-ficity does not elide the colonial aspects of the play but rather draws our attention to the perceived "exotic" and othered figures who people the is-land-space. Like Caliban's body, the island is suspended "between what it is and what it is said to be."[38]

"Nature Does Not Comprehend Itself, My Gentle Ariel": Thus Utters the "Moon-Calf"[39]

Before bringing Caliban on stage, Shakespeare has Prospero relate the ex-traordinary origin of the islander's mother, "this damned witch Sycorax," preconceiving Caliban as otherworldly, both geographically and existen-tially.[40] It is important to Prospero to highlight her physical deformity—she, "who with age and envy / Was grown into a hoop." But Sycorax is also de-scribed as "blue-eyed" and, like Prospero himself, was exiled for her "sorcer-ies terrible." Shakespeare consistently entreats audiences to make connec-tions between the subtle, or sometimes not-so-subtle, similarities of the exotic mother and son and the European father and daughter.[41]

Prospero's suspicious and demonic account of Sycorax forecasts her son as a preternaturally dangerous devil-spawn, but when Caliban clownishly stumbles on stage, he is largely unimpressive despite his remarkable body. Perhaps he is "blue-ey'd" like his mother, and maybe "freckled" because his fair-skinned mother mated with a dark-skinned Algerian. He has "long nails," and we may assume other aspects in productions of the play that cause Pros-pero to deride him as "filth" and "savage." And, in the drama's most memo-rable epithet, Caliban is "a thing most brutish," a pun that playfully parallels the *brute* with the *Brit*, what is "brutish" with what is "British," and what is foreign with what is familiar. Caliban's status as human is constantly nego-tiated, as when Prospero claims Caliban was born to a human woman but without "a human shape."[42]

Due to Prospero's characterization that he is a "born devil" that was "got by the devil himself," early critics like John Dryden and Joseph Warton read him as demonic.[43] Later images looked to various derisions like "earth" and "mountain" in order to imagine Caliban as a natural overgrowth from the island itself.[44] Elsewhere he has been described as reptilian (as in "tortoise" and "poisonous") or amphibian (as in a "debosh'd fish" and "half a fish and half a man").[45] Caliban's various forms produced by the characters' descrip-tions, staged productions, and scholarship signify his unintelligibility and irreducibility. Shakespeare purposefully wrote in a body that raises more questions than it answers.[46] To Trinculo, he is at first a fish, then he says, "This is no fish but an islander," identifying his at least human-looking form, to then only a few lines later call him a "puppy-headed monster" with "eyes . . . almost set in [his] head."[47] Like with the "uninhabitable and inaccessible" island, Trinculo struggles to apprehend and comprehend—that is, to even access—the figure before him.[48]

It has been argued that *The Tempest* owes much of its discourse on the comparisons between European, "civilized" persons and Indigenous natives to the essay "Of Cannibals" (1580), wherein Montaigne writes, "There is nothing savage or barbarous about those peoples, but that every man calls barbarous anything he is not accustomed to."[49] To be sure, Montaigne's essay reeks of the same obsession with the "rustic" type we see heralded in the Romanticism (one need only read a handful of poems by Wordsworth to sense it) and then by the antiquarians of the later nineteenth century. "These nations," he observes early in the essay, "seem to me to be . . . not much remote from their original simplicity. The laws of nature . . . govern them still."[50] Montaigne's "defense" was radical at the time, but even so it fails to capture the complexity of the Other. Caliban's earthiness is "savage" to the observably European characters (and to most audiences), but it is in the lessons of Prospero and through the symbolic power of language that he can imagine far more treacherous and barbaric behaviors as in when he plots with Trinculo and Stephano to murder Prospero. Consider also how Trinculo, upon first seeing Caliban, imagines a way to transport and exploit Caliban's corporeal variation:

> Were I in England now (as once I was) and had but this fish painted, not a holiday-fool there but would give a piece of silver. There would this monster make a man. Any strange beast there makes a man. When they will not give a doit to relieve a lame beggar, they will lay out ten to see a dead Indian.[51]

Trinculo's fantasy was not at all an uncommon enterprise during the period, saying little of the cabinets of curiosity parallel. In this same speech, Trinculo detects the realization of Gonzalo's wish in the opening scene: "Here's neither bush nor shrub."[52] The barren land that should (and for Gonzalo, indeed would) offer a more suitable and useful environment somehow presents itself just as treacherous for the ship-wrecked Europeans. The inhospitable land will not help them "to bear off any weather at all" and in a thrilling move toward transgressing the privileged European body, there will be no place for them "to hide [their] head[s]."[53] The natural world *does* present inherent disadvantages for specific, particular bodies, but in this case, it is with the body of difference, the inchoate muddiness of Caliban,[54] that advantage lies.

Despite his insistence that language has only given him the ability to curse his master (and later plot against him), Caliban's are some of the most graceful and poetic speeches in all of Shakespeare. As we should expect, his language swells and prospers most when he talks about the natural world of the island's beautiful landscapes. It is by Prospero's pedagogy, we are told, that he has "made much of [Caliban]" giving him the power "to name" and endowing his "purposes / With words that made them known."[55] Caliban's education involves a mimetic performance of reclaiming the natural world via interpellation. In return, Caliban has "showed [Prospero] all the qualities o'th' isle: / The fresh springs, brine pits, barren place and fertile."[56] The interaction seems ethical enough, with particular capabilities and knowledge traded to enable one another; however, the magus gives with a closed fist. He usurps Caliban's spatial mobility: "And here you sty me," asserts Caliban, "in this hard rock, whiles you do keep from me / The rest oath' island." He also refuses to allow Caliban a freedom with said speech: "thou most lying slave."[57] Audiences should notice how Prospero is constantly asking questions of other characters to immediately reject their answers and scold them. His leitmotif is one of punishment and discipline.

Leaning in to this mutability, Lauren Eriks Cline embraces Caliban's many monstrous renderings throughout *The Tempest*'s performance history to bring forth "a baggy 'assemblage' of shifting embodiment, whose opaque surfaces present opportunities for thought rather than demand resolution."[58] In her reading of the play, Caliban's monstrosity is linked to both his native speech and, following Deleuze and Guattari, his "facialization," two of the primary ways Caliban is identified within the play and through its various performance iterations. Cline encourages us to read the "language lessons as an attempted facialization of Caliban" so that the island's native might "translate the 'qualities' of the island . . . into discourse of knowledge that he shares with Prospero."[59] Language is both a symbolic leverage of power and, once "translated," particularized knowledge and material resource. Thus, the citational potency of Caliban's learned speech—which remains tied up in the way he is hailed, named, imagined—is meant to create distance between him and the island (his embodied knowledge) while also providing simulated access to Prospero of that same knowledge.

Unlike Prospero, however, Caliban has a somewhat nuanced understanding of ownership when it comes to the island. He acknowledges Prospero's immediate power over its natural resources, due to his master's continued efforts to "crip" its ecology, but he also braves the claim, "This island's mine . . . which thou tak'st from me."[60] Many scholars read this regarding native populations and their rights to land or as a political remark on inheritance and law, and indeed, Caliban's claim is a political act of resistance. But a greener interpretation connects Caliban to *his* island in more suggestive ways. If Prospero, the colonizer, is seen as a disease, infecting the island ("All the infections the sun sucks up / From the bogs, fens, flats, on Prospero fall, and make him / By inch-meal a disease"),[61] then Caliban, the native visionary, situates himself as the harmony to come. Prophetic and beautifully scripted, Caliban signals us toward a final communion where the disabled bodies of Ariel and Caliban are liberated, and their ecological functions might become harmoniously balanced. In fact, by the ending, Caliban is left ostensibly in isolation on the island once the settlers abandon it. In many productions of the play, Caliban can be seen sitting alone and not speaking, which has historically been interpreted through "notions of powerlessness and passivity."[62] Recent work in the social sciences, however, are reorienting this view considering indigeneity. For example, Darrien Morton et al. describe non-"Western" absences and silences "as incompletions free of error and reconcilement, not hidden Otherness, and correlates of what it means to be hear and seen, [that] may invigorate sites of inquiry" into nonstandard ways of being and knowing.[63] The authors refer to these moments of silence as "closings," "a strategic matter of self-preservation and protection" that comes "from a solitary quietness and ceremonial place of not knowing and wanting to find out about self—what is unexplored and untold."[64] Within this framework, Caliban's isolation is a kind of liberation whereby he may purposefully explore, cultivate, and preserve his own sense of self not through the tools of the colonizing agents (i.e., language, dialectic, etc.) but rather by his relationship to the environs around him. Access to autobiography that Prospero represses in various characters throughout the play is reimagined in the silence of a now remote Caliban.

"From Strange to Stranger," or from the Inhuman to the Humanly Unthinkable

Juxtaposed to the grounded Caliban, Ariel is the air and fire of the island, and his spectacle is that which "flame[s] amazement" when he does "divide / And burn in many places."[65] To all but Prospero, Ariel's form is invisible. His interactions with the other characters take more natural and material forms, like wind, water, fire, and especially noteworthy, music—vibrations that register as harmonious or dissonant to those who might overhear. If he is regularly read as disembodied, or rather as taking on many bodies and forms, then the fact he still experiences pain and anguish are noteworthy.[66] Shakespeare means to imply a kind of invisible, silent suffering of the oppressed native. Ariel is able to "take [any] shape" and be "invisible" all at once; he is no form and every form, like the multifaceted flora and fauna of the island itself.[67] When he "groans / [he does] make wolves howl and penetrate the breasts / Of ever-angry bears," signifying his previously situated interconnectedness with the island's ecology.[68] The call of the island is matched and returned. Drawing on Michel Foucault's "Heterotopia," I argue that the island's status as elsewhere heightens Ariel's position as a paradoxically embodied and disembodied space of otherness, a "place that is outside all places."[69] Foucault posits this as a space wherein other real spaces are represented, contested, and reversed. Ariel's ecological commitment, somewhat similar to Caliban's, gives shape and body to this space.

The revelation of Ariel's intimate connection to the island's wildlife comes at a moment when Prospero becomes increasingly annoyed with Ariel's nearly incessant interruptions. Like with Miranda and Caliban, Prospero recounts Ariel's past, framing his servitude as liberation. And likewise, as we saw with the Miranda exchange early on, Ariel attempts to employ the same power of interruption and articulation Prospero commands, to which the latter scolds, calling him a "Dull thing."[70] He then threatens Ariel, "If thou more murmur'st, I will rend an oak / And peg thee in his knotty entrails till / Thou has howled away twelve winters."[71] In his intrusion on the island's ecology, two outcomes yet remain for the island's spiritual shape: silence or isolation. Indeed, for Prospero, this outcome is "crippling" as he reminds Ariel "within which rift / Imprisoned thou didst painfully remain."[72]

The tactic is not new nor is it unique to the subjugation of Ariel. As punishment for Caliban's sexual advances to Miranda, Prospero promises "urchins / Shall forth at vast of night that they may work / All exercise on thee; thou shalt be pinched / As thick as honeycomb, each pinch more stinging / Than bees that made 'em."[73] As with much of the history prior to the play's plot, we are never given a full account of these events, and though it is difficult to know to what degree Prospero is once again revising historical record for his own purpose, what we do know is his proclivity to do so. Jyotsna Singh deftly reviews this relationship in one of the earliest readings of the play to combine both feminist theory and postcolonial studies. She notes, "While Miranda ultimately aligns herself to the colonizing father and husband, the play . . . also gestures toward an alliance . . . in a childhood prehistory" between she and Caliban.[74] Prospero's recollections are prescriptive and procreative. Always below the surface of his speeches, a current of rampant fear and anxiety freely flows. At the heart of this instance is miscegenation. On the one hand, there is the irrational fear that his lineage may be "tainted" in some way by the blood of Sycorax, a fear subtly expressed elsewhere in the shared traits that land too close for comfort for the colonial architect (i.e., her unusually blue eyes and artful, occult knowledge). On the other hand, there is the period's entrenched xenophobia. As Karen Newman has argued, "Always we find the link between blackness and the monstrous, and particularly a monstrous sexuality."[75] By narrating Caliban thus, Prospero is able to falsely legitimize his sense of superiority and subsequent subjugation of the Indigenous figure before him. Whether Shakespeare intended to do this or if it is a consequence of the time, the play thus invites reflection on how the singular rage of one figure might encapsulate the latent ideology of an entire era.

Although he accuses Caliban of exaggerating his chores in previous scenes, Prospero's overarching project bleeds into his rhetoric during an admonishment of Ariel as well:

Thou dost, and think'st much to tread the ooze
Of the salt deep,
To run upon the sharp wind of the north,
To do me business in the veins o'th' earth
When it is baked with frost.[76]

The descriptions serve as a reminder of Ariel's past immobilization at the hands of Sycorax and of Prospero's "generosity" in freeing him. In either case, Ariel is stilted and requests liberation, but Prospero's linguistic-prowess recasts Ariel's current condition. He does so to set himself apart from the Othered "devil-witch" while also to garner power and authority on the island and over its natural (and extranatural) resources. Set apart, "of the salt deep" serves as a moniker for the island itself. Here things come from nature and to the salt they return, forcing the temporary inhabitants to flee by the play's close. According to Arne Naess, who coined the philosophical term *deep ecology* in 1972, "The aim of . . . the deep ecology movement is not a slight reform of our present society, but a substantial reorientation of our whole civilization."[77] This is perhaps where Montaigne's reductive apology fails to decenter his own latent commitments to a strictly "Western" narrative and aligns instead with my reading of Caliban and Ariel as agents of a kind of ecojustice, made more prescient in their "monstrous" and supernatural forms.

It is in Ariel's music and singing, for example, that we are given a glimpse into the harmonious influence environments and their inhabitants may have. To Ferdinand, Ariel sings of his father's return to nature in a "sea-change / Into something rich and strange."[78] Nature is, for the shipwrecked aliens, so strange that they struggle to understand its meaning and their own ecological responsibilities. In that same scene, when Miranda first observes Ferdinand, she articulates this incomprehension: "I might call him / A thing divine, for nothing *natural* / I ever saw so noble."[79] She fails to understand and know the noble environment that has sustained and enabled her; in their limited perspective, the island's "rich and strange" ontologies are mere "spirits" and "sprites" and are desperately Othered by the European occupants.

Upon hearing the music, Ferdinand is amazed and confused. "Where should this music be?" he asks. "I'th' air, or th' earth?"[80] The music invites apprehension and comprehension. The music may offer the possibility for redemption, and Caliban, "the earth," appears to be the only inhabitant open to Ariel's—that is, "the air's"—call for harmony. Caliban beautifully meditates on the island's soundscape when he offers assurance to Stephano and Trinculo in act three:

> *Be not afeared, the isle is full of noises,*
> *Sounds, and sweet airs, that give delight and hurt not.*
> *Sometimes a thousand twangling instruments*
> *Will hum about mine ears; and sometime voices,*
> *That if I then had wak'd after long sleep,*
> *Will make me sleep again . . .*[81]

Because Caliban is "confined *into* this rock," he is of it, a part of it, and thus an elemental kindred of Ariel.[82] His open ear opens him to fine feeling, which representationally might translate into a kind of futurity—an ability that is aided by the island and likewise aids it.

In the final act, Prospero's continued eco-illiteracy conceals from him Ariel's material disability in interacting with the island and its space in a liberated manner.[83] After Ariel confirms the others are "confined together . . . all prisoners," Prospero unwisely asks, "Hast thou, which art but air, a touch, a feeling / Of their afflictions?"[84] As he had done with the plot to end Ariel's life and take the island, Prospero has forgotten the previous conversation about Ariel's imprisoned pain and suffering and disregards his social confinement under the threat and intimidation of further isolation. It is in oppression (the limitation of space, we might say) and repression (in this case, the usurpation of the material self and autobiography) that these two body-texts are disabled by and through interaction with Prospero. They are cut off, so to speak, from their environments, from each other, and from their shared and personal histories. Severed from others and from their own histories, we find the two islanders existing outside what John Kunat has argued is the driving plot of the play: "The action of *The Tempest* is in effect a staging of the trauma through which humans move from the natural into the civil state."[85] At the play's close, Caliban and Ariel are not afforded such movement, but the ending nonetheless asks audiences to consider if this assumed restriction is wholesale a negative outcome. In other words, it is the "civil state," no matter how compromised or incomplete it is on the island, that has caused them trauma—not the natural.

"Stranger Always Rhymes with Danger"[86]

Ultimately, this is a play of strangers and their dangers. The danger of an un-finished figure, an inhuman but with "a human shape," speaks to the rest of Nabokov's popularly quoted line: "So, let us bless the freak; for in the natural evolution of things, the ape would perhaps never have become man had not a freak appeared in the family."[87] In the final act, Alonso echoes the bewil-derment of the others when his eyes fall on Caliban: "This is a *strange* thing as e'er I looked on," to which Prospero responds, "He is as disproportioned in his manners / As in his shape." Caliban is *The Tempest*'s freak, and indeed deserves blessing. Enabled by the "heavenly music" of his elemental sibling, he "will be wiser hereafter / And seek for grace."[88] While other critics read this as remorse and repentance toward Prospero and his treacherous plot with Stephano and Trinculo, I read it in shades of green. When the European settlers leave the island, the ecological place transforms (or rather, re-forms) into an enabling space.[89] The harmony that has been foreshadowed in the music, revelries, and masque full of nature imagery becomes manifest when what remains is the singing wind and listening earth. The text's persistence in situating Caliban both in and of the land demands a reconsideration of how we listen to the varied parts of our natural and social spaces—not so that we might "cure deafness," as Miranda puts it, but perhaps that we may iden-tify the incredible excluded bodies and excluded sites in our own ecologies and, rather than disable them, recognize how they, in turn, are enabling.[90]

NOTES

1. Judith Butler, *Bodies That Matter* (London: Routledge Classics, 2011), 8, my emphasis.

2. William Shakespeare, *The Tempest*, Arden Shakespeare, 3rd series, ed. Virginia Mason Vaughan and Alden T. Vaughan (London: Arden Shakespeare, 2011), 1.2.107, all other citations will come from this edition unless otherwise noted.

3. 1.2.106.

4. Consider with this Miranda's own dissembling nature when she hints at the pos-sible fabrication and deception of her father's story: "The *strangeness* of your story put / Heaviness in me" (1.2.307–8, my emphasis). The strange, the stranger, and their strange-ness are all players in my underlying rumination of *la Différance* within the play.

5. See James Olney's *Memory and Narrative: The Weave of Life-Writing* (Chicago: University of Chicago Press, 1998) for an exceptional consideration of historiographic-narration where he situates memory as the vexed methodology for any who engage with autobiographical and biographical materials. This approach to *The Tempest* might reveal its tendency toward "auto/biografiction" and "auto/biographic metafiction."

6. 1.2.33–5.

7. 1.2.250, 257.

8. Mark Sherry, "(Post)colonizing Disability," in "Intersecting Gender and Disability Perspectives in Rethinking Postcolonial Identities," ed. Pushpa Parekh, special issue, *Waga-du* 4 (Summer 2007): 10–22, 10.

9. Ibid., 11.

10. 3.2.11.

11. Peter Greenaway, *Prospero's Books* (film script) (New York, 1991), 12.

12. Rosmarie Garland-Thomson, *Extraordinary Bodies: Figuring Physical Disability in American Culture and Literature* (New York: Columbia University Press, 1997), 8.

13. Karen Barad, "Posthumanist Performativity: Toward an Understanding of How Matter Comes to Matter," *Signs: Journal of Women in Culture and Society* 28, no. 3 (2003): 801–31, 816, 821.

14. Rosmarie Garland-Thomson, *Freakery: Cultural Spectacles of the Extraordinary Body* (New York: New York University Press, 1996), 10.

15. See John G. Demary's "Symbolism in the Tempest" for a more detailed analysis into the role of symbol, spectacle, and history from the perspective of "utopian literature and the literature of exploration" in *Shakespeare and the Spectacle of Strangeness: The Tempest and the Transformation of Renaissance Theatrical Forms*, ed. Albert C. Labriola (Pennsylvania: Duquesne University Press, 1998), 110–34.

16. *The Tempest* has been compared to the cabinets of curiosity that became popular in early modern Europe. The island invites us to tour and look on a series of natural and preternatural "wonders" as the plot takes a back seat to visual spectacles.

17. I should note here that two definitions of disability are operative throughout this essay. As is being suggested in this section, disability is distinct from impairment in that it is a socially constructed phenomenon that discursively shapes identity and social interaction (i.e., stigma). There is another definition of disability that underlines my treatment of Caliban and Ariel, however: disability as identity, in line with what has been dubbed the cultural model of disability. For a thorough discussion of disability models and frameworks, see Anne Waldschmidt, "Disability-Culture-Society: Strengths and Weaknesses of a Cultural Model of Dis/ability," *Alter* 12, no. 2 (June 2018): 65–78.

18. 2.2.29–30, 1.2.315.

19. 2.1.40.

20. 2.1.55.

21. Though it has waned considerably in the last decade or so. Consider, for instance, Tom Shakespeare's admission in "The Social Model of Disability: An Outdated Ideology?" (*Research in Social Science and Disability* 2 [2002]: 9–28) that "people with impairments will always be disadvantaged by their bodies" when encountering natural land features such as rock cliffs, mountains, heavily wooded forests, and sandy beaches.

22. Robert McRuer, "Coming Out Crip," in *Crip Theory: Cultural Signs of Queerness and Disability* (New York: New York University Press, 2006), 61.

23. Alison Kafer, "Bodies of Nature," in *Feminist, Queer, Crip* (Bloomington: Indiana University Press, 2013), 130.

24. Ibid.

25. While I am aware of the criticism of potential anachronism in using this terminology, I deliberately choose to include it because any presence of impairment or "deformity" in a society inevitably does shade the way people view themselves and others; it is the phenomenon of disability rather than a stylized identity category that is of interest to this essay. See Allison Hobgood and David Houston Wood, *Recovering Disability in Early Modern England* (Athens: Ohio State University Press, 2013), for a promising and compelling defense of using "disabled" retrospectively in historicist scholarship.

26. Miguel De la Torre, *Introducing Liberative Theologies* (Mryknoll, NY: Orbis, 2015), 78.

27. Ernest Renan, *Caliban: A Philosophical Drama Continuing* The Tempest *of William Shakespeare*, trans. Eleanor Grant Vickery (New York: Shakespeare Press, 1896; repr. 1971), 6. This short volume places Ariel and Caliban in conversation with each other after having left the island with Prospero. It is an interesting reflection on how these two ontologies "of the island" might dwell and adapt in other ecologies, but it lacks the spirit of its source material and languishes into philosophical amusement by its close.

28. Geraldo U. De Sousa, "Alien Habitats in *The Tempest*," in *The Tempest: Critical Essays*, ed. Patrick Murphy (London: Routledge, 2010), 448.

29. Paul Shepard, *Man in the Landscape: A Historic View of Esthetics of Nature* (College Station: Texas A&M University Press, 1991), 41, 43.

30. *The Tempest* in *Shakespeare After All* (New York: Pantheon, 2004), 853.

31. 1.2.312–4.

32. 1.2.315.

33. Caliban is cast as the "savage and deformed slave" in the dramatis personae of the play; 3.3.80.

34. Allison Hobgood, *Beholding Disability in Renaissance England* (Ann Arbor: University of Michigan Press, 2021), 25.

35. Ibid., 26.

36. The postcolonial reading of *The Tempest* began with D. O. Mannoni, *Prospero and Caliban: The Psychology of Colonization* (1950), trans. Pamela Powesland (New York: Praeger, 1956). For an overview of this reception of the play, see Jonathan Bate, "Caliban and Ariel Write Back," *Shakespeare Survey: An Annual Survey of Shakespeare Studies and Production* 48 (1995): 155–62.

37. Garber, *Shakespeare*, 856.

38. Jeffrey Wilson, "'Savage and Deformed': Stigma and Drama in *The Tempest*," *Medieval and Renaissance Drama in England*, 31 (2018): 146–77, 147.

39. The first quotation comes from Ernest Renan's *Caliban* and echoes Richard III's accusation of "dissembling nature," in the most treated work of Shakespeare in disability studies. But here it is with an inflection of nature's impossibility rather than purposed counterfeit—it is the "inhuman" of Butler's "excluded sites." The second is another of Caliban's sobriquets that dominates much of scene two, along with the most common, "monster," often accompanied with a qualifier.

40. 1.2.263. See Daniel Wilson's "The Monster Caliban" in *The Tempest: Critical Essays*, ed. Patrick M. Murphy (New York: Routledge, 2001), 123–39, for a useful chapter on Caliban as monster and the process of stigmatization, wherein Wilson focuses on how "monsters" are figured in the play but does, toward the end, offer a similar sentiment to the ecocritical argument in this essay: "[Caliban] has that poetry of the senses which seems natural to his companionship with the creatures of the forest and the seashore" (138). A more recent claim by Jeffrey Wilson that "Caliban nowhere suffers the hardships of disability," however, is cautious at best and moralizing at worst. We know that bodies and identities are intertwined and that the focus of disability studies lies in onto-epistemologies rather than axiology. Jeffrey R. Wilson, "'Savage and Deformed': Stigma as Drama in *The Tempest*," *Medieval and Renaissance Drama in England: An Annual Gathering of Research, Criticism and Reviews* 31 (2018): 146–77.

41. 1.2.257–8, 69, 263.

42. 1.2.283, 168, 346, 355–57, 281–84; see also Wilson, "'Savage and Deformed,'" 15.

43. See John Dryden, "The Grounds of Criticism in Tragedy," in *Troilus and Cressida* (London: Able Swall and Jacob Tonson, 1679); Joseph Warton, *The Adventurer* 97 (October 9, 1753): 142.

44. 1.2.313–14 and 4.1.255, respectively; see also August Wilhelm Schlegel, "Lecture XXI," in *A Course of Lectures on Dramatic Art and Literature* (1815), trans. John Black, rev. A. J. W. Morrison (London: Henry G. Bohn, 1846), 395; Samuel Taylor Coleridge, "Lecture IX," in *Lectures and Notes on Shakespeare and Other English Poets* (1811–12), ed. Thomas Ashe (London: G. Bell and Sons, 1883), 142; William Hazlitt, "The Tempest," in vol. 1 of *Leigh Hunt's London Journal* (London: Charles Knight, 1834), 43; and Paul Franssen, "A Muddy Mirror," in *Constellation Caliban: Figurations of a Character*, ed. Nadia Lie and Theo D'Haen (Amsterdam: Rodopi, 1997), 27.

45. 2.3.316–19 and 3.2.26–9, respectively; for criticism that focuses on these physical aspects, see John W. Draper, "Monster Caliban," *Revue de Litterature Comparee* 40 (1966): 605; Barry Gaines and Michael Lofaro, "What Did Caliban Look Like?" *Mississippi Folklore Register* 10 (1976): 175–86; and Michael Baird Saenger, "The Costumes of Caliban and Ariel Qua Sea-Nymph," *Notes and Queries* 42, no. 3 (1995): 334–36.

46. See appendix A for photographs and illustrations of Caliban's various renderings.

47. 2.2.34–5; 2.2.154–55; 3.2.9.

48. 2.1.39.

49. Michel de Montaigne, "Of Cannibals," in *The Essays of Michel de Montaigne*, trans. and ed. M. A. Screech (London: Allen Lane/Penguin, 1991), 236.

50. Ibid., 93.

51. 2.2.27–32.

52. 2.2.18.

53. 2.2.22.

54. See Julia Reinhard Lupton's "Creature Caliban" (*Shakespeare Quarterly* 51, no. 1 [2000]), where she links Caliban's uncertainty in shape with his "faceless and featureless being" (8).

55. 1.2.334, 336; 1.2.358–9.

56. 1.2.338–9.

57. 1.2.343–5.

58. Lauren Eriks Cline, "Becoming Caliban: Monster Methods and Performance Theories," in *The Oxford Handbook of Shakespeare and Embodiment: Gender, Sexuality, and Race*, ed. Valerie Traub (Oxford: Oxford University Press, 2016): 709–23, 712.

59. Ibid., 713.

60. 1.2.332–3.

61. 2.2.1–3.

62. Darrien Morton, Kelley Bird-Naytowhow, and Andrew Hatala, "Silent Voices, Absent Bodies, and Quiet Methods: Revisiting the Processes and Outcomes of Personal Knowledge Production through Body-Mapping Methodologies among Indigenous Youth," *International Journal of Qualitative Methods* 20 (2021): 1–14, 3.

63. Ibid.

64. Ibid., 9.

65. 1.2.198–99.

66. See 1.2.198–99, for example.

67. 1.2.304.

68. 1.2.287–8.

69. Michel Foucault, "Different Spaces," in *Michel Foucault: Aesthetics, Methods and Epistemology*, trans. Robert Hurley and ed. James D. Faubion (London: Penguin, 1998), 178.

70. 1.2.285.

71. 1.2.294–6.

72. 2.277–8, my emphasis.

73. 1.2.327–31.

74. Jystona Singh, "Caliban vs. Miranda: Race and Gender Conflicts in Post-Colonial Rewritings of *The Tempest*," in *Feminist Readings of Early Modern Culture*, ed. Valerie Traub, M. Kaplan, and Dympna Callaghan (Cambridge: Cambridge University Press, 1996), 203.

75. Karen Newman, "'And Wash the Ethiop White': Femininity and the Monstrous in *Othello*," in *Shakespeare Reproduced*, ed. Jean Howard and Marion O'Connor (London: Routledge, 1990), 148.

76. 1.2.252–6.

77. This essay is not wholly wedded to the concept of "deep ecology," and I recognize its relatively outdated use here. While an analysis of *The Tempest* with regard to deep ecology's controversial debate over individual reform versus institutional reform would be both interesting and important, that is a project I have not set out to do here and so I use the term simply to point toward a political motivation in offering "greener" and disability-inflected readings of Shakespeare.

78. 1.2.401–2.

79. 1.2.417–9.

80. 1.2.388.

81. 3.2.13308.

82. 1.2.362, my emphasis.

83. Aimé Césaire's brilliant adaptation of *The Tempest* strikingly revises this ending by keeping Prospero on the island. As a postcolonial reboot, Césaire's play makes clear the colonizer's dependence on the Other for a sense of self and identity. *A Tempest*, trans. Richard Miller (Theatre Communications, 2002). See also Joseph Khoury, "*The Tempest* Revisited in Martinique: Aimé Césaire's Shakespeare," *Journal for Early Modern Cultural Studies* 6, no. 2 (Fall–Winter 2006): 22–37.

84. 5.1.7–8, 21–2.

85. John Kunat, "'Play Me False': Rape, Race, and Conquest in *The Tempest*," *Shakespeare Quarterly* 65, no. 3 (Fall 2014): 307–27, 323.

86. Vladimir Nabokov, *Lectures on Literature*, ed. Fredson Bowers, 1st ed. (New York: Harcourt Brace Jovanovich; B. Clark, 1982), 337.

87. Ibid.

88. 5.1.290 (my emphasis), 291–92, 295–96.

89. See also Julia Watts Belser, "Disability, Climate Change, and Environmental Violence: The Politics of Invisibility and the Horizon of Hope" (*Disability Studies Quarterly* 40, no. 4 [2020]), for a rally to read disability into discourses of ecological disaster and hope. Both disability studies and ecocriticism are founded upon and ethically bound to respective political movements, and as Belser notes, they require an orientation toward justice and response to "core inequities," which is thus highlighted in this chapter through a postcolonial reading of Shakespeare.

90. 1.2.107.

9

The Superfluous Who "Neither Produce like the Poor nor Consume like the Rich"

Eugenics and the "Coloniality of Ability" in Edward Thomas's The Happy-Go-Lucky Morgans *(1913)*

ANNA STENNING

The Welshman cannot but look back on that early age to which the historian has given so much space and, and ask, if Arthur will come back?

—EDWARD THOMAS, "REVIEWS"[1]

Critical disability studies (CDS) has begun to consider how the intersections of disability with race, gender, class, and culture provide the means to understand neoliberal constraints on personhood and action for those who are marginalized.[2] While traditional disability studies has focused on the social origins of dis/ablism and the changes that are needed in attitudes toward disabled individuals in mainstream cultural life, CDS considers the historically enacted constructions of disabilities through ableism and the occlusion of "socially constructed privileges and affordances—tools, technologies, infrastructures, and human networks—that enable normate activity."[3] Through its origins in critical social theory, CDS denies the possibility of studying societies through "atheoretical, context-free science."[4] Drawing on critical race theory (CRT), CDS has identified the possessive investments of those with dominant identities in technologies and structures that naturalize the apparent superiority of white/abled ways of producing knowledge. For instance, Thomas P. Dirth and Glenn A. Adams refer to the dubious histories of identity-based ability testing (within eugenic theory and phrenology) as a way to render legitimacy to practices of isolation and segregation.[5] This means that a "CDS lens helps to reveal how investments in ability not only relegate (raced/disabled) non-normate bodies to the margins, but also leads people more generally to pursue (untenable) normate ways of being predicated on high levels of resource consumption."[6]

In this essay, I introduce the circumstances surrounding the formulation of "moral deficiency" in the UK Mental Deficiency Act of 1913. I do not believe this is a unique moment in the cultural production of disability within the West; rather, it suggests a particular change in attitudes toward subjectivity and personhood within Britain that resulted from (a) the dominance of instrumental reason in all fields of life, brought about by the project of empire and the material benefits of industrialization; and (b) scientific practices that sought to reduce complex forms of life and personhood and subjectivity to traits that could be seen as "developed." The first idea shares terrain with Hannah Arendt's observations on the "superfluous" condition of Western subjects in the late industrial period, even if her work did not address eugenic theory or its origins in British and American scientific thought.[7]

In what follows, I focus on one particular novel by Edward Thomas as part of a critical need to engage with human differences as the means to engage the "political potentialities of the otherwise."[8] I am interested in works that explore disturbances in Western social, political, and economic orders—such as those that emerged in the lead-up to World War I—and that "open up novel spaces of the political in order to think and enact alternatives, potentially with others."[9] The subject of my engagement is therefore my own field of the health humanities and its relationship to literary and cultural studies more generally, specifically insofar as practitioners of the literary medical humanities tend to shy away from critical engagement with positivism.[10] I contend that prevailing constructs of literary merit in the West are underpinned by the same concepts of individual excellence that buttressed eugenic policies in the long nineteenth century. I do not intend to direct attention away from the politics and epistemologies of those who are more fundamentally "otherwise" to the neoliberal centers of power in the late stages of capitalism nor to hide from the conditions that make living otherwise increasingly dangerous.[11] Within Edward Thomas's "minor" novel, I find an idea of community and a cultural "otherwise" to the state of exception that prevailed in the colonial wars of the nineteenth century and its intensification leading up to World War I.[12] For me, as a neurodivergent and otherwise disabled academic seeking to intervene in cultural conversations around neuromedical differences,[13] Thomas's often-overlooked novel and prose essays highlight the role of literature in enabling cultural and philosophical exchange as an antidote to reductive sociobiological explanations of life.

In his only novel, *The Happy-Go-Lucky Morgans* (1913), the poet and critic Edward Thomas (1878–1917) responded to a phase in the development of eugenic social policy during the final stages of industrialization. I argue that the early decades of the twentieth century mark a transition in social attitudes toward personhood and subjectivity that responded not only to the burgeoning field of biostatistics and sociology but also to the visible presence of unemployment and poverty within the metropolis. Like Arendt, he shows that there are political issues that are often neglected through an exclusive focus on economic organization under capitalism or socialism; these issues concern the ways that social life can be understood through centralized and "neutral" structural designations. I argue that a complex range of political, social, and economic conditions in early twentieth-century Britain led to cultural understandings of social otherness that have implications for how we conceive of disability today. Within this context, I suggest how the tools of critical disability studies may inform reading practices that illuminate contingent constructions of ability and their relationship to our current standards of measuring literary and human worth within and beyond the Global North.

Global disability studies offers a basis from which to consider how disability studies in the West has focused on environmental constraints to personal independence at the exclusion of "networks of connection that, for better and worse, provide people with identity and meaning"; these networks include local ecologies that are essentially different from those of the minority world.[14] From a majority world perspective, disability can be understood as resulting from both the physical reality of colonial violence and the imperial ideology of the colonial other as "unfit" and in need of civilization and development.[15] For Dirth and Adams, this ideology informs current practices in Western psychology and health that reproduce colonial violence within an ongoing project of modernity. This draws attention to the way that health is often framed as the ability to pursue normative lifestyles for a privileged few, depicted by Adams and Dirth as

> the violence of a neoliberal economic regime that enables the unconstrained pursuit of happiness among a privileged global minority, but uproots others from lifestyles oriented toward collective self-sufficiency and requires them to seek exploitative forms of employment that regard them as disposable or that expose them to hazardous working conditions.[16]

Working within the institutional confines of psychology, Dirth and Adams describe how "hegemonic psychological science elevates [individualistic] ways of being to the status of prescriptive standard against which to measure individual and collective adjustment"; at the same time, psychological practices obscure the "disabling costs associated with enablement of normate subjectivity," both to individuals and to our shared lifeworld.[17] This essay aims to present the historical emergence of modern social constructions of personhood and its entanglement with a particular literary context: the emergence of Anglocentric modernism. Furthermore, it may be argued that the medicalization of social difference contributed to the erasure of "networks of connection" within colonial centers, which itself comprised a form of violence that undermined the possibilities for resisting what David Mitchell and Sharon Snyder have termed as "able-nationalism."[18] Vernacular literatures may serve as a repository of alternative conceptualizations of subjectivity, including those that model interdependent personhood.

Rather than seeking a global model of oppression that could unite experiences of the Other within the contemporary Global North and Global South, I am interested in destabilizing the assumed naturalness of what Dirth and Adams describe as a modern/Westernized way of being. This is one that promotes "impressive achievements, exploration and expression of personal desires."[19] These are not "natural endowments of the human organism or inherent features of the normate body abstracted from context" and are only "available to the privileged few," since they "reflect appropriation and extraction of the Other's productivity."[20] I extend Dirth and Adams's analysis by exploring how institutions and practices within the West, including not only hegemonic psychology but also literary studies, have suppressed recognition of the "disabling costs associated with enablement of normate subjectivity."[21] To do so, I argue for the need to renew critical attention to the heterogeneous cultural ecologies within the Global North, such as those recorded by the Anglo-Welsh poet and critic Edward Thomas, which were evident in his peers' celebration of Anglicized non-English national traditions from Ireland and Wales.

Andrew Webb has noted that apart from John Kerrigan's *Archipelagic English: Literature, History, and Politics 1603–1707*,[22] there has been little attention to how dominated nations within Britain and Ireland were subject to the imposition of imperialistic projects of education in English literary sensibility. From the sixteenth century, Wales was the first nation under English colonial rule, and its history since has been one of cultural and linguistic domination. For instance, Webb cites the 1847 "Black Books Report into the State of Education in Wales, which attacked the language, morality, and learning of the Welsh."[23] At Oxford, Thomas was introduced to decolonial thinking *avant la lettre* by O. M. Edwards, a leading figure in the Welsh "literary renaissance." Throughout his life, Thomas was also close friends with two Welsh language poets, Gwili and Watcyn Wyn.[24]

In this context, I argue that Edward Thomas's semiautobiographical novel *The Happy-Go-Lucky Morgans* (1913) contributes to our understanding of both Thomas's poetry and "the dark side of Western modernity"[25]—the influences of colonialism and coloniality on Western liberal thought. This corresponds to Nelson Maldonado-Torres's exploration of an ongoing "lack of recognition of the greater part of humanity as givers, which legitimizes dynamics of possession, rather than generous exchange."[26] Edward Thomas was a keen observer of changes in language that traced the growth in instrumental ways of organizing social life, which were increasingly informed by a logic of aggressive competition, and the pseudoscience of eugenics. In this way, I seek to supplement Dirth and Adams's analysis by drawing attention to the interconnections between literary culture and resistance to normative ways of being in communities of giving and exchange—including practices of cultural exchange of ideas and stories—within the centers of the empire. This literary context cannot be comprehended without addressing the coloniality of literary culture through a standardized set of aesthetic criteria centered on "uniqueness" rather than affordances for collective understanding.

The Happy-Go-Lucky Morgans and Edward Thomas

Through the novel, Thomas re-created his childhood as the coming-of-age narrative of a fictionalized middle-class Welsh family living in suburban South London, as recorded by the English narrator, Arthur Froxfield. We learn about the history of the Morgan family and their friends on either side of the turn of the nineteenth century, which provided Thomas with the opportunity to present a microcosm of attitudes toward social change, including those that originated in Welsh dissenting traditions within the community of Abercorran House. However, given the centrality of Welsh folklore in the story, it is not coincidental that the narrator—a school friend of the youngest Morgan—is named Arthur, who, according to Geoffrey of Monmouth, was the mythical Romano-Welsh king of the Britons.[27] While most family members are skeptical of the changes going on around them, Mr. Morgan is more optimistic that "there is a long future for men and women, if they have more and more air, and they have enough sixpences to let them bathe, for example, in peace," and he articulates nineteenth-century progressive attitudes toward welfare policy focused on labor conditions and environmental improvement.[28]

For the other members of the household, Welsh nonconformist protestant and Unitarian approaches to charity dominate, most often voiced by Ann, the housekeeper.[29] She says of Mr. Torrance, the scholar, "There are people born that can do nothing else, and they must live like the rest of us."[30] We are told that "Ann is good to all beggars" because, as she describes in her story about "The Castle of the Leaves," they may have fallen on hard times through no fault of their own.[31] Ann reinterprets the story with a much older story of her own. Many beggars of her own childhood had been young men before they went to fight in English imperial wars and had come back injured, "strange idols and images crawling and jiggering home" with "no more legs or arms than a fish." Their wives and children "had no more tears left to cry."[32] While others had accused the men of sin, Ann wonders, "What had the young men and women done? They were but mankind."

Early in the text, we learn how Jessie, the daughter of the Morgan family, had first encountered a man called Aurelius when he was working as a bookseller's assistant on the Charing Cross Road until he "wearied of dried goods."[33] Jessie admires Aurelius's appearance "as one of those young men in the *Arabian Nights*" who "longed to capture someone long lost or much desired," but it is Arthur who introduces Aurelius to Abercorran House. We are told that, within the household, "all liked" Aurelius, partly because his visits "brought quite little children."[34] Arthur says that Aurelius liked to "read in old books about Paradise" and had become "determined to make its equal on earth."[35] He is described as "foreign," "Italian," and "a gypsy," although his actual origins are unclear. Arthur says he has a "face like Merlin."[36] The stories he narrates within the book are not specific to any tradition, but he joins in with the Morgans and the Englishman, Mr. Torrance, in what they call "wool gathering," which is sharing stories based on real and imagined places and events "without profit or applause."[37] In response, Aurelius tells the Christian story of creation from the perspective of birds.[38]

While Philip's death marks the first step in the narrator's journey from innocence to experience, the later disappearance of Aurelius creates a rupture that is never fully resolved within the novel. Aurelius serves as both a symbol of a type that is explicitly named in the text—the superfluous man—and as a character-narrator who contributes to the frames through which we can interpret the story. When he disappears—and we do not find out whether he has died or is "put out of the way" in squire's agent's terms—Arthur finds himself further uprooted from his connections to this extended family.[39] Furthermore, the trope of the "superfluous" man appears extensively throughout Thomas's other prose, and I argue that at the time of writing (prior to his work as a poet), it provided him with a way to think about his own fate. "Superfluous" is the epithet Arthur uses to describe Aurelius after learning about his disappearance, but it is a term Arthur refines to contradict the terms that Aurelius's former employer uses to describe him. The employer—a squire's agent by the name of Theobold—says that "such people were unnecessary. Nothing could be done with them. They were no better than wild birds compared with pheasants, even when they could sing, which some of them could do, but not Aurelius."[40] We learn that Theobold had fired Aurelius for releasing a hare from a trap, which he regarded as poaching. Comparing Aurelius to a wild animal, he describes him as both "unnecessary" and as having "something wrong with him" because he could "neither produce like the poor nor consume like the rich."[41] The adult Arthur explains to the reader that this man had been "brutal" but not incorrect in his depiction of Aurelius: "Sometimes I think it was some of these superfluous men who invented God and all the gods and godlets. Some of them have been killed, some enthroned, some sainted, for it. But in a civilization like ours the super-fluous abound and even flourish."[42] Arthur's continued meditation on the condition of the "superfluous" moves away from the heroic masculinity of the Romantic tradition and toward a metaphysical difference that cannot be fully comprehended within class-based or racialized schemas. While Arthur thinks it is "unsympathetic" to describe Aurelius as a foreigner, he explains, "There is something in it." Arthur resists casting any of the household into naturalistic categories of race or speciation. Jessie is defined by her "radiant sweetness"; Ann is "half bird" and "half angel" though "not a mere human travesty."[43] Aurelius is described as "lightsome," which is the word Mr. Mor-gan uses to describe "swan-women" in a story he tells Arthur: "A stranger could hardly have told that they were not human, except for the cold, greenish light about them and their gait which was like the swimming of swans."[44]

We also hear about the death of David Morgan, the oldest son; his moth-er reads his letters to the family. David had thought himself to be descended from "a race who had kept themselves apart from the rest of men, though found among many nations, perhaps all." As reported by Arthur, David believed that "these, untainted with the blood of Cain, knew not the guilt of shame—but neither had they souls. They were a careless and godless race, knowing not good or evil. They had never been cast out of Eden." While Mrs. Morgan thinks this applies to Aurelius, we are told that David believed himself to have been born of a mixed parentage, one of many "unions of violent happiness and of calamity" between this race and humankind, which led to the "birth of a poet or musician who could abide neither with the strange race nor with the children of Adam." He believed he was feared because this meant he "retained what men had lost by civilization, because they lived as if time was not, yet could not be persuaded to believe in the future." Predicting his own fate, we learn that David died alone in a tower in Carmarthenshire, where he had tried to "think about his life before he began to live." He had wanted to "learn to see in human life, as we see in the life of bees, the unity, which perhaps some higher order of beings can see through the complexity which confuses us."[45] He had "set out to seek at first by means of science, but [later] he thought that science was an end, not a means,"[46] and this led him to believe that in "a hundred years" . . . "men had been reading science and investigating, as they had been reading history, with the end result that they knew some science and some history."[47]

David's discussions of race and parentage echo eugenicist ideas manifest in a Royal Commission Report from 1908, which argued for the direct in-heritance of social deficits: "It is important to consider the point of the im-provement of the race, if any means can be taken to prevent these 'undesir-ables' from producing their like."[48] The authors of the report refer to children who, judging from their parents, they considered likely to grow into adults who are only capable of "unskilled labour" and posing a burden in their need for "care and discipline." Through David Morgan, however, Thomas suggested that these ideas come from insufficient familiarity with history.

Like contemporary social reformers, David had discerned a "dark power" in humanity and yet had become "dismayed by numbers, by variety, by the grotesque."[49] His drive for naturalistic understandings becomes thwarted by the loneliness it brings; his poetry is suppressed by his quest for a naturalistic understanding. It is the search for knowing, as opposed to intuiting or feeling, that suppresses his poetry. As Thomas explained in *The South Country*:

> How little do we know of the business of the earth, not to speak of the universe; of time, not to speak of eternity. It was not by taking thought that man survived the mastodon. The acts and thoughts that will serve the race, that will profit this commonwealth of things that live in the sun, the air, the earth, the sea, now and through all time, are not known and never will be known.[50]

Thomas, who studied history rather than science while at Oxford, suggested a different understanding from race—one that is, in *The South Country*, metonymically connected to "commonwealth." As Stan Smith observed, Thomas, "who had read History under G. M. Trevelyan, knew the full seventeenth-century resonance of this word: if individuals are interdependent, mutually sustaining, on the ground of a nature which is a 'common,' shared wealth, then 'inheritance' has theological implications."[51] Thomas's invocation of "race" through Arthur suggests an alternative inflection of Darwinian theory that recognizes interdependence, not just between men but between humans and all life, since Aurelius was "the first man I ever met who really proved that man is above the other animals *as an animal*."[52] If Aurelius is inefficient, this does not mean that he should be seen as having no use in the greater scheme of things. Thomas suggests that social Darwinism is simply a newer articulation of aristocratic ethics.

In *The Happy-Go-Lucky Morgans*, Aurelius signified the possibility that "what we value not at all, are not conscious of, may break the surface of eternity with endless ripples of good."[53] He symbolizes how the "unvalued" may be advantageous for collective survival, including capacities for awe, wonder, and imagination. We are told that Aurelius is a poet; in one of his stories, he tells the family about an army who defeats its enemy by dancing and singing, since the soldiers' arts are "so divine and moving."[54] While he cannot tell how he came across this story, his fascination with the beauty of heroic deeds suggests a Keatsian "negative capability" that deals with "uncertainties, mysteries, doubts, without any irritable reaching after fact and reason."[55]

Through other people's responses to Aurelius, Thomas records emerging attitudes to social difference. Thomas would have been aware of the urge to construct social deviance in medicalized terms, which was increasingly a part of mainstream social life. When Thomas was writing *The Happy-Go-Lucky Morgans*, most Liberal Party members were invested in eugenics as a way of dealing with unemployment, inequality, poverty, and crime. The British media was complicit in the dissemination of eugenic ideas. As a reviewer for newspapers including *The Daily Chronicle*, Thomas would have been exposed to shifting editorial attitudes. In *The South Country*, Thomas fictionalizes the response of the crowd to a demonstration by the unemployed:

> Comfortable clerks and others of the servile realized that here were the unemployed of whom the newspapers had said this and that—("a pressing question"—"a very complicated question not to be decided in a hurry"—"it is receiving the attention of some of the best intellects of the time" . . . "who are the genuine and who are the imposters?"— "connected with Socialist intrigues")—and they repeated the word "Socialism" and smiled at the bare legs of the son of man.[56]

Here, and in his observations on changing attitudes to patriotism in the coming year, Thomas records a specific cultural shift driven by the media and industrial classes toward the valorization of an independent self who is economically productive.

While nineteenth century social policy had focused on environmental improvements, medicine, and education—with financial aid only available for the most obviously disenfranchised—there was a general sense that a laissez-faire attitude was not working, as poverty and ill health remained widespread. The Liberal government of 1906, under David Lloyd George and Winston Churchill, thought the state should intervene to produce an economically and militarily strong nation. In the early decades of the twentieth century, the middle classes viewed New Liberalism as a more appealing alternative to socialism or communism.

Thomas's father, Philip, was a high-ranking civil servant in the Board of Trade, who, upon retiring, stood as a parliamentary candidate for the Liberal Party in 1914. From around 1910, Philip Henry Thomas had an active role in the British school of positivist humanism, called the Church of Humanity.[57] Positivism originated with the nineteenth-century French philosopher Auguste Comte. Through his *Course in Positive Philosophy* and *A General View of Positivism*, Comte is widely recognized as the first modern philosopher of science and as the father of sociology and Progressivism (radical utopian liberalism). However, he is less often recognized as the author of a *System of Positive Polity*, which advocated a "religion of humanity" founded on science and designed to replace all other religions. The aim of the religion was the "divinification" of humanity, through the tenets of altruism, order, and progress, and a program for public worship.[58] Comte's ethical perspective was founded on an evolutionary ethics that saw altruism as a capacity unique to humans, one that should be deliberately produced by interventions in medicine and philosophy.[59] For Comte, the sociologist's role was to discover the mechanisms through which a society may become more "developed," by abandoning theological or metaphysical speculation.[60] The British Church of Humanity drew on these ideas in translations by Harriet Martineau and Richard Congreve, and Philip Thomas was a frequent chronicler of their activities.[61]

In the aftermath of Francis Galton's interpretation of Darwin's as an evolutionary model of human society, Comte's proposed scientific study of society became a branch of sociology that concerned itself with an interventionist role for the state. While Galton advocated the centrality of biostatistical data to legislation that would create a better society (through better people), Karl Pearson believed in the need to intervene to prevent reproduction by inferior "races."[62] Within the early decades of the twentieth century and following the formation in 1907 of the "Eugenics Education Society," these informed the negative eugenic measures that were legislated for in the Mental Deficiency Act of 1913.

The act was an outcome of the Royal Commission of Inquiry into the Care and Control of the Feeble-Minded (1904–1908), which had been set up by Churchill, and it proposed new categories of "imbeciles, feeble-minded persons, moral imbeciles, and such inebriates, epileptics, deaf and dumb, and blind persons as are also mentally defective."[63] "Moral imbeciles" were "persons who from an 'early age display some permanent mental defect coupled with strong vicious or criminal propensities on which punishment has had little or no deterrent effect.'"[64] According to Stephen Watson, the category developed out of the practices of prison medical officers in the nineteenth century. The "moral imbecile" was someone who presented problems for administration and control in prison settings.[65] The Eugenics Education Society "was able to exploit existing concern with the problems of habitual recidivism, 'feebleminded' school children and pauper 'imbeciles,' and connect them to wider anxieties over differential fertility and 'national efficiency.'"[66] The original definition of "feebleminded" was applied to a class of prisoners "who, though not certifiably insane, were nevertheless 'unfit for discipline.'"[67] That such inmates could not respond to punishment was used as an explanation for their status as "habitual offenders," who were believed to lack a "moral sense."[68] In the 1908 report, the "morally deficient" came to be seen as a distinct category from the "feebleminded," who were thought "incapable from mental defect existing from birth or from an early age (a) of competing on equal terms with their normal fellows; or (b) of managing themselves and their affairs with ordinary prudence."[69]

While the so-called moral imbecile was a category lacking clear inclusion criteria "social and political attitudes to the problem of the 'feebleminded' gave it a social and cultural authority."[70] Feeblemindedness was linked to innate failure to become an economic citizen, and moral imbecility became, under eugenic ideology, an inherited tendency toward nonconformity, as judged by a medical professional.

Attitudes toward Aurelius in Thomas's novel suggested a conflation of ideas about the "feebleminded" and "moral imbeciles" described in the Mental Deficiency Act. Within the eugenic climate of the era, the act legislated that anyone (including children) who met the criteria of the legislation should be seen as a risk to the welfare of the nation. The act stipulated that the "mentally deficient" would be segregated from society in "mental deficiency colonies" and further separated from members of the opposite sex, since they were seen as incapable of resisting base instincts. The 1909 report identified 149,628 people as "mentally deficient."[71]

Aurelius could have been regarded as a "moral imbecile" on the grounds that he was unable to find stable employment, that he broke the law by releasing a hare from a game-keeper's trap for no logical reason, and that he was regarded by many older people as lacking a religious sense.[72] He could also be seen to be "feebleminded," or incapable of "competing on equal terms" with contemporaries, since he did not contribute economically through either consumption or production. Edward Thomas described himself in similar terms, that he was neither an "average man" nor the "intelligent man."[73] Both he and the fictional character of Aurelius may have been seen to fall short of prevailing ideals of personhood, with its imperative of "becoming more independent, self-sufficient, enterprising, competitive, flexible, adaptable, risk-seeking, less reliant on government support, and oriented toward pursuing self-interest."[74] While the negative eugenic measures of the 1913 act were directed at poor children and adults, Thomas hinted that the ideology of the mental deficiency act was in danger of making all but the most self-oriented superfluous.

Through the novel and elsewhere in his prose writing, Thomas questions the validity of scientist approaches to morality. Rather than supposing that we should see ethics as something that could be formulated according to abstract rules, *The Happy-Go-Lucky Morgans* recognized the possibility of a culture based on generous exchange, whether that was of stories or hospitality and charity. Edward Thomas was happy with the novel, even though it did not sell.[75] In the coming months—until his enlistment in August 1914—

he recorded how a friend had observed the fusing of eugenic ideology to fuel anti-German sentiment and hatred:

> In print, men become capable of anything. The bards and journalists say extraordinary things. I supposed they do it to encourage the others. They feel that they are addressing the world; they are intoxicated with the social sense.[76]

The Superfluous Man in England

Studies of Edward Thomas's poetry, essays, and fiction focus on Thomas's love of nature and see his work as a critique of Progressive politics and a continuation of an Anglocentric culture in contrast to "foreign" modernism. *The Happy-Go-Lucky Morgans* contributes to our understanding of Thomas's sense of the meaning of social upheavals, but it has seldom been read in this way.

The term *superfluous* was one that Thomas had used before in his nonfiction prose and may stem from the English translation of Ivan Turgenev's "The Diary of a Superfluous Man."[77] Unlike either the Byronic or early Russian "superfluous men," aristocrats who rejected the limited role assigned to them within an increasingly regulated society, Turgenev's protagonist did not *choose* his fate. Like Aurelius, Tchulkaturin is unable to fulfill the social role he finds himself in even if, according to the requirement of narrative storytelling, he may seem to be responsible for his own undoing. For Arthur, it is more of a surprise that Aurelius survived for as long as he had, and at the end of the novel, his fate is determined by ongoing social circumstances.

While the majority of Thomas's novel takes place in the nineteenth century, the narrative occasion is the lead-up to World War I, during which time nationalism contributed a new dimension to discourses around social pathologies in England. We learn about Aurelius's response to English nationalism in the chapter entitled "Mr. Stodham speaks for England." The lodger, Mr. Stodham, invokes Arthur and the Morgans to understand that "the more you love and know England, the more you can love the Wilderness and Wales."[78] We are told that Arthur replies by shouting "Home Rule for Ireland," but Aurelius exerts a more decisive effect on the mood: "I really did not know before that England was not a shocking fiction of journalists and politicians. I am the richer, and, according to Mr. Stodham, so is England. But what about the London fog? What is the correct attitude of a patriot toward London fog and the manufacturers who make it what it is?"[79] This episode ends ambiguously as Aurelius points to the trees in the street, which are dimly lit by lamplight through the fog. Before stepping outside, he asks, "What are these / So withered and so wild in their attire, / That look not like th' inhabitants o' the earth/ And yet are on't?" before suggesting that the trees are less likely to inspire patriotism than the Elephant and Castle on a Saturday night.[80] Aurelius identifies problems with relying on human preferences, or judgments about what is natural, as guides to ethical goodness through his metonymic reference to G. E. Moore.[81]

The withered trees outside of Abercorran House on that Saturday night in the late nineteenth-century prefigure changes narrated later in the novel. We have learned from Arthur that the wilderness consisted of three acres of land that had become "attached" to Abercorran House by some accident of planning. The wilderness was an area of abandoned land comprising many elms, jackdaws, and a fishpond that was full of carp and lilies, which had become a victim to the "Board of Works, School Board inspectors, Rate Collectors, surveyors of taxes, bailiffs and recoverer of debts."[82] Arthur explains,

> The lilies and carp are no longer in the pond, and there is no pond. I can understand people cutting down trees—it is a trade and brings profit—but not draining a pond in such a garden as the Wilderness and taking all its carp home to fry in the same fat as bloaters, all for the sake of building a house that might just as well have been anywhere else or nowhere at all.[83]

A similar observation could be made about the "superfluous" people who were either put to "use" for the sake of short-term profit (such as in colonial warfare), or expelled according to a rhetoric of "efficiency" that exceeded logical justification.

Edward Thomas and World Literature

While Edward Thomas is commonly thought of as a poet, most of his work consisted of biographies, essays, countryside writing, and an extensive body of reviews and journalism. Thomas's death in the Battle of Arras during World War I has inspired the contemporary depiction of his entire work as that of an "accidental" English patriot who, despite Welsh familial origins, was willing to sacrifice his life for a British nation that was essentially defined by an English culture. Since Thomas's poetry and journalism written after the start of the war focus on the changes to England that occurred because of mass enlistment, influential readers have sought in his work a repository of images either of a "lost England"[84] or of enduring connectedness to the landscapes that remain and, despite change, are central to a sense of national belonging.[85]

Yet drawing on Pascale Casanova's *The World Republic of Letters*,[86] Andrew Webb considers Thomas as a Welsh poet who sought to define himself within a global literary tradition. For Casanova, culturally dominated nations within the West could gain recognition by appealing to the literary elite of Paris, New York, Berlin, London, and Barcelona, with Paris as the center of literary cultural capital. However, through his postcolonial critique of Casanova's imperialistic imposition of universalized measures of literary progress, Webb argues that Thomas's case demonstrates how the evaluative methods of global literary culture can develop recognition for specific authors while simultaneously reducing autonomy for dominated nations.[87] Webb points out that Thomas's (now underacknowledged) contributions to Welsh literary culture during his lifetime show how such dominance can be resisted—and explains why Thomas drew on the aesthetics of poetry in Welsh in his own verse.[88] I would argue that Thomas's subversiveness consists not only in his allegiance to Welsh literary traditions but to a much wider circle of cosmopolitan influences, including nineteenth-century Russian literature.

Thomas's wide-ranging literary influences are clear in *The Happy-Go-Lucky Morgans*, including his interest in folk stories (he had already published English editions of Welsh, Irish, and Nordic folk stories). The closest counterparts to the novel are Richard Jefferies's semiautobiographical novels *Bevis* and *Amaryllis*. Stan Smith suggests that Thomas shared Jefferies's belief in the redemptive power of the imagination, which, following Traherne, meant that God "hath made you able to create worlds in your own minds which are far more precious unto Him than those which He created. . . . That power to create worlds in the mind is the imagination and is the proof that the creature liveth and is divine."[89] Thomas's thoughts on the contemporary obsession with "efficiency" may have origins in his readings of H. D. Thoreau, who reflected throughout his life on the possibility of self-cultivation through meaningful work that did not require the exploitation of others.[90]

During his time as a critic and reviewer, Thomas developed extensive knowledge of poetry, history, and criticism, but it is seldom noted that he was also widely read in world literature. In 1914, he finished a draft of his essay "Ecstasy," in which he made unlikely connections between his contemporary Georgian poets and writers in other periods and traditions, including Fyodor Dostoevsky, Leo Tolstoy, Edward Carpenter, Rabindranath Tagore, and Hafiz of Shiraz. With such writers, Thomas shared his skepticism of collective utopianism and a commitment to self-transcendence in the form of mystical and aesthetic experiences. Speaking of this wider circle of peers, he says, "We ask for something that will suddenly knot up our science and illuminate it or maybe altogether blot it out." This meant achieving a condition of "boundlessness" that could lead one to become a "citizen of eternity." Thomas described aesthetic ecstasy as similar to the state of "distraction" that others had come to be seen as madness: "Earlier ages seem to have treated [the mad] less as human beings lacking something than as distinct, even favoured, species, like birds or beasts, with some uncanniness added by their superficial humanity."[91]

Thomas's friend Joseph Conrad shared an interest in the negative epiphany of terror at loneliness, which Thomas describes as "the opposite" of ecstasy.[92] For both Thomas and Conrad, this experience came through realization of the vastness of nature or human civilization, voiced by the sailor Charles Marlow as the "wilderness" that threatened to engulf him (*Heart of Darkness*) and by Thomas in his realization during *The Icknield Way* that "all that was once lovely and alive in the world, all that had once been alive and was memorable and now dead is now dung for a future that is infinitely less than the dark falling rain."[93] Conrad saw this negative social epiphany as the precursor to the moral descent of the superfluous man in colonial conquests, embodied in Mr. Kurtz (*Heart of Darkness*) and Nikita Necator (*Under Western Eyes*), who share a moral shallowness, characterized by Marlow as being "hollow at the core."[94] These same characters are archetypes for Arendt in her later *Origins of Totalitarianism*: "Expelled from a world with accepted social values, they had been thrown back upon themselves and still had nothing to fall back upon except, here and there, a streak of talent which made them as dangerous as Kurtz if they were ever allowed to return to their homelands."[95] Arendt describes the colonialists of Africa in terms evocative of Arthur's characterization of Aurelius: "The luck hunters were not distinctly outside civilized society but, on the contrary, very clearly a by-product of this society, an inevitable residue of the capitalist system and even the representatives of an economy that relentlessly produced a superfluity of men and capital."[96]

Thomas's superfluous men in his later prose and poetry were displaced from civilized society, unable to perform the roles assigned to them even if they were born into the middle classes. In a similar way, for Arendt, the social changes that produced the superfluous among the elite in the nineteenth century transformed during the first decades of the twentieth century, extending to include all citizens who were redundant if they did not follow the logic of a system they did not care about. For Arendt, in *The Human Condition*, the focus on maximizing production in modern life has encroached on the capacity for humans to contribute to a shared human world: "The process of wealth accumulation, as we know it, is stimulated by the life process and in turn stimulating human life is possible only if the world and very worldliness of man are sacrificed."[97] She notes the failure of modern life to provide conceptual resources for meaningful relationships through its monolithic focus on the material reproduction of bare life. This meant that "what was not needed, not necessitated by life's metabolism with nature, was either superfluous or could be justified only in terms of a peculiarity of human as opposed to other animal life."[98] In Aristotelian terms, Arendt saw that the "higher functions" of man consisted in a sense of a shared "world-liness"—but this was precisely what was lost through the impulse to accelerated wealth accumulation. For Arendt, modern superfluity is always a negative condition rather than a potential basis for resistance. However, in citing anthropocentric "higher functions" as the basis of what was lost, she echoes the instrumentalist reasoning of the eugenicists.

Nelson Maldonado-Torres is clearer that the conditions for "generous exchange" were obliterated by "non-ethics of war" that defined European Imperial society and legislated for racism.[99] However, he sees resistance as possible and draws on Frantz Fanon's radical "receptive generosity" as the means through which ethics can be reinserted into the social realm.[100] For Maldonado-Torres, it is not a purported innate or exclusive capacity of humans but a deliberate "absolute responsibility for the Other that gives birth to human subjectivity."[101] A similar sentiment can be found in Dostoevsky, who Thomas quotes in his essay on ecstasy: "Love life above everything in the world . . . love it, regardless of logic . . . it must be regardless of logic, and it's only then one will understand the meaning of it."[102]

Thomas's Superfluous Men

In his book *The South Country*, Thomas describes himself superfluous in the senses of "unfortunate" and depending on "sanitation, improved housing, police, charities, medicine" for survival.[103] Within an otherwise nonfictional text, Thomas uses the word *superfluous* to describe a fictional Carmarthenshire clerk who felt both "helpless" and "superfluous" since he experienced the "intimation of the endless pale road, before and behind, which the soul has to travel."[104] Thomas imagines the clerk now working as a farm laborer during the summer but returning to London in the winter where he could make more money in a job he described as "slavery" since it offered no satisfaction.[105] Thomas envisions meeting him again as a part of a "contemptible" procession of men who are a spectacle of "unbrotherliness" and also "gentle with hunger."[106]

Stan Smith connected Thomas's interest in the superfluous man to the social conditions of the early 1900s, where office workers were doubly removed from having either a secure social or economic status.[107] This was the situation of the newly expanded lower middle class that had no geographical roots and who worked in newly emerging industries. Smith quotes Thomas's imagined clerk in *The South Country*: "I realize that I belong to the suburbs still. I belong to no class or race; and have no traditions. We of the suburbs are a confused, hesitating mass, of small courage though much endurance. As for myself, I am world-conscious and hence suffer unutterable loneliness."[108] While Smith focuses on class anxieties—a concern for status within an increasingly homogenized labor force—it does not seem to do justice to the nature of spiritual crisis that Thomas identified. In a prose essay from 1913, *The Country*, Thomas described this "world-consciousness" in more favorable terms. Here, it meant being a "citizen of the world" while retaining, or even amplifying, our attachment to those around us:

> Calming us with its space and patience, the country relates us all to Eternity. We go to it as would-be poets, or as solitaries, vagabonds, lovers, to escape foul air, noise, hard hats, black uniforms, multitudes, confusion, incompleteness, elaborate means without clear ends,—to escape ourselves; and we do more than escape them. So vastly do we increase the circle of which we are the centre that we become as nothing. The larger the circle the less seems our distance from other men each at his separate centre; and at last that distance is nothing at all in the mighty circle, and all have but one circumference. And thus we truly find ourselves.[109]

In the same essay, he describes how another fictionalized Welshman, now living in London, denies this possibility. This character is writing his memoirs and "trying to prove by autobiography that all was over for him and the world" because of "his imprisonment in a London office."[110] Echoing Turgenev's superfluous man and Thomas's own plight, he explains that science has stripped the world of mystery, and empire consolidated this through its insistence on secular education that overrides the sense of what is "incalculable." He says, "We have been robbed [. . .] of the small, intelligible England of Elizabeth and given the word Imperialism instead [. . .] There is nothing left for us to rest upon, nothing venerable or great or mysterious, which can take us out of ourselves."[111] In the novel, Mr. Torrance echoes this feeling in his lament that "[T]here is nothing to rest on, nothing to make a man last like the old men I used to see in cottage gardens, or at gateways in the valley of the Uther."[112]

The clerk in *The Country* experiences both a cultural and dispositional dislocation, the latter of which prefigures Aurelius, of whom we are told that "the magic circle drawn round us all surrounds these in such a way that it will never overlap, far less become concentric with, the circles of any other in the whirling multitudes."[113] The clerk in *South Country* similarly seeks an "under-cowman's place" in the country but anticipates that, unlike the countryman, he is "lacking in those strong tastes and impulses which, blinding men to what does not concern them, enables them to live with a high heart."[114] He is also alienated from his London peers, since he lacked any pleasure in showing "outward scorn for those who were outlandish, and for all things that were not like those of the richer people of their acquaintance or envy."[115] This comment by the fictional clerk may have been based on Thomas's own brief experiences of office work. Despite having had success as a literary reviewer, he accepted a post as a secretary for a new Royal Commission on Ancient Monuments while completing *The South Country*. He lasted less than a year because of declining mental health, which he attributed to London air and feeling that he was "not really earning his stipend."[116]

In *Fiction* (1914), an autobiography of his early life, Thomas describes a similar feeling toward his peers when he was training for the civil service entry exam:

> Already, I found it painful to see so much vacuity without leisure, indolence without refinement. The young men of my own age twirling their canes, pushing into one another sideways, made me angry—was it because they at least had achieved contentment, and I only contempt?[117]

The Carmarthen-born clerk in *The South Country* finds it strange that his officemates do not criticize their bosses but instead despise "everyone armed not with the power to take away our bread—to the old, the poor, the women, the children."[118] The clerk finds no solace in this because he recognizes that he is one of a "people" who had "always been oil or grit in a great machine" rather than one of the "powers above."[119] Perhaps, because of his keen sense of familial history as laborers and artisans, he cannot find meaning in seeing himself as part of a class apart from his ancestors. Thomas was aware that the recent social elevation of white-collar work was simply another step in the progression of "respect for surfaces" that obscured the real conditions of the poor as a "tyranny that poisons quietly without blows."[120]

Virginia Woolf famously said in her 1924 essay "Mr. Bennett and Mrs. Brown" that there was a change in human nature in 1910, where relations between "masters and servants, husbands and wives, parents and children" meant that a novel would need to convey individuals as individuals rather than in terms of their earlier social roles. Edward Thomas suggested otherwise.[121] *The Happy-Go-Lucky Morgans* searches for sources of interdependence outside established orders. In this way, the text can be seen as an act of resistance against new social realities.

In his extensive countryside writing, Thomas often spent his time recording the "happy-go-lucky" human and nonhuman inhabitants of patches of neglected waste ground or woodland, including the "no man's land" that was the name first given to borders of towns that were the site of gypsy and traveler settlements. As he recorded the encroachment of "urban development" on the London edge lands in *The Happy-Go-Lucky Morgans*, his poetry records the continued drive for agricultural efficiency:

> Common 'tis named
> And calls itself, because the bracken and gorse
> Still hold the hedge where plough and scythe have chased them.

"Up in the Wind" evokes a remote country pub that has become more isolated in the first decades of the twentieth century. Like earlier dissenting poets, Thomas showed that modern agricultural reformation consolidated changes that had begun with the enclosures. In other poems, such as "A Private," Thomas connects the changes to the countryside to a different sort of displacement—to the battlefields of France. In "Lob," Thomas suggests that the mythical countryman has become tragically "one of the lords of No Man's Land." While there is much more to say on this theme, I mention this here to highlight that Thomas's sensitivity to changes would combine to produce a unique set of conditions in which the "socially inefficient" could be controlled and effectively erased.

Conclusion

Critical responses to Edward Thomas's novel *The Happy-Go-Lucky Morgans* have been few, and, where they exist, they mine the text for autobiographical data rather than seeing it as a potential insight into Thomas's sense of his own historical location. While it would be false to claim that Thomas is a postcolonial or decolonial writer, he responds to the connections between colonialism and disablism. I argue that Thomas's observations on his historical moment are relevant to a critique of modernity's enthronement of instrumental reason as a guide to social life. Specifically, his interest in history and Welsh nationalism had led him to understand that British history was "a thousand years . . . of bloody tyranny."[122]

For this reason, I agree with Andrew Webb that Thomas's novel deserves to be explored within the cultural ecology of world literature, specifically as he champions the independence of Anglicized national literatures of Wales and Ireland as a source of cultural autonomy outside colonial Britishness. Therefore, while Thomas did not challenge Eurocentrism, he was alert to the conditions by which a colonized nation may begin to resist the impositions of a colonizing language and culture. For Webb, Thomas's poetry was informed by his concern with how "oral language might be inserted into written forms, as a way of undermining the dominant English literary standards and building an alternative national tradition within a re-appropriated English language."[123]

While most critics focus on Robert Frost's influence in alerting Thomas to a Wordsworthian project of incorporating speech rhythms in poetry, Webb notes that Thomas deployed what he learned from nineteenth-century symbolism against the "rhetoric" of Victorian poetry and, in so doing, found inspiration in Walt Whitman's "American internationalism."[124]

Therefore, Thomas's modernism proposed a critical rupture from certain, more recent traditions, which he saw as Prometheanist. He was not a reactionary advocate of a return to English Romanticism (as could be claimed of some of his Georgian contemporaries) nor did he desire to return to classical literature as Ezra Pound and T.S. Eliot did. Thomas was pragmatic as far as he accepted the inevitability of modern conveniences and admonished the naivety of many contemporary "back to nature" movements. However, he sought literary autonomy to question the idealization of "independent" personhood within both literary and political discourses. Through the character of the "superfluous man" in *The Happy-Go-Lucky Morgans* and elsewhere in his prose writing, Thomas connected cultural homogenization to the erasure of specific kinds of people who had formerly been valued within the domestic or cultural realm.

Thomas's awareness of the colonization of Welsh culture through the Black Book study and his familiarity with cultural resistance in dissenting religious tradition during his own childhood and through his tutelage under O. M. Edwards at Oxford provided a unique context to critique both changes in welfare policy toward those who were seen as morally or intellectually underdeveloped and the assumption that economic efficiency should drive all fields of social life. Thomas's characters in *The Happy-Go-Lucky Morgans* and elsewhere resist "socially constructed privileges and affordances—tools, technologies, infrastructures, and human networks—that enable normate activity."[125] In so-doing, the novel offers a blueprint for a community, with roots in the oral storytelling and dissenting religious traditions of Wales but also exceeding those through recognition of technological change and globalization, where the economically and socially marginal, including the disabled, could endure.

This manifests at the level of form with the novel's episodic and polyvocal narration producing a text whose meaning is greater than its constituent parts. Both the form and content of the novel weigh against the idea that, under modernity, individuals are necessarily isolated both from each other and from a world beyond them for the sake of socioeconomic development. Aurelius embodies the possibility of collective resistance against efficiency via "networks of connection" that are both material and symbolic, where superfluity may even form the basis of new communities. Ann reminds readers of those nineteenth-century wars in which young men were rendered superfluous.

Liberal ideas about subjectivity, recorded by Woolf and others, contributed to the apparent "naturalness" of independent selfhood registered as "impressive achievements, exploration and expression of personal desires."[126] The authorized contemporary readings of Thomas's novel provided by Andrew Motion and Edna Longley—as an expression of a uniquely individualistic English patriotism—can be read within Mitchel and Snyder's frame of "ablenationalism" as a strategic evasion of Thomas's own neuroatypicality and ambivalence about Imperial Britain.

Within this essay, I have argued that Thomas's investment in Welsh cultural traditions enabled him to challenge the idea of efficiency that was manifest in both the historical emergence of new diagnostic classifications and in land management practices that were detrimental to wildlife. Through the characters of Ann and Aurelius in *The Happy-Go-Lucky Morgans*, Thomas suggested that "networks of connection" could be preserved through literature despite these changes. I have argued that literary scholars of disability and health must participate in a more generous exchange of ideas with disability and decolonial theory, to recognize how literary culture is enriched by its engagement with the "otherwise." This would include reevaluating criteria for literary and scholarly merit so that they no longer simply reinforce normative sensibilities.

My focus in this essay has been tracing Thomas's responses to the conditions within Britain during the first decade of the twentieth century that led to the construction of categories of "moral imbeciles" and "feebleminded" that were manifest in his contemporaries' attitudes. This includes attitudes toward work, bureaucracy, and welfare, which, he noted earlier, included "outward scorn for those who were outlandish, and for all things that were not like those of the richer people of their acquaintance or envy."[127] Finally, it is through this context, I suggest, that we must understand both the historical emergence of Western ideas about cognitive and developmental disability and the coloniality of literary culture in its own scorn for the "outlandish" and marginal. I have argued that the construction of the categories of the "moral imbecile" and the "feebleminded" reflect a cultural change masked as scientific progress.

The Liberal investment in ideas about cognitive difference as either moral deficiency or an inability to manage one's own financial affairs represent the endurance of nineteenth-century Comtean ideas about the divinification of society through science and the urge to render ongoing social problems as the fault of marginalized individuals. Edward Thomas shows that other cultural traditions—including Ann's nonconformist Protestantism and Mr. Morgan's philanthropism—recognized the inherent value of all individuals, even if they require care or are accustomed to devalued, manual labor. In so doing, Thomas's work is itself an act of "receptive generosity" that demonstrates the centrality of the moral imagination to recognizing the worth of those rendered superfluous to capitalistic production. To make the "equal" of paradise on earth is not to make "a better world" but to make a community such as Abercorran House, where all "earned a living."[128]

ACKNOWLEDGMENTS

With thanks to Alice Hagopian for comments on a draft of this manuscript. This work was produced while working under the Wellcome Trust grant 218124/A/19/Z.

NOTES

1. Edward Thomas, "Reviews," scrapbooks 1901–1913, vol. 3, no. 6. Review of O. M. Edwards's *Wales* in *The Academy*, 1902.

2. Dan Goodley, "Dis/entangling Critical Disability Studies," *Disability & Society* 28, no. 5 (2013): 631–44; Helen Meekosha and Roger Shuttleworth, "What's So 'Critical' about Critical Disability Studies?" *Australian Journal of Human Rights* 15, no. 1 (2009): 47–55.

3. Thomas P. Dirth and Glen A. Adams, "Decolonial Theory and Disability Studies: On the Modernity/Coloniality of Ability," *Journal of Social and Political Psychology* (2019): 270. The "normate" is a term coined by Rosemarie Garland-Thompson to describe "the corporeal incarnation of culture's collective, unmarked, normative characteristics"—see *Extra-ordinary Bodies: Figuring Disability in American Culture and Literature* (New York: Columbia University Press, 1997), 8.

4. Helen Meekosha and Russell Shuttleworth, "What's So Critical?," 52.

5. Dirth and Adams, "Decolonial," 27.

6. Dirth and Adams, "Decolonial," 272.

7. Hannah Arendt, *The Origins of Totalitarianism* (1951); *The Human Condition* (1958).

8. Janina Kehr, "Toward the Otherwise: Anthropology, Politics, Medicine," *Journal of Social and Cultural Anthropology* (2020): 28.

9. Kehr, "Toward the Otherwise," 29.

10. William Viney, Felicity Callard, and Angela Woods, "Critical Medical Humanities: Embracing Entanglement, Taking Risks," *BMJ Medical Humanities* (2015).

11. Marisol de la Cadena, *Earth-Beings: Ecologies of Practice across Andean Worlds* (Durham, NC: Duke University Press, 2015); Ghassan Hage, *Alter-politics: Critical Anthropology and the Radical Imagination* (Melbourne: Melbourne University Press, 2015); Achille Mbembe, *Necropolitics* (Durham, NC: Duke University Press, 2019); Elizabeth Povinelli, *Geontologies: A Requiem to Late Liberalism* (Durham, NC: Duke University Press, 2014).

12. Giorgio Agamben, *State of Exception* (Chicago: University of Chicago Press, 2005).

13. See, for example, my "Misfits and Ecological Saints: Strategies for Non-normative Living in Autistic Life Writing," *Disability Studies Quarterly* 42, no. 1 (2022).

14. Dirth and Adams, "Decolonial," 273.

15. Dirth and Adams, "Decolonial," 274.

16. Dirth and Adams, "Decolonial," 275.

17. Dirth and Adams, "Decolonial," 275.

18. "Ablenationalism and the Geo-Politics of Disability," *Journal of Literary & Cultural Disability Studies* 4, no. 2 (2010): 113–25.

19. Dirth and Adams, "Decolonial," 275.

20. Dirth and Adams, "Decolonial," 275.

21. Dirth and Adams, "Decolonial," 275.

22. John Kerrigan, 2008. Webb observes that Kerrigan's observations on the Welshness of Henry Vaughn echo comments made by M. Wynn Thomas in *Corresponding Culture: The Two Literatures of Wales* (Cardiff: University of Wales Press, 1999).

23. Andrew Webb, *Edward Thomas and World Literary Studies: Wales, Anglocentrism and English Literature* (Cardiff: University of Wales Press, 2013), 13.

24. Webb, *Edward Thomas*, 93.

25. Walter D. Mignolo, *The Darker Side of Western Modernity: Global Futures, Decolonial Options* (Durham, NC: Duke University Press, 2011).

26. Neldon Maldonado-Torres, "On the Coloniality of Being: Contributions to the Development of a Concept," *Cultural Studies* 21:240–70.

27. Stan Smith notes, with reference to Thomas's poem "The Combe," "There is another more subversive dimension to the idea of Britain, which takes us back to . . . that legendary darkness which preceded the English ultimately Roman Empire, too—a Britain of obscure and hidden corners . . . surviving only in the swarthy, taciturn peoples of Wales and the West." In *Edward Thomas: Student Guides* (London: Faber and Faber, 1986), 22.

28. Edward Thomas, *The Happy-Go-Lucky Morgans*, in *Edward Thomas: Prose Writings, A Selected Edition, Volume I, Autobiographies*, ed. Guy Cuthbertson (Oxford: Oxford University Press, 2011), 105.

29. Until 1828, nonconformists were subject to civil "disabilities" that made it impossible for them to attain a public office or to study at Oxford or Cambridge. See Owen Chadwick, *The Victorian Church*, Part One: 1829–1859 (1966): 60–95, 142–58.

30. Thomas, *Happy-Go-Lucky Morgans*, 94.

31. Thomas, *Happy-Go-Lucky Morgans*, 121.

32. Thomas, *Happy-Go-Lucky Morgans*, 120. Ann's characterization within the novel suggests the influence of Welsh nonconformist religious culture on an English-language Welsh tradition that survived despite cultural dominance by the Anglican church. See M. Wynn Thomas, *In the Shadow of the Pulpit: Literature and Nonconformist Wales* (Lampeter: University of Wales Press, 2010).

33. Thomas, *Happy-Go-Lucky Morgans*, 45.

34. Thomas, *Happy-Go-Lucky Morgans*, 36.

35. Thomas, *Happy-Go-Lucky Morgans*, 55.

36. Guy Cuthbertson notes that Aurelius Ambrosius was "a military leader who resisted the Anglo-Saxon advance" and "became a legendary figure and was associated with exploits attributed elsewhere to either Merlin or Arthur"; see Thomas, *Happy-Go-Lucky Morgans*, 55.

37. Thomas, *Happy-Go-Lucky Morgans*, 55.

38. Thomas, *Happy-Go-Lucky Morgans*, 55.

39. Thomas, *Happy-Go-Lucky Morgans*, 28.

40. Thomas, *Happy-Go-Lucky Morgans*, 38.

41. Thomas, *Happy-Go-Lucky Morgans*, 38.

42. Thomas, *Happy-Go-Lucky Morgans*, 39.

43. Thomas, *Happy-Go-Lucky Morgans*, 17.

44. Thomas, *Happy-Go-Lucky Morgans*, 31.

45. Thomas, *Happy-Go-Lucky Morgans*, 65–67.

46. Thomas, *Happy-Go-Lucky Morgans*, 67.

47. Thomas, *Happy-Go-Lucky Morgans*, 67.

48. Royal College of Physicians, "Report of Royal Commission on Care and Control of the Feeble-Minded" (London: HMSO, 1908), 117.

49. Thomas, *Happy-Go-Lucky Morgans*, 68.

50. Edward Thomas, *The South Country* (London: J. M. Dent, 1909), 26.

51. Stan Smith, "The Public Mind: Edward Thomas's Social Mysticism," *Critical Survey* 11, no. 3 (1999): 68. Smith refers to Thomas's quote from Traherne's *Centuries* in *The South Country*.

52. Thomas, *Happy-Go-Lucky Morgans*, 36.

53. Thomas, *South Country*, 26.

54. Thomas, *Happy-Go-Lucky Morgans*, 109.

55. *The Letters of John Keats*, ed. by H. E. Rollins, 2 vols. (Cambridge: Cambridge University Press, 1958), 193–94.

56. Thomas, *South Country*, 110.

57. See Jean Moorcroft Wilson, *Edward Thomas: From Addlestrop to Arras* (London: Bloomsbury, 2015), 17.

58. Auguste Comte, *System of Positive Polity; or, Treatise on Sociology, Instituting the Religion of Humanity* (1851–1854), 4 vols.

59. See Michel Bourdeau, "Auguste Comte," Stanford Encyclopaedia of Philosophy, University of Stanford, accessed December 2021, https://plato.stanford.edu/entries/comte/#RelHum.

60. Leonard Beeghley, "The Sociology of Auguste Comte," in *The Emergence of Sociological Theory*, 7th ed. (Newbury Park, CA: Sage, 2012), 37–54.

61. See Gladys Bryson, "Early English Positivists and the Religion of Humanity," *American Sociological Review* 1, no. 3 (1936): 343–62.

62. Karl Pearson, "National Life from the Stand-Point of Science: An *Address* Delivered at Newcastle" (1901) (London: Adam & Charles Black, 1908).

63. Royal College of Physicians, "Report of Royal Commission on Care and Control of the Feeble-Minded" (London: HMSO, 1908), 42.

64. HMSO, "Mental Deficiency Act of 1913," *Education England: The History of Our Schools* (2019), accessed December 2021, http://www.educationengland.org.uk/documents/acts/1913-mental-deficiency-act.html.

65. Stephen Watson, "Malingerers, the 'Weakminded' Criminal and the 'Moral Imbecile': How the English Prison Medical Officer Became an Expert in Mental Deficiency, 1880–1930," in *Legal Medicine in History*, ed. Michael Clark and Catherine Crawford (Cambridge: Cambridge University Press, 1994), 223–42.

66. Watson, "Malingerers," 224.

67. UK Parliament, "Mental Deficiency Act of 1913," 137.

68. Watson, "Malingerers," 233.

69. Royal College of Physicians, "Report," 36.

70. Watson, "Malingerers," 236.

71. Royal College of Physicians, "Report," 6.

72. Arthur explains that "older people said that Aurelius had no perception of religion, or beauty, or human suffering" (Thomas, *Happy-Go-Lucky Morgans*, 43). One of the last things that Edward Thomas wrote in his diary during World War I was, "I never understood quite what was meant by God"; quoted in Matthew Hollis, *Edward Thomas: Selected Poems* (Faber and Faber 2011), 168.

73. Thomas, *South Country*, 6.

74. Jeff Sugarman, "Neoliberalism and Psychological ethics," *Journal of Theoretical and Philosophical Psychology* 35, no. 2: 103–16.

75. R. George Thomas, *Edward Thomas: A Portrait* (Oxford: Oxford University Press, 1985), 26.

76. Edward Thomas, "England" (1914), in *The Last Sheaf*.

77. Ivan Turgenev, *The Diary of a Superfluous Man: And Other Stories* (London: William Heinemann, [1850] 1894).

78. Thomas, *Happy-Go-Lucky Morgans*, 130.

79. Thomas, *Happy-Go-Lucky Morgans*, 130.

80. The Elephant and Castle is an area in South London. In the early twentieth century, it was a thriving center of shopping and entertainment known as the "Piccadilly of the South." See https://www.elephantandcastle.org.uk/a-brief-history/the-piccadilly-of -the-south/.

81. I am taking Thomas as being ironic when he writes, "Both are good, as they say at Cambridge" (Thomas, *Happy-Go-Lucky Morgans*, 130). G. E. Moore, one of the most influential philosophers of the period and based at Cambridge alongside Russell and Wittgenstein, wrote that ethical judgments cannot be justified through reference to natural facts, but they belong to a separate domain of enquiry. Moore's ideas were seen by modernist thinkers, including Woolf and T. E. Hulme, as having freed the generation from utilitarianism. See Principia Ethica (Cambridge: Cambridge University Press, 1903).

82. Thomas, *Happy-Go-Lucky Morgans*, 15.

83. Thomas, *Happy-Go-Lucky Morgans*, 15.

84. The quote comes from J. M. Coetzee's autobiographical novel about his time in London, *Youth: Scenes from a Provincial Life II* (London: Secker and Warburg, 2002), 58: "What has happened to the ambitions of poets here in Britain? Have they not digested the news that Edward Thomas and his world are gone forever?"

85. This is the argument of Robert Macfarlane's *The Old Ways: A Journey on Foot* (London: Penguin, 2013), which reinterprets some of Thomas's writing within Macfarlane's own political vision.

86. Pascale Casanova, *The World Republic of Letters*, trans. Malcolm DeBevoise (Cambridge, MA: Harvard University Press, [1999] 2004).

87. Webb, *Edward Thomas*, 2013.

88. In the chapter titled "Edward Thomas and the Welsh Cultural Tradition," Webb also identifies the Welsh cultural influences on *The Happy-Go-Lucky Morgans*; see Andrew Webb, *World Literary*, 109–38.

89. Edward Thomas, review of Thomas Traherne's Poems of Felicity, *Daily Chronicle*, June 10, 1908, quoted in Smith's "Public Mind," 69.

90. For more on this theme, see David B. Raymond's "Henry David Thoreau and the American Work Ethic Author," *Concord Saunterer* 17 (2009): 137–56.

91. Anna Stenning, "Edward Thomas's 'Ecstasy': An Unpublished Essay," *Essays in Criticism* 66, no. 4 (2016): 466–87.

92. Stenning, "'Ecstasy,'" 475.

93. Edward Thomas, *The Icknield Way* (London: Constable, 1913), 282.

94. Joseph Conrad, *Heart of Darkness*, 71.

95. Arendt, *Origins of Totalitarianism*, vol. 2, 69.

96. Arendt, *Origins of Totalitarianism*, vol. 2, 69.

97. Arendt, *Human Condition*, 25.

98. Arendt, *Human Condition*, 321.

99. Maldonado-Torres, "Coloniality," 259.

100. Maldonado-Torres, "Coloniality," 260.

101. Maldonado-Torres, "Coloniality," 260.

102. Stenning, "'Ecstasy,'" 177.

103. Thomas, *South Country*, 6.

104. Thomas, *South Country*, 74.

105. Thomas, *South Country*, 81.

106. Thomas, *South Country*, 92–94.

107. Stan Smith, *Edward Thomas* (London: Faber and Faber, 1989), 11–58.

108. Thomas, *South Country*, 86.

109. Edward Thomas, *The Country* (London: Batsford, 1913), 55.

110. Thomas, *Country*, 1.

111. Thomas, *Country*, 6.

112. Thomas, *Happy-Go-Lucky Morgans*, 93.

113. Thomas, *Happy-Go-Lucky Morgans*, 39.

114. Thomas, *South Country*, 86.

115. Thomas, *South Country*, 78.

116. Thomas, *Portrait*, 157.

117. Edward Thomas, *Fiction* [1913], in *Edward Thomas: Selected Prose Writings, Volume I: Autobiographies*, ed. Guy Cuthbertson (Oxford: Oxford University Press, 2011), 326.

118. Thomas, *South Country*, 79.

119. Thomas, *South Country*, 87.

120. Thomas, *South Country*, 121.

121. Virginia Woolf, "Mr. Bennett and Mrs. Brown" (London: Hogarth, 1924).

122. Thomas, *South Country*, 29.

123. Webb, *Edward Thomas*, 174.

124. Webb, *Edward Thomas*, 175.

125. Dirth and Adams, "Decolonial," 270.

126. Dirth and Adams, "Decolonial," 275.

127. Thomas, *South Country*, 78.

128. Thomas, *Happy-Go-Lucky Morgans*, 122. By the end of the novel, Abercorran House has been sold.

10

The Damaging Effects of Western Neoliberal Policies and Local Corruption in Indra Sinha's *Animal's People*

Suha Kudsieh

The themes of nature and disability are not alien to Anglophone South Asian novels. However, deploying both themes simultaneously and making them central to a work of fiction is a rare phenomenon. Indra Sinha's novel *Animal's People* is a unique example in this regard. The novel retells the chemical disaster that unfolded in Bhopal in December 2–3 of 1984, when a gas leak at the Union Carbide India Limited (UCIL) caused the release of thirty tons of a highly toxic gas called methyl isocyanate, among other poisonous gases. The pesticide plant was surrounded by overcrowded slums and shanty towns—over six hundred thousand people were exposed to the deadly gas on those nights, causing victims' throats and eyes to burn. According to the estimates of the Indian government, fifteen thousand people were killed over the years, and many of the survivors have given birth to physically and mentally disabled children.[1]

Indra Sinha utilizes the theme of disability to reveal the impact of Western neoliberal policies in India and in other countries once colonized by the West. He also exposes the complicity of local governments in that process. Subsequently, disability becomes a suitable vehicle to examine the issue of injustice. In addition, he depicts the ease with which Western corporations are held responsible for work accidents in the West, whereas they flaunt the same laws in the ex-colonies. As Sinha sheds light on the struggle of the victims who suffered the deadly aftermath of the leak, he details the mercurial efforts of Western companies to shift blame, which renders the quest for justice a "transnational maze."[2] As a result, the novel reflects the struggle for human rights in the era of "transnational capitalism."[3]

The theme of disability in the novel transcends the realm of the personal to include the communal. By depicting the quest for social justice by a community that suffers from physical deformities and persistent ailments resulting from chemical pollution, Sinha unveils not only postcolonial entanglements but also the elusive struggle for human rights in marginalized communities. Although a decisive victory seems elusive at the end, change seems possible, but on a limited, micro level if one embraces hope and starts planning for the future as Animal, the titular narrator, does. Both actions, being hopeful and thinking of tomorrow, are integral to the human condition.

Environmental Disasters and the Bildungsroman in South Asian Fiction

When India and Pakistan were partitioned after obtaining their independence from Britain in 1947, the budding agrarian nations relied heavily on seasonal rain and the intricate mesh of fluvial arteries that connected their vast terrains. Floods, rainfall, and droughts were therefore recurring motifs in Indian fiction written at the time. The first wave of Anglophone South Asian authors invoked those themes to depict the hardships of village life and to highlight caste and class struggles between the landowners and their landless tenants (i.e., the *zamindari* system) and the social and environmental circumstances that hindered the sharecroppers' social mobility. Kamala Markandaya's novel *Nectar in a Sieve*, published in 1954, represents this wave.[4] The precarity of the human condition before the forces of nature remained a prominent theme in Anglophone novels published afterward, as evidenced by *The Ibis Trilogy* by Amitav Ghosh[5] and *The Last Jet Engine Laugh* by Ruchir Joshi.[6] The novels written by the second wave authors not only depicted natural floods and storms as destructive forces but also deployed them to describe inadequate sewage systems in crowded cities and to criticize the inadequate planning of governments in the colonial and postcolonial eras, particularly after the rise of neoliberal ideologies that transformed transnational economies since the 1970s.[7] During the same period, that is to say, at the turn of the twenty-first century, Anglophone authors began to explore the theme of disability as a suitable medium to examine the violence unleashed by religious and caste conflicts. Bapsi Sidhwa,[8] Rohinton Mistry,[9] Arundhati Roy,[10] and Salman Rushdie[11] exemplify this trend.

Indra Sinha takes this criticism a step further, targeting globalization and Western neoliberal policies, which increase the wretchedness of the exploited poor. Moreover, the amalgamation of the themes of disability and the environment in the novel is not haphazard, for industrial disasters cause the disability and disfigurement of those who are exposed to their toxins. Industrial accidents impact the poor more widely than the rest of society. In the case of Bhopal, for example, the poor took on more dangerous jobs and handled more toxic materials by hand because of the high rate of illiteracy and lack of training. Since most international companies did not offer protective gear or training to cut costs, those unfair conditions were aggravated.[12]

Like most postcolonial Anglophone novels, *Animal's People* is structured as a bildungsroman, a coming-of-age novel. Determining the genre of fiction Sinha uses is crucial because the novel reveals how the interactions between Animal and the people of Kaufpur conditioned his personality and molded it according to established social norms.[13] Joseph Slaughter explains how "human rights and the *Bildungsroman* are mutually enabling fictions: each projects an image of the human personality that ratifies the other's version of the ideal relations between individual and society."[14] The novel starts when Animal, the protagonist, is negotiating the price of being interviewed by an Australian journalist. However, when he narrates his story on the journalist's recorder, he begins with his childhood memories. As we listen, we quickly learn that he is a surly, unabashed nineteen-year-old adult, who grew up without developing close bonds with his fellow humans. Although his demeanor reflects his illiteracy and poor class, his ability to converse in French, the mother tongue of Ma Franci, tempers his outbursts in English.[15]

Animal has no recollection of his biological family, but he remembers Ma Franci, the French nun who brought him up. She tells him that he used to be a normal child before "that night" when the gas leaked in the "Kampani" (i.e., "company"). The disaster caused his spine to be so twisted and deformed that he must walk on all four. The leakage wreaked havoc on the people who lived in the slums of Kaufpur, the fictional city that represents Bhopal. Many died and a large number lost their sight while the throats of others were damaged. Some developed serious respiratory conditions, whereas others, like Ma Franci, went mad.

Alexandra Schultheis Moore observes that Animal's disability "serves as a synecdoche for the disaster itself, a symbol of human vulnerability to nefarious corporate interests."[16] Therefore, the invisibility of the workers and the people of Bhopal in the eyes of powerful transnational corporations mirrors Animal's isolation in the novel. For Michael Davidson, Animal is "literally invisible to justice."[17] Street children refused to play with him when he was a child and denied his human identity by calling him animal. When he became an adult, he remained invisible. To better understand the invisibility of the victims in Bhopal before the law, we must look at the colonial history of India.

Postcolonial Ecologies and Neoliberal Entanglements

Human disasters in Bhopal can be traced back to the British Raj, when India was still governed by Britain. Union Carbide India Limited (UCIL) was founded in 1934, when Union Carbide Corporation (UCC) became one of the first U.S. companies to invest in India. The company specialized in producing pesticides that were useful in protecting crops from seasonal pests.[18] In the 1960s, the newly independent country launched India's Green Revolution. The name refers to the government's attempts to increase the yield of agrarian lands by encouraging farmers and land tenants to increase the use of pesticides and fertilizers. The government also encouraged landowners to modernize their farming techniques, switching from traditional methods to industrial forms of farming. The plant in Bhopal was built in the late 1970s in an overpopulated slum area. It was owned by UCIL, an Indian company. Union Carbide owned half the stocks, while Indian financial institutions and thousands of private investors in India owned the remainder. The diffusion of ownership meant that the company could easily shift the blame to locals, relying on the backing of India's wealthy shareholders and the full cooperation of Indian governmental institutions.[19]

Those changes coincided with the rise of transnational neoliberalism in the 1970s, which influenced worldwide economic policies, especially those promoted by the World Trade Organization (WTO) in developing countries such as India.[20] David Harvey defines neoliberal economies as

> a theory of political economic practices that proposes that human well-being can best be advanced by liberating individual entrepreneurial freedoms and skills within an institutionalized framework characterized by strong private property rights, free market, and free trade. The role of the state is to create and preserve an institutional framework appropriate to such practices. The state has to guarantee, for example, the quality and integrity of money. It must also set up those military, defence, police, and legal structures and functions required to secure private property rights and to guarantee, by force if need be the proper functioning of markets. [. . .] State interventions in markets (once created) must be kept to a bare minimum.[21]

Although neoliberal policies were meant to allow the economy of Western countries to flourish naturally, outside state control, they had a devastating impact on bilateral agreements struck between the West and developing countries. Whereas Western enterprises and local powerful classes reaped the benefits of those deals, the policies impoverished the lower classes and stripped newly independent countries of their natural resources. Rob Nixon cites the example of the World Bank, which encouraged the shipment of industrial and nuclear waste from the West to Africa in return for monetary support and writing off the interest on loans offered to underdeveloped countries. Those deals, struck between uneven parties, the rich West and the developing nations (Africa, the Middle East, South Asia, and the Caribbean, among other regions) were legitimized under the guise of the West's desire to aid the newly independent nations, but the ramifications of those deals were catastrophic for local populations. Nuclear toxins polluted local lands, acidified rivers, and contaminated water resources, among other misfortunes.[22]

The neoliberal paradigm established among unequal parties is reproduced within the social hierarchies of developing countries. The poor were forced to work in unsafe jobs and were paid a pittance for their labor. In contrast, the rich increased their powers, especially since local governments supported them. They pocketed a considerable portion of the profits, whereas the shareholders in the West were given the lion's share.[23] Indra Sinha unveils those unequal relationships in the novel. Rob Nixon points out that the author gives focus to three defining characteristics of contemporary neoliberal order. Sinha highlights "the widening chasm—within and between nations—that separates the mega-rich from the destitute." He also sheds light on the "burden of unsustainable ecological degradation that impacts the health and livelihood of the poor most directly." Lastly, he reveals how "powerful transnational corporations exploit the lopsided universe of deregulation, whereby laws and loopholes are selectively applied in a marketplace a lot freer for some societies and classes than for others."[24] Those conflicting attitudes are laid bare at the beginning of the novel, when Animal derides the Australian journalist who is eager to hear what happened on the night that changed the fate of Kaufpur and its residents. Animal tells him that "many books have been written about this place, not one has changed anything for the better, how will yours be different? You will bleat like all of the rest." Animal adds, "You all talk of *rights, laws, justice.* Those words sound the same in my mouth as in yours but they don't mean the same thing."[25]

Disability and Hope

Animal's disfigurement marks him as different from his peers. He is an outsider who "locates himself both within and outside"[26] of Kaufpur. According to Michael Davidson, "inválid" members of society are given "outlier status" because they are "marked by atypical bodies or non-traditional forms of cognition." While Animal's disability prevents him from enjoying human company, his unique status positions him as a keen observer of the events that transpire in Kaufpur.[27] However, since he wavers between being human and animal, he can be perceived as a hybrid, as someone who straddles the world of humans and animals at the same time. Homi Bhabha discusses the concept of hybridity and applies it to cultural signs, arguing that cultures typically amalgamate more than one strand of influence. This process opens up a new space, a "Third Space of enunciation," which is a contradictory and ambivalent space.[28] Bhabha's analysis aptly fits Animal, who embodies the space that exists between the world of humans and animals. His contradictory and ambivalent identity is evident when he states that he is endowed with the ability "to hear people's thoughts" and "the comments of all types of things, animals, birds, trees, rocks."[29] He is fully aware that people are driven by money and greed. When he looks at people's souls, he notices, "Most were ugly, some shone like green birds, but all without exception were full of fear." This prompts him to protect himself by hiding his true feelings.[30] Although Animal appears hard-hearted and snarls and bites his enemies like a dog, he is kind to those who are close to him, like Ma Franci; Aliya, the sick child; and similar children in Kaufpur, as he often gives them free rides on his back.[31]

Though he appears to be confident, even arrogant, Animal has internalized the insults his peers throw at him. He considers his disability a lack, an imperfection. As a result, he rejects his human condition. The rejection liberates him from social conventions, and he transcends typical identity markers such as religion and ethnicity. He often repeats, "I'm not a Muslim, I am not a Hindu, I'm not Isayi [Christian], I'm an animal."[32] Nevertheless, his rejection is not entirely genuine. It is a mechanism to avoid the responsibility that comes with being human, as Ma Franci and Farouq, his close friend, inform him.[33]

Animal's aloofness casts him as an objective commentator on the slums' seedy reality. Animal's twisted back means he cannot stand upright, but the world of humans "is meant to be viewed from eye level." Whenever he lifts his head, he finds himself "staring into someone's crotch."[34] His character stands in sharp contrast with that of Zafar's, the idealist activist, "who is tall, handsome, whose beard curls like a raja's and who's robed in the odour of sainthood."[35] Although both men are each other's foil, with Animal being the pragmatist and Zafar the optimist, they are very much alike. They both side with the poor in their own ways, and they are both in love with Nisha; yet their outlook on the conditions of Kaufpur are completely different. When the company's victims are disheartened by the court's decision, Zafar raises the crowd's spirits by telling people that although the managers of the company have money and powerful friends, "they don't understand us, they've never come up against people like us before. . . . Having nothing means we have nothing to lose. So you see, armed with the power of nothing we are invincible."[36] In contrast, Animal does not trust the legal system, and he does not entertain any hope for the people. For him, hope "is a crutch for the weaklings."[37] He adds that in the "kingdom of the poor," there is no place for hope.[38]

When Animal notices the eagerness of the Australian journalist to record his story at the beginning of the novel, Animal remarks, "For his sort we are not really people. We don't have names. We flit in crowds at the corner of his eyes. Extra's we're, in his movies."[39] Animal is protective of the people of Kaufpur and refers to them as *his* people.[40] His solidarity with the people demonstrates the common characteristics that animals and humans share. Michael Davidson suggests that being human "is a discursive rather than a natural fact."[41] Both groups are social beings: animals move in packs while humans live in communities. When Elli, the American medical doctor who volunteers to cure the poor, arrives at Kaufpur, she asks Animal to show her the slums. After witnessing the miserable conditions, Elli cannot comprehend why they turned down her "genuine and good offer of help" when they "have nothing." Animal informs her, "I understand [them] because these are my people."[42]

In *Orientalism*, Edward Said examines the scholarly bias of Western experts when they discuss the Orient and the people who live there. He outlines the "nexus of knowledge and power" that creates an "Oriental," which obliterates him as a human being and reduces him to an academic subject.[43] For those Western experts, "he is first an Oriental, second a human being."[44] Such acts of Othering can be observed in the company's apathy toward the people of Kaufpur. When Elli cannot fully grasp why people associate her with the company or why they boycott her clinic, Pandit Somraj, Nisha's father, informs her about their concern regarding the data and statistics she will gather, which could be used by the company to overturn the legal case. He explains, "The studies need not be real. All they need's someone willing to falsify them. A doctor, for example."[45] Those events mirror what took place in Bhopal, where a group of doctors who were friendly to Union Carbide exonerated the company from blame, whereas a group of volunteer doctors, who offered to treat the patients and victims for free, incurred the wrath of the company and its powerful clique because their treatment confirmed that cyanide had been one of the killer gases that escaped from the plant.[46] Those differences reflect the apathy not only of the rich toward the poor but also of the Global North toward the Global South.[47] This is nowhere more evident than in 2002 when Dow Chemical's spokesperson, Kathy Hunt, "defended Union Carbide's settlement by claiming, 'You can't really do more than that, can you? $500 is plenty good for an Indian.'"[48]

While the novel sheds light on the gap between the rich and the poor, it also criticizes the head figures of local authorities and government officials who stand by Western corporations. The opinion of one of those officials reflects the antipathy of the class that enjoys power when he explains to Elli, "Those poor people never had a chance. If it had not been the factory it would have been cholera, TB, exhaustion, hunger. They would have died anyway."[49] For those officials, the poor are subhuman.

Hope and the Struggle for Human Identity

Animal's People examines the chasm between the boundaries that set humans and animals apart, especially since it corresponds to the boundaries that separate the rich from the poor.[50] While the rich can set their eye on tomorrow and plan for the future, the poor are unable to do that. The latter live for the moment because they are unsure what will happen tomorrow. Animal explains to Elli, "I don't need a watch because I know what time it is. It's now o'clock. Look, over there are the roofs of Nutcracker. Know what time it's in there? Now o'clock, always now o'clock. In the kingdom of the Poor, time doesn't exist."[51] The difference between the rich's and the poor's attitudes about the future signals the hopefulness of the former group in contrast to the unpreparedness of the latter. The poor are reduced to the level of animals because animals do not understand hope or how to plan for tomorrow. In Animal's words, "Hope dies in places like [Kaufpur], because hope lives in the future and there's no future here, how can you think about tomorrow when all your strength is used up trying to get through today?"[52]

When Animal's peers tease him by calling him animal for fighting back aggressively,[53] he turns the tables against them by adopting the pejorative term as his nickname. According to Adele Holoch, Animal's "tongue-in-cheek reappropriation of the term 'Animal' seeks to destabilize those broad divisions between 'animal' and 'human.'" The strategy reflects "the ways in which the processes of naming and categorizing define the one who names as much as the one who is named."[54] Marked as nonhuman, Animal boasts that he can do whatever he wants without being constrained by social conventions and rules, what is right and wrong, or proper and improper. He is aware that he is free because he has nothing to lose. Ma Franci took him to see several doctors when he was young, but they all decided his case was incurable. Having lost hope, he does not bother to conform or act responsibly.

The situation changes when Elli gives him the confidence to hope and to change his deformity. She assures him they both would seek a seventh medical opinion, even a ninth opinion.[55] Animal's love for Nisha fuels his desire to alter his condition and forces him to change his mind about being an outsider. He acknowledges that he "never mentioned" his "yearning to walk upright."[56] In his confession, Animal correlates walking upright with being human. Justin O. Johnson examines the link between posture and the human condition by looking at Sigmund Freud's analysis in *Civilization and Its Discontents*, published in 1930. According to Freud, "the bipedal body" lifts the head, "directing the human gaze upward into the world and away from the abdomen."

Freud links this change to civilization: the erect gait causes civilizations to flourish, whereas walking on four is associated with being nonhuman.[57] Viewed from this perspective, Animal's twisted posture represents a regression, a relapse, from the progress made by humankind. Moreover, Freud links the difference in gait to sexual drive—while animals do not curb their desires, humans are expected to do that. Freud attributes this difference to walking upright, which increases the distance "between the human nose and genitalia."[58] Animal's thoughts echo Freud's analysis when he admits, "Sex was the one thing I could never forget, my second impossible wish. My first wish was to stand upright, but did I want that if not because it led to the second?"[59]

When Elli offers him hope, Animal begins to entertain thoughts about the future. For the first time in the novel, he uses the present future tense: "I will walk up and down the Claw. Nisha will not recognize me. She will see a young stranger upright, and handsome, there and then she'll fall in love. She'll forget Zafar, phhht, he's gone. She will be besotted with her new love, desperate to marry him."[60] However, those plans evaporate when Animal loses his friend Farouq, after he participates in a hunger strike to force the company and the local authorities to accept their legal case. Animal also feels guilty about Zafar's death during the hunger strike. The final blow to his plans comes when Nisha rejects his advances. Dejected and filled with disappointment, Animal flees to the forest to live among the animals. After swallowing the datura pills he used to sneak into Zafar's tea, to make him ill and keep him away from Nisha, Animal begins to hallucinate. During one of his trances, he catches a lizard, which pleads with him to set it free. When he does, the lizard confronts him by telling him that his nature "can never change," adding, "if you were an animal you would have eaten me."[61]

Difference and (Dis)Ability

Christopher Krentz highlights the way disability is deployed in modern novels produced by the West and the Global South. He notes that disability is typically "removed at the end of Euro-American narratives, ultimately shoring up some notion of normalcy elsewhere." A similar phenomenon can be observed in the early waves of South Asian fiction, whereby disability played a peripheral role. It was used symbolically as an allegorical prosthesis to push the plot forward or to induce the readers to sympathize with the characters. Krentz attributes this proclivity to society's desire to eradicate "impairments" in the modern period, whereas in the postmodern neoliberal era, disability becomes a site of "profitability and normativization." He contends that in novels from the Global South, characters with disability "are almost never rehabilitated." In Salman Rushdie's *Midnight's Children*, for example, Salim's "extraordinary" body is left uncured. Indra Sinha's *Animal's People* follows a similar path.[62]

An essential problem with Animal's attitude regarding his identity is that he inherited the social paradigms that prevail in Kaufpur, where nonhumans are seen as subhuman. The latter rank at the bottom of the social order, which mirrors class hierarchy, which places the poor at the bottom and the rich at the top. Disability rights activists, however, do not regard disability as bad or harmful. They argue it does not deserve the negative attention it typically receives.[63] For example, despite his physical deformity, Animal can fend for himself, run errands, and move agilely and quickly in the narrow streets of Kaufpur. He even describes his upper body as strong as that of a bodybuilder.[64] Nisha and Zafar see him "as [an] especially abled" human being rather than disabled.[65] When Animal inquires about the meaning of their words, Zafar replies, "It means okay you don't walk on two legs like most people, but you have skills and talents that they don't."[66] Taking all those details together, it is difficult to see Animal as disabled.

This realization brings to the fore the debate about medical and social disability. Athena Engman and Cynthia Cranford outline the difference between those concepts:

> The social model of disability provides a discursive framework for thinking about disability as a social phenomenon rather than one that arises from the objective character of the physical bodies of people with disabilities. As such, it is explicitly contrasted with the medical model of disability. The medical model, paradigmatic for understanding disability for much of the twentieth century, conceives of disability as an individual, medical problem to which the appropriate response is the intervention of medical expertise.[67]

Subsequently, although Animal is different from other humans, he is not disabled. Despite his repeated proclamations that he lives outside the world of humans, he has many friends who care for him and are close to him. His ties to the human world are solidified after he gets close to Farouq, Nisha, and Zafar. Farouq tells him, "You're well enough now, looked after now," adding, "We are your friends. Don't we care about you?" He reminds him that if he wants to be accepted as a human being, "you must behave like one."[68] Zafar, Farouq, and Nisha emphasize the significance of acting, speaking, and behaving like a human being—that is to say, Animal must modify his behavior. But Animal's attention is fixed on his physical deformity, a condition he cannot change. Consequently, he is hesitant about accepting his human identity, for "if I agree to be a human being, I'll also have to agree that I'm wrong-shaped and abnormal. But let me be a quatrepattes animal, four-footed and free, then I'm whole, my own proper shape, just a different kind of animal."[69]

Michael Davidson argues that "disability unsettle[s] modernist aesthetics" by refusing to acknowledge the depiction of modern bodies as the epitome of harmony, beauty, and good health. Deformed and unwholesome bodies disrupt those aesthetics. Quoting Tobin Siebers, Davidson points out that "non-traditional" bodies have directly "impacted modernist art while creating a critical framework" to rethink "the nature of the human."[70] Animal's disability represents those contingencies. He is both human and nonhuman. He is an outsider despite witnessing how the people of Kaufpur have suffered at the hands of the company and the unjust treatment they receive in local courts. According to Davidson, "Overcoming the *lack* of some bodily function"—in Animal's case, it is his inability to walk upright—"is necessary to produce rational order and power." Therefore, like the clowns in Shakespeare's plays, Animal's viewpoint represents the voice of reason that speaks truth to power.[71]

Elli's efforts in finding a medical cure for his condition fills Animal with the hope that he will impress Nisha. However, in this context, the language of cure is pejorative because it implies that Animal's condition will "change for the better."[72] Moreover, Western science offers him a false hope—Elli informs Animal that he will need to use crutches after the operation. At first, he is content, but when Nisha rejects him and he flees to the forest, he recognizes that he is better off without the operation. He realizes that although he walks on all fours, he can fight, run, evade his enemies, and live freely, but if he ends up on crutches, he will be weak and dependent on the kindness of others. He wisely realizes that his relationship with his surroundings will change and that his daily habits will subsequently change.[73] He therefore decides to reject the solution Western science offers him and does not go ahead with the operation.

Conclusion

Animal's decision demonstrates his resilience, which reflects the ability of the people of Kaufpur to adapt and change with time.[74] After accepting his physical difference, he starts to plan for his future. Left alone after the disappearance of Ma Franci and the death of his friends, he decides he will "go to buy Anjali free and she will come to live with me." Anjali is Animal's childhood friend, who ends up working as a prostitute in a brothel. His decision is not a compromise on his part, for he understands that "if I'm an upright human, I would be one of millions, not even a healthy one at that. Stay fourfoot, I'm the one and only Animal."[75]

Although Animal does not think his life is "so bad,"[76] the struggle of the activists and the people of Bhopal continues. The fight against transnational corporations who evade their responsibilities to local communities is not over, not as long as the descendants are born with various types of disabilities because earth and water remain polluted. As Zafar predicted before he died, "Is Kaufpur the only poisoned city? It is not. There are others and each one has its own Zafar. There'll be a Zafar in Mexico City and others in Hanoi, and Manila and Halabja and there are Zafars of Minamata and Seveso, of São Paulo and Toulouse."[77] The novel ends on a hopeful note, with Animal making plans for his future and envisioning the descendants of current activists following in their fathers' steps. Although this glimmer of hope will not affect the slow pace of the wheels of justice for the company's victims, it improves Animal's life and his prospects for a better future.

NOTES

1. See Arthur Rose, "Imagining Breath, Imagining 9/11 in Indra Sinha's *Animal's People*," *Studies in the Novel* 53, no. 1 (Spring 2021): 69–70; and Alan Taylor, "Bhopal: The World's Worst Industrial Disaster, 30 Years Later," *Atlantic*, December 2, 2014, accessed September 26, 2021, https://www.theatlantic.com/photo/2014/12/bhopal-the-worlds-worst-industrial-disaster-30-years-later/100864/.

2. Rob Nixon refers to those agreements as a form of "slow violence" in *Slow Violence and the Environmentalism of the Poor* (Cambridge, MA: Harvard University Press, 2013), 46.

3. See Alexandra Schultheis Moore's discussion of this concept and how it stands in opposition to "national sovereignty" in the article "Disaster Capitalism and Human Rights: Embodiment and Subalternity in Indra Sinha's *Animal's People*" in *Theoretical Perspectives on Human Rights and Literature*, ed. Elizabeth Swanson Goldberg and Alexandra Schultheis Moore (New York: Routledge, 2012), 232.

4. In addition to literature, the Zamindari system was a popular theme in Indian cinema from the 1940s to 1980s. The farmers' attachment to the land was intertwined with nationalism. As such, it became a convenient tool to expose the injustices of the feudal system; see, for example, *Mother India*, directed by Mehboob Khan (1957; India, produced by Mehboob Productions, Eros Entertainment, 172 minutes), DVD.

5. *Ibis Trilogy* is a name given to three historical novels written by Amitav Ghosh set in the nineteenth century in the Indian Ocean when India was ruled by Britain. The novels depict the various methods the East India Company utilized to exploit India's economy, reaping profits by trading in opium and trafficking impoverished Indians as indentured laborers to its colonies in the Caribbean. The three novels are *Sea of Poppies* (New York: Picador, 2009), *River of Smoke* (New York: Picador, 2012), and *Flood of Fire* (New York: Picador, 2016).

6. See Ruchir Josh, *The Last Jet Engine Laugh* (New York: Harper Collins, 2002).

7. Upamanyu Pablo Mukherjee attributes the effects of those policies to the rise of environmental fiction in South Asian literature; see *Postcolonial Environments: Nature, Culture and the Contemporary Indian Novel in English* (London: Palgrave Macmillan, 2010), 2–3. This shift is evidenced by the nonfictional works of Arundhati Roy and Amitav Ghosh. Roy was vocal in opposing the government's planned displacement and rehabilitation of

tribes from their ancestral lands in Sikka, Surung, Neemgavan, and Domkhedi to imple-ment the Narmada River Development (NRD), a project that involves building several dams on the river and its tributaries. See Arundhati Roy, "Lies, Dam Lies and Statistics," *Guardian*, June 4, 1999, https://www.theguardian.com/books/1999/jun/05/arundhatiroy? view=mobile. Roy also published *My Seditious Heart: Collected Nonfiction* (Chicago: Hay-market, 2019), a collection of essays that examine human rights, justice, political activ-ism, democracy, and the outcomes of capitalism in India. Likewise, Ghosh published two works that focus on climate change and the ensuing crises it has unleashed worldwide; see *The Great Derangement: Climate Change and the Unthinkable* (Chicago: University of Chi-cago Press, 2017) and *The Nutmeg's Curse: Parables for a Planet in Crisis* (Chicago: Univer-sity of Chicago Press, 2021).

8. See *Cracking India* (Minneapolis, MN: Milkweed Editions, 1991). The protagonist in the novel is a young girl who limps because she was struck by polio when she was an infant. The novel depicts the religious violence that erupted when India and Pakistan were partitioned. Sidhwa is a Pakistani author who is a member of the Parsi community, a minority in Pakistan.

9. See, for example, Rohinton Mistry, *Such a Long Journey* (New York: Vintage, 1992). Tehmul, a central character in the novel, is mentally disabled.

10. See Arundhati Roy, *The God of Small Things* (New York: Random House, 2008). One of the main characters, Estha, becomes mute following traumatic events he experiences. The river plays a symbolic role in the novel, as its placid surface contrasts with the com-munal and familial disturbances and the ensuing tragedies the novel depicts.

11. Salman Rushdie wrote several novels that explore disability as a metaphor; among the most well-known are *Midnight Children* (New York: Random House, 1981) and *The Moor's Last Sigh* (New York: Vintage, 1995). In the first novel, the protagonist is a mutant who is endowed with superhuman powers, yet he is unable to put his extraordinary abilities to good use. In the second novel, the protagonist suffers from progeria and was born with a deformed hand. Both novels trace the complex history of India.

12. Mukherjee, *Postcolonial Environments*, 140.

13. See Joseph R. Slaughter's "Enabling Fiction and Novel Subjects: The *Bildungsro-man* and International Human Rights Law," published in *Theoretical Perspectives on Human Rights and Literature*, ed. Elizabeth Swanson Goldberg and Alexandra Schultheis Moore (New York: Routledge, 2013), 41–42. In this regard, Christopher Krentz states in *Elusive Kingship: Disability and Human Rights in Postcolonial Literature* (Philadelphia: Temple University Press, 2022), 148, that Animal's account "resembles a bildungsroman."

14. Slaughter, "Enabling Fiction and Novel Subjects," 44.

15. To understand the significance of the various languages and accents that Indra Sinha deploys in the novel, see Brigitte Rath, "'His Words Only?' Indra Sinha's Pseudotrans-lation *Animal's People* as Hallucinations of a Subaltern Voice," *AAA: Arbeitenaus Anglistik und Amerikanistik* 38, no. 2 (2013): 161–83. Rath examines Ma Franci's references to the Book of John, Animal's metonymic use of "Eyes" to refer to the imagined audience he is telling his story to, and the use of Hinglish words in the novel and Tudor English by one of the characters. See also Adele Marian Holoch, "Profanity and the Grotesque in Indra Sinha's *Animal's People*," *International Journal of Postcolonial Studies* 18, no. 1 (2015): 127. On that page, Holoch argues that Sinha targets different audiences by mixing profane words with French. This method narrows the gap between international readers and the subaltern characters that are at the center of Sinha's novel.

16. Alexandra Schultheis Moore, "Disaster Capitalism and Human Rights: Embodiment and Subalternity in Indra Sinha's *Animal People*," in *Theoretical Perspectives on Human*

Rights and Literature, ed. Elizabeth Swanson Goldberg and Alexandra Schultheis Moore (New York: Routledge, 2012), 238.

17. Michael Davidson, *Invalid Modernism: Disability and the Missing Body of the Aesthetic* (Oxford: Oxford University Press, 2019), 151.

18. See the section on "History of Union Carbide India Limited" on the *Union Carbide Corporation Bhopal Information Center* website, accessed September 22, 2021, https://www.bhopal.com/uc-india-limited-history.html.

19. See Kim Fortun, *Advocacy after Bhopal: Environmentalism, Disaster, New Global Orders* (Chicago: University of Chicago Press, 2001), 115–17; and Mukherjee, *Postcolonial Environments*, 138–41. See also Jesse Oak Taylor, "Powers of Zero: Aggregation, Negation, and the Dimensions of Scale in Indra Sinha's *Animal's People*," *Literature and Medicine* 31, no. 2 (Fall 2013): 178; and Andrew Mahlstedt, "Animal's Eyes: Spectacular Invisibility and the Terms of Recognition in Indra Sinha's *Animal's People*," *Mosaic: A Journal for the Interdisciplinary Study of Literature* 46, no. 3 (September 2013): 60.

20. Justin O. Johnston, "'A Nother World' in Indra Sinha's *Animal's People*," *Twentieth-Century Literature* 62, no. 2 (June 2016): 125.

21. David Harvey, *A Brief History of Neoliberalism* (Oxford: Oxford University Press, 2005), 2.

22. See Nixon, *Slow Violence and the Environmentalism of the Poor*, 1–3. See also Patrick D. Murphy, "Community Resilience and the Cosmopolitan Role in the Environmental Challenge-Response Novels of Ghosh, Grace, and Sinha," *Comparative Literature Studies* 50, no. 1, Special Issue: Sustaining Ecocriticism: Comparative Perspectives (2013): 151; and Oak Taylor, "Powers of Zero," 180–81.

23. Nixon, *Slow Violence and the Environmentalism of the Poor*, 8–9.

24. Nixon, *Slow Violence and the Environmentalism of the Poor*, 46.

25. Indra Sinha, *Animal's People* (New York: Simon & Schuster, 2009), 3.

26. Moore, "Disaster Capitalism and Human Rights," 235.

27. See Michael Davidson, *Invalid Modernism: Disability and the Missing Body of the Aesthetic* (Oxford: Oxford University Press, 2019).

28. Homi Bhabha, *The Location of Culture* (New York: Routledge, 1994), 37, 54–55.

29. Sinha, *Animal's People*, 8.

30. Sinha, *Animal's People*, 11.

31. Sinha, *Animal's People*, 110.

32. Sinha, *Animal's People*, 14, 313, among other instances.

33. Sinha, *Animal's People*, 38, 109.

34. Sinha, *Animal's People*, 2.

35. Sinha, *Animal's People*, 39.

36. Sinha, *Animal's People*, 54. Jesse Oak Taylor discusses Zafar's words by quoting from Arjun Appadurai, who equates the question of the future with "the capacity to aspire;" see Oak Taylor, "Powers of Zero," 189.

37. Sinha, *Animal's People*, 75.

38. Sinha, *Animal's People*, 172.

39. Sinha, *Animal's People*, 284.

40. Emphasis here is mine.

41. Davidson, *Invalid Modernism*, 149–50.

42. Sinha, *Animal's People*, 183.

43. Edward Said, *Orientalism* (New York: Vintage, 1979), 27.

44. Said, *Orientalism*, 102.

45. Sinha, *Animal's People*, 160.

46. Mukherjee, *Postcolonial Environments*, 138–39, 142–43.

47. Robert P. Marzec describes this process as the "ecological degradation [of] the poor, and the corporate control vis-à-vis the judicial system"; see "Speaking Before the Environment: Modern Fiction and the Ecological," *MFS Modern Fiction Studies* 55, no. 3 (Fall 2009): 436.

48. Johnston, "'A Nother World' in Indra Sinha's *Animal's People*," 128.

49. Sinha, *Animal's People*, 153.

50. Michael Davidson contends that disability is "often equated with poverty, illiteracy, or sexuality"; see *Invalid Modernism*, 11.

51. Sinha, *Animal's People*, 185.

52. Sinha, *Animal's People*, 185.

53. Sinha, *Animal's People*, 15–16.

54. Holoch, "Profanity and the Grotesque in Indra Sinha's *Animal's People*," 132.

55. Sinha, *Animal's People*, 140.

56. Sinha, *Animal's People*, 23.

57. Johnston, "'A Nother World' in Indra Sinha's *Animal's People*," 122.

58. Johnston, "'A Nother World' in Indra Sinha's *Animal's People*," 122.

59. Sinha, *Animal's People*, 75–76.

60. Sinha, *Animal's People*, 187.

61. Sinha, *Animal's People*, 346.

62. See Krentz, *Elusive Kingship*, 9. For Krentz's analysis of Rushdie's *Midnight Children*, see pages 64–78 of the same book.

63. Elizabeth Barnes, "Valuing Disability, Causing Disability," *Ethics* 125, no. 1 (October 2014): 89.

64. Sinha, *Animal's People*, 15.

65. Sinha, *Animal's People*, 23.

66. Sinha, *Animal's People*, 23.

67. Athena Engman and Cynthia Cranford, "Habit and the Body: Lessons for Social Theories of Habit from the Experiences of People with Physical Disabilities," *Sociological Theory* 34, no. 1 (March 2016): 31.

68. Sinha, *Animal's People*, 209. See also the examples that Davidson sites in *Invalid Modernism*, 150.

69. Sinha, *Animal's People*, 208.

70. Davidson, *Invalid Modernism*, 2.

71. Davidson, *Invalid Modernism*, 4.

72. Barnes, "Valuing Disability, Causing Disability," 110.

73. Engman and Cranford, "Habit and the Body," 29–31.

74. Murphy defines resilience as "the ability of a system to absorb disturbance and still retain its basic function and structure"; see "Community Resilience and the Cosmopolitan Role in the Environmental Challenge," 14.

75. Sinha, *Animal's People*, 366. See also Krentz's discussion of Animal's identity in *Elusive Kingship*, 149–51.

76. Sinha, *Animal's People*, 366.

77. Sinha, *Animal's People*, 269.

IV

Colonialism, (Dis)Ability, and Nature in and through America

11

American Degeneracy

Colonial Science and Environmental
Anxiety in the Eighteenth Century

Gordon M. Sayre

The Finnish-Swedish naturalist Pehr Kalm traveled through colonial America in 1748–1751, from Philadelphia to Quebec and back. He visited the settlement of New Sweden in what is now New Jersey. He consulted with political leaders including Benjamin Franklin and Roland-Michel Barrin de la Galissonière, commandant general of New France, and with naturalists including John Bartram, Michel Sarrazin, and Jean-François Gaulthier. On his return Kalm published in Swedish *En resa til norra America* in three volumes starting in 1753.[1] At many points in this long book, Kalm reported that the American climate and environment was harmful to life there:

> It is remarkable that the inhabitants of this country commonly acquire understanding sooner but likewise grow old sooner than the people in Europe. . . . Those who are born in Europe attain a greater age than those who are born here of European parents. In the last war it plainly appeared that these new Americans were by far less hardy than the Europeans in expeditions, sieges, and long sea voyages.[2]

This claim impugns the American-born as deficient compared to Europeans. Kalm wrote several times of this vague malaise as well as of health issues which, from a modern perspective, have clear etiologies, such as an association of malarial fevers or "agues" with swamplands. In the lines quoted, however, he pointed to deficiencies such as premature aging that remain obscure.[3] Disability studies scholar Rosemary Garland Thompson draws on Aristotle's natural history treatise *Generation of Animals* to show how the notion of monstrous births "arranges somatic diversity into a hierarchy of value that assigns completeness to some bodies and deficiency to others."[4] Americans, both Natives and immigrants, might not appear monstrous at birth but were believed to suffer deficiencies related to the natural environment of the New World, and inasmuch as these health problems were chronic, invisible, and conjectural, they likely manifested through doubt and anxiety, not injury and trauma.

Kalm's insinuations about the health of American Creoles—people born on that continent to parents of European or African origin, the "new Americans" of the passage above—were among the earliest volleys in the controversy over American degeneracy. Previous scholarship has referred to it as "The Dispute of the New World" (from the title of the 1955 intellectual history by Italian-Peruvian scholar Antonello Gerbi), as "Criolian Degeneracy" (from Massachusetts minister Cotton Mather in his sermon "The Way to Prosperity" and other writings), or as the "Querelle d'Amérique" (from the *Voyage aux régions équinoxiales du Nouveau Continent* by Alexander von Humboldt).[5] By the 1770s a shrill polemic over American degeneracy engaged naturalists, historians, intellectuals, and politicians on both sides of the Atlantic, and the dispute became part of the ideological battles of the Creole revolutions, even more in Spanish America than in the United States. Mary Louise Pratt described it as "the long and arrogant dispute among European intellectuals over the relative size, value, and variety of American flora and fauna, in comparison with those of Europe and the other continents."[6]

In this paper I consider American degeneracy as a discourse of environmental toxicity that afflicted colonists, Creoles, and Natives, both with anxiety about the risks they faced living in America, and with prejudice arising from their alleged deficiencies in growth, health, and fertility. As Garland Thompson writes, "According to such logic, physical alterations caused by time or the environment—the changes we call disability—are hostile incursions from the outside, the effects of cruel contingencies that an individual does not adequately resist."[7] My inquiry here will be tentative, not just because the allegations were vague and unsubstantiated but because the intersecting fields of disability studies and environmental justice have rarely been applied to the early modern period; discourses of medicine, social work, and epidemiology on which the two fields rely today can only awkwardly be applied to eighteenth-century settings.[8] Nonetheless, I propose that the writings of Pehr Kalm and of American Creole scientists, including Thomas Jefferson and William Byrd II, express what Jina B. Kim has called "the epistemology of somatic witness," the testimony of individuals who face bodily risk and suffering caused by living in an environment considered unhealthy, and whose testimony might be dismissed as a consequence of that disability.[9] The rhetoric of their writings often tries to refute or erase the purported degeneracy. In the 1998 article that helped inspire the commitment to environmental justice by scholars of literature and environment, Lawrence Buell defined *toxic discourse* as "a discourse of allegation rather than of proof. Its moralism and intensity proceeds in good part precisely because of the awareness that its charges have not yet been proven, at least to the satisfaction of the requisite authorities."[10] Buell's lines also characterize the discourses of American degeneracy two centuries earlier. But before considering some more specific allegations of America as toxic, let me describe the larger shape of the controversy.

The most widely read theories of American degeneracy arose in the 1760s and 1770s from French naturalist Georges-Louis Leclerc, Comte de Buffon; Dutch geographer Cornelius de Pauw; French political economist Guillaume-Thomas Raynal; and Scottish historian William Robertson. None of the four ever traveled to America.[11] Their views of American nature were picked up secondhand, motivated by prejudice against Native Americans as primitives, against Spanish colonizers as oppressive slave drivers, and against promoters of colonial plantation and land speculation schemes as dishonest and exploitative. Their biased arguments benefitted from shifting standards of historical epistemology and analysis of sources, as Jorge Cañizares-Esguerra has argued and as I will further explore here.[12]

The most committed defenders of American nature were Spanish American intellectuals and historians such as Mexican Jesuit Francisco Javier Clavijero, Ecuadorean Jesuit Juan de Velasco, and Chilean natural historian Juan Ignacio Molina. All entered the debate in order to defend America, and all identified as *criollos* set apart from the privileged class of Spanish *peninsulares*. Ralph Bauer and José Antonio Mazzotti extend this dynamic to the North American colonies: "In British America, a creole consciousness developed largely as a phenomenon among the colonial elite in response to negative metropolitan attitudes regarding the creoles' social origins in Europe and to their cultural difference in the new environment in America."[13] Mather, Jefferson, and Byrd did not self-identify as Creoles but wished to defend their social status and corporeal integrity; for similar reasons, modern American scholars have joined in the defense of American nature and culture espoused by these colonial Creole intellectuals, whereas European scholars have been much less concerned with the dispute. The debate was articulated within a discourse of natural history that asserted European scientific authority at a time when the major imperial powers—Britain, France, and Spain—all were devoting considerable effort and expense to scientific exploration, both to profit from the colonies and to justify imperial hegemony in the face of rebellions and inter-imperial warfare. As Bauer and Mazzotti put it, "a dialectical and rhetorical response to environmental determinism in neoclassical natural history" was bound up with questions of race, place, and identity, specifically how place and environment affected health and intellect.[14]

For scholars and students in the United States today, the best-known, most read text of the dispute is the sixth query (or chapter) of Jefferson's *Notes on the State of Virginia* (1786), in which the future U.S. president and chairman of the American Philosophical Society enthusiastically refuted the opinions of Buffon, who had claimed that the quadruped animals of the Americas were smaller than those in the Old World and who impugned the fertility of America's native people and the wholesomeness of its climate. In a treatise on "Animals common to the two continents," Buffon had written of American Indians, "The savage is feeble, and has small organs of generation; he has neither hair nor beard, and no ardor whatever for his female."[15] Jefferson set out to refute this claim by the most prominent naturalist in Europe, and he took aim at Pehr Kalm as well, for whereas Buffon never traveled to America, Kalm knew it firsthand:

> All the cattle [near Philadelphia] have originally been brought over from Europe . . . But the cattle degenerate here and gradually become smaller. The cows, horses, sheep, and hogs are all larger in England, though those which are brought over here are of the same breed. But the first generation decreases a little in build and the third and fourth is the same size as the cattle already common here. The climate, the soils, and the food together contribute towards producing this change.[16]

According to Kalm, de Pauw, Robertson, and other European intellectuals, the American environment harmed both people and domestic animals who had been brought from Europe. If the American climate was excessively humid and cool, as Buffon claimed, or its soil deleterious to growth and fertility, as Kalm wrote, then Americans faced subtle deficiencies they had to overcome if they were to compete with Europe intellectually or economically. Over several generations, animals and people in America gradually but noticeably became smaller, weaker, and less venerable, Kalm wrote. In Quebec, for instance, "everyone agreed that the cattle, which are born of the original French breed, never grow to the same size as the parent stock"; the same held true for sheep, an observation attributed to the cold winters there.[17] Even plants degenerated when brought across the Atlantic: "Those who have been employed in sowing and planting kitchen herbs in Canada and have had some experience in gardening told me that they were obliged to send for fresh seeds from France every year, because they commonly loose [sic] their strength here in the third generation and do not produce such plants as would equal the original ones."[18] Because women, peasants, and enslaved workers were often treated as akin to animals, they were considered more susceptible than elite men to the alleged environmental toxicity. But under the empiricist methods of natural history writing, this superiority complex began to crumble. Thomas Jefferson, at the same time he began a long affair with his enslaved servant Sally Hemings, tried to refute American degeneracy in *Notes on the State of Virginia*, which he published in English and French versions in 1785–1786. He sought out measurements of livestock in America and Europe and of wild animal specimens from North and South America as documented by Buffon in the many volumes of *Histoire naturelle, générale et particulière*, which Jefferson carefully read during the 1770s and 1780s.[19] His analysis of animals was intended to buttress his arguments that American scientists Benjamin Franklin and David Rittenhouse had made discoveries equal to those of the greatest natural philosophers of Europe (particularly Buffon).

The American degeneracy debate holds interest for disability studies, I argue, because it links environmental humanities to social studies of science and expands research in disability and environment to the early modern period. This analysis brings to light the anxiety of some colonists, who even if they remained healthy in America, feared their offspring might suffer ailments or deficiencies. It also offers an opportunity to study how the climatic determinism promoted by Enlightenment thinkers such as Montesquieu, Buffon, and Hume was applied to migrants as well as to Indigenous peoples. As Bauer and Mazzotti put it, "Observations about the Euro-American creoles' changes in complexion, dress, custom, or morality compared with the English-born were typically explained, not through racial mixture, but rather through the influence of climate, environment, and cultural contact with Africans and Native Americans."[20] How did colonial Creoles perceive the risks of living in an unfamiliar environment? What places, what foods, what weather or climatic phenomena did they believe lay behind these risks? The myth of American degeneracy and the role that Creole Americans played in the debate lie at the intersection of race and disability, and of natural history and public health.

Since Gerbi's *Dispute of the New World*, the topic has been studied in a fractured and foreshortened manner. In one line of attack, pursued by American scholars, it is treated as a political/ideological debate essential to American independence or patriotism, and it often comes up in biographies and historical scholarship about Creole American leaders, notably Mather, Jefferson, William Byrd, and Simon Bolivar.[21] A second approach, pursued by European as well as American scholars, examines the health problems faced by European colonizers and enslaved Africans, most often with reference to plantation economies in the subtropical climate of the Caribbean and Central America, where these migrants suffered high rates of malaria, cholera, yellow fever, and yaws.[22] One approach dismisses American degeneracy as a myth while the other examines genuine environmental health issues, illnesses poorly understood at the time and treated with remedies that were often ineffective, thus exacerbating the fear and anxiety about the American environment.

In this paper, however, I am interested in North America's temperate climates, such as those Kalm visited. Historians of colonial America who have reconstructed demographic data for the colonies in this region have drawn conclusions contrary to what Kalm reported about accelerated aging. Indigenous peoples of America suffered horrific mortality from diseases like smallpox and influenza, for which they had little immunity and few effective treatments amid war, dislocation, and genocide. Prior to these epidemics, however, most Native Americans were taller and better fed than the average European. After all, the European invaders were sickly people who had built herd immunity to diseases like smallpox and influenza because they had grown to maturity either in densely populated cities like London, where poor sanitation, polluted air, and insect and rodent pests spread diseases, or as rural peasants who lived closely alongside livestock and passed pathogens back and forth with their animals. Colonizers who landed on the coast of North America in the early 1600s were lucky to occupy lands Native Americans had fertilized and husbanded for centuries before their populations were decimated by disease. Notwithstanding these advantages, Kalm's own observations and his reports of local beliefs among Swedish-, English-, German-, and French-speaking settlers between New Jersey and Quebec suggest that some colonists perceived environmental health risks to their own bodies and to the introduced species of animals on which they relied for food, fiber, and labor.

Because the available demographic evidence on human health and reproductive rates in eighteenth-century America does not confirm Kalm's observations, from a modern perspective American degeneracy appears to be a phenomenon of anxiety and prejudice. But this is not to say one should dismiss its importance. My goal is not to show how modern scientific understanding has displaced prejudice and error. I want instead to understand how, when, and why European colonists speculated about the effects of the American climate, air, water, and food on their bodies, and whether they internalized the prejudice against Creoles based on their potential deficiency. The phenomenon is comparable to influential concepts in environmental humanities such as Buell's "toxic discourse," Stacy Alaimo's "trans-corporeality," and Ulrich Beck's "ecological risk society." These concepts were developed to explain industrial modernity and its toxic emissions, but they can also be applied to American degeneracy in the early modern period. American degeneracy was, in effect, an inverse of the doctrine of American Exceptionalism. Rather than proclaiming America (or more specifically, the United States of America) to be favored by nature or chosen by God, the continent is instead seen as inferior or harmful. Both were rhetorical statements, and the works of the loudest degenerationists, de Pauw and Raynal, were likely motivated by a desire to prevent increased emigration of European peasants (de Pauw enjoyed the patronage of Prussian noblemen whose serfs were leaving for America) or the transport of enslaved Africans (Raynal was an early abolitionist) to North America during the period in the eighteenth century that saw the highest rates of such movement.

In the rest of this essay, I propose two possible reasons why the American degeneracy controversy arose when it did. Both draw evidence from Kalm's *Travels*. The first emphasizes Kalm's role in applying the new system of Latinate binomial nomenclature to the flora of North America. Carl Linnaeus's *Systema Naturae* and the system of binomial nomenclature based on it were decisive for establishing modern concepts of species and biogeography. Only with a single system for describing and naming biological species—in the Eurocentric and imperial language of Latin—could scientists study nature on a global scale and use this knowledge to expand proto-capitalist markets for commodities that were based on key species of plants and animals used as foods, spices, furs, dyewoods, and medicines.[23] However, this new methodology discredited local traditions of herbalism and *materia medica*. As these traditions were abandoned (a process of agnatology, or willed forgetting), some people felt that their illnesses could not be treated, because traditional herbal remedies were no longer considered valid.[24]

The second reason involved the rise in the mid-1700s of techniques in stratigraphy and comparative anatomy that made possible the description of extinct species of animals. This in turn contributed to new theories of the deep history of the earth, including the gradually changing forms of animals across time, which brought new evidence and new complications to the theory of American degeneracy. Considering this history, it becomes apparent how the eighteenth-century prejudice against the American climate might be compared to today's concerns over climate change and toxic industrial pollution.

Herbalism, Pharmacopeia, and Epistemic Shifts in Botanical Species Identities

Kalm traveled to America as one of seventeen so-called "apostles" of the Swedish botanist Carl Linnaeus. These collectors were sent to distant lands including China, Russia, Egypt, Suriname, South Africa, and the East Indies, charged by Linnaeus and the Royal Swedish Academy of Sciences to collect seeds and pressed plant specimens and return them to Sweden. Linnaeus wanted new specimens to add to his encyclopedic catalog of nature (begun in the

Species plantarum of 1735) and for his quixotic effort to obtain and acclimatize exotic plant species and varieties that might improve Swedish agriculture
and replace imports. Kalm, for example, was tasked with finding a mulberry
tree in North America that might grow in Scandinavia and support a local
silk industry. Linnaeus dreamed of acclimatizing key exotic plants including
tea, coffee, and even bananas to grow them in Sweden. He failed at this goal,
even as his scheme for a new taxonomic structure and nomenclature succeed-
ed brilliantly.

Kalm's was among the first books about North American nature to employ Linnaean nomenclature for species. Its impact has not been recognized
to the same degree as William Bartram's 1791 *Travels*, which turned the Latinate Linnaean vocabulary of plant and animal species into fodder for romantic spiritual soliloquies. Both men traveled with the purpose of identifying and
collecting unfamiliar species of plants and animals useful for agriculture and
horticulture and then sending specimens of them to European collectors.
Peter Collinson, a British Quaker businessman who was the most important
patron of John and William Bartram, was an enthusiastic Linnaean. But
whereas the Quaker Creole Bartram effused about the beauties of Florida
and Appalachia and rarely complained about hazards like mosquitoes and
rattlesnakes, Kalm expressed fears and anxieties about the American environment. Kalm's interests began with botany and extended to medicine and
to what today would be called public health:

> Many people are of the opinion that the air of this country hurts the
> teeth. So much is certain, that the weather can nowhere be subject
> to more frequent and sudden changes; for the end of a hot day often
> turns out to be piercing cold and vice versa. Yet this change of weath-
> er cannot be looked upon as having any effect upon the shedding of
> the teeth, for the Indians prove the contrary. They live in the same air,
> and always keep their teeth in a fine, white condition as long as they
> live. This I have seen myself and have been assured of by everybody.
> Others ascribe it to the great quantities of fruits and sweetmeats which
> are here eaten. But I have known many people who never eat any fruit,
> and still have hardly a tooth left.[25]

Loss of teeth was common in the eighteenth century, but it would constitute
a disability by modern standards. Kalm's analysis of this dental problem begins by considering a cause that modern dentists have confirmed: sugary foods.
Kalm then considers tea as the culprit, because "there is hardly a farmer's wife
or poor woman who does not drink tea in the morning" and because William
Johnson, the superintendent of Indian affairs in New York and reputed au-

thority on Native American culture, "told me at that time, that several of the Indians who lived close to the European settlements had learned to drink tea."[26] However, Kalm writes how he

> found afterwards that the use of tea could not entirely cause this condition. Several young women who lived in this country but were born in Europe, complained that they had lost most of their teeth after they had come to America. I asked whether they did not think that it arose from the frequent use of tea, as it was known that strong tea, as it were, entered into and corroded the teeth. But they answered that they had lost their teeth before they had begun to drink tea.[27]

Kalm concluded that the cause was not the tea itself but the heat at which it and other food and drink were consumed, for "those Indians whose teeth were sound never ate anything hot."[28] He sought empirical evidence in Native Americans' diets, and he did not assume that as people of a different "race" their health patterns would differ from Europeans. Similarly, in the inquiry about tea, Kalm did not assert a distinction between those born in America and colonists born in Europe, as in the observation of life expectancy I quoted at the beginning of this essay. Scholars have traced the emergence of concepts of inherited racial difference to this period, as the notion of American degeneracy spread alongside shifts in how status and identity were conceived in the Atlantic world. As Ralph Bauer observed, "In the course of the seventeenth century, when second-generation colonials born in America were replacing their immigrant parents, the implications of an American birth rather than of non-aristocratic lineage became increasingly of interest to English officials, travelers, and natural historians."[29]

Kalm had several theories for the causes of tooth decay and for the premature aging of Americans, but he wrote little about treatments for these afflictions. In truth there was little need for remedies. The population of the thirteen colonies of British America grew from around a million in 1749 to 1.5 million in 1754, roughly the period Kalm was traveling, and then to 2.4–2.6 million by 1775.[30] This was a period of continuing immigration, but the natural increase in eighteenth-century America was also much higher than in Europe due to lower rates of child mortality. So why did the theory of American degeneracy become so influential in France, England, and the low countries during a period when the American colonies were prospering and populations growing? It was in part a propaganda campaign to stanch the flow of emigrants, particularly from regions such as Ireland and the Rhineland that had no empire in the Americas and thus no interest in sending people to colonies there. But American degeneracy also had a lot to do with changes in natural history and medicine. Kalm was among Linnaeus's apostles, and from the 1750s to 1780s, Linnaean taxonomy was spreading quickly both in Europe and America.[31]

As Michel Foucault argued in his influential history of science *The Order of Things*, in natural history prior to Linnaeus, a Renaissance episteme prevailed, and "to write the history of a plant or an animal was as much a matter of describing the resemblances that could be found in it, the virtues that it was thought to possess, the legends and stories with which it had been involved."[32] Among these traditional narratives was the "doctrine of signatures," which held that for all the illnesses and poisons endemic to a region, remedies and herbal curatives could also be found there. As the Linnaean binomials Kalm brought from his mentor replaced local names for plant species, however, a traditional pharmacopeia was displaced as well. Staffan Müller-Wille studied the correspondence between Kalm and Linnaeus and traced how the great botanist selectively incorporated Kalm's work into his taxonomic catalogs. In this process, "all the care that he [Kalm] had invested in recording the morphology, geographic distribution, natural habitats, and uses of North American plants seems to have been in vain." Kalm's observations and analysis of health and healing in North America, among both Creole settlers and Indigenous peoples, found no place in Linnaeus's work, and "botanical knowledge was thus purged, so to speak, of all context-dependent meaning, resulting in a taxonomic system that consisted of little more than extensional relations of signifiers to signifieds."[33] If a plant or animal in America came to bear a new, unfamiliar name, based on the name of a botanist's patron or of a similar species in Europe, its value for the treatment of local illnesses was likely to be obscured.

A comparison between Kalm and an earlier traveler to North America, John Josselyn, reveals the extent of this shift in epistemologies. Josselyn traveled to New England in 1638–1639 and 1663–1671 and published two books: *New England's Rarities Discovered in Birds, Beasts, Fishes, Serpents and Plants of That Country* (1672) and *An Account of Two Voyages to New England* (1674). He was heir to an aristocratic family from Essex, had studied popular English plant books, and aspired to contribute reports to the Royal Society, which published a notice about Josselyn's books in its *Philosophical Transactions*. Josselyn devoted much attention to the remedies New Englanders derived from local plants and animals. Many of these follow the doctrine of signatures, of "like heals like." For instance, "a stone found in the bellies of Cod is present remedy for the stone," and the Dogfish is described as "a ravenous fish, upon whose back grows a Thorn two or three inches long, that helps the Toothache, scarrifying the Gums therewith."[34] Josselyn's book included crude woodcuts of some local plants. When names of familiar plants and trees from Europe were unsuitable for describing those he found in America, Josselyn listed "plants as are proper to the country, and have no Name."[35] These included "wound herbs" and others identified by their therapeutic applications. Local people passed along their medical knowledge directly and did not need to read about plants in books or to describe them with technical Latinate terminology. The local techniques were of little use to Josselyn's readers, however, if he could not provide a distinct name or a high-quality image that would enable them to find the plant in the field in America.

Josselyn's writings acknowledged the imperial context of New England's colonization, but unlike Kalm he believed in inherent ecological and medical differences among various places and cultures, and his praise for New England plants was expressed using Foucault's Renaissance episteme: "The plants in *New England* for the variety, number, beauty, and vertues, may stand in Competition with the plants of any Countrey in Europe. *Johnson* hath added to *Gerard*'s herbal 300. and *Parkinson* mentioneth many more; had they been in New England they might have found 1000 at least never heard nor seen by any Englishman before."[36] So whereas New England had plants not found in Old England, it also had many similar plants that nonetheless displayed contrasting medical effects when used by various people who responded differently to the same herbal remedies. Josselyn did not assume, as Linnaeus would, the principle that a species of plant was the same no matter where it grew. The "American Mary-Gold, the Earth-nut," and other plants "are generally of (somewhat) a more masculine virtue, than any of the same species in England, but not in so terrible a degree, as to be mischievous or ineffectual to our English bodies."[37] He cites as an example: "The English in New-England take white Hellebore [American hellebore, *Veratrum viride*] which operates as fairly with them, as with the Indians," who gradually accustomed their bodies to its poisonous alkaloids.[38]

Josselyn was not trained as a physician, but in his natural history he occasionally wrote of his experience prescribing *materia medica*, such as when

> a neighbor of mine in Hay-time, having overheated himself, and melted his grease, with striving to out-mowe another man, fell dangerously sick, not being able to turn himself in his bed, his stomach gon, and his heart fainting ever and anon; to whom I administered the decoction of Avens-Roots and leaves in water and wine, sweetning it with Syrup of Clove-Gilliflowers, in one weeks time it recovered him, so that he was able to perform his daily work, being a poor planter or husbandman as we call them.[39]

A more famous seventeenth-century New England episode of herbal healing involved transcultural encounters of medical techniques. The sacham Massassoit of Wessagusset, whose assistance was essential to the Plymouth colonists in the 1620s, fell ill in 1623, and the Pilgrim colonist Edward Winslow, according to his own account in *Good Newes from New England*, was able to cure him with "a confection of many comfortable conserues," or fruit jam, and then a broth from boiled leaves and roots that he gathered nearby.[40] Winslow writes that he could not administer a "physicke" brought from England, because the bottle containing it had broken, and so he turned to local remedies. Winslow's *materia media* was derived from a combination of indigenous herbal traditions and European folk medicine, although he does not specify his medical theory. He writes that he "could not find any but strawberry leaves" and sassafras roots.[41] Strawberry varieties (*Fragaria sp.*) are native to many temperate regions of the northern hemisphere. *Sassafras albidum* is a tree native to North America, but a different species found in South America was also called sassafras and was widely used in the fifteenth through eighteenth centuries to treat syphilis.[42]

Before Linnaean taxonomy, many herbals identified and described plants based on their medical applications, and a name like "sassafras" could apply to different plants from different regions so long as they shared these healing properties. Similarly, Josselyn writes of a treatment for epilepsy: "The Indians tell of a Tree that growes far up in the land, that is as big as an Oake, that will cure the falling-sickness infallibly, what part there ove they use, Bark, Wood, leaves or fruit, I could never learn; they promised to bring it to me, but did not."[43] Because Josselyn's episteme focused on medicine or herbalism, not botany as we know it today, the use of the tree as a treatment for epilepsy, not its place in a taxonomy of species, genus, and family, was what defined the identity of the plant at issue. Kalm would likely have tried to identify the plant and given it a Latin name, while not endorsing its power to cure the disease.

Kalm's methods thus differed from Josselyn's, even as they also differed from those of his patron Linnaeus. Kalm did not see himself as a physician or healer, but he was interested in identifying plants that would have global commercial value, so he documented medical applications of a new global botanical pharmacopeia, such as ginseng:

> An ounce of ginseng brings the surprising price of eight ounces of silver at Peking. When the French botanists in Canada first saw a picture of it, they remembered to have seen a similar plant in this country. They were confirmed in their conjecture by considering that several settlements in Canada lie in the same latitude as those parts of the Chinese Tartary, and China, where the true ginseng grows wild. They succeeded in their attempt and found the same plant wild and abundant in several parts of North America. . . . The French use this root for curing asthma, as a stomachic, and promoting fertility in

women. The trade which is carried on with it here is very brisk, for they gather great quantities of it and send them to France, whence they are brought to China and sold there to great advantage.[44]

Here Kalm assumes that the plant found in America (today known as *Panax quinquifolius*) is the same as that known in China and Korea (*Panax ginseng*), which is extinct in the wild today, having been over gathered. However, his proof lies in the efficacy of the two plants' herbal applications and of their common marketability, for Kalm was not able to compare live specimens of the two types of ginseng.

"Giants in the Earth": The Emergence of Deep Time, Comparative Anatomy, and Extinct Megafauna

As Linnaean taxonomy was adopted by botanical explorers who circled the globe collecting specimens and sending them back to centers of calculation in Europe, the local knowledge of medical applications for plants was overshadowed by the growing market value of plant products as food, spices, medicine, fibers, and dyes. Linnaeus was a devout Lutheran who believed all species had been created by God; he did not see them as having evolved in distinct habitats, and this view supported his efforts to acclimatize tropical plants into the Scandinavian climate. However, leading naturalists in Britain and France, including Linnaeus's rival Buffon, developed early evolutionary theories as they tried to explain how, in the distant past, now-extinct species of plants and animals had inhabited the earth. This opened the door to new evidence in support of the theory of American degeneracy. Kalm himself was at the cutting edge of these discoveries. He wrote from the Philadelphia area,

> I met with people here who maintained that giants had formerly lived in these parts, and the following particulars confirmed them in this opinion. A few years ago some people digging in the ground met with a grave which contained human bones of an astonishing size. The *tibia* is said to have been fourteen feet long.[45]

Kalm went on to summarize a local legend related to the bones: "in this neighborhood on the banks of the river there lived a very tall and strong man, in ancient times, who carried the people over the river on his back."[46] Folk beliefs about the origins of bones and other vestiges dug out of the earth are examples of "fossil legends," which Adrienne Mayor has studied in the context of both ancient Mediterranean mythology and Native North America.

Kalm also wrote of a "huge skeleton" and explained, "The Indians who were there . . . reported that it must be the skeleton of the chief or father of all the beavers."[47] The huge beaver was just one of many larger versions of common mammals that thrived during the Ice Ages in both America and Eurasia.

Two generations before Kalm's voyage, in 1705, huge bones had been discovered at Claverack, in the Hudson Valley near Albany, New York. English and Dutch colonists as well as local Indigenous peoples speculated about their origins. Were these bones the remains of a human giant? The New England minister and poet Edward Taylor believed they were and wrote a poem about the "Claverack Giant." He did not publish this or any of his poems. Cotton Mather also considered Indian myths of a giant ancestor called "Maughkompos" that he believed may have been destroyed in a biblical flood. Mather wrote to the Royal Society: "There has lately been brought into our Light from the Subterraneous World in our Neighborhood, a Rarity, which appears to me worthy of a consideration with all mankind."[48] Reexaminations of the bones later in the eighteenth century proved that the Claverack bones were not from a giant human but from a mammoth.[49]

Paul Semonin, Claudine Cohen, and Elizabeth Kolbert have shown how bones of the mammoth and mastodon, found in the 1700s at Claverack, at Big Bone Lick on the south bank of the Ohio River, and at many other sites in North America, were decisive for the development of the theory of extinction by elite European natural historians, notably Buffon and Georges Cuvier. As Thomas Jefferson completed his *Notes on the State of Virginia*, he sent a copy to Buffon and urged him to retract his claims about American degeneracy, because the mammoth was the largest of all land animals and might still inhabit the western parts of North America. Buffon had already acknowledged the extinction of the mammoth: "The enormous animal of which the species is lost, came to us from Canada, and others just like it have come from Siberia and Tartary."[50] And because the mammoth and mastodon were ancient ancestors of, but much larger than, the modern elephant, "these great bones and enormous teeth are the surviving witnesses of the great power of nature in those primitive times."[51] Buffon's conjectural history of the earth held that it had contained more heat and more power in "those primitive times" and had been gradually cooling, and thus losing energy, ever since. Buffon's assertion of a deep history of the earth and of a gradual decline in the size of its largest animals not only in North America but all around the globe was based in part on the evidence presented by Kalm in his scientific travel narrative. Kalm, like Indigenous people in America who interpreted fossil bones through legends of Maughkompos or of the father of the beavers, saw the fossil bones as evidence that animals and people had shrunk in stature. To propose that America had once had giant humans or giant versions of familiar animals would be to accept evidence that they had gradually shrunk and, therefore, that Americans really had declined compared with their ancient ancestors.

Environmental Anxiety and Environmental Medicine from Early Modern to Modern Eras

I have argued that the American degeneracy controversy arose in the late 1700s following shifting paradigms for plant species, pharmacopeia, and the temporal scales of natural history. Plants that had been known by local people for their healing properties were now more often studied by cosmopolitan scientists according to the rigid global taxonomy conceived by Carl Linnaeus. Animals familiar to hunters, herders, and farmers were also now understood to be related to animals on other continents and to extinct species of the deep past, based on the study of fossil bones transported, collected, and examined by cosmopolitan scientists. As a result, settlers in American colonies felt less capable of treating their common ailments with plant remedies, and some began to believe accusations that the size and vigor of plants and animals around them were gradually shrinking and that the climate and environment in the New World must be harmful to growth and fertility. Moreover, because the debilitating effects of the American environment that Kalm had described were most immediately issues of human health, the paradigms of eighteenth-century medicine were also at issue. From Hippocrates in ancient Greece to the European Renaissance, climate had been understood in relation to human health, often as part of humoral theories of the four elements—earth, air, fire, and water—and associated bodily fluids and temperaments. Warm and cool, dry and moist were qualities not only of weather and climate but of soils, minerals, and human and animal bodies, and changing one's environment was believed to change one's body. Colonial American Creoles developed a distinct identity in response to suspicions that their bodies might differ from Europeans. As William Robertson wrote in his history of America, "The external form of the Americans leads us to suspect that there is some natural debility in their frame."[52] The phenomenon of transcorporeality advanced by Stacy Alaimo is not new, for early modern people saw transcorporeality as self-evident but not as caused by anthropogenic chemical toxins. In the eighteenth century, humoral theory came under challenge, but the history of humans on Earth was still believed to be as lengthy as that of animals. Consequently, changes in climates and landforms and changes of human bodies and intellects were understood to take place concurrently and in response to the same forces. The discourse of American Creole degeneracy is important not because it was true or false but because of the anxiety it aroused and the inquiries it inspired on the part of natural historians and scientific travelers, whether Europeans such as Pehr Kalm or Creole Americans such as Jefferson.

Among a handful of Anglophone American Creoles who participated in natural history research before the American degeneracy polemic began was another Virginia planter, William Byrd II. Byrd was proud to have been elected to the Royal Society in 1696 when he was twenty-two years old. He sent natural history specimens to Sir Hans Sloane, secretary of the Society, and maintained an ongoing correspondence with him. In his study of Byrd, Ralph Bauer proposes what he calls a "natural history of scientific authorship," a recursive effect whereby the writings of a Creole American natural historian were suspect (in the estimation of European readers at least) because a Creole may have been influenced by the climate of the land where he was born.[53] Bauer's idea resembles Kim's "epistemology of somatic witness" and when applied to Byrd helps explain his "obsessively methodical entries in his diaries, containing information about what he ate, what he read, about the weather's effects upon his body as well as about his neglect of his nightly prayers, [which] may thus be seen as a pathological exercise in scientific self-objectification."[54] In effect, a Creole American scientist was forced to consider himself as a subject of his own research; he was unable to maintain his critical objectivity or sense of superiority over the Indigenous peoples or animals he described. Byrd's diaries expressed self-consciousness about how his Creole origins damaged his status in the eyes of British gentry and of young women he wooed during visits to England. Susan Scott Parrish describes Byrd as "a semi-outsider as a native-born Virginian and subject to anxieties about what Cotton Mather termed 'criolian degeneracy,' as many elite colonials were."[55] In response, Parrish adds, "he worked hard at disciplining his body (through a devoutly followed exercise regime and careful food consumption)."[56] As a planter reliant on the production of enslaved workers, Byrd also wanted to be able to prescribe "physick" or medicine to the inhabitants of his estate, because he shared the concerns of Caribbean planters about the local environment and its effects on health. For instance, in his narrative of the survey of the border between Virginia and North Carolina, he wrote, "The Inhabitants of N Carolina devour so much Swine's flesh, that it fils them with grow Humours" causing "the Yaws, called there very justly the country-Distemper. This has all the symptoms of the Pox, with this Aggravation, that no Preparation of Mercury will touch it."[57]

Byrd's anxiety was a neurotic complex particular to colonial plantation slaveholders, whose knowledge or ignorance of the local pharmacopeia exposed their precarious dependence on those whom they oppressed. Enslaved Africans in British America often knew the local flora and fauna better than those who enslaved them, either due to their interactions with local Indigenous peoples or from folk healing methods brought from ecosystems in

West Africa that resembled the Caribbean Islands and the Carolina low country. As Byrd was trying to develop expertise in the natural history of Virginia and Carolina that might earn him recognition from the Royal Society, he was advised by James Petiver, a Society member, prominent London attorney, and botanical collector, to order his slaves to gather specimens of local plants and animals for him. But, as Parrish writes, "at the same time that colonials used slaves as collectors, they also associated slaves with poison . . . not only in the South and the Caribbean but in the metropolitan centers of the North as well."[58] Byrd's epistemology of somatic witness was highly unstable; he tried to assert knowledge and mastery of the American environment from a position of relative ignorance and anxiety. The anxiety was in part driven by fear of uprisings by enslaved people, and Parrish and others have traced how accusations against supposed leaders of slave revolts included allegations of poisoning with local plant and animal products.

This fear of poisons reflects the notion of American degeneracy as a form of environmental toxicity, which in turn can provide some insight on contemporary public health politics. Many modern people fear environmental hazards in the form of pollution or toxic contaminants that affect their bodies and/or the bodies of future generations. Toxins may lie undetected in the ground until they ooze out and wreak havoc on local people's health, as at Love Canal, New York, in the 1980s, or may be deposited from the skies by nuclear bomb testing in Nevada and Utah, as Terry Tempest Williams wrote of in her somatic witness memoir *Refuge*.[59] These chemical and radiological poisons are envisioned as monstrous invaders of a benign natural environment. They do not have an ancient provenance; they are anthropogenic, and they lie on the modern side of Bill McKibben's "End of Nature." The early modern anxiety about the American environment, by contrast, was a suspicion of diffuse, autochthonous environmental poisons, distinct from the refined or active poisons attributed to enslaved Africans, which might have been obtained from rattlesnakes or other poisonous animals (these were relatively rare in North America compared to other theaters of European imperialism). Kalm and others believed the American climate held a deep legacy of place and environment that had mysterious health impacts, faintly legible in the organisms living in that place.

Environmental justice examines relationships between class, status, place, and health and seeks to show why hazardous places are socioeconomic phenomena, a consequence of science, power, and capital in modern society. In the eighteenth century, as we have seen, the relationships between colonial beliefs about health and imperial science, power, and capital were rather different. The science of Linnaean taxonomy was alienating colonists from their practices of herbal medicine, and imperial conquest was marginalizing the medical knowledge of Indigenous people. By the 1790s, however, the study of the remains of extinct animals led to a new sense of deep time, including a deep past of megafauna species that had gradually diminished, not only in the Americas but also in isolate habitats such as Australia and Madagascar. Deep time accentuated a division between human culture (now confined to a brief anthropogenic modernity) and nonhuman nature (the legacy of a distant prehistory). Only since the late twentieth century have new archives of Earth's history and climate emerged from the study of palynology, dendrochronology, and polar and glacial ice cores that reconnect the temporal scales of human history and of deep time. Strata of annual seasonal deposits have been correlated to produce finely grained time lines of climate and environment going back several hundred thousand years. From these stratigraphic archives, the history of Earth's climate can now be examined with the same epistemic methods that have brought to light its past life forms, including human somatic history. Consistent with this epistemology, Stacy Alaimo proposes a concept of the "trans-corporeal" that "link[s] corporeal interiority with the more-than-human life processes. This trans-corporeal space may help us to imagine an epistemological time-space in which, because they are always acting and being acted upon, human bodies and nonhuman natures transform, unfold, and thereby resist categorization," and this time-space blends the immediate with the historical or archival.[60] Alaimo cites Sandra Steingraber, who concludes "our bodies, too, are living scrolls of sorts. What is written there—inside the fibers of our cells and chromosomes—is a record of our exposure to environmental contaminants."[61] We can thus read our bodies much like a dendrochronologist intuits past growing conditions from the rings of a fossilized tree. The historical is collapsed into the organismic. Eighteenth-century Europeans also understood the body as a delicate balance of humors that could be upset by foods, climate, or environmental toxins, and they began to integrate this medical theory with an environmental history of the type Alaimo describes. Kalm's writings contributed to the early steps in this new epistemology, whereby the causes of the demise of ancient giants might or might not be linked to the environmental health of contemporary human and quadruped inhabitants of the same regions.

American degeneracy was "a discourse of allegation rather than of proof."[62] Part of the value of Lawrence Buell's humanistic approach was to show how modern societies should not expect to be able to manage the dangers of pollution and contamination simply by perfecting the sciences of microbiology, epidemiology, and public health, of teasing causation out of correlations. Jefferson's attempts to disprove Buffon's accusations did not prevent other degenerationists from continuing to make claims about America's feeble Indians, seething reptiles, and pestilential swamps, because American degeneracy was not only a scientific theory but a polemic, a quarrel. Anxieties about local climates and health, often linked to the still-unknown causes of malaria, continued into the nineteenth century. By examining American degeneracy as a form of disability or as prejudice against people perceived to suffer from a deficiency in their bodily integrity, one can better understand the complex theories of environment and identity in early America.

NOTES

1. The second and third volumes of *En resa til norra America* appeared in 1756 and 1761, and a fourth was planned but was not published in Kalm's lifetime. An English translation, *Travels to North America* by Johann Reinhold Forster, followed in 1770, as well as translations into French and other languages. Forster became a well-known naturalist after he accompanied James Cook on his second voyage to the Pacific in 1772–1775. Citations here are from the Dover Books edition, which includes a translation of the manuscript of the planned fourth volume, and a narrative of Kalm's visit to Niagara Falls.

2. Pehr [Peter] Kalm, *Travels in North America: The English Version of 1770*, ed. Adolph D. Benson, trans. John Forster and Benson (New York: Dover, 1964), 56.

3. "For it has been observed in this country, that such people as live in the neighborhood of morasses or swamps, or in places where a stagnant, stinking water is to be found, are commonly infested with the fever and ague every year, and get it more readily than others" (ibid., 193).

4. Rosemary Garland Thompson, *Extraordinary Bodies: Figuring Physical Disability in American Culture and Literature* (New York: Columbia University Press, 1997), 20.

5. See Antonello Gerbi, *La disputa de Nuovo Mondo: Storia di una polemica, 1750–1900* (Milano-Napoli, 1955), trans. Jeffrey Moyle as *The Dispute of the New World: The History of a Polemic, 1750–1900* (Pittsburgh, PA: University of Pittsburgh Press, 1973); John Canup, "Cotton Mather and Criolian Degeneracy," *Early American Literature* 24, no. 1 (1989): 24–40. In the abridged Penguin Classics edition of *Personal Narrative of a Voyage to the Equinoctial Regions of the New Continent*, Humboldt refers to the Indians as a "degenerate race" (194). The book was first translated into English by Helena Williams and was widely read in Britain and North America starting in 1815.

6. Mary Louise Pratt, *Imperial Eyes: Travel Writing and Transculturation* (London: Routledge, 1992; 2nd ed. 2008), 120.

7. Thompson, *Extraordinary Bodies*, op. cit. 45.

8. Among the most influential recent theorists of environmental toxicity: Stacy Alaimo, *Bodily Natures: Science, Environment, and the Material Self* (Bloomington: University of Indiana Press, 2010); Beck, *Risk Society: Towards a New Modernity* (London: Sage, 1992), a translation of *Risikogesellschaft: Auf dem Weg in eine andere Monderne* (1986).

9. The phrase "epistemology of somatic witness" has been used by Jina B. Kim, "Cripping East Los Angeles: Enabling Environmental Justice in Helena Maria Viramontes's *Their Dogs Came with Them*," in *Disability Studies and the Environmental Humanities: Toward an Eco-Crip Theory*, ed. Sarah Jaquette Ray and Jay Sibara (Lincoln: University of Nebraska Press, 2017), chap. 18.

10. Lawrence Buell, "Toxic Discourse," *Critical Inquiry* 24, no. 3 (Spring 1998): 659.

11. Buffon's short treatise "Animaux Communs aux Deux Continents" in vol. 9 of *Histoire naturelle*, published in 1761, is a foundational statement of American degeneracy. Cornelius de Pauw's *Recherches Philosophiques sur les Américains* was first published in Berlin in 1768–1769 and subsequently in many editions and several translations of the French original. De Pauw cherry-picked quotes and misinterpreted ideas from colonial

travel texts to argue that America was a sickly place and that American Indians were few, stupid, and lazy. A rhetoric of anticlerical, anti-imperial skepticism in the book appealed to French Enlightenment thinkers and later to French revolutionaries, as did de Pauw's lurid fascination with sexuality and disability, such as syphilis. Raynal's *Histoire philosophique et politique des établissements et du commerce des Européens dans les deux Indes* was first published anonymously in Amsterdam in 1770 and in some thirty editions thereafter, as well as many translations and abridgements. It was attributed to Raynal, who served as editor and compiler, while other Enlightenment men of letters including Denis Diderot and Melchior Grimm contributed to the work. The 1780 Geneva edition included notable revisions, such as a new chapter on the American Revolution likely written by Diderot, which retracted the derogatory view of American colonists, due to the success of their revolution against Britain. Robertson, *The History of America* (Edinburgh, 1777) treated primarily Spanish colonies in Central and South America and recapitulated the anti-American theories of Buffon and de Pauw.

12. Jorge Cañizares-Esguerra, *How to Write the History of the New World: Histories, Epistemologies, and Identities in the Eighteenth-Century Atlantic World* (Stanford, CA: Stanford University Press, 2001).

13. "Introduction," in *Creole Subjects in the Colonial Americas: Empires, Texts, Identities*, ed. Ralph Bauer and José-Antonio Mazzotti (Chapel Hill: University of North Carolina Press, 2009), 28.

14. Ibid., 33.

15. "Le Sauvage est faible et petit par les organes de la génération; il n'a ni poil, ni barbe, ni nulle ardeur pour sa femelle." (*Histoire naturelle* IX, 104); Thomas Jefferson, *Notes on the State of Virginia*, ed. William Peden (Chapel Hill: University of North Carolina Press, 1955), 58.

16. Kalm, *Travels in America*, 55–56 (see also 409 for the bison, which is the "cattle already common here"). Jefferson (*Notes on the State of Virginia*, 85) attempted to refute Buffon's claims using Buffon's own evidence about the size of animals native to America, and in the same manner he also cited Kalm for evidence that "the lynx, badger, red fox, and flying squirrel, are the same in America as in Europe."

17. Kalm, *Travels in North America*, 477.

18. Kalm, *Travels in North America*, 438–39.

19. See Gordon M. Sayre, "Jefferson Takes on Buffon: The Polemic over American Animals in *Notes on the State of Virginia*," *William and Mary Quarterly*, 3d ser., 78, no. 1 (January 2021): 79–116.

20. Bauer and Mazzotti, *Creole Subjects in the Colonial Americas*, 41.

21. See David Brading, *The First America: The Spanish Monarchy, Creole Patriots, and the Liberal State, 1492–1867*, esp. chap. 19. Brading's study is among the best in English on the social conflict in the Spanish Empire between Creoles or *criollos* and Spanish-born *peninsulares*, who were systematically favored for appointments to top posts in the church, the military, and the crown administration. As a result of this prejudice, the sense of political identity among Creoles was stronger in Spanish America. See also Joshua Simon, *The Ideology of Creole Revolution: Imperialism and Independence in American and Latin American Political Thought* (Cambridge, UK: Cambridge University Press, 2017).

22. See Karen Kupperman, "Fear of Hot Climates in the Anglo-American Colonial Experience," *William and Mary Quarterly* 41, no. 2 (1984): 213–40; Seth Quinlan, "Colonial Bodies, Hygiene and Abolitionist Politics in Eighteenth-Century France," *History Workshop Journal* 42 (1996): 106–25.

23. "Linnaeus's nomenclature, noncolonial as it was in origin, later became one of the prime instruments of colonial exploration." Staffan Müller-Wille, "Walnuts at Hudson Bay, Coral Reefs in Gotland: The Colonialism of Linnaean Botany," in *Colonial Botany: Science, Commerce and Politics in the Early Modern World*, ed. Londa Schiebinger and Claudia Swan (Philadelphia: University of Pennsylvania Press, 2009), 35; see also Pratt, *Imperial Eyes*, 1–37.

24. On agnatology, see Robert Proctor and Londa Schiebinger, *Agnatology: The Making and Unmaking of Ignorance* (Stanford, CA: Stanford University Press, 2008). The process has continued into the modern era; on the loss of herbal healing expertise in the developing world, see Robert A. Voeks, *The Ethnobotany of Eden: Rethinking the Jungle Medicine Narrative* (Chicago: University of Chicago Press, 2018), 17.

25. Kalm, *Travels to North America*, 190.

26. Ibid., 190.

27. Ibid., 190–91.

28. Ibid., 191.

29. Ralph Bauer, *The Cultural Geography of Colonial American Literatures* (Cambridge, UK: Cambridge University Press, 2000), 183.

30. *Colonial and Pre-Federal Statistics* (Washington, DC: United States Census Bureau, 2004), 1168; Edwin J. Perkins, *The Economy of Colonial America* (New York: Columbia University Press, 1980), 2.

31. "The Spanish crown imposed the Linnaean system on all botanical institutions." Antonia Lafuente and Nuria Valverde, "Linnaean Botany and Spanish Imperial Biopolitics," in *Colonial Botany*, 136.

32. Foucault, *The Order of Things: An Archaeology of the Human Sciences* (New York: Vintage, 1970), 129.

33. Müller-White, "Walnuts at Hudson Bay," in *Colonial Botany*, 36–48.

34. John Josselyn, *New England's Rarities Discovered* (Bedford, MA: Applewood, n.d.), 33.

35. Ibid., 33.

36. John Josselyn, *Colonial Traveler: A Critical Edition of Two Voyages to New England*, ed. Paul J. Lindholdt (Hanover, NH: Dartmouth University Press, 1988), 43. John Gerard published *An Herball: or Generall History of Plants* in 1597 and many subsequent editions, including revised and improved versions edited by Thomas Johnson in 1633 and 1636. John Parkinson was an apothecary, herbalist, and gardener whose *Theatrum Botanicum* was published in 1640. These were three of the most important figures in the study of herbal medicine at the time Josselyn wrote.

37. Ibid., 43.

38. Ibid., 44.

39. Ibid., 56–57.

40. Edward Winslow, *Good Newes from New England*, ed. Kelly Wisecup (Amherst, MA: University of Massachusetts Press, 2014), 28–29.

41. Ibid., 29. For analysis of this episode, see Wisecup, *Medical Encounters: Knowledge and History in Early American Literature* (Amherst, MA: University of Massachusetts Press, 2013), 78–79.

42. See Voeks, *Ethnobotany of Eden*, 106.

43. Josselyn, *Two Voyages*, 51.

44. Kalm, *Travels to North America*, 435–36.

45. Ibid., 54–55.

46. Ibid., 55; Adrienne Mayor, *Fossil Legends of the First Americans* (Princeton, NJ: Princeton University Press, 2005).

47. Ibid., 378. On Native American knowledge of the *Castoroides* or Giant Beaver, see also *David Thompson's Narrative of His Explorations in Western America*, ed. J. B. Tyrell (Toronto: Champlain Society, 1916), 151.

48. David Levin, "'Giants in the Earth': Science and the Occult in Cotton Mather's Letters to the Royal Society," *William and Mary Quarterly* 45, no. 4 (October 1988): 758.

49. Amy Morris writes, "Ezra Stiles, president of Yale College, believed in fossil evidence of giant [human]s until about 1786, when Thomas Jefferson convinced him otherwise. Stiles was inspired by the Indian geomyths and the poem fragment passed down to him from his grandfather, Edward Taylor." "Geomythology on the Colonial Frontier: Edward Taylor, Cotton Mather, and the Claverack Giant," *William and Mary Quarterly* 70, no. 4 (October 2013): 701–24, quotation at 716.

50. Buffon, *Les Époques de la Nature* in *Œuvres* (Paris: Pleaide, 2007), 1293–94; "l'énorme animal dont l'espèce est perdue, nous sont arrivées du Canada, et d'autres tout semblable sont venues de Tartarie et de Sibérie."

51. Ibid., 1294; "Ces grands ossements et ces énormes dents sont des témoins subsistant de la grande force de la Nature dans ces premiers âges."

52. Qtd. in *Was America a Mistake? An Eighteenth-Century Controversy*, ed. Henry Steele Commager and Elmo Giordanetti (Columbia: University of South Carolina Press, 1967), 147. This is a concise anthology of important volleys in the debate, some excerpted from texts that are obscure or difficult to find.

53. Bauer, *The Cultural Geography of Colonial American Literatures* (Cambridge, 2000), 180.

54. Ibid., 184.

55. Susan Scott Parrish, "William Byrd II and the Crossed Languages of Science, Satire, and Empire in British America," in *Creole Subjects in the Colonial Americas: Empires, Texts, Identities*, ed. Ralph Bauer and José Antonio Mazzotti (Chapel Hill: University of North Carolina Press, 2009), 361.

56. Ibid., 361.

57. *William Byrd's Histories of the Dividing Line betwixt Virginia and North Carolina* (New York: Dover, 1967) 46, 54.

58. Susan Scott Parrish, *American Curiosity: Cultures of Natural History in the Colonial British Atlantic World* (Chapel Hill: University of North Carolina Press, 2006), 271, 276.

59. Lois Marie Gibbs, *Love Canal: The Story Continues* (Stony Creek, CT: New Society, 1998), a rev. ed of *Love Canal: My Story* (1982); Terry Tempest Williams, *Refuge: An Unnatural History of Family and Place* (New York: Vintage, 1991).

60. Stacy Alaimo, "Trans-Corporeal Feminisms and the Ethical Space of Nature," in *Material Feminisms*, ed. Stacy Alaimo and Susan Hekman (Bloomington: Indiana University Press, 2008), 237–64, quotation at 252–53.

61. Steingraber, *Living Downstream: An Ecologist Looks at Cancer and the Environment* (Reading, MA: Addison-Wesley, 1997), qtd. in Alaimo and Hekman, *Material Feminisms*, 261.

62. Buell, "Toxic Discourse," 659.

12

The Bison and the Plow

Eco-Ableism and the Conquest of the Great Plains

Matthew J. C. Cella

Near the end of *Black Elk Speaks*, a narrative recounting of Black Elk's life story as told to John Neihardt, the Oglala Sioux spiritual leader laments a major alteration to the Great Plains landscape precipitated by the expansion of Euro-American settler colonialism into the region: the relative absence of bison. He says, "That fall [of 1883], they say, the last of the bison herds was slaughtered by the Wasichus. I can remember when the bison were so many that they could not be counted, but more and more Wasichus came to kill them until there were only heaps of bones scattered where they used to be."[1] Black Elk bemoans this transformation from a landscape teeming with seemingly countless bison to one riddled with the remains of the nearly eradicated species because it fundamentally impacted the lifeways and well-being of the Oglala Sioux and the other bison-hunting tribes who relied on the species for sustenance and whose cultural and spiritual practices were tied to the bison hunt. Indeed, this equivalence—that the eradication of the bison would likely lead to the ultimate subjugation of the Plains Indians—was supported by the U.S. Army, which regarded the prolific work of the hide hunters in the 1870s and 1880s as an important piece of the overall effort to subdue the hostile tribes of America's last frontier.[2] From this perspective, the destruction of the great bison herds of the Great Plains was a crucial aspect of America's pursuit of its manifest destiny.

For Black Elk, of course, the wasteful ways of the hide hunters did not signal the triumph of a superior civilization but instead demonstrated the inherent degeneracy of the colonizers. Of the American hunters' slaughter

274 / Matthew J. C. Cella

of the bison, he says, "The Wasichus did not kill them to eat; they killed them for the metal that makes them *crazy*, and they took only the hides to sell. Sometimes they did not even take the hides, only the tongues. . . . You can see that the men who did this were *crazy*."[3] The metal he is referring to here is likely gold, as the discovery of gold in the Black Hills of Dakota Territory in the 1870s triggered a rush of Euro-American settlers into territory that was supposed to be protected by the Treaty of Fort Laramie of 1868. More generally, however, Black Elk's reference to "the metal that makes them crazy" registers his general disdain for a Euro-American worldview that condones killing for the sake of commerce and financial gain. That he twice refers to Euro-American greed as "crazy" is both fitting and ironic. It is fitting because when compared to the ethic of interdependency that informs the Siouan bison hunts—"when we hunted bison, we killed only what we needed," he says—the act of wiping out whole herds of buffalo for only their skins and tongues would appear to be deviant behavior and a sign of madness.[4] The irony, however, is that while Black Elk pathologizes the greed of the Wasichus here, the Euro-American colonizers similarly pathologized the bison-hunting Plains Indians as mentally and socially undeveloped. From the perspective of most Euro-Americans, the Plains Indians' continued reliance on hunting as a means of subsistence verified their savagery and therefore their moral and social deviance; this pathologization of Native "savagery" served to justify the subjugation of the Plains Indians and the erasure of the bison, as both needed to be removed for the sake of Euro-American progress. A key component of fulfilling America's manifest destiny included replacing the bison and the hunter with the plow and the farmer. The image of the bison-less prairies thus provokes two conflicting responses that then reflect two colliding worldviews. For the colonized Plains Indians, it is a sign of the inherent madness of the white colonizers who regard natural resources as mere commodities to be traded for the "metal that makes them crazy"; for the colonizing Euro-Americans, the absence of bison signals a landscape reclaimed from a state of primitive savagery and ready for cultivation by the homesteader and the plow.

This essay uses the dual lenses of disability studies and ecocriticism to examine the cultural and environmental significance of the transition from bison to plow on the Great Plains. More to the point, I will read the annihilation of the so-called buffalo plains—a landscape shaped by the nomadic bison-hunting tribes of the arid grasslands of the West—as a tragic manifestation of eco-ableism.[5] Eco-ableism is the antithesis of *eco-ability*, a concept first proposed and developed in *Earth, Animal, and Disability Liberation: The Rise of the Eco-Ability Movement*, a collection of essays that explore practical and theoretical intersections between animal studies, disability studies, and environmental justice. In their introduction to the book, the editors note that eco-ability "argues for the respect of difference and diversity, challenging social constructions of what is considered normal and equal" and works toward "building a sustainable future void of exploitation of all life and elements by a system of domination."[6] Eco-ability aims to disrupt divisive dichotomies—normal/abnormal, human/animal, able-bodied/disabled, commodifiable/useless—in favor of a paradigm of inclusivity that emphasizes the interdependent relationships between different bodies (human and animal) and the various structured and natural environments that these bodies maneuver in. Its goal is to shift "away from acts of domination and towards compassion."[7]

Eco-ableism, on the other hand, is a worldview that depends on domination and the eradication of difference to enforce socially constructed standards of normalcy for both bodies and environments. As such, it is one of the driving forces behind global colonialism, as the colonizers conquer occupied land to harvest its natural resources while expunging the Indigenous communities who they deem unfit to make proper use of the landscapes they occupy. As Anthony Nocella demonstrates, the notion of advancing civilization, one of the core components of imperialism, relies on a dichotomy that pits culture against nature while simultaneously constructing a normative standard of culture. He writes, "The marginalization of those who are different was first fostered and reinforced by the concept of *civilization* and its divide between nature and humans. . . . Those considered wild, savage, or primitive were situated on the one side, with those considered civilized, privileged, and normal on the other."[8] Viewed through this framework, eco-ableism concomitantly promotes the exploitation of the physical environment and the suppression of the "primitive" people who obstruct the progress of civilization.

In other words, as a manifestation of eco-ableism, settler colonialism is inherently ecocidal and genocidal, a point that Dina Gilio-Whitaker (Colville Confederated Tribes) makes in her book *As Long as the Grass Grows: The Indigenous Fight for Environmental Justice, from Colonization to Standing Rock*. Drawing on work by scholars like Patrick Wolfe and Kyle Powys Whyte (Potawatomi), Gilio-Whitaker highlights the eliminatory and disruptive nature of settler colonialism and demonstrates how it is at the root of persistent acts of environmental injustices against Native people. Building on Wolfe's notion that colonization is "fundamentally genocidal," she explains that "elimination as a process hinges on the expropriation of Indigenous lands and their transfer into settler possession via regimes of private property ownership, beginning with war, killing, and forced removal."[9] Indeed, both Gilio-Whitaker and Karen Jarrett-Snider identify the long-term impact of colonization on Native peoples as one of the key facets of Indigenous Environmental Justice (IEJ). As Jarret-Snider notes, a primary difference between IEJ and the mainstream environmental justice movement is "the continuing effects of colonization. These include changes in the ability to subsist—to live off the land—gathering, growing, and fishing or hunting for primary food sources."[10]

The "environment disruptions" enacted by settler colonialism are part of a process of replacing an inferior biocultural landscape with a more productive one. As I shall demonstrate in my analysis of the conquest of the buffalo plains, an act of environmental disruption on America's final frontier, justification for the elimination of the Plains Indians was often couched in the rhetoric of disability, as the "wild, savage, or primitive" Indigenous population was regularly cast as mentally and morally deficient and therefore undeserving of their ties to the Plains landscape. Ultimately, my goal in this essay is to explore the historical, social, and environmental forces that led to the eradication of American bison during the nineteenth century and, more particularly, to show how the trope of disability was deployed by supporters of manifest destiny as a defense for the conquest of the Plains Indians.[11] While the geographical focus of this essay is on the Global North, the United States in particular, my emphasis on the destructive impact of the colonizers' imposition of a Euro-American paradigm of disability on a local, Native culture aligns with the goals of scholars of disability and the Global South who seek to challenge universalizing discourses of disability by demonstrating the ways that disability is constructed differently in a range of geopolitical and temporal realities. Ultimately, by examining the "historical event of colonialism" as it pertains to the conquest of the Plains Indians and the buffalo plains, I hope to highlight how the intersection between Euro-American concepts of disability, imperialist ideology, and eco-ableism impelled this conquest and thereby contextualized the colonialism-disability nexus as it shaped Americans' pursuit of "manifest destiny."[12]

I will approach the history and legacy of the annihilation of the buffalo plains from two related angles. First, I will demonstrate how the destruction of the bison population during this period was part of an overall attempt to regulate the deviance of Native American bodies—that is, the campaign to eliminate bison was an attempt to "cure" the Indigenous buffalo-hunting cultures of the American West of their "savagery." As Native Americans—and Plains Indians in particular—were regarded as unfit for civilization and citizenship because of their perceived moral and intellectual deficiencies, the destruction of bison—along with the emergence of Indian boarding schools and the reservation system—was intended to subdue and eradicate the pathology of Native savagery. Conversely, and somewhat ironically, the colonizing acts of bison destruction and assimilationist policies had a widespread debilitating impact on the colonized Native population, as revealed in, among other places, the writings of Zitkala-Sâ. Second, I will demonstrate how the near destruction of the bison herds and the subsequent colonization of the Plains Indians was motivated by an eco-ableist paradigm that regarded the arid grasslands—and the bison-hunting culture it supported—as a nonnormative biocultural landscape that needed to be conquered, subdued, and rehabilitated. The eradication of the bison and the subjugation of the Plains tribes who hunted the animal was part of an overall effort to redeem the Great Plains and transform it—through the work of the plow and other technological innovations—into a viable agricultural landscape. I will read the impetus behind this transformation within the context of postbellum attitudes regarding science, technology, and disability. Before examining the specific historical and regional factors that contributed to the destruction of the buffalo plains, I would first like to review the broader historical and cultural contexts behind the eco-ableist nature of American colonialism.

The Pathologization of Native Savagery: Historical and Cultural Contexts

The conquest of the Plains Indians was essentially the closing chapter of America's centuries-long effort to colonize the continental United States as attention shifted after the Civil War to the formerly neglected and as-yet sparsely populated arid grasslands east of the Rockies. Thus, while there were key regional components to the conquest of the buffalo plains, which I'll address more directly in the next section, it is important to acknowledge that this conquest ultimately represents a regional manifestation of a larger pattern of conquest that began when the first permanent European settlers arrived in Virginia in 1607. The expansion of the Euro-American frontier into occupied territories led to repeated conflicts between white settlers and the various Indigenous communities that populated North America. The racist and ethnocentric logic used to justify the expansion of Euro-American civilization and the erasure and removal of Native people was present from the beginning. Native Americans were regarded as racially inferior, an inferiority that was purportedly observable through their primitive and savage behavior and cultural practices. Their less-than-human biological status disqualified their claims on the land: they did not deserve their ties to the land because they did not properly use and cultivate it.

This is admittedly an oversimplification of the ideology that drove frontier expansion, but in examining this logic through the lens of disability, I want to highlight two interrelated components of what would come to be known as the ideology of manifest destiny: the dehumanization of Native people and the pathologization of hunting and gathering as land-use practices. As Kim Nielsen documents in her *Disability History of the United States*, the destructive impact of colonization on Native people was fueled, in part, by Euro-American standards of physical, cultural, and economic well-being that clashed with the precontact emphasis on an interdependent and communal ethic sustained by most tribes. While instances of bodily impairments were common among Indigenous people, Nielsen argues that precontact Native Americans had no real "concept for what in American English we today call 'disability.'"[13] There was no real stigma attached to bodily impairments because ability was largely measured in relational terms; as long as individuals could participate in and contribute to the community on some level, they were not regarded as disabled. As Nielsen writes, "Though individuals might experience impairment, disability would only come if or when a person was removed from or was unable to participate in community reciprocity."[14] One of the more disruptive consequences of colonization was that the worldview of the European colonizers directly challenged this ethic of reciprocity. As Nielsen notes, "Western concepts of wellness and medicine directly and tragically conflicted with the indigenous embrace of body, mind, spirit as one. Any sense of mutuality between European and Native cultures was extinguished by disease, greed, and notions of cultural superiority."[15] From the perspective of the Europeans, the Native people were inherently disabled: their barbaric rituals and primitive existence were viewed as proof of their backwardness and their lack of social and intellectual development.[16]

The dehumanization of Indigenous people and the notion of the Native-as-disabled was fostered by the correlation drawn within the Euro-American mindset between Native people and the wilderness. The very idea of "wilderness," of course, is a social construction, and its meaning has shifted over the course of American history; within the context of Euro-American colonization and the expansion of agrarian-based civilization, however, wilderness signified uncultivated land (literally, the terrain of the wild deer).[17] Though precontact Native Americans had developed sustainable communities supported by hunting, foraging, and, in many cases, the planting and harvesting of crops, their land-use practices were seen as primitive and their humanity was subsequently diminished because they were regarded as part and parcel of the untamed wilderness. Through their association with one another, both the wilderness and its "savage" inhabitants were mutually denigrated: the Natives' inhabitation of the wilderness made them no different than the other "beasts" of the forests, and, conversely, the presence of the Natives in the wilderness confirmed the inconsequential value of uncultivated land. The goal of colonization then was to remove the Natives and reclaim and improve the wilderness through agricultural and commercial development. In other words, from the time of the initial arrival of European settlers in the New World, the Native-inhabited wilderness—whether in the mountains, forests, or grasslands—was perpetually a target for eradication and then rehabilitation. As Cameron Wolfe notes, "Settler colonialism is at base a winner-takes-all project whose dominant feature is not exploitation but replacement."[18] The conquest of the Great Plains, like all colonial projects, was about replacing an undesirable biocultural landscape with one more suited to dominant Western standards of economic and aesthetic values.

The pathologization of Native savagery and the characterization of Native people as deviant was thus informed by Euro-American perceptions about their own racial and cultural superiority; furthermore, this sense of superiority was tied to the notion that Euro-Americans were better equipped to make proper use of the natural resources of the New World because their land-use practices were more advanced. The implicit eco-ableism behind this denigration of the Native wilderness was further bolstered by the influence of the stadial model of social development and the emergence in the early American period of agrarianism as the cornerstone of Jeffersonian democracy. In the introduction to his book-length examination of American literary responses to the expanding globalism of the post–World War II period, Guy Reynolds highlights the lingering influence of stadialism on American ideas about social evolution and progress. Rooted in Enlightenment ideas initially developed in Scotland, stadialism holds that "societies evolved from a 'savage' state through the 'barbarian' stage, then on to a 'civilized' culture of herding, followed by a contemporary scene of commerce and manufacturing."[19] This linear model of social development establishes a correlation between a society's dominant land-use practice—from hunting and gathering, to herding, to cultivation, to manufacturing—and the degree of social advancement. One of the most widely recognized expressions of this theory in American literature is in the third letter of John Hector St. John de Crèvecoeur's *Letters from an American Farmer* (1782), in which Farmer James explains how the westward expansion of the Euro-American frontier offered a unique snapshot of the evolution of human society. As one moves west from the manufacturing towns and cities of the Eastern Seaboard—the epicenter of advanced civilization—to the frontier outposts of the unsettled regions of the West, one can observe the regression of human society from the sophisticated cosmopolitan of the East Coast to the savage backwoodsman of the untamed wilderness. Farmer James's disdain for the white frontier hunter, whom he regards as a "mongrel breed," registers the deep stigma attached to the lower forms of social development.[20] Indeed, for Farmer James the white frontiersman is even more sinister and savage than the more "respectable" Natives because he represents a regression in social development as he gives up the plow to follow the hunt.[21] Even so, Crèvecoeur's Letter III reflects a belief in social progress that relegates hunters to almost subhuman status.

Even as the metropolis represented the final phase of social advancement within the stadial model of social development and therefore the opposite pole of the wilderness, it was also the site of potential greed and corruption. The actual peak of social evolution—the true pinnacle of civilization and the keystone of democracy—was the agrarian state. Within the framework of Jeffersonian democracy and its vision of an agrarian America, the tillers of the soil embodied the best of civilization. In an oft-quoted passage from his *Notes on the State of Virginia*, Thomas Jefferson posits the yeoman as the centerpiece of democracy:

> We have an immensity of land courting the industry of the husbandman. Is it best then that all our citizens should be employed in its improvement, or that one half should be called off from that to exercise manufactures and handicraft arts for the other? Those who labor in the earth are the chosen people of God, if ever He had a chosen people, whose breasts He has made His peculiar deposit for substantial and genuine virtue. It is the focus in which he keeps alive that sacred fire, which otherwise might escape from the face of the earth.[22]

As the "chosen people," farmers engage in a land-use practice that was regarded as the standard from the early American period through the nineteenth century. Within the agrarian vision of America, the well-ordered and cultivated field of the independent farmer is the basic unit of an ideal society, and the farm represents a biocultural standard or normative landscape against which other working landscapes are measured.

When viewed through the lens of stadialism and the agrarian ideal, the impetus behind the Euro-American effort to pathologize Native land-use practices becomes clear. Native people's continued reliance on hunting and gathering as a means of subsistence and their supposed inability to rise above their boundedness to the wilderness confirmed their social deviance. Conversely, the rapid social evolution of Euro-American settlements at each phase of frontier expansion, where the white hunter is soon replaced by the cultivators who drive the progression of civilization, offered proof of the racial superiority of white civilization. Whereas Euro-Americans were capable of (and had achieved) social evolution, Native Americans were perpetually stuck at the most primitive stage of development. When evaluated against the socially constructed biocultural ideal of the farm, the hunting grounds of Indigenous people were viewed as an inferior working landscape, one destined to be replaced by cultivated fields.

Manifest Destiny and the Destruction of the Buffalo Plains

On one level, then, the eradication of the buffalo plains and the bison-hunting tribes of the Great Plains echoes the cycle of conquest reproduced at each frontier of America's westward expansion. The primitive hunters must give way to the superior agrarians whose manifest destiny it was to change the wild grasslands into the domesticated fields of grain and meat. On another level, though, there are a few environmental and historical factors that make the tragedy of the buffalo plains stand out as a particularly salient example of the implicit eco-ableism of the Euro-American colonization of Native land. First, the destruction of the buffalo plains during the first few decades of the postbellum period occurred in the wake of American Romanticism, which introduced the figure of the Noble Savage that complicated the Euro-American perception of Native Americans. While the romanticization of the Native hunter countered contemporary calls for the eradication and subjugation of the bison-hunting tribes, the Euro-American defenders of the Plains Indians still saw them as essentially doomed. Second, the colonization of the buffalo plains was unique because it required major environmental revisionism to overcome the Euro-American bias against a region that was long considered the Great American Desert. The arid and relatively treeless landscape was regarded as uncultivatable, fit only for the nomadic hunters who occupied the area. Finally, a variety of historical changes—including a heightened commitment to fulfilling America's manifest destiny, widespread industrialization, and the emergence of postbellum principles of reform in the decades leading into the Progressive Era—combined to hasten the effort to eradicate the bison, subdue the Plains Indians, and permanently alter the working landscape of the buffalo plains.

During the Romantic period, writers like James Fenimore Cooper, Catherine Maria Sedgwick, and George Catlin, to name a few prominent examples, recast Native Americans as noble rather than bloodthirsty savages. Within the context of evolving ideas about the benefits of wilderness and the morally uplifting quality of the natural world, the primitivism of Native American land-use practices was heralded by many Romantics as a potential boon rather than a definitive deficit. The best illustration of this shift in perspective, and the one most relevant to my focus here, is Catlin's call to preserve the buffalo plains in the form of a "nation's Park."[23] Catlin traveled throughout the West from 1831 to 1837 to record—in both his paintings and his journals—the lifeways of the bison-hunting tribes of the Great Plains. This mission to "fix and preserve" the image of the Plains Indians on canvas and through the written word was motivated by a sense, shared by many Romantic artists, that the Plains Indians were on the brink of extinction.[24] Not unlike Farmer James, Catlin described his westward journey in stadialist terms, characterizing the physical movement toward the Plains frontier as a regression "through the different grades of civilization, which gradually sink to the most deplorable condition along the extreme frontier."[25] Also like Farmer James, he draws a distinction between the savagery of the white backwoodsman of this "extreme" frontier and the noble savagery of the Native dweller of the still Wild West beyond the frontier. In his ninth letter, he explains that after passing through the "savage degradation" of the frontier outpost of white civilization, one "gradually rises again into the proud and chivalrous pale of savage society, in its state of *original nature* beyond the reach of civilized contamination" where the Native people display the "noblest traits of honour and magnamity."[26] The Natives' close association with the "original nature" of the undomesticated wilderness still marks them as savages, but this wilderness condition endows them with positive rather than negative traits.

Catlin is particularly taken with the aesthetic presented by the bison-hunting tribes of the Great Plains, as he considers the buffalo plains something of a biocultural ideal. His romanticization of the Native bison hunters is best captured in letter thirty-one when he proposes the creation of a national preserve to essentially protect and maintain the buffalo plains as a working landscape. He writes,

> And what a splendid contemplation too, when one (who has travelled these realms, and can duly appreciate them) imagines them as they *might* in future be seen, (by some great protecting policy of government) preserved in their pristine beauty and wildness, in a *magnificent park*, where the world could see for ages to come, the native Indian in his classic attire, galloping his wild horse, with sinewy bow, and shield and lance, amid the fleeting herds of elks and buffaloes.... A *nation's Park*, containing man and beast, in all the wild and freshness of their nature's beauty.[27]

His vision of a "nation's Park" casts the wildness of the bison hunters in idyllic terms. He sees them as embodying a pure state of "nature's beauty" that is otherwise lacking from the more advanced stages of civilization. Catlin's desire to freeze the Plains Indians in time to preserve them from contamination by white civilization is fueled in part by his sense that the bison-hunting tribes were doomed. His celebration of the biocultural ideal of the buffalo plains is thus tinged with nostalgia, bred by the recognition—shared by most Romantics who lauded the Noble Savage—that "the buffalo's doom is sealed, and with their extinction must assuredly sink into real despair and starvation, the inhabitants of these vast plains."[28] While he expresses consternation about this fate, he understands that the primitive society of the bison hunters will inevitably be extinguished to make room for the more advanced white civilization.

When examined through the lens of eco-ableism, Catlin's call to monumentalize the buffalo plains draws attention to a couple of key points. First, while a desire to preserve is, of course, an improvement over the desire to annihilate Indigenous people, both desires are rooted in the same ableist principle. That is, both view Native people in essentialist terms and consider them socially undeveloped and intellectually incapable of changing and adapting to shifts in the social and natural environment. For Catlin, the encroachment of white settlers into the Native hunting grounds can only have a contaminating effect on Native people who will succumb to the corrupt aspects of civilization—like greed and alcoholism—and will inevitably fall into a life of "despair and starvation." They only have the capacity to react and not to adapt. Therefore, the only alternative to the outright destruction of the Plains Indians is to enclose them within the boundaries of a park where their culture can remain static and pure, unsullied by the unavoidable march of progress.

The irony here is that this view that the nomadic bison-hunting culture of the Plains Indians was a static and pure manifestation of "original nature" lacks historical perspective. As Andrew Isenberg notes continually throughout his environmental history of the buffalo plains, what was regarded as the "classic" culture of the Plains Indians was actually the result of a dynamic adaptation to European colonization, particularly the introduction of the horse. Before the adoption of the horse, many of the tribes in the middle of North America relied on a mixture of agriculture and hunting. The introduction of the horse, however, made the pursuit of game—and particularly the plentiful bison—easier and more productive. Isenberg writes, "In essence, the horse regularized food procurement in the unpredictable environment of the western plains. . . . [T]he diffusion of the horse into the plains made nomadic bison hunting a more secure land-use strategy than the combination of hunting and sedentary horticulture—at least in the short term."[29] While the nomadism of the Plains Indians was read by most contemporary Euro-Americans, including Catlin, as a sign of their primitivism and lack of social advancement, it was, in fact, an example of a dynamic adaptation to the natural environment. Indeed, Isenberg argues that in a direct contradiction to the stadial model, the Plains Indians' transformation from planter-hunters into horse-mounted bison hunters was *not* a backward step. He writes, "Rather than exhibiting backwardness, the nomads—characterized by mobility, social anomie, and economic specialization—anticipated later social and economic developments in the plains."[30] What Catlin viewed as savagery, even if it was a noble savagery, was "an adaptation to the volatile and desiccated plains environment" and therefore an example of a social evolution.[31]

A second takeaway from Catlin's proposal for a "nation's Park" ties directly to the "volatile and desiccated" quality of the Great Plains that Isenberg mentions. For Catlin, the idea of setting aside a vast tract of the Plains landscape for the purpose of a bison preserve was feasible, in part, because he held the view common at that time that the interior grasslands were not suitable for agricultural development and therefore were otherwise expendable. He even goes so far as to suggest that the Great Plains were divinely ordained for use by the bison-hunting tribes of the West. He contends that the "plain of grass . . . is, and ever must be, *useless* to cultivating man. It is here, and here chiefly, that the buffaloes dwell; and with, and hovering about them, live and flourish the tribes of Indians, whom God made for the enjoyment of that fair land and its luxuries."[32] In characterizing the Plains environment as "useless to cultivating man," Catlin echoes a widely held view during the antebellum period that the arid grasslands were destined to remain an uncultivated wilderness because the climate and soil were not suitable for traditional agriculture. In the 1830s, when Catlin was traveling throughout the American West, the Plains region was still commonly regarded as the Great American Desert, a label introduced by Edwin James in his chronicle of the 1820 expedition to the area led by Major Stephen Long. He affixed this label to the map of the region included in his chronicle, as it captured his impression that this desert was "wholly unfit for cultivation, and of course uninhabitable by a people depending on agriculture for their subsistence."[33] This rejection of the uselessness of the Great Plains delayed the conquest of the nomadic bison hunter, as the westward expanding Euro-Americans temporarily leapfrogged the region to the more fertile and mineral-rich land west of the grasslands.

The cycles of boom and bust that define the historical record of agriculture on the post-settlement Plains, of course, bear out this characterization of the landscape as "unfit for cultivation," but what I want to emphasize here is the eco-ableism implicit in this "useless" designation. As I noted at the outset of this essay, such a designation stems from a Euro-American bias toward an agrarian ideal that requires arable land like that found in the moister environment east of the Mississippi and west of the Rockies. The Great Plains were dismissed by Euro-American agrarians because they did not resemble the more familiar landscapes of Europe and the eastern states and because they were not viable for agriculture. The presence of the nomadic bison hunters only served to foster this bias against the Great American Desert; that the area was inhabited by savages who depended on hunting as their means of subsistence confirmed the uselessness of the landscape. While Catlin attaches some aesthetic value to the buffalo plains—an aesthetic he wants to preserve with his "nation's Park"—the general assessment of the region during the antebellum period was that it was, as Josiah Gregg notes in his *Commerce of the Prairies* (1844), destined to remain "the haunts of the mustang, the buffalo, the antelope, and their migratory lord, the prairie Indian."[34] This eco-ableist construction of the buffalo plains paints the arid grasslands as an inferior landscape inhabited by an inferior people.

Gregg's prediction that the Great American Desert would forever remain the domain of the nomadic "prairie Indian," of course, did not come to fruition. In the second half of the nineteenth century, the Euro-American attitude toward the economic potential of the Great Plains shifted substantially; rather than dismiss the Plains as viable only for the savage bison-hunting nomads, the arid grasslands came to be viewed as redeemable and therefore desirable, especially as a site for the continued expansion of Euro-American civilization. As I will document in the remainder of this section, there were a few social and historical factors that contributed to this revised outlook about the value of the Plains landscape, most notably an invigorated commitment to the doctrine of "manifest destiny" and widescale urbanization and industrialization. Coupled with an emerging faith in science and education as tools of social and environmental reform, these factors hastened the destruction of the buffalo plains and the subsequent conquest of the bison-hunting tribes of the Plains.

The term *manifest destiny* is often attributed to John L. O'Sullivan, a newspaper editor who invoked the phrase in an 1845 column as part of an argument in defense of the annexation of Texas. In the column he argues that America has a "manifest destiny to overspread the continent allotted by Providence for the free development of our yearly multiplying millions."[35] This notion of a providential right to territorial expansion across the continent continued a long tradition of American exceptionalism and served as a justification for the colonization of the Native tribes of the West. Within the framework of manifest destiny, the conquest of the buffalo plains became not only a political necessity but part of a divinely ordained mission to spread American agrarianism and democracy across the West.[36] To fulfill this mission required a rhetorical makeover of the dominant contemporary image of the Great Plains in order to sell it as a feasible site for agricultural development. According to Andrew Menard, such a makeover was in progress in the form of John Frémont's *Report on an Exploration of the Country Lying between the Missouri River and the Rocky Mountains*, which he submitted to Congress in 1843, one year before Gregg declared the Plains unfit for cultivation. Menard argues that Frémont's report aimed to verify the fertility not the sterility of the so-called Great American Desert; he did so through his use of the picturesque to describe the topography and geography of the region in specific and diverse terms, illuminating the fecundity and dimensionality of the landscape rather than its alleged monotony. A primarily "aesthetic enterprise," the *Report* presents an empirical description of the Plains landscape that was intended to debunk the perception that the grasslands were impervious to agriculture.[37] The goal of the *Report* was to encourage emigration to the region. As Menard explains, it had to "demonstrate that nature itself granted the right of manifest destiny. With everyone from Washington Irving to Daniel Webster arguing that the vast, essentially treeless region was a natural barrier to the nation, Frémont had to show that it was not—and mainly by showing it was not a desert at all."[38] According to Menard, the *Report* encouraged some movement toward fulfilling America's manifest destiny, as it inspired a "sudden spike in western emigration which occurred a little more than two months after it was published."[39] While widespread migration to the Plains was still a few decades away, Frémont's *Report* represents an early effort to rhetorically reconstruct the image of the region as part of a larger project of encouraging Euro-American settlement.

Complementing this rhetorical makeover of the Great American Desert were scientific (and pseudoscientific) advances made in the latter part of the nineteenth century that promised to correct the Plains environment and make it suitable for agriculture despite its aridity. One widely held belief was that cultivation of the grasslands itself would transform the desert into a garden; by unleashing the moisture in the soil, the theory went, the plowman would gradually change the climate of the region in a way favorable to further cultivation. This pseudoscientific theory that "rain follows the plow" was popularized by Charles Dana Wilber; in 1881 he couched the theory in terms of America's manifest destiny by lauding the white plowman as the redeemer of the Great Plains. Furthermore, he articulates an eco-ableist claim that Plains Indians were responsible for the desert conditions of the region because they pursued inferior—that is, nonagrarian—land-use practices. He writes, "The Indians are, and, as far as we know, have always been, co-workers with the natural forces that maintain and extend desert conditions. He will neither plant nor sow. . . . He, by his law, or economy of life, makes the desert still more a desert, and when the desolation is complete, he can either disappear as the exit of the *non-fittest*, or retreat to other wilds."[40] That the removal of the unfit savages and their replacement by the plowman would transform the Plains into a garden is here presented not just as a divine prophecy but as a scientific fact. The relatively moist decades of the 1870s and 1880s seemed to support this notion that the rain follows the plow, and Wilber's book is replete with tables and charts to prove the theory.

Although the severe drought of the 1890s ultimately debunked this pseudoscientific theory that cultivation could alter the climate, the emergence of scientific agriculture during this time offered more promising techniques that were alleged to be feasible even in times of drought. In particular, the practice of "dryland farming," introduced by Hardy Campbell, proscribed more methodical techniques to tap into and make use of the limited moisture of the prairie soils without costly irrigation. As Manning explains, in addition to the introduction of drought-resistant grains, Campbell "recommended a regime of plowing, of summer fallow in alternate years, and a relatively diverse system of crop rotation with wheat at its center."[41] Like the rain-follows-the-plow theory, the dryland farming methods ultimately proved unsuccessful—with doubt about their validity spectacularly confirmed by the Dust Bowl phenomenon of the 1930s—but the theories were widely promoted to enhance migration to the arid West and therefore fulfilled the ideological and cultural goals of manifest destiny.[42]

In terms of policy, the twin goals of reclaiming the Great American Desert and fulfilling the nation's manifest destiny were supported through the passage of the Homestead Act of 1862. This piece of legislation made millions of acres of western public lands available for free if claimants of the 160-acre tracts could "prove up" their claims by living on the land for at least five years and by making improvements in the form of cultivation. The homesteads were organized into square plots in alignment with Thomas Jefferson's vision of a well-ordered agrarian society. The goal of the act, in other words, was to not only encourage the settlement of the arid West but to utterly transform the landscape by imposing the agrarian ideal upon it. The influx of Euro-American homesteaders to the region increased steadily in the postbellum period, fostered by the completion of the first transcontinental railroad in 1869 as well as the passage of the Timber Culture Act of 1873, a companion to the Homestead Act that offered additional acreage to claimants provided they planted trees on a quarter section of their land. The promise of the plow to reshape the buffalo plains into a facsimile of the eastern United States was beginning to take hold in the waning decades of the nineteenth century as the Euro-American frontier expanded into the region.

If the perception of the sterility was one impediment to the agricultural conquest of the buffalo plains, the other major barrier was the presence of the Plains Indians. The increasing encroachment of white ranchers, gold seekers, and homesteaders into the bison-hunting grounds led to an uptick in violent conflicts between the Plains Indians and the Euro-American settlers. After the Civil War, the U.S. Army directed its attention to the Great Plains with the goal of subduing the few remaining tribes not yet settled on reservations. As Isenberg notes, "The army was the forward arm of federal government policy in the plains, which in turn reflected dominant cultural notions of the rightness of Euroamerican conquest of the West." In essence, the army's purpose in the region was to act on the "belief in the inevitability of Euroamerican triumph over Indians and the wilderness" and to enforce America's manifest destiny.[43]

Warfare was a major component of this effort to conquer the buffalo plains, of course, but military leaders like Colonel Richard Dodge and Generals William Sherman and Philip Sheridan also understood that a key to victory in the West was the eradication of the bison. According to Mari Sandoz's history of the buffalo hunters, Dodge once encouraged a hide hunter who was feeling guilt over a massacre of dozens of bison bulls by prodding him to "kill every buffalo you can. Every buffalo dead is an Indian gone."[44] Historians debate whether the army had a direct policy to exterminate the bison as a wartime strategy, and even if it was not part of an official policy, there are recorded instances of uniformed soldiers leading wasteful hunts.[45] Regardless, the heavy influx of white hide hunters into the region in the 1870s was welcomed and encouraged as a potential tipping point in the conquest of the Plains Indians. Of the white hide hunters, Sheridan said, "These men have done more in the last two years, and will do more in the next year, to settle the vexed Indian question than the entire regular army has done in the last thirty years. . . . Let them skin, kill and sell until the buffaloes are exterminated."[46] This market-driven extermination of the keystone species of the buffalo plains was necessary for progress, Sheridan argued, because it would open up the prairies for the "speckled cattle" and "festive cowboy" who are the "forerunner[s] of an advanced civilization."[47] As vital actors in the pursuit of manifest destiny, the hide hunters were the advanced guard of the forthcoming biocultural evolution of the buffalo plains from savage hunting grounds to the more advanced agrarian patchwork of pastures and cultivated fields.[48] In addition to clearing the way for Euro-American settlers, the prolific work of the hide hunters would also subdue the Plains Indians into a state of dependency. Columbus Delano, the secretary of the interior who was adamantly opposed to legislation proposed in 1874 to protect bison from extermination, explained the benefit of bison extermination in clear terms, noting that he would not "regret the total disappearance of the buffalo from our western prairies, in its effects on Indians, regarding it rather as a means to hasten their sense of dependence on the products of the soil and their labor."[49]

As Isenberg notes, the commanding general of the army at the time, William Tecumseh Sherman, certainly "commended the hunters" even if he "did not command them" to partake in the bison slaughter.[50] What did compel the hide hunters to come to the region in droves was the growing American "industrial economy's appetite for natural resources."[51] Increased urbanization and industrialization in the second half of the nineteenth century expanded the market for bison, and the completion of the transcontinental railroad assured access to this market for those seeking to harvest the animal for profit. It is important to note, as Isenberg does, that trade in bison furs was a well-established component of trade between the Plains Indians and the Euro-American economy from the 1830s, as their thick winter furs were valuable to produce blankets and coats.[52] Demand for bison escalated in the last decades of the nineteenth century, however, dramatically increasing their commercial value. Isenberg explains, "A spasm of industrial expansion was the primary cause of the bison's near extinction in the 1870s and early 1880s. During this period, Euroamericans hunted bison to satisfy an increasing demand for hides in industrializing America. Leather belts were the sinews of nineteenth-century industrial production: mills relied on heavy leather belting to animate their machinery."[53] With advances in the technology required to tan the hides for the mass production of leather belts, bison hides became an invaluable resource for the rapidly expanding industrial economy. The mass harvesting of bison hides therefore offered a lucrative venture with little overhead for the hunters who could follow the herds and slaughter the bison in massive quantities. Because it was only the hides that were needed, the image of hundreds of rotting bison carcasses strewn throughout the prairies was not uncommon. By the middle of the 1880s, the last of the bison herds was essentially wiped out, with even their bones being harvested for commercial purposes.[54] While a few more years of warfare followed the demise of the last buffalo herd, the eradication of the buffalo plains as a working landscape was essentially accomplished by the middle of the 1880s. As Gilio-White puts it, the "environmental disruption" of the buffalo plains—an act of ecocide and genocide—represents "one of the most destructive and tragic outcomes of the United States' industrial expansion."[55]

If the destruction of the bison was a major facet of the effort to subdue the Plains Indians and reduce them, as Delano suggested, to a state of dependency, another was the advent of the boarding school system with its assimilationist objectives. It is fitting, indeed, that the emergence of the Indian boarding schools was contemporaneous with the intensification of bison eradication, as the first of the boarding schools was established by Richard Pratt in Carlisle in 1874. Like the unofficial bison extermination policy, the mission of the Indian boarding schools was to essentially "cure" Native savagery through education. Indeed, Dodge's statement that each dead buffalo meant one gone Indian echoes a phrase attributed to Pratt about the goal of the boarding schools: "Kill the Indian, and save the man." In teaching the "savages" English, converting them to Christianity, and training them to learn a trade, the goal of the schools was to strip them of their culture and integrate them into Euro-American civilization. The emergence of the Indian boarding schools at this time parallels a broader trend in postbellum America of using institutionalization as a means to fix—or in some cases simply warehouse—deviant bodies. As Nielsen notes, "The period from the Civil War until the 1890s is one in which disability became increasingly institutionalized."[56] Just as scientific agriculture in the late nineteenth century was touted to correct a deviant landscape, so, too, was institutionalization and the professionalization of medicine touted as the means to correct individuals whose bodies did not conform to the normative standard. Nielsen explains, "The nation sought to transform the questionable citizen into a good one and confine those either refusing or incapable of transformation. While institutions each had varying histories, they shared the underlying assumption that human behavior could be managed and altered through professional intervention."[57] The schools for the "deaf," "blind," "insane," and "feeble minded" that were created to address supposed bodily deficits through "professional intervention" and the reservations and boarding schools that were meant to address or otherwise contain the savagery of Native Americans had the same objectives: to regulate and control bodies deemed unfit for participation in Euro-American civic life. The extermination of the bison and the coerced assimilation of Native people through the boarding school system thus worked in tandem to rein in the deviant savagery of the bison-hunting culture of the buffalo plains.

Conclusion: Legacies of the Conquest of the Buffalo Plains

In her autobiography about her experience as an Indian boarding school student and then teacher, Zitkala-Ša highlights the deep personal and cultural trauma that the experience caused. In the second section of the autobiography, "The School Days of an Indian Girl," she recounts some of the indignities she suffered as the result of the schoolteachers' effort to sever her connection to her Yankton Dakota Sioux heritage, including the cutting of her hair—a taboo within Sioux culture—and excessive punishments for lapses in the acquisition of the English language.[58] A more long-term impact of her ultimately successful completion of her studies at the Indiana Manual Labor Institute was the way in which it fundamentally changed her relationship with her tribal community and, in particular, her mother who never fully approved of her daughter's choice to leave the Yankton Indian Reservation. Stuck in between two worlds, Zitkala-Ša notes how she feels "homeless and heavy hearted," not fully at home on the reservation or among the strangers of the towns and cities of white civilization.[59]

Aside from giving expression to the psychologically debilitating consequences of the Indian boarding system, what is notable about Zitkala-Ša's account for the purposes of this essay is how often she invokes the dichotomy of wildness and domestication to describe the effect of assimilation on her cultural identity. The first section of her autobiography, "Impressions of an Indian Childhood," for example, depicts her early childhood on the reservation as one of wild freedom and pleasure where she felt a strong connection to her mother and to the stories and legends of her people. In contrast to her youthful "happy dreams of Western rolling lands and unlassoed freedom," the boarding school experience is one that fetters her wildness, as the "iron routine" of the "civilizing machine" makes her feel like "only one of many little animals driven by a herder."[60] This figurative description of herself as a victim of domestication is again expressed toward the end of her auto-biography when she compares herself to a telegraph pole. She writes, "Like a slender tree, I had been uprooted from my mother, nature, and God. I was shorn of my branches, which had waved in sympathy and love for home and friends. The natural coat of bark which had protected my oversensitive nature was scraped off to the very quick. Now a cold bare pole I seemed to be, plant-ed in a strange earth."[61] Taken together, the images of a herded animal and an uprooted tree collectively resist the eco-ableist narrative of Euro-American colonization that reads the domestication of wildness as a desired outcome of the conquest of civilization over savagery. The movement from "unlassoed freedom" to tamed animal, in other words, is presented as a loss and a neg-ative outcome, one that challenges the notion that the shift from the buffalo plains to the checkerboard of fields and pastures was a movement forward.

What Zitkala-Ŝa's memoir draws attention to is the irony that the Euro-American drive to "cure" the savagery of the Native people and to likewise "cure" the economic deviance of the buffalo plains through colonization was a disabling phenomenon, the cause of profound cultural and environmental destruction with long-term negative consequences the region continues to overcome. The arrival of the plow on the Great Plains toward the end of the nineteenth century was celebrated as the ultimate example of the triumph of Euro-American agrarianism over an indomitable landscape and its wild inhabitants, a manifestation of America's frontier myth. This victory of the plow over the buffalo plains is perhaps most poignantly captured in Willa Cather's *My Antonia* (1918) in an iconic image of a plow laying idle at the top of a swell in the prairies, framed heroically against the backdrop of the set-ting sun. The novel's narrator, Jim Burden, is awed by the image, taken as he is with the Euro-American mythology surrounding the plowman-pioneers who tamed the wilderness of grass. The significance of the plow within the region's history, however, as this essay has shown, is much more complex than what Cather's image suggests. As one of the primary tools of the de-cades-long effort to subdue the buffalo plains, the plow also symbolizes the eco-ableist attempt to manipulate and correct a biocultural landscape that was considered impaired only because it did not fit a socially constructed standard for land-use practices. The history of the region shows that the triumph of the plow over the buffalo led to a cultural and environmental catastrophe, the consequences of which were manifest in the barren fields and great dust storms that defined the Plains landscape of the drought-stricken 1930s. Jim Burden's cherished memory of the plow against the sun, then, must be juxtaposed with the characterization of the plow expressed in Pare Lorentz's 1936 documentary, *The Plow That Broke the Plains*. Lorentz's film tells the tragic story of the Dust Bowl, where the great plow-up of the prairies transformed the "old grass lands" into the "new wheat lands" to satisfy the demand for "war wheat." The aggressive cultivation of the plains de-stroyed the complex root system of the grasslands, leaving the land even more vulnerable to the extreme droughts that often inflicted the region. When the drought of the 1930s hit, it left the plowman "baked out—blown out" and left the land barren and the soil spent. While the "sun and winds wrote the most tragic chapter in American agriculture," as the narrator proclaims in the clos-ing lines, it was ultimately the plow, and the agrarian ideal it represents, that broke the plains. The image of the dusted-out grasslands, coupled with Black Elk's image of the prairies emptied of the bison referenced at the beginning of this essay, thus register the negative legacy of the eco-ableist conquest of the Great Plains.

NOTES

1. John G. Neihardt, *Black Elk Speaks* (Lincoln: University of Nebraska, 1979), 213.
2. In addition to the Sioux, the bison-hunting tribes of the West include the Blackfeet, Hidastas, Crows, Mandans, Arapahos, Assiniboines, Kiowa, Cheyenne, and Pawnees. Although it is important to note the divergent histories, culture, and experiences of these various tribes, this essay takes a pan-tribal approach to focus on a key component that ties these tribes together, which is their reliance on bison hunting. Therefore, throughout this paper I will refer to them collectively as the Plains Indians. I use the terms *Native* and *Native Americans* when discussing the Indigenous people and communities of North America more broadly and use specific tribal designations when the context warrants such naming.
3. Ibid. (emphasis added).
4. Ibid.
5. I use the phrase "buffalo plains" throughout this essay as a shorthand way to refer to the bison hunting-grounds of the Plains Indians, a landscape that took shape in a par-ticular place, the Great Plains, at a particular time when the bison was the keystone spe-cies and bison hunting the primary land-use practice.
6. Anthony J. Nocella II, Judy K. C. Bentley, and Janet M. Duncan, eds., *Earth, Animal, and Disability Liberation: The Rise of the Eco-Ability Movement* (New York: Peter Lang, 2012), xvi, xvii.
7. Ibid., xviii.
8. Anthony J. Nocella II, "Defining Eco-Ability: Social Justice and the Intersectional-ity of Disability, Nonhuman Animals, and Ecology," in *Earth, Animal, and Disability Lib-eration: The Rise of the Eco-Ability Movement*, ed. Anthony J. Nocella II, Judy K. C. Bentley, and Janet M. Duncan (New York: Peter Lang, 2012), 6.
9. Dina Gilio-Whitaker, *As Long as the Grass Grows: The Indigenous Fight for Environ-mental Justice, from Colonization to Standing Rock* (Boston: Beacon, 2019), 60–61.
10. Karen Jarrett-Snider, "Environmental Injustice, Land, and American Indian Reli-gious Freedom," in *Indigenous Environmental Justice*, ed. Karen Jarrett-Snider and Mari-anne O. Nielsen (Tucson: University of Arizona Press, 2020), 41.
11. It is important to note that I am not a historian and it is therefore not my intention to add anything new to our historical understanding of the circumstances that led to the near extinction of bison in the 1870s and 1880s. Indeed, I will rely heavily on the com-prehensive cultural and environmental history of this phenomenon presented in Andrew Isenberger's *The Destruction of Bison*. My aim here is to examine this historical moment

through the lens of eco-ableism in order to highlight how the social construction of normative landscapes and normative land-use practices supported the colonization of the buffalo plains.

12. Shaun Grech, "Decolonising Eurocentric Disability Studies: Why Colonialism Matters in the and Global South Debate," *Social Identities* 21 (2015): 7.

13. Kim E. Nielsen, *A Disability History of the United States* (Boston: Beacon, 2012), 2.

14. Ibid., 3.

15. Ibid., 11.

16. The tragic irony of this is that the arrival of the Europeans significantly increased the rates of death and disability among Indigenous people due to exposure to foreign diseases, warfare, and competition for natural resources in the wake of deforestation and loss of land (see Nielsen, *Disability History*, 15–19).

17. Some studies that examine shifting ideas about wilderness in American culture—and regarding the social construction of nature and wilderness in general—include the following: William Cronon, ed., *Uncommon Ground: Rethinking the Human Place in Nature* (New York: Norton, 1995); Michael J. Lewis, *American Wilderness: Anew History* (New York: Oxford University Press, 2007); Roderick Nash, *Wilderness and the American Mind* (New Haven, CT: Yale University Press, 2014); and Mark David Spence, *Dispossessing the Wilderness: Indian Removal and the Making of the National Parks* (New York: Oxford University Press, 1999).

18. Qtd. in "Introduction," in *Indigenous Environmental Justice*, ed. Karen Jarrett-Snider and Marianne O. Nielsen (Tucson: University of Arizona Press, 2020), 10.

19. Guy Reynolds, *Apostles of Modernity: American Writers in the Age of Development* (Lincoln: University of Nebraska Press, 2008), 16.

20. John Hector St. John de Crèvecoeur, *Letters from an American Farmer and Sketches of Eighteenth-Century America* (New York: Penguin, 1986), 77.

21. Ibid., 76–77.

22. Thomas Jefferson, *Notes on the State of Virginia*, ed. William Peden (New York: Norton, 1956), 164–65.

23. George Catlin, *North American Indians* (New York: Penguin, 1989), 263.

24. Ibid., 4.

25. Ibid., 61.

26. Ibid., 61 (emphasis added).

27. Ibid., 263 (emphasis in original).

28. Ibid., 264.

29. Andrew C. Isenberg, *The Destruction of Bison: An Environmental History, 1750–1920* (New York: Cambridge University Press, 2000), 44. For a comprehensive history of the development of "classic" nomadic cultures of the Great Plains, see James Wilson, *The Earth Shall Weep: A History of Native America* (New York: Grove, 1998).

30. Ibid., 62.

31. Ibid., 74.

32. Catlin, *North American Indians*, 262–63 (emphasis added).

33. Qtd. in Richard Manning, *Grassland: The History, Biology, Politics, and Promise of the American Prairie* (New York: Penguin, 1995), 99.

34. Josiah Gregg, *The Commerce of the Prairies* (New York: Henry G. Langley, 1844), 192.

35. John L. O'Sullivan, "Annexation," *United States Magazine and Democratic Review* 18 (1845): 5.

36. The religious undertones of "manifest destiny" align it with the fifteenth-century Doctrine of Discovery, the moral justification used by Europeans to defend colonization

and to promote the "discovery" of new lands. As Jarrett-Snider explains, "From the beginning of civilization, Native peoples were considered uncivilized by virtue of the fact that they were not Christians. . . . The ideas of Indians as 'heathens' became institutionalized into federal Indian policy from the birth of the United States" (38). Their status as "heathens" further bolstered Euro-American claims about the inferiority and expendability of Native lives. For more on the correlation between the Doctrine of Discovery and Indigenous environmental justice, see Gilio-Whitaker, *As Long as the Grass Grows*, 56.

37. Andrew Menard, "Striking a Line through the Great American Desert," *Journal of American Studies* 45 (2011): 276.

38. Ibid., 268.

39. Ibid., 268.

40. Charles Dana Wilber, *The Great Valleys and Prairies of Nebraska and the Northwest* (Omaha, NE: Daily Republican Print, 1881), 70–71 (emphasis added).

41. Manning, *Rewilding the West*, 89.

42. Manning (*Rewilding the West*, 89) notes that one of the ironies behind the illegitimacy of the dryland farming theory was that Campbell "bought a large dryland farm in Montana and eventually went broke, just as did most who tried his system."

43. Isenberg, *Destruction of Bison*, 130.

44. Mari Sandoz, *The Buffalo Hunters: The Story of the Hide Men*, 2nd ed. (Lincoln, NE: Bison, 1978), 88.

45. See Isenberg, *Destruction of Bison*, 129.

46. Sandoz, *Buffalo Hunters*, 173.

47. Ibid., 173.

48. It is important to acknowledge here that the Plains Indians themselves were also complicit to some degree in the eradication of bison during the 1870s and 1880s; though they were compelled to do so by the increased demand for bison, many Native bison hunters partook in the wasteful hunts that led to the depletion of the species. This is a point that Isenberg stresses throughout his history (see, for example, *Destruction of Bison*, 103–9).

49. Manning, *Rewilding the West*, 38.

50. Isenberg, *Destruction of Bison*, 129.

51. Ibid., 129.

52. Ibid., 105.

53. Ibid., 130.

54. Isenberg, *Destruction of Bison*, 160–62.

55. Gilio-Whitaker, *As Long as the Grass Grows*, 58.

56. Nielsen, *Disability History*, 99.

57. Ibid., 51.

58. Zitkala-Ša, *American Indian Stories* (Lincoln, NE: Bison, 1985), 54, 57–59.

59. Ibid., 76.

60. Ibid., 65, 66, 56.

61. Ibid., 97.

13

The (Un)Making of Voice

Nuclear Colonialism, Disability, and Toxic
Environmentalism in Marshallese Music

JESSICA A. SCHWARTZ

This essay is organized around Marshallese songs, which I refer to as "radiation songs" because they help me discuss what I call the (un)making of voices in the *longue durée* of colonialism. I examine contemporary musical performances to trace the biopolitical controls placed on the voice whereby some voices are positioned to speak over and for others per representative democracy, coded in moralized terms of "harmony." In the aftermath of World War II, the United States promoted the United Nations as an organization to "harmonize" the recently decolonized nations. The Republic of the Marshall Islands (RMI) has been officially sovereign from the United Nations Trust Territory of the Pacific Islands, administered by the United States, since the 1986 joint signing of the Compact of Free Association (COFA). The COFA was part of the broader Pacific independence movement that included nuclear demilitarization. However, the Marshall Islands, which has been subject to centuries of colonialism, including nuclear colonialism, remains bound to the U.S. nuclear military projects. As Sebastian F. Braun writes in "Imagining Un-Imagined Communities," "Part of every nationalistic program has to be the silencing of heterogeneous voices, to render the harmony—or, depending on the perspective, cacophony—of historically diverse voices into a repetitive monotone and monologue."[1] In processes of harmonization, some voices are "made" or made to matter, materialize, or be heard and others are not. U.S. military projects, the COFA, and legacies of (nuclear) colonialism have provided the structural means for ordering the "political" from the "environment" and the "public" from the "private" in gendered, racialized ways that are at the core of the capitalist, ablest system. This essay draws on songs to contemplate compulsory vocal disability or how political voices come to be heard (or not) by unpacking generational injustice as environmental injustice—where injustice is the perpetuation of colonial hierarchical ordering that is paradoxically referred to as harmony (in the pursuit of justice). European notions of harmony or order have been part of colonial governance and extend from the ordering of the environment (e.g., copra plantations in the Marshall Islands) through the ordering of people (and their labor) in corporate structures. The Global South has been made through disabling bodies and voices in ways that make their subjugated, silenced position (of humans and nonhumans) in support of the Global North. For Indigenous communities, this process has been the forceful reordering of human and nonhuman communities into systematic difference.[2]

"Global harmony" was an ideal, a geopolitical social theory conceptualized by the United States—the architects of the "new world order"—as they considered immigration, decolonization, and media presence following World War II.[3] Referencing Michel Foucault's *The Order of Things* (1970), Christopher Hight argues that harmony "can be read as integral to the story of racial representation."[4] Following Jacques Attali, he writes that harmony "is based on proportional ratios between units' places on a single axis of variation (pitch), an organic unity of these increments in both pitch and time, and a rich mathematics of their combinations in whole units. This harmonic system," Hight contends, "contributed to the conceptual organization of the colonial."[5] From 1946 through 1958, the United States detonated sixty-seven nuclear weapons at Bikini Atoll and Enewetak Atoll in the northern and western part of the RMI, an archipelago in the north-central Pacific Ocean. The radioactivity did not stay in those atolls. It spread throughout the country and throughout the world. In 1954, Castle Bravo, the largest thermonuclear weapon detonated by the United States, became known as a nuclear catastrophe for the radiation it unleashed, prompting fears worldwide. Given the large media attention paid to the Bravo story, Bikinians and their neighbors, the Rongelapese, who were showered with radioactive debris and left for nearly two days on their atoll until the United States relocated them, have become some of the most vocal Marshallese communities in the push for nuclear justice.

Political independence from the United States has a limited meaning; the RMI asserted its constitutional independence in 1979, and yet, the U.S. military retains its lease of Kwajalein and strategic denial over the archipelagic country. RMI citizens can move, live, and work "freely" in the United States without a special visa, and the United States provides economic support. Legal theorists have distinguished between the "classic protectorate" and "the contemporary associate" by explaining that in the former arrangement, only the purview of the elite would have mattered; in the contemporary arrangement, "the demand for a plebiscite or some other reliable consultation of popular will indicates that dispositions of territorial communities can be effected lawfully only with the free and informed consent of the members of that community."[6] In a contemporary association, like COFA, "form is not determinative: the lawfulness of particular associations is determined by content and not form."[7] I offer a critical, musicological approach to decolonization along the lines of provincializing musical harmony through listening to interruptions in form that signal differently comprised content that challenges the biopolitical split of voice. The harmonization of "the environment" as "property" shapes atoll groups' pursuits for nuclear justice; humans learn to work and speak over the land. Geopolitics and musical harmony are formal means of relating or engaging. Songs are often approached as consent forms to listen in particular ways.

Since Marshallese songs are shaped by the hymns, national anthems, folk songs, and popular music brought during the colonial, missionary, postwar, and independence periods, when non-Marshallese audiences listen, they do so with an affective sociality shaped by generational orientations, behavioral etiquette, and expectations—as well as assumptions concerning how care, protection, and kindness manifest as feelings of empathy. As such, Western musical harmony is heard as the structure of these expressive gestures; with it, there are certain assumptions made about how to listen to songs and how to approach singers. Intercultural listening is part of the persistence of nuclear coloniality where domination is wrought through the insensible splits that create centers (of emotion, attention, focus, atolls) and peripheries (where some feelings and groups are excised). These disconnections then become part of the aesthetic experience of listening in political justice movements and feeling empathy or other emotions from the affective sociality engendered. I draw on Allen Feldman's concept of "*cultural anaesthesia*," or what he defines as "the banishment of disconcerting, discordant and anarchic sensory practices and agents that undermine the normalizing and often silent premises of everyday life."[8] Songs amplify the silenced sensory practices that have been subject to processual dis-ablement (temporal such that it is rendered invisible) because they are deemed neither efficient, profitable, nor coherent within the language or law of the capitalist state, which has its hierarchical propertied ways of managing the environment.

I spent two years in the Marshall Islands (2008–2010) and have been working with Marshallese of the diaspora in the United States since then, including on nuclear issues. I focus on how Marshallese songs resound the possibilities, limits, and challenges of intercultural communication, as a colonial legacy, with respect to hearing disability. Hearing necessitates listening, or attunements to circumstances and how they have changed (here, for example, due to radiation). Many studies understand hearing as a precondition for listening:

to borrow from Jonathan Sterne, "listening requires hearing but is not simply reducible to hearing."[9] I would offer the same about hearing: hearing requires listening but is not simply reducible to listening. By suggesting that hearing requires space and time to perceive vibratory forces and begin to register them anew (through critical listening and sensing practices), this work upends the commonplace assumption that maintains hearing *a priori* to listening, which is predicated on modernity's positivistic and individualistic orientation. This orientation is crucial for a discussion concerning the listening-hearing interplay that is constitutive in the law, language, and contingent spacings through which individuals and individuation of dis-ability becomes produced, over time in ways that are insensible to modern temporal constructs. Although these changes might be insensible to modern temporal values through which humans make sense of and order their lifetimes—seconds, hours, days, months, years—the "voices" of nonhumans, or that which has been relegated to the voiceless environment, resound in movements that are shared, like human voices, between living entities. Musical movements help people hear that which has been relegated to the surrounds, excesses, or environment through colonial hierarchical operations, but this requires listening beyond the individualized structure of the self, the ear, and the voice that are bound in ableist performances of politics. Songs resound temporal means of coloniality that become mapped from the colonial power to the reproductive bodies of women and the environment. Here, reproductive management is equated with protection, a mode of "care" or oversight, within masculine militarization and patriarchal decision-making structures that are, for all intents and purposes, arms-strong, androcentric, and optically oriented feedback loops of textual reification.

I trace codification of Western, tonal harmony as a pitch-based mechanism, through which singers' voices are ordered through gendered constructs (e.g., SATB) and in racialized hierarchies through which colonial dispossession and religious conversion (i.e., civilizing missions) were justified. As Aleksey Nikolsky et al. have explored, "Rationally defined pitches have made the corresponding music practices rely on the frequency aspect. Civilizations that cultivated frequency-based music imposed their influence on the music cultures of neighboring peoples. On a global scale, this must have resulted in a steady decline of the alternative form of TO [tonal organization] that was based on timbre."[10] Timbre, the authors explain, places an emphasis on relations, such as that of the mother–child and human–nonhuman. Through such relations, unique personalized realizations of these relations manifest, vocally. Pitches are individualized (notes) and affirm the modern-bounded notion of the individual and individuated identity that can also be uniform. Nonhuman sounds, or voices, inform human movements. They literally inform humans' decision-making, and, in this instance, I show how songs archive nonhuman sounds—from the winds to the oceans to the bomb to pills—and can therefore be significant means of extending and expanding American-ized hearing spaces, such as the courts, modern media, and education. I listen to songs to respect Marshallese indigenous, matrilineal sense-making, which comes from customary practices of land tenure and lineage (rather than the modern law), without simply folding Marshallese matrilineal voices into Western, colonial institutional structures.

"Forever Marshall Islands"

"Forever Marshall Islands," parenthetically "Forever Marshalls," is the RMI's national anthem; it was adopted in 1991, when the RMI officially entered the United Nations. The musical and geopolitical harmonization of the archipel-ago are therefore related in material reification. Political independence for the Marshall Islands also meant a break from what would become the Fed-erated States of Micronesia. First President, Iroijlaplap (paramount chief) Amata Kabua, who composed the words and music for the national anthem, revised in 1995, led the party invested in the political "Break Away" or "Sail Away" leading up to the 1979 Marshallese constitutional declaration of its independence. Kabua inherited the colonial power or title of paramount chief that was conferred to his ancestor during the German administration. He codified customary law and was able to profit from the monies paid by the United States to lease Kwajalein Atoll and for nuclear compensation. Dissent-ing parties, such as atoll communities most impacted by nuclear testing or that had lingering ties with the United States (through missionization, for ex-ample) did not want to "break" with the United States in the ways the COFA outlines. The COFA is a document that stages history and politics to mani-fest through the discursive delineation of "nuclear affected" atolls that reify nuclear violence through inscriptions of (financial) "settlements" whereby the United States assumes "responsibility" for the damages done by nuclear testing with a lump-sum payment that is said to cover all nuclear "past, present, and future." Whereas atoll polities could submit claims against the United States prior to the COFA, as I will discuss in more detail, the terms of the COFA make it so the RMI is the political intermediary, which is a key part of neo-colonial arrangements. I provide a brief history of the national anthems in the short period of the country's independence to move to "radiation songs," which detail that, although "land" is represented as the foundation, the ac-tual treatment of the land and people through which the national imaginary emerges is predicated on environmental disablement that is formally written out of official modes of political representation and become effaced when women or "non-nuclear affected" atolls groups aim to share their lived ex-periences with the disabling force of the U.S. military.

Marshallese national belonging, as a harmonizing project, evinces the coproduction of the environment and disability through the patriarchal sociality that orients androcentric, nationalistic listening in the broader geopolitical milieu. "Forever Marshall Islands" and the anthem it replaced, "Ij Iọkwe Ḷọk Aelōñ Eo Aō" ("I Love My Islands/Atolls"), frame the conversation on how the (un)making of voice in the colonial era is central to modern notions of progress, the individual, and mobility that are wrapped into nation-state ideologies. To perform national mobility and progress as meaningful discourses that validate the individual citizen and the nation-state, colonialism, imperialism, and globalism must reify *feelings of togetherness* as an intent of unification within unequally realized conditions. These inequitable conditions are, I maintain, wrought through structural, systematized means of disablement that are positioned in hierarchical arrangement. For example, the Republic of the Marshall Islands, as a nation-state, has developed a national identity through modern structures and media institutions; the twenty-four atoll polities have unique identities and political representation. When the RMI first achieved political independence, it marked its cohesion with the national anthem "Ij Iọkwe Ḷọk Aelōñ Eo Aō" (1979). The song moves from birth to death and speaks to love for one's homeland, heritage, and the pathways that interconnect the archipelago.

The national anthem "Forever Marshall Islands" was composed in the context of postwar decolonization and the United States's goal to "harmonize" nations through political independence and conscription into the UN as a "harmonizing" mechanism. The biopolitical line of gendered land and spirit is inscribed into the anthem as well, with reference to the Motherland and the concluding lyrics prior to the repeated chorus: "God of our forefathers, protect and bless forever Marshall Islands." Gendered protection serves as a basis of the problematic national alliance, the COFA's nuclear militarism, and the burden placed on the RMI as an intermediary to "take care" and be the "voice" for its complex national milieu, shaped through the nuclear cracks that persist precisely through the splits that allow for the utterances of "Forever Marshall Islands" to be sung in melodious harmony. What the normalization of such affective alliance does, however, is neutralize the actual processes of quotidian disablement that cease to make sense when they are silenced as the boundaries of song. These songs, performed to create feelings of togetherness and affirm a united goal, are the very means of cultural anesthesia that can be called "polite" or retain the polity through policing modern mediated modes of affective sociality that have framed history and politics in paternalistic, patriarchal, and protective hierarchies bounded on audiovisual streams and screens.

The Marshall Islands was part of the United Nations Trust Territory of the Pacific Islands (TTPI), administered by the United States from 1947 to

1986. In 1986, the Republic of the Marshall Islands was granted sovereignty under the Compact of Free Association that allowed RMI citizens to travel back and forth between the United States and the RMI "freely" and live and work in the United States without visas. The COFA provided lease payments for the military base on Kwajalein and, in Section 177, nuclear compensation for Four Atolls officially recognized by the United States and the RMI governments, even though the entire archipelago has been subject to U.S. military tests—nuclear, radiological, and biological. The Four Atolls that are considered nuclear affected are Enewetak, Rongelap, Utrik, and Bikini. Their acronym spells "ERUB," which can refer to the sound of the bomb (also, erūp) and to something that is "broken." The acronym literally marks the "bio" and "political" breaks through ecological or atoll-based demarcations through which moral and legal action coalesce. The break also marks the political split from Marshallese considered "not" nuclear affected, from the cleanup workers to nearby atolls where people recount the fallout.

In 2004, the U.S. Congress, under the George W. Bush administration, dismissed the RMI's Changed Circumstances Petition, which was part of Section 177 of the COFA. Section 177 outlined four nuclear-affected atolls, established a Nuclear Claims Tribunal (NCT), and "granted $150 million as part of a 'full and final settlement' of legal claims against the U.S. government, and provided for possible additional compensation, if loss or damages to persons or property arose or were discovered that could not reasonably have been identified as of the effective date of the agreement, and if such injuries rendered the provisions of the Compact 'manifestly inadequate.'"[11] The Four Atolls have also been stigmatized within their nation, and they have had to labor for the RMI government to maintain moral pressure on the U.S. government and American visitors in speech and song. With the COFA, the RMI must be the petitioning intermediary to request additional compensation through a stipulation in the COFA called the Changed Circumstances Petition (CCP), which specifies that nuclear issues are a political rather than legal question to be adjudicated by the U.S. Congress based on the scientific evidence of whether additional funds are warranted for additional information (changed circumstances) with respect to "injuries," "persons," and "damages" to "property" (land/environment): "The Petition requests additional compensation for *personal injuries* and *property damages* and restoration costs, medical care programs, health services infrastructure and training, and radiological monitoring."[12]

As Rebecca M. Herzig proposed, "Battles over whose suffering gets to matter have been waged, in large part, over who is authorized to speak about natural facts."[13] The submitted CCP argued that there was a wider breadth of radioactive damages than known at the time of the COFA signing, but Congress asserted that there was no legal basis for additional compensation. The

RMI's submission of the CCP came from momentum garnered around the mid-1990s declassification of Department of Energy records, which included papers that showed how Marshallese from different atoll communities—in particular, Rongelap and Bikini atolls—were subject to human radiation experiments. While humans were being experimented on without their knowledge or consent, American scientists were using their homelands as laboratories in the reification of new "ecological" and "ecosystems" languages that would come to frame how the environment and environmental injustice (activism) is approached in our contemporary moment.[14] In short, both "person" and "property"—split—have been appreciated in U.S. nuclear coloniality (nuclear colonialism, proper, and COFA neocolonialism) as the raw materials of U.S. geopolitical supremacy by defining the parameters of who and what can speak and for whom.

Teresia K. Teaiwa has argued that colonial domination in the Pacific divided men and women, amplifying the former while silencing the latter. Her aptly titled essay, "US Colonialism and Micronesian Women Activists," addresses the gendered political dichotomy through the split of the public and private, wherein domestic decision-making is equally as important politically as public decision-making. Teaiwa, who has written poetry through which neological frameworks for gendered equity among violence manifest embodied empowerment, speaks to women's activistic work that spans the public and private; yet, she is cautious to valorize the public as the end goal for the inclusion of women or their political empowerment, and she provides an incisive critique about the politically, socially, and economically consequential decision-making that has been privatized or domesticated and thus materially devalued along with the bodies that labor within such spaces. Stressing the Pacific gender roles distorted by centuries of colonialism that shift Pacific customary values of complementarity to equality between the sexes, Teaiwa concludes, "A woman-centered view of history and politics is vital for accurate understanding of the power dynamics and change involved in colonialism."[15] Following Teaiwa's provocation to approach history and politics by displacing the ableist strand of activism that is androcentric (patriarchal culture) and humancentric, I move from the patriarchal political language of the national anthem to Marshallese matrilineal poetics, embodiments, and sensibilities to contemplate U.S. nuclear colonialism's expressive legacy in contemporary U.S. neocolonial relations.

Radiation Songs

"Radiation songs" work to make invisible disability heard, or resonate, I argue, across more-than-human communities and socialities that span from the Indigenous matrilineal organizations to the political construct of the national body politic. Radiation songs amplify invisible disability through evincing breaks wrought by the "insensible" toxicity that has severed relations and, with it, voices that resound socialities. While there are Four Atolls officially recognized as nuclear affected, other atolls were irradiated as well, such as Likiep Atoll, which was acknowledged in the *Final Report of the President's Advisory Committee on Human Radiation Experiments* under the Clinton administration in 1994. I trace the resonant silences through repertoires that have not been heard in the public performances that strive for nuclear justice by sharing the radioactive movements between "person" and "environment." Such political splitting must be analyzed with the human–nonhuman splitting (person–environment) in the (un)making of voices.

Radiation songs resound American and Marshallese relations over 150 years; these relations are routed through European colonialism, Japanese imperialism, and U.S. nuclear colonialism, which was foundational in Marshallese political independence and continuing decolonizing and demilitarizing movements. Colonialism has persisted under the names postcolonial, neocolonial, and decolonization in the postwar period since the United States endeavored to distance itself from the European colonial powers. However, it is important to recognize that the same processes of categorical inscription that separate person from environment persist through geopolitical arrangements that bolster U.S. military supremacy as a patriarchal power that marginalizes groups through performances and discourses of ableness, strength, and loudness. My contribution to conversations in disability studies and on environmental justice is in listening to the singing voice in songs that trace these ongoing impacts of U.S. nuclear colonialism from nineteenth-century European colonialism and missionization of the Marshall Islands. By tracing the voice through Marshallese matrilineal poetics, bodily metaphors, and cultural values, I listen to the material grounds of disabling that are denigrated via throat-based movements that connect more-than-human communities. I argue that listening to the disembodied voice can perpetuate colonial modes of disablement that are racialized and gendered.

Julie Avril Minich explains, "Bodily metaphors used to define nations are a subject of theoretical inquiry for disability scholars, certainly, but they are relevant for scholars in any field that takes seriously the issue of political belonging."[16] The body politic can be read in terms of effaced disability as transgenerational personalization of the split from—as split in—the environment. The delineation of who is in or out (included or excluded) from the national polity or "representative body," and how, are matters of systematized disablement as much as they are outright rejection and denial; yet, it is often up to those who have been disabled in the making of the individualized person and environment, those who have been depressed by the environmental and political pressures placed on them to make sense in a senseless system (e.g., radioactive, nuclear colonialism). Minich continues, "The image of the nation as a whole, nondisabled body whose health must be protected from external pollutants justifies the political marginalization not only of immigrants but also of citizens, including those with disabilities and diseases (whose bodies challenge the image of the healthy national body) and racialized and sexual minorities (whose claims to social and political rights are seen to imperil national unity)."[17]

Sound studies scholarship has shown how the individuation of the senses has been central to colonization and capitalist economies (able-bodied worker). Similarly, the development of a modern nation, the national public sphere, and representative democracy have depended on the individuation of the voice that is articulated as identity. The political voice is meant to be relational between the "head" and "body"; however, the political voice is often dominated by those persons that represent the "head" or the able-minded visionary, auditor, and adjudicator to design and regulate "the environment," while the "body" (historically, colonized, enslaved, in indentured servitude, and paid low-wage) labors to build it according to the blueprint and moves through it as per the laws (rules and codes) established by the "heads" of state (ideological institutions). Colonialism functioned through networked intermediaries that imposed uniform models, such as laws, onto established cultural systems as means of domination. The normative liberal subject, whose voice was projected as law, was positioned as the center of the colonial world with all else being peripheral. Taking the human—a western European culturally Protestant/secular or "white" man of means—as center, the construct of the human itself as distinct from environment, race, and gender became the prominent means to debase and justify dispossession through which capitalistic and colonial accruals happened.

The separation of the senses is corollary to the separation of classes from a two-tier, complementary (reciprocal) relation (chiefs and commoners) to the nineteenth-century development of the German copra trade in the Marshall Islands, which saw the formation of a distinct elite class, an intermediary class, and a working class. The German copra trade was based from Jaluit Atoll in the southern Marshall Islands. Anglo-American Protestant missionaries' aims to convert commoners through humancentric hymn singing, Bible recitation, and education in Western-style schools (reading, writing, arithmetic) were also in the southern atolls. The German colonial administration and Anglo-American Protestant missionaries, followed by Japanese imperial rule through the end of World War II, proved foundational in U.S. postwar declarations of victory that preceded nuclear colonialism of the Marshall Islands. The Truman administration encouraged troops to instrumentalize the missionaries' work to gain the trust and respect of Marshallese through hymn singing and religious reference. Affective alliance formalizes hearing through listening convention articulated to the assumed in-common sensibility, here musical form (predicated on pitch). When we shift to the actual contents of the songs, the insidious movements of raw materials of nuclear injustice through which Marshallese singers must prove suffering and request redress are amplified.

The two songs I discuss, "Kōṃṃan Baaṃ" ("Making Bombs") and "Kajjitok in Aō Nan Kwe Kiio" ("These Are My Questions for You Now") amplify the disabling mechanisms of environmental toxification through the *longue durée* of colonialism and the imposition of not being listened to or heard by the COFA government. Scholars Joseph Straus, Michael Bakan, Jessica A. Holmes, Blake Howe, and Stephanie Jensen-Moulton have approached Tobin Siebers's disability aesthetics by applying it to studies on modernism in the musical realm.[18] Music, like art, can be approached through modern notions of the individual wherein the break becomes part of a body, albeit within a cultural system, and music, like art, can be assessed from the relational perspective wherein the cultural system that delineates norms and scaled variations is also relational. My feeling is that it is at the interstices of systemic relationality that we must be looking, hearing, feeling, touching, tasting, smelling, and otherwise engaging synesthetic sensibilities to thoroughly address the meaningful practices—as part of the colonial (modern) *longue durée*—of disablement that become normalized into quotidian "injustice," on the one hand, and "environmental issues," on the other. Radiation songs amplify the so-called exceptional means of transgenerational disablement and their morphic modulations into everyday protocol (e.g., working, pilltaking, lack of sleep, underemployment, nightmares). Disability, then, must be appreciated as the disabling wear and tear on bodies that are intimately connected to one another that come apart at the seams when the interlocutions are violated. By interlocutions, I refer to the interlocking means of any community that reifies it as such—communication as transgenerational process—through caring for and being cared for.

"Kōṃṃan Baaṃ" ("Making Bombs")

The nuclear issues have contributed to the Marshallese popular musical repertoire. There is even a Marshallese nursery rhyme from the nuclear testing period. . . . The nursery rhyme is called "*Kōṃṃan Baaṃ*" ("Making Bombs"). It's from Likiep. I grew up hearing it on Likiep, and I am sure that most youngsters in the Northern Marshalls will remember it. When the teachers' training program was set up, I think the song they were supposed to be working with was [called] "Making Farms" or "Gardens," but it turned up "Making Bombs." When it came up to the outer islands, everybody understood it as a "making bomb song" because it was during the bomb-testing period.[19]

"Kōṃṃan Baaṃ" tells the story of colonial transits through radioactive biopolitics; farms turn to radioactive plantations on which all bodies labor while no crops are planted and no gardens grow. A children's nursery rhyme, accompanied by silent, still choreography, shares how radiation animates the voice by disabling interconnected bodies. I read "Kōṃṃan Baaṃ" as sonic history that depicts how sensorial entrainment works in the "invisible" disabling practices of the U.S. military—here, specifically in the (Northern) Marshall Islands, as nuclear colony. I use the parenthetical (Northern) since the northern Marshall Islands, as my interlocutor explained, were most impacted by Bravo's fallout, even though it reached the entirety of the Marshall Islands materially, politically, and culturally—changing the entire foundation from which independence was realized. Marking the "Northern" atolls, however, leads to an important discussion about the recent colonial history (150 years) and missionization of the archipelago. By tracing the connection between my interlocutor's genealogical connection to Likiep Atoll from the German period onward, the U.S. colonial mode of exclusion and inclusion (disablement and enablement) through center-peripheral relations, as it is mapped onto political-environmental relations mediated by the human voice, is amplified.

The dispiriting labor of those forced to work in the U.S. nuclear colony can be heard in "Kōṃṃan Baaṃ" ("Making Bombs"), which the late Senator Tony deBrum shared with me. DeBrum had been on Likiep when he sang this with his peers as a youth. Likiep is not part of the officially designated nuclear-affected atolls under COFA's Section 177: Nuclear Affected Atolls (Four Atolls) that would enable it to have nuclear compensation and medical benefits from the United States. The song's collective memory, which contains the melody from a Filipino song about planting rice, connects the Marshall Islands to the Philippines, recalling the "militarized currents" of the Asia-Pacific region.[20] The modified lyrics speak to the insidious movements that connect the Filipino and Marshallese populations as laborers in American imperial movements of bodies across the Asia-Pacific region, connecting the imperial movements to the toxic movements of breath, food, and echoes of the bomb through the throat into and out from the bodies of Marshallese.

Children's nursery rhymes are meant to be fun and educational, and the song was indeed educational. This song, at the level of the lyrics and beyond in its communicative and gestural capacities, was forced to accommodate the consequences of nuclear testing. It tells a story of a violent presence (radiation) and the restructuring of life worlds caused by the radiation. The children's bodies as they danced and their voices as they sang were forced to "make bomb." The activity of "making bomb" was all-consuming. Marshallese had to learn how to register new sensorial experiences without information from the U.S. government on the impact of radiation, which is insensible in and of itself. They had to learn how to deal with or attempt to assuage their suffering, and they had to learn how to articulate this suffering, which is fundamentally impossible.

Senator deBrum's performance of "Kōṃṃan Baaṃ" uncovers the removal of the Marshallese from their indigenous way of life—that is, existing as a subsistence-based economy and tending to the land—and places them as *central* in the modernizing process. The Marshallese are the ones who "make" the bombs insofar as they have created the spaces (land and corporeal) for the "testing" to occur. This entails the positioning of human voice and labor over the land. Marshallese have expressed in a myriad of ways how deeply connected they feel to the land, since the land is what has allowed their lineage to survive. A Marshallese landowner said that it is not merely land but *place* (one's homeland) that is the most important thing in the world to Marshallese. Without your land, he said, you are nothing, you do not exist. Land rights and inheritance are based on kinship systems, or lineage (*bwij*). Land rights come from the mother's *bwij* (*bwije-* is the word for "navel" and *bwijen* is the word for "umbilical cord"), but "within the *bwij*, both matrilineal and patrilineal heirs possessed land rights." There are also matriclans (*jowi*) in which the members of various related *bwij* can "trace their ancestry back to a single woman," and the name of the *jowi* "recalls . . . the place of origin." The relationship between women and the responsibility to protect the land and names is therefore important in Marshallese sociality and cultural authority; yet, protection in U.S. terms deals with militarism, bombs, and paternalistic decision-making that critically excise "reason" from the "rational" or proportional movements of harmonized life and law.

The gendered violence from dislocation emerges in the absence of matrilineal expression where "making" or producing dominates. Children were now learning how to show their pain in song and choreograph a dance instead of learning how to plant the foods that comprise the neatly ordered gardens that had been imposed in the ordering of the land as civilization. The song also emphasizes the immobility of the children, "the bomb has frozen your limbs." What is *of* the land, the ants, are referenced only in the metaphorical capacity—they are associated with pain. The land, instead of belonging to the normal register of a place that protects and provides, is now a place that is contaminated and causes pain as well as the slow violence of communal and matrilineal expressive disablement.

Senator deBrum also explained that the melody was from a Filipino song. Interspersed in his description of the song were memories of the physical pain and other issues related to nuclear testing. Senator deBrum performed the song, recalling such memories and issues. In place of the Filipino melody, his performance sounded like a Marshallese chant, a *roro*. Mary E. Lawson Burke and Barbara B. Smith note that "some older people perform historical narratives (*bwebwenato*), interspersed with brief *roro* highlighting important moments in the story." *Roro* are recited in a rhythmically consistent fashion. They have been described as progressing stepwise or as monotonic, but on close listen, the chants have expressive microtonal variations and cadential patterns; they are performed "initially slowly, but usually ending hurriedly with a rising inflection."

Western musical scholarship, like law and international geopolitics, aims to harmonize or place into pitched relations, sound-based movements. While I do not know whether Senator deBrum attempted to create a *roro* from the nursery rhyme or utilized the function of the *roro* or was doing something different is not the point. The point is that deBrum's timbral attunements to the matrilineal breaks, the pain and suffering, and the stillness felt reflected in the performance. *Roro* attune Marshallese to nonhuman socialities and more-than-human communities through which they can make sense of their positionality.

Senator deBrum's performance trailed off into a description of the final lines of the lyrics:

> During the testing, I think it was one of the effects, I have no proof for it, but *kinaḷnaḷ* is common among students at Holy Rosary. Sometimes we would show up for school and a lot of the kids would complain of these *kinaḷnaḷ* pains in their bones, and they would be administered aspirin or APC—half tablet. But, *kinaḷnaḷ*, that occurs in the song.

The notion that there is "no proof" resounds the fact that the Marshallese must continue to "make [the effects of] bomb" known and to search for ways to summon strength and creativity to "prove" they deserve redress. There is proof, however. As deBrum writes, it is *in the song*: the dis-abling mechanisms that have rendered musical performance to that which exists outside the law or as part of political movements and moral pressure. That the content of the song *isn't proof* challenges the legal theories that not only speak of COFA consent but that content is more important than form. If all things are indeed just, then the form of the song should not belie its content as the sonic history or archival wealth of evidence, or proof, of materials through which nonhuman bodies move in ways that profit the nuclear colonial power—from APC tablets to learning in schools how to make gardens or bombs. The problematic framing of the COFA and the CCP is that "radiation"—as a scientific fact—becomes the basis of what "nuclear damages" are judged on through the split terms of personal injury and property damages. Such objectification excises the real profit making in colonial organization that has become the military-industrial complex, and it obfuscates the disabling mechanisms of the military in the quotidian modes of humiliation, debasement, and devaluation that enervate groups from memory and sustained, inventive political action. When they are not protected by the law, they are seen as trying to manipulate it; "illegal" proof becomes an affront to the system, which has figured colonized subjects as criminals in need of policing and developing.

Marshallese labor under nuclear colonialism—while denied through the passivity articulated or relegated to environmental devastation, property damage, or individual injury—as an accident, is proven in songs like "Kōṃṃan Baaṃ" because they are the ongoing labor in the production of nuclear knowledge. The song shares how Marshallese have labored or been active in "making" the bomb precisely through the freezing of their bodies and language, as means of making sense of suffering. In the middle of the song is a question, "for what is their suffering?" This question, both literal and rhetorical, is neither of the past nor present, but it is of both—connecting the central role of the Marshallese to the power of the Americans, in dissent of their role as passive victims. Over the course of the performance, the recitation can be relistened to with musical form in mind as means of rethinking the content—the freezing of bodies that are perpetually laboring in their "growing pains" for the nuclear power—through relational movements of more-than-human communities that have been colonized not only by radiation but pharmaceutical corporations, educational institutions, political systems, communications systems, and all other means of wearing the Native bodies and their means of empowerment through relations with the land. In the Cold War that afforded the United States such geopolitical clout, it was the Marshallese who made the bombs, through the transformation of *their* ancestral lands and bodies into factory-style production lines where the making of bombs never stops. And it is sustained through biopolitical inscription of voicelessness per the COFA's terms.

Disability becomes personalized and collectivized through the making of toxic environments, yet the individualization of communication and privatization of listening, as hearing, recursively marginalizes nondominant expressions and therefore access to participation in decision-making when it comes to health and healing from environmental, as social, toxification. "Dis-ability, as the literature points out, is not in the individual but in social and spatial conditions that limit social inclusion," writes Victor M. Torres-Vélez.[21] Adding to Torres-Vélez's insights, I want to add that dis-ability is also in the temporal conditions that limit social inclusion. Songs are significant means of thinking the interstices of dis-ability and the environment through the *longue durée* processes of colonialism precisely because they demarcate stages from which to hear the passage of time that structure the spatial and social conditions of inclusion and exclusion. This essay traces the sounds of bombs and their often-insensible yields over time from the postwar through the present to contemplate neocolonial foundations; it does so through the singing voice, structured by pitch-based harmony, to contemplate colonial and missionary foundations of nuclear colonial-as-neocolonial foundations. In doing so, it dialogues critical Indigenous studies with disability studies to rethink the political identifications of "Indigenous" and "disabled" from the environmental justice standpoint that, as a matter of non-Western space-time, shifts the individual being disabled to the generational process of relations, specifically in terms of the voice or coming to voice disablement.

Unheard voices can be gestured to in performances that use colonial structures as platforms, and yet, these platforms cannot overdetermine or dis-able non-Western, relational perceptual, affective, emotional, and political modes of empowerment. Listening to hear matrilineal modes of empowerment—that is, the unheard movements of what has been reduced to the environment or the periphery (including women from politics)—demands hearing timbral organization of harmonies. Timbral organization is not simply another way of listening for sound quality or an auxiliary "tone color" that can be stripped from the objective pitch; the making of it as excess is precisely the work of colonial harmonization. Both "Kōṃṃan Baaṃ" and "Kajjitok" share the equivocal split between indigenous attunements to more-than-human sociality through timbral organizing mechanisms, which is throat-based singing, and attunements to universal objects through which subjects "come to voice" in imperial Western, pitch-based harmony. The throat, in Marshallese bodily metaphors, is akin to the heart insofar as it is considered the seat of emotion; however, the throat speaks to the more-than-human movements and socialities that challenge the individualization of disability (personal injury) and environment (property damage) from "radiation" as a scientific fact. Nuclear colonialism must be approached in a much more capacious way where the actual means of accumulation through movements—musical and otherwise—are dialogued. These two songs attune listeners to what can and cannot be heard within the limits of COFA neocoloniality.

"These Are My Questions for You Now"

Radiation has compelled movements, from outmigration from individual atolls and the Marshall Islands to the energetic transference that becomes perceived as cellular mutation to the songs that singers have composed to stage their voices through layers of voicelessness. Voice and voicelessness are relational, like radiation and disability, and they become shared with and mapped onto future generations' modalities of belonging. In the Marshall Islands, women had to contend with the embodiment of compounded voicelessness when they miscarried or when their children were born with physical and mental disabilities, diseases, and deformities—or when they had stillborn deliveries (deaths) or the birthing of tumors (instead of a newborn). The privatization of such illness, which was continually denied by U.S. doctors and scientists due to the "classified" research (and who left Rongelapese on their highly contaminated atoll), was in part possible because the United States relocated Rongelapese back to their irradiated homeland that was relatively further from the political capital, Western medical care, and news outlets or a public space to share concerns. The return of the Rongelapese community created a reperipheralization or a rereduction to the environmental surrounds, meaning a reinscription of the insensible radiation that rendered Rongelapese bodies within their environs, insensible or nonsense, due to the pain and suffering they would experience that was not being accounted for or discussed by the nuclear colonial power that, for the most part, silently demanded Rongelapese labor without consent, compensation, care, or concern.

The RMI officially marks its complex nuclear legacy with commemorative reflection, diplomatic engagement, and performances on contemporary nuclear issues on March 1. The RMI's annual holiday has borne different names over the years, such as Memorial Day, Nuclear Victims' and Survivors' Remembrance Day (NVSRD), Bravo Day, and Nuclear Remembrance Day. The event moves the discourse from "survivor" and "victim" to how Marshallese remember and how public memory can serve in remediating the "nuclear legacy" through the frame of a nuclear future by focusing on how nuclear damages have yet to be equitably resolved and prevented. For now, every day brings with it persistent questions left unanswered; confusion and unrest not quelled; and medical conditions, illness, and constant trips to the hospital and funerals, marking the realities of shortened life spans, compromised futures at the expense of the postwar "booming" American population, and quality of life, which continues with, for example, the Americans' demands for ready-made poultry. *Every day* is Nuclear Remembrance Day. Its memory cannot be bound, stepped away from, or forced into a calendar day.

I attended NVSRD (2009) in Majuro, the RMI capital. The Rongelapese ladies' group Iju in Eañ (North Star) performed. Iju in Eañ was initiated by the Rongelapese women when they were displaced to Majuro. Iju in Eañ is a metaphor for Rongelap, in the North, that guides them and orients them in their struggles. Away from their customary homeland, they were subject to new rules, laws, and regulations. They watched as the men went without employment, causing hardship for the entire community. The Rongelapese women came together to guide their community and share their struggles in political outreach. "Kajjitok," composed in 2008, was inspired by political silencing of Rongelapese women and Utrikese women. When the U.S. Department of Energy officials visited the RMI, they met in an official capacity with the RMI government. When the women asked to be present for the meeting, so that their concerns could be addressed, their request was declined. They realized they would have to compile their questions and health concerns as well as detail the repercussions in a way that would help the Department of Energy hear them. As Lijon, a Rongelapese female composer, antinuclear activist, and "good politician" in her words, explained, she had a host of questions that she heard resonate with her sisters, referring to the women in her atoll community and the Utrikese community, younger and older. These Marshallese communities have a long history with the Department of Energy, previously the Atomic Energy Commission. When it comes to asking questions and not being heard, they have been subject to race-based and gender bias in medical examinations and ignored time and again as political persons—their "humanity" valued only insofar as they were used, as human test subjects, or human bodies to provide the raw materials for science in human radiation experiments.[22]

Songs, therefore, refuse being ignored and treated like "humans" solely based on being subject to the male medical gaze without an appreciation of Marshallese voices and all that resonates in these voices (e.g., the women's intelligence, knowledge, and sensibilities). Lijon had, like her sisters, suffered greatly from U.S. nuclear testing, which had been with her since she was a small child. She had been irradiated by Bravo's fallout when she was eight years old during a birthday picnic with her grandparents. Along with her atoll family, the Rongelapese, she was taken to Kwajalein Atoll. Rongelapese were put in camps and became human radiation experiments before being returned to their highly irradiated land after a few years. In the interim, without their land, Rongelapese were without their means of health—their sustenance, exercise, inspiration, grounding, and so forth. American doctors isolated the Rongelapese from their fellow Marshallese and controlled their space-time and movements. They were fed processed foods with high sodium and sugar content and they were given American television shows and movies; otherwise, they would pace around their enclosed areas until it was time to get poked, probed, and prodded. The Rongelapese community was subject to fear, stress, and isolation; women (girls at the time) were subject to compounded humiliation because of the U.S. patriarchal culture.

The song, performed *a cappella*, begins with the statement, "These are my questions for you now, still." The word "*kiiō*" (now, still) refers to something that is happening now and that is ongoing. Here, Marshallese language remembers temporal currencies where the "now" is the "still," which refute the point-based conceptions of the "just now" that undergirds American jurisdiction and spatiotemporal controls placed around the "nuclear affected." Kiiō animates the concept of currency, and with it current and currents, that is central to hearing beyond modern temporal constructs of the now or current. Listening can be an act of denuclearization when the core of songs—that is, sound, opens from percussive attack to resonant decay into an acoustical silence—all of which are part of the more-than-human movements of nuclear culture personalized by singers. In "Kajjitok," the lyrics mark something that is current and has currency; it is present in the word and moves through them, creating value within the relational context of the song.

Radiation songs take up Marshallese legal and political petitions and give them currency. The musical petition contains the rhetorical and literal (figures of) questions, which work to engage the listener in a call to respond. The singers' lyrics give clues to what has been shared with them, as processes, that have become their lived experiences. Amid the questions are lists of medicines that become embodiments of digestive time and side-effect half-lives, like radiation, which then becomes preoccupation, concern, and medical visits. The "side-effects" are part of the full effects that enervate the women and bolster financial returns for the pharmaceutical corporations. Without sufficient responses to their calls prompted by imperial returns, the women sing that they have lost sleep—they are perpetually laboring for the neonuclear colony—and have no peace of mind, since the United States has used atomic power as means to promote peace at their expense.[23]

The reinscription of voicelessness is an internalization of shame, fear, sadness, and blame. "Toxicity, like disability, is not contained in individually bounded bodies; it circulates, altering the life chances of future generations. . . . This circulation is entrenched in social, political, economic, and environmental regulations and policies," Kelly Fritsch explains in an affirmation of disabled futurities (lives) within a broader critique that draws on feminist science studies and critical disability studies to evaluate structural intricacies of systemic disablement (exposure to environmental toxicity of pregnant women).[24] Atomic energy research, a constitutive component of U.S. national security, was allowed to be kept secret as restricted data or "private law"—the Atomic Energy Act of 1946, for example, placed a restriction on free speech (a constitutional right). That scientific research on radiation, for weapons, privileged U.S. national silence or national security and the growth of the biomedical, pharmacological corporations over the health and healing of Marshallese shows how *health* is a fraught word since, in the U.S. system, it is very much a part of the efficient, modern system that cannot appreciate the time of care. These questions amplify the continual (un)making of Marshallese matrilineal voices in their lack of being answered; they are the rhetorical fissures that perform voice-based disablement amid the women's assertion of their voice-based enablement.

Nuclear violences, which are gendered violences, strikes the Marshall Islands' matrilineal customs in which the political power was customarily afforded to women, in particular the eldest sister. Although men would "voice" the political issues in negotiations, they developed practices that founded their positional orientations in gender complementarity with the women, since the women practiced communicative mediations (listened to) with the spiritual landscape and lineage (including humans and more-than-human animate spirits). As Kristina Stege recalls, women, customarily, were given the power as *leejmaanjuri* or the peacemaker (and peace-breaker) and caretaker; "Kajjitok" resounds how Western oppositional frameworks—here the refusal of non-state-based political complementarity that maps onto the refusal of gender complementarity—has disabled their means of peacemaking. The singers' voices, as women in their roles as peacemakers or breakers, amplify how their peacefulness has been broken, such that their voices break; as peacemakers, their voices return. Over the course of the song, the interplay of voiced and unvoiced moments can be read in the context of their struggle for peace and justice, which entails being part of the decision-making process, as Marshallese women.

During Iju in Eañ's NVSRD performance of "Kajjitok," the women's harmonies began to disentangle as their voices fell in volume in a rapid domino effect. The audience immediately began to clap. The conductor, Betty, turned to the audience. As she pointed to her neck, she shook her head and said, "Ah, tyroit!" The audience applause diminished, and the women picked up the song with slight acoustical dissonance that lessened as the women approached the final cadence. The vocal aphonia, I realized, was political and a recurring physiomusical technique employed during this and other Rongelapese songs to amplify the radioactive movements that had stripped their energetic centers (thyroid, metabolism), spiritual connections (land-humans), and literal voices through layered biomedical, nutritional, and overall subjection to toxicity. The singers mark and must endure their subjection to ongoing radiation issues; they must use it to educate audiences that cannot hear and clap over this resonant space. It is in this resonant aphonic space where the framework from a future resilience (the singers sing again) or a past fullness (when the singers sang before their voices fell) to get to the "heart," as it were, of Marshallese Indigenous spiritual connectedness.

The Rongelapese were stigmatized when they tried to sing or speak, especially women, given that their voices would sound lower, like men. They were called "*ri-baam*" and shunned for fear, early on, of contracting radiation diseases. The thyroidectomies would alter their voices, with some atolls experiencing numerous extractions given their proximity to the detonations.

The thyroid can be considered part of the throat complex (*boro*), which, in Marshallese epistemologies, is an intermediary from the person and the collective spirit (the vital world). Ionizing radiation can compromise the thyroid; many Marshallese had operations on their thyroids and thyroid problems, which altered their energy, their vitality. The throat, in Marshallese body perceptions, is discussed in terms of the heart in Western body perceptions. It is the seat of the soul, the emotions, and vital currencies where things come in and out (like the heart in the circulatory system and oxygenation of blood). The heart transits, as well, in inspiration. It rests on the "inside" and needs the throat and nose to bring in air, oxygen. The throat also moves solids, liquids, tenses up and relaxes, and produces voice through the larynx, vocal folds, and resonator that is the mouth, which can be thought of as part of the throat complex. Without understanding of how radiation spreads, Marshallese were fearful of contagion through Marshallese bodies when the Rongelapese would speak with altered voices. This is because sound intimates contagion.

The U.S. government has generally refused to listen to Marshallese matrilineal, indigenous epistemic, sensible, and practical modalities of care. This does not stop the generational persistence of radiogenic disease (compounded by nuclear culture); it does not stop the radioactivity from maintaining its half-life in their homeland atoll. Radioactive toxicity endures in the materialized traces of its precarious transits as toxic material, toxic militant masculinity, and toxic ignorance of American professionals who used Marshallese women, men, and children—and their homelands—as the raw materials of projected unilateral military power to pursue space-based colonization and the colonization of the deep sea. As such, Marshallese refuse to stop generational education that takes place daily and in the NVSRD space. As pictured, young girls sing along and learn to voice their mothers, grandmothers, and aunt's timbres, albeit here, the inscription of maternal timbre is a complex of (un)making voices—it is matrilineal empowerment displaced in an energetic transference to an assertion of radioactive belonging through the nation-state that requires the political voice to proprietarily represent inscriptions that become potential entitlements: "personal injuries" (as self) and "property damages" (as homeland).

Conclusion

This essay has explored the colonial coproduction of transgenerational disablement and environmental injustices through a repertoire of radiation songs, stories, and interviews. I find these expressive platforms and our intersubjective engagements to be pivotal in reflecting on the means of Marshallese political independence from the colonial Pacific. The nation-state, as a means of harmonization, has publicly replicated the male-focused, ableist, and humancentric biopolitics of ordering (managing) life that denigrate matrilineal labor, lives, and land. Unofficial means of intercultural expression, such as commemorative events, songs, dances, slam poetry, visual arts, and storytelling afford Marshallese platforms to communicate with Americans and with each other in ways that are not overdetermined by breaks constitutive of colonialism. These breaks are realized through the discursive production and material reification of individuals in hierarchical arrangements, such that the human and nonhuman are understood within an oppositional framework and the human is afforded voice and/as ability to care for the nonhuman contingent that is thought to be passive or voiceless. Modern institutions and their specialized languages attune participants to that which is present; while they are deeply informed by the originary breaks mapped onto bodies through colonial categorical constructs such as gender and race (to justify dispossession and debasement of labor), they cannot see, hear, or touch the breaks because such categories have been normalized as part of society. It is through the officialized means of redress, then, that Marshallese disablement—as generational (un)making of voice that violently injures communities (human–nonhuman) and compels the political voice be heard in ways that make sense to Americanized adjudicative powers—ties into interlocutional domination that is realized through the silencing of nonhuman voices. Songs that resonate nuclear issues and the movements of environmental toxicity demonstrate that U.S. nuclear colonialism, although officially over with the political independence of the archipelago, is decidedly not over.

NOTES

1. Sebastian F. Braun, "Imagining Un-Imagined Communities: The Politics of Indigenous Nationalism," in *Tribal Worlds: Critical Studies in American Indian Nation Building*, ed. Brian Hosmer and Larry Nesper (Albany, NY: SUNY Press, 2013), 141.

2. I am a non-Marshallese U.S. citizen. I grapple with environmental sensitivities, chronic health issues, and disabilities. Accommodations to such issues have been difficult at times and impossible at others due to normative, institutional systems. I am sensitive to how the imposition of toxicity and formal systems create and exacerbate disabilities, particularly through the environment that in our Western society is not understood to have a voice to listen to or is not considered as an intimate part of our relational being. While I am not writing for Marshallese people, I want to draw attention to their voices and their stories because they exemplify such issues and impediments, communally and through their individual stories. I believe these are global issues that disproportionately impact BIPOC and Global South communities.

3. Y. J. Lee, "From GI Sweethearts to Lock and Lollers: *The Kim Sisters' Performances in the Early Cold War United States, 1959–67*," *Journal of Asian American Studies* 20, no. 3 (2017): 405–39, *Project MUSE*, doi:10.1353/jaas.2017.0034.

4. Christopher Hight, "Stereo Types: The Operation of Sound in the Production of Racial Identity," *Leonardo* 36, no. 1 (2003): 13.

5. Hight, "Stereo Types," 14.

6. Chimène Keitner and W. Michael Reisman, "Free Association: The United States Experience," *Texas International Law Journal* 1, no. 39 (2006): 6, accessed August 29, 2020, https://ssrn.com/abstract=933738.

7. Keitner and Reisman, "Free Association," 5.

8. Allen Feldman, "From Desert Storm to Rodney King via Ex-Yugoslavia: On Cultural Anesthesia," in *The Senses Still: Perception and Memory as Material Culture in Modernity*, ed. C. Nadia Seremetakis (Chicago: University of Chicago Press, 1994), 89.

9. Jonathan Sterne, *The Audible Past: Cultural Origins of Sound Reproduction* (Durham, NC: Duke University Press, 2003).

10. Aleksey Nikolsky, Eduard Alekseyev, Ivan Alekseev, and Varvara Dyakonova, "The Overlooked Tradition of 'Personal Music' and Its Place in the Evolution of Music," *Frontiers in Psychology* 10 (2020), doi: 10.3389/fpsyg.2019.03051.

11. Library of Congress, CRS Report for Congress, "Republic of the Marshall Islands Changed Circumstances Petition to Congress," May 16, 2005, accessed August 29, 2020, https://fas.org/sgp/crs/row/RL32811.pdf.

12. "Changed Circumstances Petition to Congress."

13. Rebecca M. Herzig, *Plucked: A History of Hair Removal* (New York: New York University Press, 2015), 5.

14. See Elizabeth M. DeLoughrey, "The Myth of Isolates: Ecosystem Ecologies in the Nuclear Pacific," ed. Godfrey Baldacchino and Erik Clark, *Cultural Geographies* 20, no. 2 (2012): 167–84.

15. Teresia K. Teaiwa, "Microwomen: US Colonialism and Micronesian Women Activists," in *The Proceedings of the Eighth Pacific History Conference*, Guam, December 1990, ed. Donald Rubinstein (Mangilao: University of Guam Press and Micronesian Area Research Center, 1992), 139.

16. Julie A. Minich, *Accessible Citizenships: Disability, Nation, and the Cultural Politics of Greater Mexico* (Philadelphia: Temple University Press, 2014), 16.

17. Minich, *Accessible Citizenships*, 16–17.

18. See Blake Howe, Stephanie Jensen-Moulton, Neil Lerner, and Joseph Straus, *The Oxford Handbook of Music and Disability Studies* (Oxford: Oxford University Press, 2015).

19. Tony deBrum, interview with author, March 4, 2010. The nursery rhyme, or song, "Kōṃṃan Baaṃ" is transcribed here in part. During the interview, it was shared in segments with commentary.

20. Setsu Shigematsu and Keith Camacho, eds., *Militarized Currents: Toward a Decolonized Future in Asia and the Pacific* (Minneapolis: University of Minnesota Press, 2010).

21. Victor M. Torres-Veléz, "Reification, Biomedicine, and Bombs: Women's Politicization in Vieques's Social Movement," in *Disability Studies and the Environmental Humanities: Toward an Eco-Crip Theory*, ed. Sarah Jaquette Ray and Jay Sibara (Lincoln: University of Nebraska Press, 2017), 333.

22. For more information on Project 4.1, the U.S. government's classified human radiation experiments, see Barbara Rose Johnston and Holly M. Barker, *Consequential Damages of Nuclear War: The Rongelap Report* (Walnut Creek, CA: Left Coast, 2008).

23. John Krige, "Atoms for Peace, Scientific Internationalism, and Scientific Intelligence," *Osiris* 21, no. 1 (2006): 161–81.

24. Kelly Fritsch, "Toxic Pregnancies: Speculative Futures, Disabling Environments, and Neoliberal Biocapital," in *Disability Studies and the Environmental Humanities: Toward an Eco-Crip Theory*, ed. Sarah Jaquette Ray and Jay Sibara (Lincoln: University of Nebraska Press, 2017), 374.

Contributors

Holly Caldwell is a scholar, writer, and editor for academic and nonfiction authors. She received her PhD in history in 2016 from the University of Delaware and has taught as an adjunct and visiting professor at Chestnut Hill College and Susquehanna University, respectively. Her current research project examines Mexico's *Escuela Nacional de Sordomudos*, the nation's first school for the Deaf, with a particular focus on public health and social welfare policies during the Porfiriato. She is author of "Surveillance, Medicine, and the Misterios de la Naturaleza: Campaigns to 'Cure' Deafness in Late Nineteenth-Century Mexico City," which appeared in *Making Surveillance States: Transnational Histories* (Robert Heynen and Emily van der Meulen, Toronto: University of Toronto Press, 2019).

Matthew J. C. Cella is an Associate Professor of English at Shippensburg University of Pennsylvania, where he is also the director of the interdisciplinary minor in Disability Studies. He is author of *Bad Land Pastoralism in Great Plains Fiction* (Iowa City: University of Iowa, 2010) and editor of *Disability and the Environment in American Literature: Toward an Ecosomatic Paradigm* (London: Lexington, 2016). His research has been published in a range of journals, including *ISLE, Journal of Rural Studies, Great Plains Quarterly*, and *Western American Literature*.

Tsitsi Chataika is the Disability Inclusion Advisor of CBM Global Disability Inclusion. She is also an Associate Professor in disability inclusion and inclusive education in the Department of Educational Foundations, University of Zimbabwe. Her research interests allow her to understand how disability intersects with rights, policy, education, gender, religion, childhood studies, poverty, development, and postcolonial theory. She is a proponent of inclusive development, universal design, and universal design learning. She is involved in several high-level national and regional (Africa) inclusive education dialogues with implications for policy and practice. She has authored several journal articles, research reports, book chapters, and policy briefs from an African perspective. Tsitsi has evaluated several inclusive education initiatives, with the view of establishing their impact in the provision of quality and equitable education. She recently completed a World Bank–commissioned scoping study on the situational analysis of albinism in Zimbabwe.

John Gulledge is Assistant Professor of English at Wittenberg University, where he teaches courses on early modern literature and disability studies. His current book project recovers the rhetorical and poetic method of *energia* in early English drama and reveals the varied ways creative invention was often patterned after encounters with disability. He is the cofounder of "The Puck Project," a Shakespeare performance and ethics program for kids facing housing insecurity in Atlanta, Georgia. You can read more of his recent work in the journal *Inscriptions* and edited volume *Inclusive Shakespeares: Identity, Pedagogy, Performance* (2023).

Nancy J. Hirschmann is Geraldine R. Segal Professor in American Social Thought and professor of Political Science and Gender, Sexuality, and Women's Studies at The University of Pennsylvania. She has served as Director of the Program on Gender, Sexuality, and Women's Studies and Vice President of the American Political Science Association. Her books include er *The Subject of Liberty: Toward a Feminist Theory of Freedom*, which won the 2004 Victoria Schuck Award from the American Political Science Association; *Gender, Class, and Freedom in Modern Political Theory*; and *Rethinking Obligation: A Feminist Method for Political Theory*, as well as several edited volumes. She has published numerous articles on domestic violence, welfare reform, Islamic veiling, freedom, disability, and women's role in the family, which have appeared in edited collections and journals such as *The American Political Science Review*, *Political Theory*, and *Constellations*. She has held many prestigious fellowships, including the Institute for Advanced Study in Princeton, The European University Institute, National Endowment for the Humanities, and the American Council of Learned Societies.

Memona Hossain is a mother, collaborator, and PhD candidate in Applied Ecopsychology and Eco-Art Therapy Certification. She has been a lecturer through the School of Environment at the University of Toronto. She teaches community-based ecopsychology courses through the University of Guelph Arboretum, Emmanuel College at the University of Toronto, and the Riverwood Conservancy in Canada. Memona is involved in eco-diverse conversations as they pertain to climate action. Memona completed her master's degree in education at the University of Toronto and has been working in the field of Mental Health, Addictions, and Developmental Disabilities for over fifteen years. She serves on the board of directors for the Muslim Association of Canada.

Iain Hutchison is an Affiliate in the School of Social Sciences and an Associate in the School of Health and Wellbeing at the University of Glasgow. He holds a PhD awarded by the University of Strathclyde and is a Fellow of the Royal Historical Society. He has served on the boards of the Disability History Association, the Scottish Records Association, and the Economic & Social History Society of Scotland. He is reviews editor for H-Disability. His main research interests embrace the experience of mental, physical, and sensory impairment in Scotland across the long nineteenth century.

Andrew B. Jenks completed a PhD in Political Science and International Relations in 2021. His research interests are in disability politics, disability social policy, and equity and access in university teaching. His work has been funded by the U.S. Social Security Administration, and he has published in *Disability and Society, Critical Social Policy* as well as in multiple volumes on teaching and learning. He currently works as an educational assessment specialist at the University of Delaware's Center for Teaching and Assessment of Learning.

Tatiana Konrad is a postdoctoral researcher in the Department of English and American Studies at the University of Vienna, Austria; the principal investigator of "Air and Environmental Health in the (Post-)COVID-19 World," funded by the Austrian Science Fund (FWF); and editor of the *Environment, Health, and Well-being* book series at Michigan State University Press. She holds a PhD in American Studies from the University of Marburg, Germany. She was a Visiting Fellow at the University of Chicago (2022), a Visiting Researcher at the Forest History Society (2019), an Ebeling Fellow at the American Antiquarian Society (2018), and a Visiting Scholar at the University of South Alabama (2016). She is author of *Docu-Fictions of War: U.S. Interventionism in Film and Literature*; the editor of *Imagining Air: Cultural Axiology and the Politics of Invisibility* (Exeter: University of Exeter Press, 2023), *Plastics, Environment, Culture, and the Politics of Waste* (Edinburgh: Edinburgh University Press, 2023), *Cold War II: Hollywood's Renewed Obsession with Russia* (Jackson: University Press of Mississippi, 2020), and *Transportation and the Culture of Climate Change: Accelerating Ride to Global Crisis* (Morgantown: West Virginia University Press, 2020); and the coeditor of *Cultures of War in Graphic Novels: Violence, Trauma, and Memory* (New Brunswick, NJ: Rutgers University Press, 2018).

Suha Kudsieh specializes in Anglophone and world literature. She received her PhD in Comparative literature from the University of Toronto in 2008. She taught at the University of Toronto and Trent University, Canada, from 2003 to 2010, and at the City University of New York (CUNY) from 2010 to 2020. She served on the Board of The Northeast Modern Language Association from 2011 to 2015. Her articles have appeared in *Alif* and *Thamyris*, and in the following edited collections: *Russian-Arab Worlds: A Documentary History*, ed. Eileen Kane et al. (New York: Oxford University Press, 2023); *The Limits of Cosmopolitanism*, ed. Aleksandar Stevic and Philip Tsang (New York: Routledge, 2019); *Roads to Paradise*, ed. Sebastian Günther and Todd Lawson (Leiden: Brill, 2016); and *Mediterranean Travels: Writing Self and Other from the Ancient World to Contemporary Society*, ed. Patrick Crowley et al. (Oxford: Legenda, 2011). She is currently an unaffiliated independent scholar.

Gordon M. Sayre is a scholar of colonial American history and literature and Professor of English, Folklore, and Environmental Studies at the University of Oregon. He is the author of *"Les Sauvages Américains": Representations of Native Americans in French and English Colonial Literature* (1997), and *The Indian Chief as Tragic Hero: Native Resistance and the Literatures of America, from Moctezuma to Tecumseh* (2005), as well as translator and coeditor of *The Memoir of Lieutenant Dumont, 1715–1747: A Sojourner in the French Atlantic* (2012). He served as President of the Society of Early Americanists from 2017–2019.

Jessica A. Schwartz is an Associate Professor of musicology at the Herb Alpert School of Music at the University of California, Los Angeles. Schwartz's work focuses on critical, creative, and poetic dissent from an interrogation of sonic histories and musical representations of imperial and military violence, as explored in *Radiation Sounds: Marshallese Music and Nuclear Silences* (Durham, NC: Duke University Press, 2021), *American Quarterly*, and *Women & Music*, as well as DIY/punk musicality/philosophy/education in *Punk Pedagogies: Music, Culture and Learning* and the journal *Punk & Post-Punk*. Schwartz is academic advisor to and cofounder of the nonprofit, the Marshallese Educational Initiative, and hosts the Punkast Series.

Anna Stenning specializes in the literary medical humanities and is currently a postdoctoral research associate at Durham University. She was awarded her PhD in 2015 from the University of Worcester for an ecocritical study of the literary friendship between Edward Thomas and Robert Frost. She is author of *Narrating the Many Autisms: Identity, Agency, Mattering* (Routledge, 2024) and coeditor of *Neurodiversity Studies: A New Critical Paradigm* with Hanna Bertilsdotter-Rosqvist and Nick Chown. She has published in *Disability Studies Quarterly, Disability and Society, Social Inclusion, Green Letters*, and *Autism*, among other places, and she is an editorial board member for *Neurodiversity*.

Aubrey Tang graduated from UC Irvine with a doctorate in Comparative Literature. Her research interests include film theory, phenomenology of perception, and Chinese and Sinophone cinemas. Her essays on Chinese cinema and Taiwanese literature appeared in *Frontiers of Literary Studies in China* and the collected volume *Li Ang's Visionary Challenges to Gender, Sex, and Politics*. Her chapter on Shanghai sensationism came out in 2017 in the Palgrave anthology *Sensationalism and the Genealogy of Modernity: A Global Nineteenth Century Approach*. Her other chapter on the American documentary film *Art and Craft* came out in the Palgrave volume *Cognitive Theory and Documentary Film*. Her dissertation chapters on Hong Kong *noir* appeared in *antae: a Journal on the Interspaces of English Studies* and the anthology *Aromas of Asia*. While revising her book manuscript, a phenomenological study of Johnnie To's cinema, she teaches film studies at Chapman University in Orange, California. She was raised by her blind grandmother in Hong Kong, so she finds her passion in phenomenology.

Alice Wexler received an EdD in Arts and Humanities from Columbia University, Teachers College. She received an MFA and graduated with distinction at the Royal College of Art in the UK. She received a BFA from Boston University, Fine and Applied Arts. As Professor of Art Education at SUNY New Paltz from 1999 to 2015, she published numerous articles in journals such as *Studies in Art Education*, the *Journal of Social Theory in Art Education*, and the *International Journal of Education through Art*. A monograph, *Art and Disability: The Social and Political Struggles Facing Education* (2009), and an anthology, *Art Education Beyond the Classroom: Pondering the Outsider and Other Sites of Learning* (2012), were published by Palgrave Macmillan. The most recent monograph, *Autism in a Decentered World* (2016), was published by Routledge. She is coeditor of *Bridging Communities through Socially Engaged Art* (2019) and of *Contemporary Art and Disability Studies* (2020), published by Routledge. Her chapter, "Exorcising the Colonialist: The Cuna Figures of San Blas Islands," was published in *The Routledge Companion to Decolonizing Art, Craft, and Visual Culture Education* in 2023. She is currently completing the monograph *Art and Resistance in Settler Colonial Australia*.

Index

www.ingramcontent.com/pod-product-compliance
Lightning Source LLC
Chambersburg PA
CBHW030639270326

41929CB00007B/128